# On Silver Wings

## The Men & Machines of the AAC, AAF, and RAAF 1919–1939

## Volume 3

**Colin A. Owers**

**This book is dedicated to all who served in the AAC, AAF and RAAF from 1919 to 1939, and their families.**

**Cover painting:** *The Visitors* painted by Norman Clifford for the RAAF Collection. Reproduced by permission of the RAAF and Vicki Sach, Norm's daughter.



**ISBN: 978-1-953201-67-6**

Design and layout: Jack Herris
Cover design: Aaron Weaver
Digital photo editing: Jack Herris

*Books for Enthusiasts by Enthusiasts*
www.aeronautbooks.com

# Table of Contents

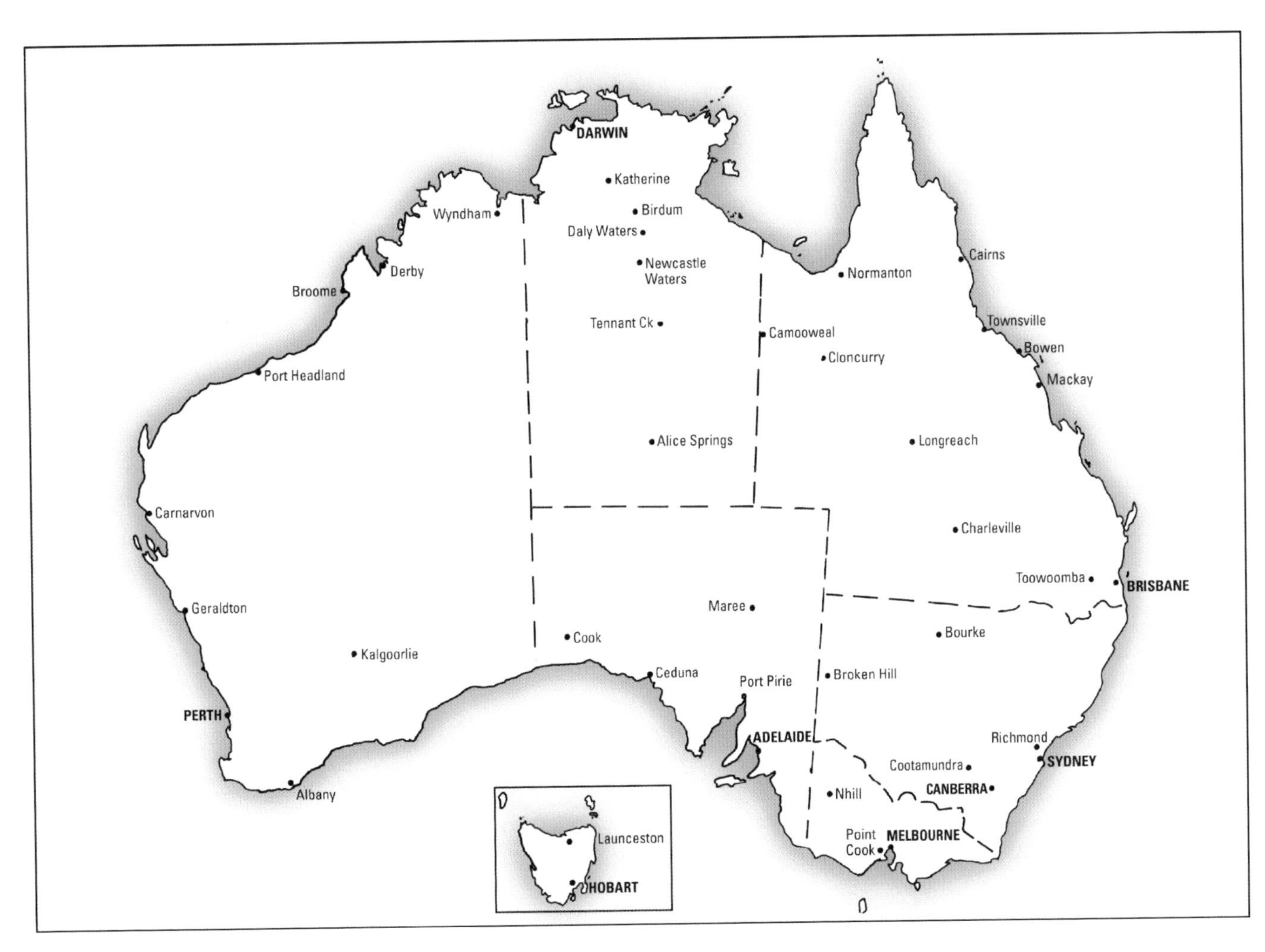


**Above:** Map showing locations of places referred to in the text.

# Chapter 20: The Supermarine Seagull V & Walrus

**Above & Facing Page:** The prototype Supermarine Seagull V carrying the registration N.1, rolled out at the manufacturer's works. For working with a seaplane carrier such as HMAS *Albatross*, the wings needed to be able to fold for stowage aboard ship. (via P London)

An onlooker, who observed the activities of Supermarine Seagull V A2-7 as it dropped 20-lb Mark I bombs in the waters off the east coast of Australia in early 1937, would be excused if he thought he was watching the RAAF practice anti-submarine work. In actual fact the targets for this aggression were schools of pelagic fish!

The aircraft taking part in this exercise was designed to meet Australian requirements for *an all-metal boat amphibian suitable for operation from H.M.A.S. 'ALBATROSS'.*[1] Williams states in his autobiography that Keith Smith, the Vickers Australian representative, presented him with the design for such a craft soon after the commissioning of *Albatross*. The Vickers proposal featured wooden wings instead of metal and as this would enable the prototype to be completed in a shorter time Williams agreed. The Air Board recommended the purchase of *two metal boat amphibians of the type submitted by them to our requirement and suitable for work in H.M.A.S. "Albatross" - the first machine to be sent to the Marine Experimental Section, ... Felixstowe, for trials, and the second to be sent straight to Australia for trials in 'Albatross'.*[2] The Minister, A.E. Green, rejected this submission. The Air Board again presented the case for purchase of the metal boat amphibian in another memorandum where the support of the 1st Naval Member, was given in that he considered that the *present equipment is obsolete and of poor performance and its continued use must mean unnecessary risk to personnel.*[3] The Minister however refused to change his stance and wrote across the Agenda, *In view of the financial position, this expenditure cannot be approved.*[4]

Despite the lack of a firm order, Vickers went ahead with the construction of a prototype amphibian at their Supermarine subsidiary as a private venture. Little information on this prototype was forthcoming, and when Williams went to London, he approached Vickers to see what the problem was and discovered that the aircraft, designated Seagull V, was being built by Supermarine at Southampton. When he visited Supermarine he found that because of a large Air Ministry order for another aircraft the nearly complete prototype had been relegated to the back of the workshop and work had ceased. Williams states he was able to get construction reactivated.[5] The prototype was registered N-1 and first flew on 20 June 1933, with Joseph *Mutt* Summers, the Chief Test Pilot, at the controls. A *short flight only attempted. Followed by successfully landing on both land and water.*[6] Six days later at the SBAC exhibition at Hendon Summers showed the capability of the new aircraft by looping the amphibian at low altitude.[7]

The Seagull V was a light reconnaissance amphibian flying boat directly descended from the earlier Seagull amphibians. It was a compact pusher biplane with folding wings for stowage in the restricted space aboard a carrier or ship. The shoulder mounted lower wing had a stabilising float mounted outboard.

**Above:** The prototype Supermarine Seagull V carrying the registration N.1, rolled out at the manufacturer's works. For working with a seaplane carrier such as HMAS *Albatross*, the wings needed to be able to fold for stowage aboard ship. (via P London)

**Right & Right Below:** The prototype now marked N.2 at the Supermarine works. (via P London)

**Above & Facing Page:** The prototype, now with the serial N.2, takes to the water.

The tail surfaces were mounted high to avoid spray. The Bristol Pegasus II L2P nine- cylinder radial engine was installed in the pusher configuration as specified to enable safer hooking-on. It also gave the advantage in protecting the propeller from spray. The engine was offset a couple of degrees to overcome the aerodynamic effect the slipstream exerted with the engine being mounted so close to the tailplane. Seagulls had dual starters, incorporating the RAE gas starter, which operated from a compressed-air cylinder and hand magneto, as well as an inertia starting system.[8] The aircraft featured a fully enclosed cockpit which together with the pusher engine enabled the crew to communicate *without special 'phone equipment.*[9] Normal complement was three - pilot, observer and Telegraphist Air Gunner (TAG). A collapsible seat was fitted to starboard of the pilot's seat for dual; the spare control column was stowed at hand and could be installed easily, even in flight. The hull was constructed of Alclad light alloy fitted for catapult launching, while the main aero structure was constructed of stainless steel. The bow position was reached by crawling through an opening under the instrument panel. Behind the cockpit was the navigator's compartment. Beyond this was the telegraphist's position. The wings were of composite wood and metal construction with fabric covering. Gun stations fitted with Scarff mountings were provided at the bow and aft of the mainplanes.[10] The amphibian gear was fully retractable and incorporated oleo pneumatic shock absorbers and wheel brakes.

The test reports noted that the design *appears to be satisfactory*, however as only 38 hours of flying had been carried out *further flying experience is necessary before a final decision is reached as to the robustness of the structure.*[11] The cockpit arrangement was considered *excellent. The hinged and sliding windows and roof are strongly constructed and are efficient.*[12] The controls were considered light and effective, with little tendency to yaw or drop a wing. Take-off was easy with no tendency to swing, however a slight tendency existed *for it to be thrown off the water in a choppy sea, but there is ample air control to deal with the emergency.*[13] The aircraft was dived up to 150 knots and no difficulties were experienced.

The performance of the Seagull V was not to expectations and the installation of a Rolls Royce Kestrel was considered; however, this was complicated by this latter engine's water-cooling system which would involve a three-month delay and further testing. The Air Board was reluctant to abandon the standard Australian requirement for air cooled engines, and decided to accept the Pegasus engines in order to get the amphibians into service.

Supermarine advised it would be *eight months from date receipt order before the first machine would be ready for test and delivery and that they could complete further boats at a rate of one every three weeks.*[14] The Navy was of the opinion that the Seagull V *would appear to fulfil all the requirements for replacing the present type of aircraft carried in H.M.A. Squadron.*[15] The Air Board thought that the price was too high and instructed the ALO to 'hin' to the manufacturer that *we propose reconsidering adoption of float seaplanes* if the price was not reduced.[16] The revised price was £7,500 each for an order of six; £6,750 each for 12; and £6,450 each for 18. This included slots installed but not the royalty on same. Wings were to be of composite construction having wooden ribs with metal compression members.

The Air Board again approached the Minister, noting that the RAAF had *now reached a stage where the provision of additional Amphibious Aircraft is essential to maintain existing units in a satisfactory state of efficiency. Owing to wastage our strength of this type of aircraft, all of which have been in use for seven (7) years, has been reduced to eight (8), three (3) of which have been recommended for write off as being uneconomical to repair and two (2) are at present undergoing extensive overhaul.*

*To complete the outfit allowance of the Seaplane Carrier,*

**Right:** N.2 being tested on a catapult at RAE Farnborough during January 1934. (via P London)

**Below & Below Right:** N.2 leaving the catapult at Farnborough. Note the bombs under the lower wings. (via P London)

**Left:** A2-1, Australia's first Seagull V, thought to be photographed in the UK.

*H.M.A. Cruisers and Seaplane F.T.S. plus adequate reserves, it is necessary that twenty four (24) Amphibian Aircraft should be ordered for delivery as early as practicable.*[17]

It was suggested that six be built for development purposes before the remainder be put into production, any modification arising from service at sea could then be embodied in the later machines. Williams authorised the order for 24 in early January 1934. The Air Board confirmed the order subject to satisfactory completion of full service trials, including catapult trials with full service crew and equipment. Airframe modifications were to include supporting points for Australian type catapults and to include duraluminium ribs if their durability was considered satisfactory. The total package was to include wing slots, bomb ribs, eight spare engines and drawings.[18]

The RAN was finally to get catapults for their cruisers and *Albatross.* A cradle type trolley was being developed suitable for hull type of aircraft and would have special supporting points acceptable for the Seagull V hull. As will be related hereunder, problems were to arise with these catapult cradles.

Williams noted that, in his opinion, considering the present state of aeronautical development the *performance of (the) Seagull is as good as can reasonably be expected for a service pusher boat amphibian to Specifications we set down.*[19] Air Board Order No.415 was raised for the purchase of 24 boat amphibians powered by Bristol Pegasus 2.M.2 engines;[20] six to be delivered in ten months with the remainder to be delayed pending the outcome of the trials of the first batch. It is evident that there were delays in the fulfilling of the RAAF order as Williams noted in a letter to Supermarine in October 1934 that *you are keeping very quiet over there about the deliveries of the "Seagulls" - when are we to get them I wonder?*[21]

Australia was informed that the British had placed an order with Supermarine for *a number of Seagull Vs for use by the Fleet Air Arm and the decision to place this order was based on the performance of the Seagull V during trials with the Atlantic Fleet.*[22] Before the prototype went to Felixstowe it was discovered that a Southampton flying boat had previously been designated N-1 and so was now serialled N-2. It had undergone sea trials on several British ships including the battleship HMS *Valiant.* Its robust construction and seaworthiness had so impressed the British that they placed an order for 12 of the developed version of the Seagull V which was to be known as the Walrus in British service.[23] In view of this order by the FAA and the fact that the first three Seagull V biplanes would be allocated to the Australian cruisers, only three would be available for No. 101 Flight, and so it was decided to request the contractor to proceed with a second batch of six without delay.

A cable from the ALO caused the first feelings of unease that the Seagull V was not quite up to expectations. He informed the Air Board that the Air Ministry was installing Pegasus VI engines in their Seagulls because the Pegasus 3M was considered unsuitable owing to its gear ratio and the Pegasus 2.M.2 is non-standard and *its production will not continue except to complete our requirements.*[24] This was the first indication that the RAAF had that the Pegasus 2.M.2 was obsolescent. When it ceased production the spares position of the Australian machines would be *vitally affected.*[25] As the Pegasus VI would not be available until sometime in 1936, the British decided to install Pegasus 2.M.2 engines in their 12 Seagulls, the same as the RAAF amphibians. The RAAF agreed to the installation of Pegasus VI engines in their last 12 Seagulls and this was carried out after satisfactory trials.

The Air Ministry withdrew the experimental Seagull from service in order to test the Pegasus VI engine and requested the loan of the third RAAF machine. The reply message to the ALO was tart and to the point in that *We cannot possibly*

**Above:** A2-2, the first Seagull V taken into operation by the RAAF.
**Below:** A2-1 on HMAS *Australia's* catapult at Spithead in July 1935. A2-1 was used for experimental catapult launches in the UK before coming to Australia.

**Left:** A2-1 has just left the catapult of a cruiser. Note the serial has been repeated as a single number on the bow, indicating this is a late photograph after it left the UK.

*agree to further delay in the prolonged delivery of this type...Our Fleet Co-operation Unit is without Aircraft and waiting for* these Seagulls.[26]

*Aircraft* for March 1936 reported that the first of the new Seagull V amphibians was awaiting flight trials at 1 AD. *It is a massive craft, the stainless steel fittings look impressive, and the technical people are greatly interested in the gas starting device and the Bristol Pegasus radial engine.*[27] This was actually the third Seagull V received as both HMAS *Australia* and *Sydney* had one amphibian delivered directly to each ship as they were in the UK at the right time, attached to the Royal Navy.

Problems with the amphibian's petrol system soon became apparent. HMAS *Australia* took over its first Seagull, A2-1, on 12 September 1935. From 3 October 1935 till 11 June 1936, the following stoppages occurred while it operated with the British Mediterranean Fleet:

**3.10.1935.** Engine revolutions dropped after the petrol was changed from the starboard tank. When the starboard tank was again turned on, the engine spluttered then returned to normal running. During this temporary failure the aircraft lost 200 feet. No cause could be found for the failure.

**11.10.1935.** On this occasion an attempt was made to fly on the port tank and the same problem was experienced but was more persistent and 3,000 feet was lost while clearing it. The possibility of air remaining in or about the filter after a ten-hourly inspection was thought to be the only possible cause of the problem.

**25.11.1935.** The aircraft was catapulted and climbed to 10,000 feet. Again, the same sequence of events occurred. After returning to the ship a thorough inspection was made and again no fault was found.

**25.11.1935.** The aircraft was catapulted and climbed to 4,000 feet. Even though the filter had been vented just prior to this flight, another engine failure occurred. The aircraft was also examined by technical officers of the RAF at the floating dock, Malta. No fault could be found.

**10.01.1936.** A similar occurrence to the above led to the discovery that the master cock of the air starter system was a possible cause of air leaking into the system. A test was carried out on the 13th wherein a small quantity of air from the starter bottle was admitted to the system and after 30 seconds a failure, similar to those previously experienced, was induced. This and the fact that the engine had developed the habit of running badly for some time after starting if the air starter was used, led to the belief that air was entering the petrol system by way of the pipe between the atomiser and the filter.

**18.03.1936.** A further stoppage was experienced during flight but was readily cleared by opening the delivery and overflow cocks of the atomiser.[28]

A2-1 was badly damaged when testing out modified hoisting slings. A split pin sheared during lifting operations, dropping the aircraft onto the deck. It was replaced by A2-12 on 23 April, this amphibian receiving A2-1's service equipment. A2-12 accompanied *Australia* when she left Malta for home in August. The repairs to A2-1 were lengthy and it was not until September 1938 that the Air Board considered replacing A2-1's service equipment when it was to be allocated to HMAS *Apollo.*

Despite a modification to the petrol system, which had been incorporated in this Seagull, stoppages still occurred. On 20 May one occurred during flight but cured itself in

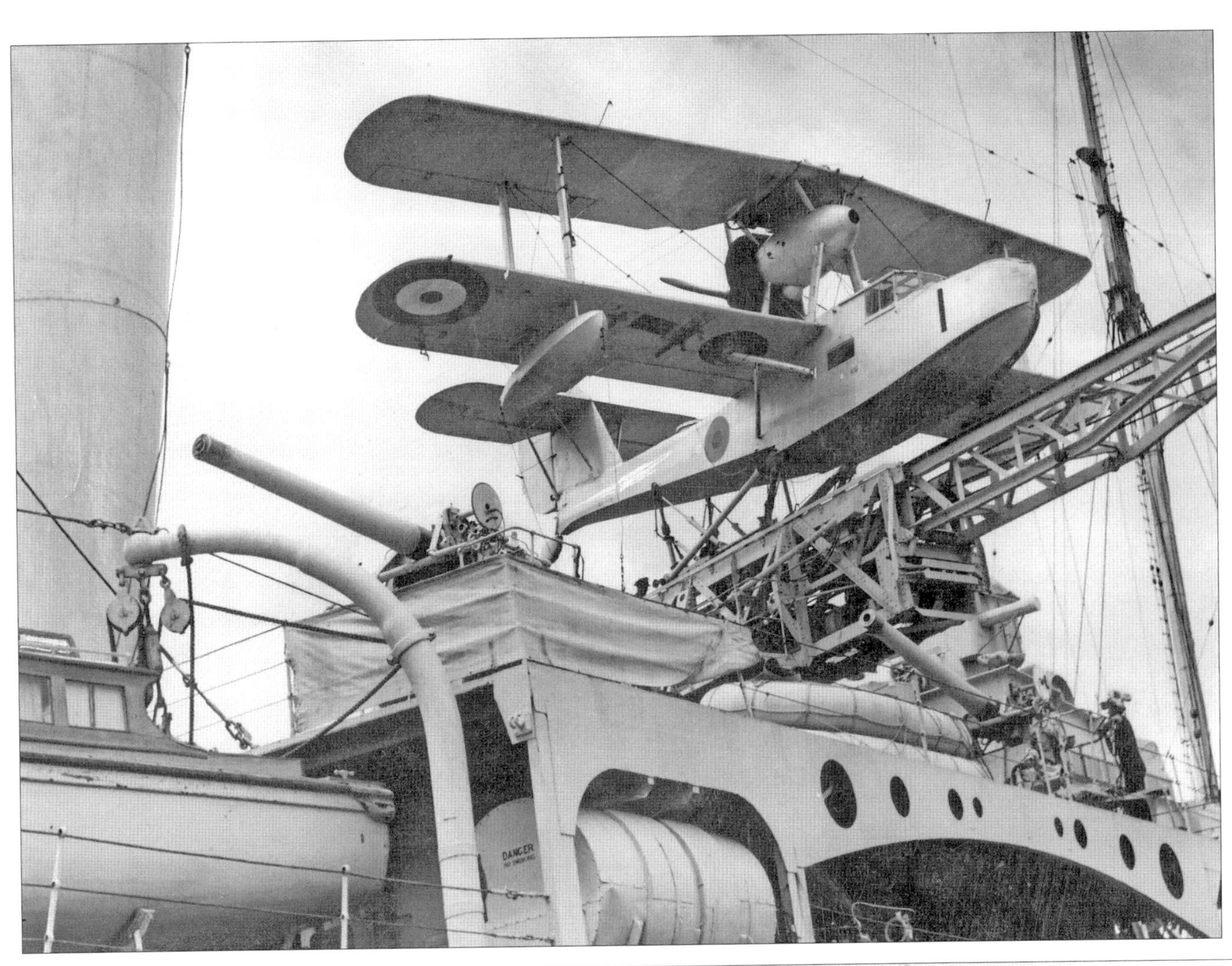


**Above:** This appears to be A2-1 on the catapult. The serial is not on the rear hull. The hull roundel is the red/ blue one adopted after the outbreak of WW2. There appear to be no rudder stripes. (*Argus* newspaper collection State Library of Victoria)

**Right:** A2-1 on the hoist. Note the 'I' on the bow and the man on the upper wing. The engine appears to be running.

**Above & Above Right:** An accident was always an opportunity to take out the camera. Here a sailor is photographing A2-1 after the accident at Alexandria on 26 March 1936. While being hoisted in after an exercise, the split pin sheared dropping the aircraft to the gun deck. It suffered extensive damage, and was returned to Supermarine for repair. (AWM P00604.016)

about five seconds. Again, on 2 June a series of stoppages persisted for about five minutes during which time the amphibian lost some 2,700 feet of height.

Seagull V amphibians were in service in Australian waters with No. 5 (Fleet Co-operation) Squadron, as No. 101 Flight became in April 1936. Three cruisers were equipped with Type EIIIH rotating cordite catapults and Seagull V amphibians, HMAS *Canberra* receiving A2-3 in Australia. The Seagulls had to be recovered by ship's crane, and hoisted back on deck for reloading on the catapult's cradle, an operation that would not be carried out in the middle of a battle. The last Seagull V was delivered in July 1937.

The May 1936 Engineering report from No. 5 (Fleet Co-operation) Squadron reveals that in addition to a number of small defects, the Pegasus engine *has a tendency to cut out for short periods in the air, for what appears to be lack of petrol. This has now occurred on four occasions in this Squadron and, although certain theories have been advanced as to the cause, no definite reason for this cutting out has as yet been found.*[29]

The cut-outs had been experienced by three separate aircraft, A2-4, A2-5 and A2-8, and would therefore *appear that it is a fault due to the design of the system.*[30]

On 6 May, A2-5, while operating from *Canberra*, force landed at Jervis Bay when the engine failed at 7,000 feet after flying for 1:05 hours. Various modifications and procedures were tried but as late as 24 February 1938, A2-14 force landed on Richmond golf course with the same problem.

The first 12 Seagulls had a number of other defects which service use brought to light. The unsplinterable glass of the cockpit windows cracked on all aircraft. This was thought due to expansion and contraction of the frames. The sliding roof of the pilot's cockpit became distorted due to continual walking on it and a strengthened unit was introduced from A2-17 onwards before delivery, the earlier aircraft being modified in service. A further problem with the roof became apparent on 22 December 1939. Flt Lt Campbell was preparing to land A2-4 in Rose Bay, NSW, and the latch on the cockpit hatch was released to slide it back before landing when the hatch flew off its rails taking most of the propeller with it, Campbell executing a forced landing in Rushcutters Bay.[31]

The gas starter systems had the pressure cocks coupled up incorrectly by the contractor on all aircraft. Wind screen wipers were considered a necessity as it was almost impossible to see through the windscreen in conditions of rain. The undercarriage required constant attention to ensure smooth operation. In taking off at sea, slight buckling of the hull occurred just aft the pilot's cockpit. Aileron ribs on HMAS *Sydney's* amphibian were broken by the force of water thrown off from the wingtip float during take-off. Enquiries revealed that the Supermarine prototype had suffered similar problems and strengthened ribs were incorporated into the design. In all 13 defects were listed for the airframe, two for the engine and three for the handling characteristics.

The Air Ministry did not consider the reported handling problems to be serious. It was noted that whilst gliding 'hands off' aircraft tended to do a mild 'falling leaf' which, however, was not very serious. In take-off, great difficulty was experienced in lifting the port wingtip float out of the water, but this was a characteristic of a pusher aircraft and could be overcome by pilot handling. Occasionally, when landing on an aerodrome, the aircraft swung towards the end of its run, and the swing, once started, could not be obviated with the use of the brakes. This was noted as being a similar characteristic of the wooden Seagull III and was due to incorrect air pressure in the oleo undercarriage legs.

More serious were the reports in May 1936, from the RAF Depot, Middle East, on A2-2 which was operating from *Sydney*. Cracks had developed in the fin skin in the vicinity of the rivets. A similar problem had occurred in A2-1 on HMAS *Australia*. The ailerons and elevators of A2-2 had insufficient clearance and had to be pared down. A2-2 then

**Above:** Only A2-8 can be identified in this line-up of at least eight Seagull V amphibians. (via J Hopton)

went on to serve for a period on HMS *Glorious*.

The report from 2 AD, when the second batch of Seagull amphibians were erected a year later in May 1937, was most disturbing. A2-13, A2-14 and A2-15 were thought to be *not up to the standard of the first aircraft delivered.*[32] On A2-14 the hand operated bilge pump was full of salt water and the connections had badly corroded requiring replacement, while on A2-15 the riveting was considered to be generally rough. The Air Board decided to wait until the next batch was received before taking the matter up with the Supermarine

**Above:** Possibly the same line up. The propeller cover is noteworthy.

**Above:** A2-8 at Richmond. Only the hull roundels have a white outline. The serial number was spaced out along the bottom surface of the lower wings.

Company.

A2-15 was assembled on 4 May and issued to No. 5 Squadron. After seven weeks in which the aircraft flew only 27 hours and alighted on water once, the fabric on the port lower mainplane *was found to be defective when an airman's hand went through it during washing.*[33] Repair entailed the replacement of 12 nose ribs, three spruce stringers and three-ply coverings to the leading edge. It was considered that the incomplete impregnation of the fabric by the red dope undercoat coupled with the fact that the wings had been stored on their leading edge with water inside, had allowed a concentrated attack by micro-organisms which had caused the damage during their shipment to Australia.

The Seagull V had been purchased to re-equip No. 101 (Fleet Co-operation) Flight, and exercises were conducted with A2-14 in HMAS *Albatross* in August 1937 to determine how many of the amphibians could be carried by that ship. It was necessary to exercise extreme caution in stowing the amphibian as clearances were only a matter of inches in most cases. The height of the aircraft when standing on its own undercarriage was such that it fouled various points on the deckhead, even when the tail was on the deck. When the tail was raised, as it had to be in order to prevent fuel leaking from the main tanks when the wings were folded, the aircraft fouled the main deck girders by four inches. It was suggested that a handling chassis be constructed which would lower the aircraft so that the keel was three inches clear of the deck. As noted below, this chassis brought the discrepancies in the hull dimensions of the Seagull V to the attention of the Air Board.

It was decided that six or seven Seagull V amphibians would be easily accommodated as the normal complement of *Albatross*, and that nine might be carried in an emergency. The compressed air catapult built for *Albatross* was rendered obsolete by the development of the cordite catapult, and the former was scrapped. A catapult, similar to that fitted to the Australian cruisers, was ordered. It was fitted to *Albatross* and on 24 August 1936, A2-6 was launched by the seaplane carrier.[34] This was to be a non-event as *Albatross* was sold to the Royal Navy in 1938 and left Sydney Harbour on 11 July bound for the United Kingdom. Seagulls flew overhead as the ship left Sydney Harbour for the last time.

A Seagull V had been embarked in *Albatross* on 5 November 1937, to test a newly constructed handling chassis and to investigate the problem of stowing and handling the Seagull V in the ship's hangar. The chassis had one disadvantage in that it was built for A2-14 and *when offered up to Seagull A2-16 could not be fitted.*[35] There was nothing that could be done about the lack of uniformity in the positioning of the catapult points on the Seagull's hull

**Above:** A2-4 bearing the 'J' code on the forward hull.

**Right:** A2-4 with the serial on the bow. This view shows the offset of the engine.

and a trolley was made which adjusted for the differences between the rear catapult spools. The Navy Board considered that this *lack of uniformity in the athwartship distance between the forward spools* would require adjustment of the catapult trolley between each launch thus causing a serious delay in flying off machines from the catapult of *Albatross*.[36] The cruisers, which carried only one Seagull V at a time, had no problem with adjusting their catapult trolleys.

No correspondence between Supermarine and the Air Board on the standard of craftsmanship of the Seagulls has been found, however as late as July 1941 it was reported the *owing to the poor standard of inter-changeability that exists in the Seagull aircraft, it is more or less necessary to tailor-make parts of the type in question (wing trailing edge) and... it becomes necessary to repair them if they are damaged rather than fit another one.*[37] Notwithstanding this further example of poor workmanship, in December 1938, the RAAF placed another order, this time, for the Walruses to allow for future requirements for No. 5 Squadron, which was to be again renumbered as No. 9 Squadron in the New Year.[38] The RAAF was to purchase four batches of the amphibians for a total of 24 machines. With loaned machines, the RAAF was to utilise 38 Mk. I and Mk. II (wooden hull) Walrus amphibians.

There were the usual number of accidents in introducing

**Above:** Another view of A2-4 with Navy personnel on the upper wing waiting for a hook up. This must have been a very precarious position; however, no documents recording any injuries from this position have been found.

a new type into service. Some of these would lead to modifications which were introduced into new aircraft on the assembly line. One such problem was the failure of the locking device for the flap which sprang up while the machine was landing and fouled the propeller blades. A2-3, A2-5 and A2-9 had suffered such occurrences. The flap referred to was *really the trailing edge of the wing hinged at the rear main spar and folds upwards to allow the wing...to be folded backwards for stowage purposes. It is not a flap in the generally understood sense of that term.*[39]

The undercarriage of the Seagull biplanes caused a number of problems and embarrassments. A2-8 suffered a brake failure when the locking release lever had sprung behind the top edge of the upper fairing of the compression such that during the subsequent lowering of the undercarriage the release lever had been activated by the top edge of the upper fairing. Seagull Order 55 introduced a modification to prevent a recurrence.

After the accident to A2-7 piloted by P/Off A.N. Hick after its undercarriage collapse on landing at Archerfield Aerodrome, Brisbane, Qld, on 20 August 1937, the CO of the Richmond base noted that the warning system on the Seagull was not as efficient as it should be as in his *Own recent experience, although the undercarriage was in the down position, the green lights would not show until after the aircraft had landed and run along the ground for some distance.*[40]

A2-5 from HMAS *Australia* suffered the collapse of the lower water rudder attachment to the hull when landing at Pari aerodrome, Port Moresby, Papua, on 28 July 1937. It was necessary to transport the aircraft to the wharf to return it to Richmond for repair. The tail unit was dismantled, the wings folded and the tail secured to the back of a truck which then towed the amphibian to the wharf. Twenty-five telephone lines had to be cut and two lamp standards removed to enable the aircraft to have access. It returned to Australia via the SS *Montoro* arriving in Sydney on 8 August.

The accident occurred because A2-5 did not have Seagull Modification No.3 carried out due to a lack of stainless-steel bolts. The Air Board was concerned that this modification had not been carried out and the whole practice of allowing aircraft to remain in service when modifications were required was re-examined. It would appear that the Board was not completely successful in overcoming this problem as there is evidence in late 1938 of a further failure to incorporate modifications in accordance with Technical Orders which could have led to an *epidemic of cracked engine mountings.*[41]

Operations exposed other defects in equipment. Seawater had a severe corrosive effect on bomb carriers and the contact plugs of the E.M. bomb release gear fitted to the Seagull V. The bombsight was mounted on a wedge-shaped plate outside the front cockpit gun mount without any protection from the slipstream. Carriers in use were required to be replaced by *clean carriers as soon as the aircraft returns to*

**Above:** Although an amphibian, the Seagulls were sometimes moored out and launches were used to carry the crew to shore. A2-8 off the pier at Point Cook, under tow. (via R Cresswell)

**Below:** A2-5 on the crane hoist. Note that the engine is running. (AHMofWA P021500)

**Above:** The caption says it all! A2-7 piloted by P/Off A.N. Hick had its undercarriage collapse on landing at Archerfield Aerodrome, Brisbane, Qld, on 20 August 1937. The chassis lock had failed to engage and Hick was blamed for not checking that the undercarriage had locked down and was required to contribute £10 to the cost of repairs.

*the ship after the last flight of the day. To minimise sea water corrosion, used carriers could then be cleaned immediately after removal from the aircraft.*[42] Unless they were immediately required, bomb carriers were to be removed from aircraft on catapults. Due to a shortage of carriers in the RAAF and no hydraulic platforms which would enable maintenance work to be carried out on board ship, it was decided to double the establishment of bomb carriers for ship borne aircraft. In September 1939 an order was issued that universal carriers on Seagull aircraft allocated to cruisers were not suitable for catapulting with bomb loads, a severe restriction on the operational capability of the aircraft. Anti-submarine patrols would be of limited value until the new carriers were obtained, the outbreak of war in Europe making this a matter of priority.

In early 1939 it was decided that all Seagull aircraft would have Sperry instruments and de-icing equipment which meant that the amphibians could be *operated from cruisers under unfair weather conditions* with additional safety.[43] It is not known if this matter was ever followed to completion.

The Seagull V carried out the multitude of duties required of RAAF aircraft attached to the RAN in this period. Their main purpose in these days before gun-laying radar was in being the eyes of the fleet, searching over the horizon for the enemy and correcting the fall of shells from the ship's guns should an engagement take place. There was always the disadvantage in operating such aircraft in that the ship had to stop to pick it up after a sortie. They also carried on with the work of photographic survey. By August 1936 work had been carried out from Gippsland to the north-east of Melbourne and along the North Queensland coast.[44]

These peace-time sorties could have their share of excitement as the following routine flight of A2-5 shows. F/Off Francis Xavier Richards was sent in A2-5, HMAS *Canberra*'s aircraft, to visit Port Molle and the anchorages of the Molle Island group on 2 September 1936. Shortly after landing west of Mid Molle island at noon the weather deteriorated rapidly. The engine would not start and a message was sent asking for new sparking plugs. Lt G.C. Oldham, RAN, left in the *Sea Trump* and found the Seagull anchored in an exposed position and dragging. He towed her into a more sheltered position under the lee of West Molle Island but though everything possible was done the engine still would not fire.

A motor boat was sent with an additional anchor, spare battery, etc. It was dark by the time Lt M.J. Clark, RAN,

**Right:** Practice bomb dropping from a Seagull V bomb carrier.

found the amphibian. He took it in tow and started to return to *Canberra*. There were no lights or other navigational aids in this area. A strong tide was running with strong winds with heavy squalls and frequent drenching showers of rain. At 2010 hours the boat's propeller coupling worked free and it was thought that the shaft had broken. Lt Clark was forced to anchor in an exposed position and a W/T message brought *Waterhen* to their assistance. The ship reached the group by 2240 and was able to pass grass lines to the Seagull with the assistance of the *Sea Trump*. By 0100 the aircraft was safely moored astern of *Waterhen*.

It was found that the very heavy rainstorms had led to saturation of the plugs and leads and water had entered the engine cylinders. This had occurred when the aircraft was on the water with the engine stopped and uncovered. Water had penetrated down the upper exhaust pipes and through such

**Above:** Four Seagull V amphibians at Rathmines. Only A2-14 can be identified.

**Above:** Flt Lt Gibson was engaged in survey work with the Naval Detachment in New Guinea. On the night of 24/25 May 1939 A2-20 broke free of its moorings and sank in three feet water in a high wind. The port wing was damaged, and there was considerable hull damage. On the 8th of the following month it was returned to Sydney for repair via SS *Macdhui*.

exhaust valves as were open.

The Captain of the *Canberra* noted that the crews had worked under extremely difficult conditions. For the greater part of the time they were in darkness with strong squally winds, strong tides, choppy sea and violent rainstorms. It was a credit to all that the Seagull was recovered without any damage whatever.[45]

In January 1937, A2-5, again with Richards at the controls, and Lt Commander Patten-Thomas, RAN, as observer and Leading Telegraphist Oxley as TAG, was

**Above:** A9-12 on HMAS *Australia* in October 1937.
**Below:** A2-2 and A2-12 flying together. Note the code '076' on the bow of A2-2.

**Left:** Working on the engine of a Seagull V.

launched from *Canberra* in Victor Harbour, South Australia, en route to Richmond. The trip took three days and the CO of *Canberra* remarked that this flight was illustrative of the good flying qualities and usefulness of the Seagull V and showed its self-sufficiency if fuel was available.

The amphibian had flown to cross the railway line to Nhill, then following the line to the town where it landed. Petrol and oil were waiting on the aerodrome and refuelling took approximately one hour. Take-off was delayed by stormy weather and the aircraft left at 1400 hours. After passing over the Grampian Range by Ararat and Ballarat a landing was made at Point Cook. The aircraft left Point Cook the next morning and landed at Metung where a permanent mooring was established. The pilot went ashore and arranged for refuelling.

Leaving Metung for Mallacoota the aircraft arrived at 1635 and stayed overnight. Two moorings were permanently established here and the amphibian was secured to one and fuel was brought out in a fishing boat. The crew spent the night in a hotel in Mallacoota except the TAG who embarked onboard the aircraft for the night. The next morning the aircraft tried to contact the *Canberra* as it was anticipated that the proposed exercise was not feasible owing to the strong wind. On cancellation of the exercise the aircraft returned to Mallacoota, refuelled and departed for Richmond. The aircraft arrived at Richmond to remain disembarked for the leave period for *Canberra's* crew.

The greatest distance that two-way W/T communication was established during the flight was 285 miles, and this was considered *ample for all normal flights*.[46] The praise of the Seagull was reinforced by the Navy Board who considered this type of exercise, involving as it did, catapulting at sea, and refuelling and maintenance at seaplane harbours and emergency seaplane anchorages, had great value in training aircraft personnel to become more self-reliant and competent in the maintenance of their machines when away from their ships.[47]

**Above:** Loading bombs into the cockpit of Seagull V A2-9 in Jervis Bay. Note sailor with *Canberra* headband.

**Above:** Unfortunately, the serial of this Seagull V cannot be read to confirm whether the 'I' on the bow means that it is A2-1. (via H Lobb)

**Above:** There is no doubt as to the serial of this Seagull V. The undercarriage is in the down position to act as a water brake. Again, the position of the crewman on the upper wing looks precarious.

**Right:** The Seagull V was never a good-looking aeroplane, none more so when everything was down as shown here by A2-6.

In 1936 the 16 foot motor launch *Mystery Star* with two men on board went missing from Lord Howe Island and the RAAF were requested to conduct a search for the craft. Two Seagull V amphibians and a Tugan Gannet were allotted to the search. They were to report the position of the launch to HMAS *Waterhen*, which was also patrolling the search area. The Seagulls could only search for a distance of 50 miles out to sea as the T21A and TF wireless receivers had a range of 200 miles allowing approximately 50 miles sea search range.[48]

Seagulls A2-2, A2-11 and A2-12 under Flt Lt Pearce, F/Off Richards and Flt Lt Alexander respectively, together with Gannet A14-1 piloted by F/Off Lerew left on the search towards Lord Howe Island on 16 October. A2-2 suffered a forced landing on the 17th and was immediately replaced by A2-8. *Aircraft on the patrol flew at a distance of two and a half miles apart as it was considered that at any greater distance it was likely that they would lose sight of each other and that possibly some area of sea might not be thoroughly searched.*

**Above:** Preparing A2-6 for a flight. Note the crew members inside the hull.

**Above:** A2-6 at a later stage in early camouflage with the yellow outer ring to the hull roundel.

**Above:** RAAF Seagulls and Walrus had some interesting nose art, usually associated with a 'duck.' The markings are blue and white, the red being omitted when Japan entered the war. Note the Catalina in the background.

**Above:** Side elevation of a pristine A2-8. Note the wireless aerial from the wings to the rudder and the open leading edge slats on the upper wing. (via P.G. Heffernan)

**Right:** The reason why flying boats had high-set tailplanes is evident in this view that shows the amount of spray a Seagull V generates when it reaches the step prior to take off.

**Above:** The float obscures the underwing serial on this Seagull V. Note the men working on the catapult, the pilot in the machine, and the engine running.

*No sign of the missing launch was seen during the patrols.*[49] On the 19th the Air Board recommended that the search cease as the weather had deteriorated with the wind reaching force 8, however the Minister directed that the Gannet carry on. The results were unsuccessful and the Gannet returned to Laverton on the 22nd.

On 15 July 1936, the *Daily Telegraph* announced that the RAAF was going to conduct aerial observations of Pelagic fish movements on behalf of the Council for Scientific and Industrial Research (predecessor of the present CSIRO). Pelagic fish are surface swimming fish such as tuna, pilchards, Australian salmon and mackerel. Seagull V, A2-11, of No. 5 Squadron was assigned to the task after repairs which had caused her to leave HMAS *Canberra* for Richmond. F/Off Richards and AC1 J *Jerry* Barnes carried Messrs Fowler and Pearse, the Commonwealth Fishery Officer and Government Cinematographer respectively, on observations *in the coastal waters of N.S.W. between Sydney and Cape HOWE, the South Eastern waters of VICTORIA, BASS STRAIT (with particular concentration in the Furneaux Group), all the East Coast of TASMANIA, and the south coast as far as PORT DAVY.*[50] Of the 42 days the aircraft was available, flying was possible on 24 days. They determined that *Aerial observation is effective.*[51]

Fowler concluded his detailed report with appreciation for the co-operation of the RAAF. *And last, but no means least, I wish - despite its extraordinary capacity for the tearing of flesh and fabric - to record my unbounded admiration for aircraft A2-11 and its trusty engine.*[52]

The next season saw the Air Board recommend that approval be given for a Seagull to be made available for the continuation of the survey work as *this work has definite training value for a pilot operating on his own away from a base.*[53] A2-7 commanded by Flt Lt James Alexander with Kerr and Barnes completing the crew, took part in the observations from 23 February to 15 March 1937. From this date to the end of the assignment on 28 March F/Off John Napier Bell was in command. On this occasion four 20-lb Mark I bombs were *released with the hope that stunned or dead fish might be observed on the surface. The experiment was unsuccessful due, possibly, to the bombs being of the direct-contact type which resulted in their bursting on the surface.*[54] Notwithstanding the results of this experiment the *effectiveness of aerial observations for the location of shoals of pelagic fish and for determining the area containing the greatest concentration of pelagic fish life has been strikingly confirmed.*[55] The RAAF thought that the experience gained whilst having little bearing on the type of training peculiar to No. 5 Squadron, *was yet of excellent value*

**Above & Right:** A2-9 in the stored position on a catapult. The engine has a canvas cover. The crowded deck with stowed motor launches is noteworthy. (via H Lobb)

*in general airmanship and afforded all members of the crew an opportunity of becoming familiar with many of the less frequented areas of the Australian coast.*[56]

A2-4 took part on the Fisheries Investigation Flight from 5 July to 8 August 1937, again under F/Off Bell with Cpl William *Bill* Bradley, AC1 A.F. *Rainbow* Thorley[57] and Mr Fowler. They observed the south-east waters of Victoria, Bass Strait, all of the eastern waters of Tasmania and from Cape Howe to Cairns. Fowler wished to extend the investigation to the waters of Queensland but was restricted as to time and funds and so an attempt was made to cover as big an area as possible. This is the last report filed and it is not known if any more such work was undertaken by the RAAF. With the expansion of the RAAF and the outbreak of war there would have been little time for this type of venture.

On 28 November 1938, A2-15, which was temporarily stationed at Archerfield Aerodrome, left to carry out a search for the Brisbane typist, Miss Marjorie Norval, who had been missing for several days. The pilot, F/Off Maxwell James Wiber, took Constable George Young of the Water Police with him as he did not have much knowledge of Brisbane and its environs. After leaving the aerodrome the aircraft headed directly to Redland Bay, then flew down the Albert River travelling low over the water and some 12 minutes later hit a span of high-tension cables which crossed the river. The time was 12.22 p.m., established by the stopping of electric clocks in the vicinity. The cables were attached to towers on either side of the river at a height of 90 feet and were 50 feet above the river at their midpoint.

The aircraft appeared to fly for some distance before veering sharply to the left and crashed into the south bank of the river bursting into flames on impact. The crew of three and Constable Young were killed. Wiber had joined the RAAF as a Cadet in January 1937. The assessment report for October 1938 for the 22 year-old had found that he was an average pilot who required supervision to prevent him

**Above:** Working on attaching A2-14 to the catapult.

**Above, Right, Below Right, & Bottom Right:** On 14 October 1936, A2-10 sank just 200 yards off the jetty at Point Cook. The accident was held to have been due to an error of the student pilot who made a bad landing and the machine capsized. The machine was considered uneconomical to repair and it, and its engine, were reduced to produce.

becoming careless. The AAIC noted that the pilot should have made himself conversant with any obstacles which were known to exist in the area where he proposed to fly at low altitude. However, considering the circumstances of the search, the flight at such a low altitude was justified although it was in contravention of Air Force Orders and Air Navigation regulations. It was believed that the crew were engaged in searching for signs of the missing woman and failed to observe the cables, which were not very conspicuous, one cable wrapping itself around the engine and causing the crash.[58] Miss Norval's body was never found.

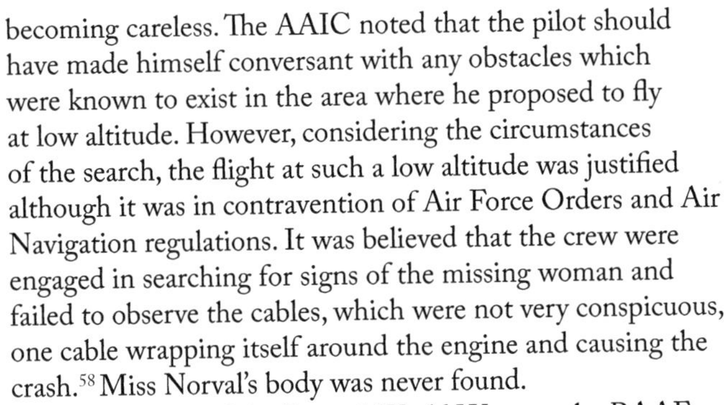

The outbreak of the Second World War saw the RAAF engaged in anti-submarine and anti-surface raider patrols. Because the Lockheed Hudson general reconnaissance bombers had not arrived there were only the Anson and Seagull V aircraft to conduct such patrols. For example, on 4 September 1939, three Ansons from Richmond, four from Canberra and three Seagulls from Mallacoota formed the reconnaissance force available to the RAAF with one Empire flying boat used to cover the outer edge of the patrol area. All aircraft were fitted with normal bomb loads.[59]

The Australian Navy kept its cruisers in Australian waters as protection against German surface raiders. Later they were to serve with the British in the Atlantic Ocean and Mediterranean Sea. Problems were soon evident in that not enough trained observers were available, a legacy of the conflict between the RAAF and the RAN for the scant resources of the 1930s.

The Seagull V amphibians attached to the cruisers were used for reconnaissance and gun-laying. The most crucial part of the operation in the use of the seaplanes was the hoisting in

**Facing Page, Below:** Walrus W2755 on a catapult showing details of the bomb carriers and the wheel wells as well as the catapult. It carries the red/blue roundel and fin flash.

**Above:** On The Seagull V was used for towing drogues for anti-aircraft gun firing practice. The drogue reel could hold up to 7,000 feet of fine wire and was installed in the rear cockpit area. Seagull V A2-6 has its landing gear down while target towing near Jervis Bay in 1937. On the original photograph the upper surface of both upper and lower wings shows large 'splotches' of colour. They do not seem to be in any pattern and their colour and use is unknown. (RAAF Museum)

**Above:** A2-22 at Rathmines. Note the serial on the hull is outlined in white.

**Above:** A2-22 on the step at Rathmines in late 1940. The serial has been applied to the nose and fin stripes added in accordance with the change adopted by the RAAF in October 1940. Although not seen in the photograph the hull roundel now had a yellow outer ring. (AHMofWA P027265)

**Above, Below Left, & Below Right:** The remains of A2-15 after its tragic crash.

**Above & Right:** The Seagulls were carried by other than the Australian Fleet cruisers. Without a catapult the ship had to stop to launch and, in most cases, to pick up the machines. Camouflaged Seagull V A2-8 on deck and hoist of HMAS *Westralia*, on 10 April 1940, off Macassar, Celebes, at about 1630. Pilot F/Off Ekins, RAAF, Observer Lt P.E. Carr, RAN; Air Gunner: Leading Telegraphist Herzell, RAN. Seagull A2-8 hoisted out for preliminary Recce of Macassar Roads to confirm reports of presence of German merchant ship *Sheer*. (via P.E. Carr)

**Above:** The motor vessel *Minoora* was built in Scotland in 1935 for the Adelaide Steamship Co. It was named after the sheep station owned by Sir Walter Duncan, a director of the Company. Following the outbreak of war, the RAN took over the vessel on 14 November 1939, as an armed merchant cruiser. Her conversion saw seven 6-in guns and two 3-in anti-aircraft guns added as well as equipment to operate a seaplane. A 6-in gun is visible on the poop deck, with a Seagull V or Walrus amphibian in front of the funnel. In 1942, the ship was converted into Australia's first infantry landing ship, and in this guise served in the Pacific. After the war she continued in RAN service shipping occupation forces to Japan and bringing refugees to Australia until 1947. Converted back to a merchant ship she was returned to the Adelaide Steamship Co. Sold to Indonesia in 1961, she survived until 1972 when she was sold for scrap.

**Above:** Manhandling a bogged A2-16. At least 21 men can be made out pushing and pulling the aircraft.

**Above:** A camouflaged A2-16 alongside HMAS *Canberra* at a later stage in its life. It still carries the tri-coloured roundel. There is a Seagull on deck with folded wings.

**Above:** An Australian cruiser with a Seagull on the catapult.

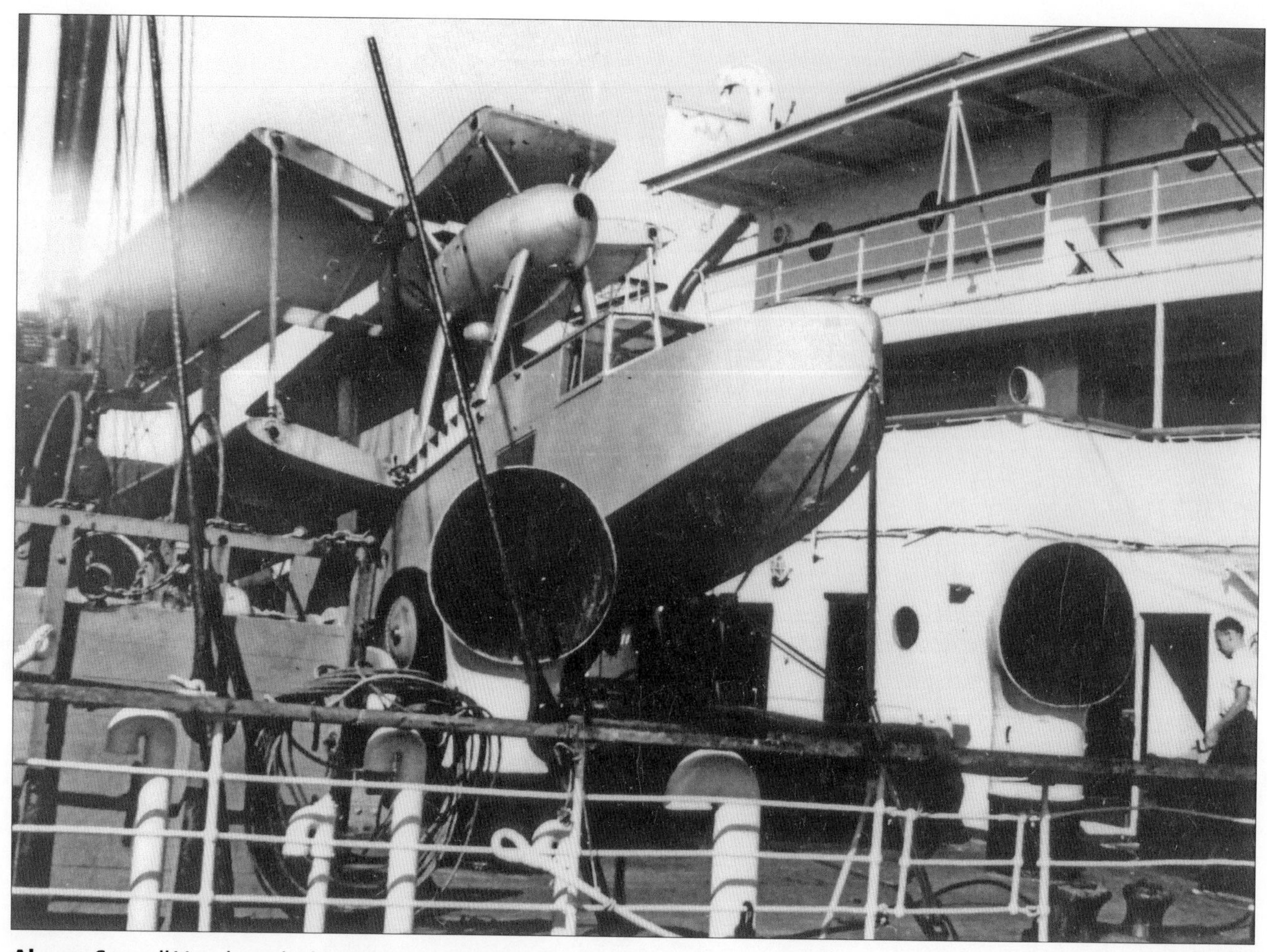

**Above:** Seagull V on board what appears to be a civilian ship.

of the aircraft. As it was desired to keep the aircraft ready for spotting, it was often not launched until just before a shoot. Changing requirements and the desire to know what was over the horizon was to lead to the aircraft being used more in the reconnaissance role, with the attendant risk that the machine would be damaged in recovery and not be available for combat as each ship only carried a single Seagull.

**Above:** A well-worn camouflaged A2-22 at No. 3 Operational Training Unit, Rathmines, circa 1943. Note the Catalina flying boats in the background and a Walrus Mk. I flying overhead. (AHMofWA P026743)

This is illustrated by the case of A2-23 on HMAS *Hobart*. In October 1939 she left for Singapore, and on the 31st, when returning from an exercise in the Malacca Strait, the aircraft crashed due to the inexperience of the crew in night landings. *Hobart* was without an aircraft until a Walrus could be obtained as a replacement, to be followed by another Walrus from Aden when the replacement seaplane came due for major maintenance. This latter Walrus engaged in hostilities against the Italians when it bombed a radio station at Massawa, Ethiopia. These replacement aircraft were often borrowed and it was some time before the official paperwork caught up with what was happening in the field.

On 21 June 1940, A2-21 was catapulted from HMAS *Sydney* to carry out spotting duties in co-operation with the attacking naval force on Bardia. Flt Lt Thomas MacBride Price took up his station directing naval gunfire when he *was intercepted by a formation of Italian fighters, two of which carried out diving attacks... The first indication of attack was the sound of machine-gun fire. At the time of the attack the Observer was engaged in spotting and the Telegraphist Air Gunner attending to the wireless. I immediately took avoiding action endeavouring to get my front and rear guns to bear...It was then that I received a second burst of fire which severed the aileron*

**Above:** This photograph of a dilapidated Seagull/Walrus shows the raised hatch of the rear cockpit and was dated 5 January 1967. Note the exposed starboard spar.

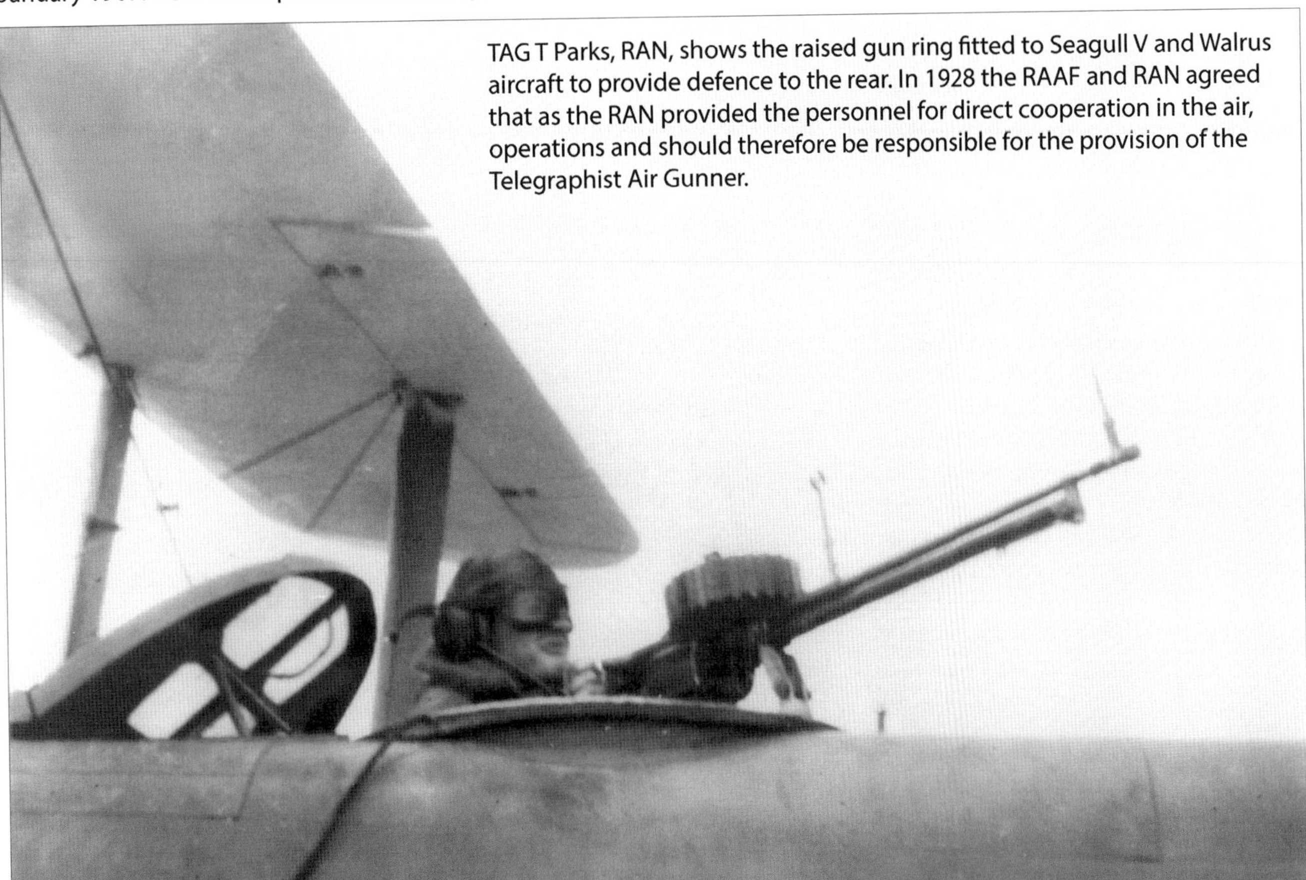

TAG T Parks, RAN, shows the raised gun ring fitted to Seagull V and Walrus aircraft to provide defence to the rear. In 1928 the RAAF and RAN agreed that as the RAN provided the personnel for direct cooperation in the air, operations and should therefore be responsible for the provision of the Telegraphist Air Gunner.

**Above & Below:** A series of photographs were taken of the Seagull V amphibians with the remaining Southampton, A11-2, in 1936. *Bull* Garing is thought to have been piloting the Southampton.

*control wires and the aircraft became out of control.*[60]

The amphibian plunged 7,000 feet before Price gained control at approximately 2,000 feet. As they were no longer under attack, he decided to lose height gradually and make for El Sollum about 10 miles inside the Egyptian border. The base proved unsuitable for forced landing owing to the nature of the surrounding country and he decided to try and make Mersa Matruh which was about 100 miles away rather than try and alight on the sea. Price was able to keep the aircraft laterally level and flew within 3/4 miles of the coastline until he reached Mersa Matruh. On landing the Seagull *the port wheel collapsed causing it to skid 180 degrees on one wing. The aircraft broke up on landing and the airframe is considered suitable for spares only. The engine is untouched and the airscrew* (sic) *has one bullet hole through it and is repairable.*[61]

In this action the tailplane struts had been almost shot away; the after part of the hull and fin badly riddled; the main spar of the port lower wing damaged; W/T aerials shot away and aileron control wires severed. Miraculously there were no casualties amongst the crew due to the action or the landing of the amphibian.

The observer, Lt Cdr J.C. Bacon, RN, had just noted where the third salvo from *Sydney* had fallen when there was *a sound of splintering wood and the next moment we were in a steep dive and I was going forward into the front gun position. It was at this time that I had my only glimpse of the aircraft which*

**Above:** HMAS *Canberra*. The catapult, sans Seagull V, is located behind the three funnels.

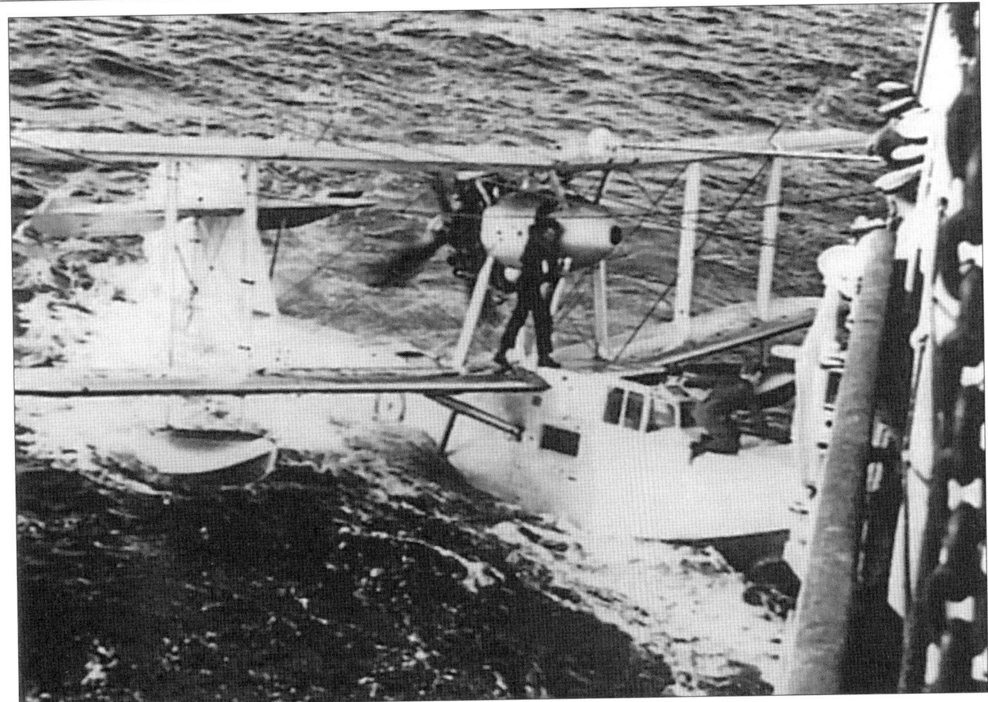

**Right, Above & Below:** A2-1 taxying up to and being hoisted aboard HMAS *Australia*. The damaged wing would have been caused by collision with the ship. Most probably while hoisting.

**Above:** Walrus L2293 damaged wing, repaired on *Canberra*, July 1942.

**Above:** Cpl L Riddell, LAC A.H. Roberts and Cpl R Bliss repairing the wing of Walrus X9510 (ZA-X) as used by the RAAF at Jacquinot Bay, New Guinea. (via Vic State Library)

After No. 107 Squadron was disbanded, the Seagull V and Walrus amphibians were lined up for disposal. Photograph dated 31 October 1945. W2705 served with No. 9 Squadron from July 1942 until July 1943. The codes YQ-H were assigned in April 1943, but they were then allocated to W2755 in July the same year. YQ was the allotted Code letters for No. 9 Squadron.

**Above:** Walrus HD812 of No. 9 Squadron taken at the same time and same location as the previous photograph. The YQ-J codes were assigned to A2-6 before it was lost on 30 August 1943, and were reallotted to HD812.

*attacked us and all I noticed was a wing...and part of the fuselage, and that the underside of the wing appeared a dark brown.* Bacon had noted that while climbing *three fighter aircraft in formation were sighted and were judged to be Gladiators. Their camouflage and fuselage markings appeared to be the same as ours.*[62] Although some historians have stated that the attacking fighters were RAF Gladiators, Bacon insisted that they were Italian aircraft.[63]

Bacon thoroughly commended the action of Price in *deciding to fly the extra 100 miles to Mersa Matruh and for arriving there safely and consider it a very creditable feat of airmanship.*[64] The Seagull V was restricted to diving at airspeeds below 150 mph and when *approaching 150 miles per hour, the greatest care is to be exercised to handle the controls gently when recovering to normal flight.*[65] Price must have exceeded these safety parameters in his wild dive and it is a tribute to the sturdiness of Supermarine's construction that the Seagull held together.

In mid-1940 it was considered that in *view of the number of unserviceable Seagull aircraft in the Service due chiefly to our inability to obtain spares, etc., from overseas, demands for which have been outstanding up to two years, it was decided to endeavour to obtain from the Air Ministry 6 Walrus aircraft to make good the deficiency in Seagull aircraft.*[66] The British agreed to release two Walrus from the Far East Command to be taken delivery of at Singapore. These were L2318 and L2319 which were shipped to 2 AD, Richmond via the *Mangola* on 5 July. The cost of these two-year-old aircraft was £21,700.

A Meeting on the overhaul and repair of aircraft in April 1941 was told that ten unserviceable Seagulls were held within the Service, two without engines and eight for repair. Stainless steel for repairs was in short supply and the CAS (Sir Charles Burnett) stressed the *absolute importance* of Seagull aircraft and urged that the overhaul of these aircraft was most important as *the demand for this type of aircraft was most urgent.*[67] No suitable replacement aircraft had been produced either in the UK or USA and as the Supermarine Sea Otter had little to offer in terms of increased performance the Air Board decided to wait until the S12/40 amphibian had been tested before deciding on which aircraft to rearm the Fleet Co-Operation Squadrons.[68]

Six Walrus were noted in November as having been ordered to meet *immediate requirements* until a new aircraft could be provided by the UK aircraft industry.[69] Further Walrus amphibians were forthcoming and in 1943 five were being erected at the QANTAS facility at Rose Bay. The Senior Maintenance Staff Officer complained that the work was being slowed by the number of modifications required to be made to the biplanes and by the fact that as few spares were available, QANTAS had to make them.[70]

When HMAS *Perth* replaced HMAS *Sydney* in the Mediterranean Fleet, she had her catapult removed at Alexandria to make room for anti-aircraft guns. Her Seagull, A2-17, was operated from Suda Bay, Crete, until German strafing attacks led to the crew, under Flt Lt E.V. Beaumont, bringing the aircraft to shore. They found a sheltered beach where it was possible to bring the amphibian up against a steep hill. A2-17 continued to operate from here until it was strafed at Heraklion by Italian fighters and had to be carefully flown to Alexandria for repair.

**Above:** A2-21 after its crash landing at Mersa Matruh on 21 June 1940.

A cartoon showing what the airmen thought of their Antarctic adventures.

**Left:** Manhandling a camouflaged Supermarine amphibian ashore in less than ideal condition in the tropics. (via Vic State Library)

**Above:** HD874 after its encounter with Antarctic weather. John Paddick poses with the remains of HD874, Herd Island, 1949. (RAAF Museum)

On 28 April 1941, A2-17 was performing a reconnaissance of the island of Kithera when it was attacked by two German Junkers Ju.88 bombers. Beaumont *made for the hilly country in the extreme South of the island and endeavoured to evade them by flying low around the hills and down the valleys.* By flying as low as possible the crew were able to evade the worst of the German attacks, but *Within the first few minutes of the combat a shot...passed through the starboard fuel tank which drained in about three minutes.* Beaumont headed for Antikithera still pursued by the German aircraft. TAG Petty Officer D.M. *Danny* Bowden, RAN, kept up return fire from the rear gun. The marine distress flares, stowed aft of the rear gunner's position, ignited from being hit by German fire. *With flames from the fuel tank passing over his head, and the distress signal going off in the confined space of the hull aft of him,* Bowden *Coolly kept up his fire until the enemy had passed out of range, and then pulled the signals from the stowage and threw them, burning, over the side.* Sub Lt (A) G.F.S. Brian, RN, the observer, had his gun jam after a few shots and he was not able to clear the stoppage. The port fuel tank was hit and burst into flames. *The engine cut out for lack of fuel, and it was necessary to land in the sea... The enemy then ceased fire.* The Germans, apparently satisfied with their work, left the area. The crew launched their dingy; Beaumont returned to the hull to recover emergency rations and only just climbed out before the burning engine and wing collapsed onto the cockpit area. The hulk sunk soon thereafter. A passing destroyer, HMS *Havoc*, picked the three crew up that night.[71]

In Australia the Seagull V was fitted with experimental self-sealing fuel tanks in 1942. These tanks were made by the Fire Proof Tank Ltd of Adelaide, and were covered using the C.I.M.A.50T process. The test tanks were a success but *several minor modifications were necessary in order to provide access for fuel gauges, drain cock and bonding clips.*[72] The tanks were returned for the necessary modifications and a program installed to convert all the amphibians to the self-sealing tanks. As no pool of self-sealing tanks was held, it became necessary to remove tanks from aircraft as they came in for inspection or repair and dispatch them to Adelaide for treatment, a procedure which entailed a minimum of three weeks unserviceability.

In addition to their other duties the Seagull V was used to tow drogues for anti-aircraft practice. The gear was available in 1939; however, it would appear that the whole process of co-operation with the Army was a very confused and unorganised affair. In 1940 the RAAF could not provide a Seagull V for co-operation with the 4th Anti-Aircraft Battery from 4 to 7 March owing to *embarkation of a Seagull in each of H.M.A.S. 'Manoora' and 'Westralia'*

**Above & Above Right:** The hull of HD874 after recovery in 1980 and in the RAAF Museum restoration facility, 12 June 1992. (via D Makowski)

*and unserviceability of remaining aircraft.*[73] It was stated that the Seagull V was the only aircraft capable of carrying sufficient cable to trail a drogue for anti-aircraft practice. These aircraft were allocated to No. 9 Squadron stationed at Rathmines. Colin Harvey flew army co-op flights in A2-19 during 1940. He recalls that the winch was fitted to operate through the starboard side window, 6,000 feet of cable being used.[74] The next year the Army was told that the *only sets of anti-aircraft towing gear available* (were) *being installed in 3 Battle aircraft at No.1 Air Depot, Laverton.* The set fitted to a Seagull V had been removed for installation in a Battle monoplane.[75] Seven months later the RAAF stated that with regard to drogue towing aircraft the Seagull was the only aircraft which carried *sufficient cable to trail drogues for AA practice. These aircraft are stationed at RATHMINES, NSW.*[76] Other problems associated with co-operation with the Army are detailed in the chapter on the Hawker Demon. These fragmentary glimpses show that as far as carrying out training in Australia the relationship between the RAAF and the Army was not smooth.

The Seaplane Training Flight of 1 FTS was transferred to Rathmines as a separate unit on 1 March 1940. No. 9 Squadron also operated from there. Problems were experienced with obtaining enough aircraft to carry out an effective training program. The first Consolidated Catalina flying boat, A24-1, arrived in February 1941 and conditions improved from then. During the month of January 1942, all other aircraft apart from the Catalinas were transferred to No. 9 Squadron who conducted initial pilot conversion courses using a Douglas Dolphin and Seagull V aircraft. The Seaplane Training Flight only conducted conversion courses onto the Catalina.[77]

The Seagull V is remembered with affection by its crews. Colin Harvey recalls that there were two *major No/No's with Seagulls - Make sure the camera hatch in the hull was secure and put the cap back on the trailing aerial fairlead after reeling in the aerial! Otherwise spectacular fire-hose effects* would occur during a landing on water.[78] Philip Mathiesen thought it was *quite an aeroplane.* It was a *remarkable aeroplane in that it was very, very strong. It was fully aerobatic... When you opened up for take-off, there was a lot of turning moment there. You used to start the take-off with full left rudder and the wheel right over to the left, then as you built up speed you gradually unwound*

**Above & Facing Page:** Restoration work on the hull of HD874. (via D Makowski)

**This Page & Facing Page:** The rebuilt HD874 rolled out for a photographic session at the RAAF Museum, Point Cook. (RAAF Museum)

RAAF Museum: Walrus HD874: Received by QANTAS at Rose Bay on 14 September 1943, HD874 was initially allotted to No 9 Squadron in December of that year. In storage until 1947, HD874 was then sent to Maintenance Squadron Rathmines for servicing before issue to the RAAF's Antarctic Flight in October of that year. Nicknamed 'Snow Goose' and painted bright yellow, HD874 was transported on HMAS Labuan LST3501 to Heard Island, for the National Antarctica Research Expedition 30 October 1947, and flew only once before being badly damaged in a storm on 21 December 1947. The damaged hull was recovered by the RAAF in 1980, and transported to Point Cook, restoration of the airframe began in 1991, and the amphibian was completed in 2002.

HD-874

**Above & Facing Page:** The rebuilt HD874 rolled out for a photographic session at the RAAF Museum, Point Cook. (RAAF Museum)

A2-4 when operating under its civil registration VH-ALB at Coffs Harbour, 1965. In January 1970, the aircraft had a forced landing the pilot not selecting both tanks for take-off, the selected tank being near empty. On landing the amphibian hit a tree stump hidden in the long grass and this tor off the undercarriage leg, the resultant damage ending the types flying career. The remains were obtained by the RAF Museum and it was airlifted back to the UK by No. 53 Squadron Belfast transports. Restored at RAF Wyton, it was displayed at the RAF Museum Hendon as a British Walrus. In 1979 it was moved to the Battle of Britain Hall and shown in RAAF camouflage and markings.

*all this.*[79] Harry Lobb recalls that the RAAF did not carry out catapult training before a pilot was assigned to a ship. *We had a new pilot come on board, a fellow named Murchinson, he was taking over from F/O LAVERACK...Murchinson had never been catapulted, so first time off Laverack flew it. Volunteers were called for to make a crew – there was a rush naturally. We recovered the plane and next time Murchinson flew it and Laverack sat beside him (volunteers not so many). The third time Murchinson flew it by himself (no volunteers), but as the Navy always said, 10 pressed men were better than one volunteer.*[80]

42 Radar Direction Finding (RDF) Wing HQ thought that the Seagull was ideally suited to the task of servicing the RDF stations which were usually situated on remote coastal locations on the mainland and small islands where landing strips were not possible and they had to be maintained by naval vessel. The unit had an allotment of one Anson and one Tiger Moth and wanted a 'Walrus' in lieu of the Tiger Moth. In making its application for such replacement the unit noted that in addition to supplying these remote stations, the Seagull, *due to its metal construction and suitability for the installation of such equipment as is required* was considered ideal for carrying out radar calibration and training duties. Unfortunately, the request was denied.[81] The type was operated by Communication Units (as the Communication Flights became) for search and rescue in the islands to the north of Australia.

The War Cabinet was informed in June 1940 that the Seagull was obsolete and that the *R.A.F. Walrus is very similar to the Seagull and is therefore unsuitable as a replacement. In any case the Air Ministry has stated that neither the Seagull nor the Walrus can be made available. Investigation must therefore be made of suitable American amphibious types.*[82] The RAAF had a requirement for 27 amphibians to re-arm the Fleet Co-operation Squadrons.[83] Despite this four Walrus amphibians, together with seven Beaufighters, were reported on board the *Port Melbourne* and were expected to arrive in Melbourne in September 1942.[84] It appears that Overseas Indent 1255 was raised in May 1943 for the supply of 12 Walrus aircraft.[85] This Indent may have been to cover the aircraft already obtained by the RAAF, but this is not clear from surviving documents. It was probably the inability to obtain a suitable replacement which led to the comment that it was *not desirable to make any further reduction in numbers (of) Seagull (and) Walrus in Service* and to complete the repairs to those at QANTAS.[86] The amphibians continued to perform valuable service and it was not until late 1945 that it was *confirmed that there is no future requirement for Walrus aircraft in the R.A.A.F.* and the type was declared obsolete on 3 December on Air Board Order E.24/15.[87]

Walrus aircraft were no longer required on the strengths of Nos. 6 and 8 Communication Units and those already held by those two units were to be withdrawn. Two serviceable Walrus aircraft were required by the RN for Air Sea Rescue duties with the British Pacific Fleet. These aircraft did not require offensive armament but would require radar and were to be delivered to Naval Air Station Schofield, immediately.[88] These were Z1804 and Z1811 which were located at 2 Flying Boat Repair Depot. No further work of a major nature was to be done on the amphibians but work which was almost complete could be finished and the aircraft allotted to Rathmines. *No further operational use of Seagull and Walrus aircraft in the R.A.A.F. is envisaged.*[89] There were four Seagull and 12 Walrus amphibians still remaining in the RAAF at this time. Two Sea Otter amphibians, the successor to the Walrus in the RAF, were *to be taken over from R.N. at Naval Air Station Bankstown (and were) to be allotted to No.11 Communication Unit for the exclusive use of the Commander Task Force 70.5 R.A.N. for survey duties.*[90] In June 1945, the RAN no longer wanted these biplanes and the requirement lapsed.

The Department of Aircraft Production declared all Pegasus engines surplus in 1947.[91] The amphibians were put up for disposal but *One Seagull aircraft, three spare Pegasus engines and a range of airframe and engine spares and associated equipment peculiar to this type of aircraft, to an approximate value of £2,000, were withdrawn from disposal for use in the Antarctic Expedition.*[92] The aircraft which was loaned to the Department of External Affairs was recorded as HD874, a wooden hull Walrus II (of batch HD904-HD936) built by Saunders Roe, however the RAAF aircraft had a metal hull and could well have been a Seagull V. In any event the orange painted amphibian made only one flight before being wrecked during storms at Heard Island in which winds of up to 120 mph battered the aircraft.

Geoffrey *Geoff* Meek was one of the crew of HD874. He recollected that the

*Walrus was in storage at Lake Boga and from there we flew her to Rathmines where she was fitted out for Antarctica. After refitting we made several flights from Rathmines to Garden Island Sydney where we did recovery and launching practice with LST3501 which was later named HMAS Labaun.*

*Part of my duties in this procedure was to kneel on the top wing and grab the hook lowered from the LST and attach it to the inboard sling on the wing. The reverse procedure was applied for launching and I might ass it was rather a hairy experience especially if there was a bit of a swell. My other duties apart from being the fitter ws to act as Co-Pilot whilst the Pilot used the sextant etc.*

*On leaving Sydney the LST berthed at Williamstown Melbourne and Freemantle Western Australia. As the walrus was cradled on the ship's main hatch we had to take it off at these ports to facilitate loading of stores. At these stopovers we encamped at Laverton Victoria and Crawley Bay Perth.*

*At Crawley Bay we were taking Air Training Corps boys for flights and using the //Walrus Amphibian capabilities.*

*After the firs flight we parked half way up the steep steel ramp to take on the nest boys and due to the attitude of the tail plane still being in the water we shipped quite a quantity of water and took off with this extra weight.*

*As we were circling over Perth I decided I would pump it out and often wonder if the residents of Perth thought they were*

*having a summer shower.*

*After leaving Freemantle we had a very rough passage to Heard Island where we only made one flight.*[93]

The pilot of HD874 was Mal Smith who was killed in a Catalina crash at Lord Howe Island in 1948.

This was the last operational RAAF Supermarine amphibian. Future aircraft requirements for Antarctic expeditions were to be limited to Kingfisher and Norseman types only.[94]

The Commonwealth Disposals Commission announced 13 Seagull and Walrus amphibians for disposal in August 1946. For some reason three ex-British aircraft, X9514, X9517 and X2705[95], were listed as Seagulls. The Department of Civil Aviation would give the type a Certificate of Airworthiness and they could allowed to be used for private, aerial work or charter, but not for regular scheduled passenger operations.[96]

Fourteen Seagull and Walrus amphibians were listed for disposal on 19 August 1948, and an auction was held at Rathmines on 2 March 1949. A Mr E McIllree purchased a hull and three brand new Pegasus VI engines. This was in addition to the three Walrus aircraft and large complement of spares he purchased two years earlier from Dubbo, Lake Boga, Richmond, etc. McIllree had purchased A2-4 with engine in 1946 for £600, and P5664 and A2-3 in 1947, the latter two being flown to Sydney. The 1949 sale carried the warning that this *equipment is to be sold for its scrap value only and purchases are to be warned that it may not be used for any purpose in contradiction of Department (of) Civil Aviation Requirements.*[97]

The remains of Walrus HD874 were recovered from Antarctica and landed from the *Cape Pillar* at Fremantle, WA, in April 1980. They comprised a badly damaged hull, engine pod and the original engine. The wing sections recovered were so badly damaged they were only useful as templates for newly constructed wings. The tail plane, including rudder, had been torn from the aircraft. Reconstructed by RAAF Museum staff and volunteers, the completed project was rolled out in 2001. It is presently displayed in the Museum at Point Cook, in its Antarctic colours. Of the civil Seagull V amphibians, VH-ALB, ex-A2-4, is preserved in the RAF Museum, Hendon, UK.

The Seagull V amphibian's robustness enabled it to operate away from special facilities for long periods. The type proved itself as a good reconnaissance and gun-laying aircraft but was vulnerable to fighter opposition. From the Arctic to the Antarctic the RAAF flew its Seagull V and Walrus aircraft. They operated against the Germans, Vichy French, Italians and Japanese. Their role was supplanted by the development of radar but they continued to soldier on to the end of the war. With their passing an era ended.

## Specifications

**Seagull V**

Dimensions: Span: 45 ft 10 in. Length 37 ft 7 in. Height 15 ft 3 in on undercarriage.
Weights: Empty 4,900 lb, Loaded 7,200 lbs.
Performance: Speed Max 135 mph. Cruising 95 mph. Range 600 mls.
Armament: Two Vickers K guns or Lewis guns. Bomb load 500 lbs. Anti-submarine bombs or depth charges alternate load.

**Walrus I**

Dimensions: Span 45 ft 10 in; Length 37 ft 7 in; Height 16 ft 10 in on undercarriage. Area mainplanes 610 ft $^2$.
Weights: Empty 4,900 lb; Loaded 7,200 lb.
Performance: Max 135 mph; 124 mph with ASV and weapons load; Range 512 mls.
Armament: Two Vickers K guns or Lewis guns, 4 x 100-lb anti-submarine bombs and eight 20-lb bombs. Two 380-lb Mk. VII depth charges was alternate load.

## End Notes

1. Williams is thought to have designed a specification for a Seagull III replacement in the mid-1920s. He did this by working with the dimensions of the hangar, hatch, and crane of *Albatross*. An air-cooled engine was standard to all RAAF specifications and a requirement of its shipboard operations was that it be installed as a pusher so that the airman, who had to sit on the top wing to pick up the crane hook, would not be in danger from the propeller. The hull was to be of metal and the aircraft was to be capable of being catapult launched. No British firm was interested in such a design until Supermarine, a division of Vickers, took up the challenge. AA ACT CRS A705/1 Item 114/6/57. Quarterly Letter. Four Months Ending 31.01.1930. The Australian connection with the design of the Seagull V is alluded to in Letterbook entries where the ALO asked for permissible dimensions for Supermarine who were proceeding with the design of an all metal amphibian. AA ACT CRS A2408 Item 200/3. Letterbook L.14 - Aircraft Carriers. Entry 266 of 24.01.1930.
2. Air Board Agendum No.1398. Memorandum by R Williams, 2.05.1930.
3. *Ibid.* Memorandum of 16.05.1930.
4. *Ibid.* Minister's handwritten comment, 9.05.1930.
5. Williams, R. *These Are Facts,* P.209.
6. NAA ACT CRS A705 Item 13/5/237. Supermarine Amphibian. Wireless message, Austair to Air Board. 26.06.1933.
7. Nicholl, G.W.R. *The Supermarine Walrus*, G T Foulis, UK, 1966, P.18.
8. Colin Harvey noted that A2-4, A2-14, A2-18, A2-19 and A2-22 were at Rathmines in 1939 and all were equipped with inertia, not gas, starters. To operate the inertia starter *one stood on the port centre section with a safety belt on (so as not to slip down into the prop). Wound a big handle and then pulled a wire to engage the clutch! Quite impressive starts, with smoke and noise from the short stub exhausts!* Notes to draft chapter.

08.1991.
9. NAA ACT CRS A705 Item 13/5/237. *Op Cit.* Supermarine Aviation Works (Vickers) Ltd, Specification No.401.C, 28.06.1933.
Colin Harvey commented that the usual method of communication before the advent of the enclosed cockpit was for the crew to yell at one another! Comments to draft chapter, 08.1991.
10. Colin Harvey recalled that *the rear gun was only about three feet astern of the 4 bladed prop. It was a noisy/windy/smelly and dangerous station. It was also used to send/receive messages by Aldis lamp - Interesting without voice intercom or any safe way to write (down) received messages.* Notes to draft chapter, August 1991.
11. NAA ACT CRS A705 Item 13/5/237. *Op Cit.* Experimental Test Report No. F/118, P.31.
12. *Ibid.* P.31B.
13. *Ibid.* P.36A.
14. *Ibid.* Letter from Robert Bryce and Co Pty Ltd to Air Board, 26.10.1933.
15. *Ibid.* Rear Admiral R.C. Dalflish to Navy Board, 4.10.1933.
16. *Ibid.* Signal Air Board to Air Liaison officer. December 1933.
17. *Ibid.* Minute to Air Member for Supply, 10.01.1934.
18. *Ibid.* Secret Wireless message, Air Board to Austair.
19. *Ibid.* Secret wireless message, Austair (Williams) to Air Board.
20. The engine was also designated II M2. That used is as recorded in RAAF documents.
21. Williams Papers, RAAF Museum Point Cook. Williams to Brigade General W.B. Caddell, Supermarine (Vickers) Aviation Ltd, 3 October 1934.
22. NAA ACT CRS A705 Item 13/5/237. *Op Cit.* Air Member for Supply, Air Board Agendum No.1724/1935.
23. The main external distinguishing feature between the Seagull V and the Walrus was that the latter did not have slots fitted as the aircraft responded well on all axes near stalling speed. On the Seagull V the jury struts that were fitted when the wings were folded were usually stowed in the rear fuselage, whilst on the Walrus they were not generally removed.
24. NAA ACT CRS A705 Item 13/5/237. *Op Cit.* Wireless message, Austair to Air Board, 16.05.1935.
25. *Ibid.* Memorandum to Air Liaison from Dept of Defence, 21.05.1935.
26. *Ibid.* Wireless Message to AUSTAIR.
27. *Aircraft*, 2.03.1936. P.35.
28. NAA Vic CRS MP124/6 Item 415/201/1100. Memo: Petrol Stoppages in Seagull, Mark V. CO, HMAS AUSTRALIA at Alexandria, to Rear-Admiral Commanding First Cruiser Squadron, 11.06.1936.
29. NAA ACT CRS A705/1 Item 9/5/194. Seagull Mainplanes and Spars - Repair Of Seagull Defects. Report from No. 5 Squadron to HQ, RAAF, Richmond, 22.05.1936.
30. NAA ACT CRS A705/1 Item 9/5/194. *Op Cit.* HQ, RAAF Richmond, to Air Board, 26.05.1936.
31. Notes to draft chapter by C Harvey, 08.1991.
32. NAA ACT CRS A705/1 Item 9/5/194. *Op Cit.* No.2 AD, Richmond, to Air Board, 25.05.1937.
33. NAA Vic MP1118/2 Item 69/2/722. Defective Fabric Seagull A2-15. Report 22.09.1937.
34. *9 Squadron Diary* via J Barr.
35. NAA ACT CRS A1196/1 Item 1/501/89. Stowage of Seagulls in ALBATROSS. Report, Flight Lieutenant J Alexander to Air Board, 29.11.1937.
36. *Ibid.* Minute; Navy Board to Air Board, 1.04.1938.
37. NAA ACT CRS A705/1 Item 9/5/213. Seagull V Folding Flap Defect. Minute, DTS to CAS, 17.07.1941.
38. Nicholl, Lt-Commander G.W.R. *The Supermarine Walrus*, G.T. Foulis and Co Ltd, UK, 1966, P.63.
39. NAA ACT CRS A705 Item 9/5/213. *Op Cit.* Minute: DTS to CAS, 17.07.1941.
40. NAA ACT CRS A705/1 Item 32/10/1863. Accident to Seagull A2-7 at Archerfield. CO, RAAF Richmond, to Air Board, 24.11.1937.
41. NAA ACT CRS A2408 Item 9/5. Walrus and Seagull. Letterbook entry No.64, 21.10.1938.
42. NAA CRS MP124/6 Item 415/201/1352. Armament Equipment on Seagull V Aircraft. Air Board to Navy Board, 27.10.1938.
43. Air Board Agendum No.2576.
44. Nicholl, G.W.R., *Op Cit,* P.57.
45. NAA Vic CRS MP124/6 Item 415/201/1105. Message: "Breakdown and Recovery of Seagull Amphibian A 2-5, 2nd and 3rd September, 1936." CO, HMAS Canberra to Rear Admiral, HMA Squadron, 7.09.1936.
46. NAA Vic CRS MP124/6 Item 415/201/1140. Commander HMA Squadron to Navy Board, 30.01.1937.
47. *Ibid.* Navy Board to Commander HMA Squadron, 3.03.1937.
48. By April 1939, A2-5, A2-21and A2-22 were fitted with R1082/T1083 radios. The earlier equipment ending up in the Signal School outstations at Laverton. Notes on draft chapter by C Harvey. 08.1991.
49. NAA ACT CRS A705/1 Item 153/1/859. Search For Missing Launch "Mystery Star" (Messrs. B Abott and L.H. Simpson). Report to CO, 5 Squadron, 26.10.1936.
50. NAA ACT CRS A705/1 Item 153/1/885. Air Observation of Pelagic Fish Movement. R.A.A.F. Operations on Behalf of the Council For Scientific And Industrial Research. 1936 and 1937. Report by F/O A.X. Richards, enclosed with letter from CO, Richmond, to Air Board, 15.12.1936.
51. *Ibid.* Report by Mr. S Fowler, 22.12.1936.
52. *Ibid.*
53. *Ibid.* Minute: "Aerial Observation of Pelagic Fish", 9.02.1937.
54. *Ibid.* Report by S Fowler, 12.04.1937.

55. *Ibid.*
56. *Ibid.* Report by Flight Lieutenant Alexander to CO, 5 Squadron, 14.04.1937.
57. *Rainbow* Thorley earned his nickname by his habit of ending W/T transmissions with "OK Rainbow". When Seagull aircraft were employed on pelagic fish surveys the Coastal Radio Net was used for Communications. Notes on draft chapter by J Gerber, 08.1991.
58. NAA Vic CRS MP187/4 ITEM 196. Aircraft Accident Report Files. "AAIC Report No.196."
59. NAA ACT CRS A9186/11 Item 246. Unit Diary RAAF Station Richmond. April 1936 to March 1952.
60. NAA ACT CRS A705/1 Item 9/5/181. Report from Flight Lieutenant T MacBride Price to CO, HMAS Sydney, 26.06.1940.
61. *Ibid.*
62. *Ibid.* Report by Lieutenant Commander J.C. Bacon, RN, to CO, HMAS Sydney, 24.06.1940.
63. For example see *Australian Aviation*, June 1990, P.41. The information from Bacon was given to Lt Cdr R Geale, Curator of the Australian Naval Aviation Museum, Nowra. Interview with Geale on 16.09.1996.
64. NAA ACT CRS A705/1 Item 9/5/181. *Op Cit.* Report by Lieutenant Commander J.C. Bacon, RN, to CO, HMAS Sydney, 24.06.1940.
65. NAA ACT CRS A705/1 Item 9/5/241. Flying Restrictions Walrus Aircraft. "Starting Procedures, etc., Seagull V."
66. NAA ACT CRS A705/1 Item 9/5/167. Supply of Walrus Aircraft from Far East. Minute from Director General Supply and Production, 24.05.1940.
67. NAA ACT CRS A705/1 Item 9/1/548. Minute: Minutes of Meeting Held at Century House, Tuesday, April 8, 1941.
68. NAA ACT CRS A5954/1 Item 230/1. Expansion of Home Defence Air Forces Aircraft Required for RAAF Home Defence Units. Supplement No.7 to War Cabinet Agenda 151/1940, considered 13.09.1941.
69. NAA ACT CRS A5954 Item 215/6. Supply of Spare Engines, Airframes and Engine Spares For Local Manufacture Beaufort Aircraft. War Cabinet Minute of 17.11.1941.
70. NAA ACT CRS A705 Item 9/5/273. Seagull V and Walrus Aircraft General Technical File. "Walrus Erection". Senior Maintenance Staff Officer to Air Board, 18.10.43.
71. Report by Flt Lt E.V. Beaumont on Loss of Seagull A2-17. 30.04.1941. Copy in Australian Naval Aviation Museum, Nowra, NSW.
72. NAA ACT CRS A705/1 Item 9/5/251. Seagull Aircraft Installation Self Seal Fuel Tanks. Minute to TS1 from TS1(b.1).
73. NAA ACT CRS A705/1 Item 208/3/488. Army Co-Operation - Southern Command. CO, No.2 Group, RAAF, Point Piper, to Air Board, 26.02.1940.
74. Notes on draft chapter, August 1991.
75. NAA ACT CRS A705/1 Item 208/3/488. Army Co-Operation. Southern Command. Copy: "RAA Anti-aircraft Practice Shoots", 17.06.1941.
76. NAA ACT CRS A705/1 Item 208/3/488. *Op Cit.* "Air Co-Op: Target Aircraft - AA Defences", 23.01.1942.
77. NAA ACT CRS A9186/14 Item 362. "Seaplane Training Flight Unit Diary" to December 1942. RAAF Form A50.
78. Notes to draft chapter, August 1991.
79. "Philip Mathiesen - Flying Boat Experiences", *Man and Aerial Machines*, No.56, March-April 1966, P.9.
80. Letter to author, 27.07.1995.
81. NAA ACT CRS A705/1 Item 9/2/238. HQ, NE Area to Air Board, 18.05.1943.
82. NAA ACT CRS A1196/2 Item 36/501/113. RAAF Development Program (Expansion Scheme Z). Organisation Policy. War Cabinet Agendum No.151/1940, 28.06.1940.
83. NAA ACT CRS A5954/1 Item 1808/3. Paper No.19 Aircraft Requirements. "Prime Minister's Visit to U.K., 1941. Aircraft Required for Royal Australian Air Force Home Defence Units", 14.01.1941.
84. NAA ACT CRS A705/1 Item 9/2/238. Vessels Enroute to Australia with Aircraft, 4.09.1942.
85. NAA ACT CRS A2408 Item 9/5. Walrus and Seagull. Letterbook entry No.293, 25.05.1943.
86. NAA ACT CRS A705 Item 9/1/1425. Seagull Aircraft Allotment Policy. Minute, 13.11.1944(?).
87. NAA ACT CRS A705/1 Item 9/1/1425. Obsolescent Aircraft - Repair and Maintenance Policy. Copy of Minute extracted from File 9/5/321, 10.12.1945.
88. NAA ACT CRS A705/1 Item 9/2/471. Seagull Aircraft Allotment Policy. Minute from S/Ldr L.M. Hurt, TOR (GR/FB), 10.09.1945.
89. *Ibid.*
90. *Ibid.* Minute 14.11.1944(?).
91. NAA ACT CRS A2408 Item 69/16. L14 - Pegasus Engines and Spares. Entry No.173 of 31.07.1947.
92. NAA ACT CRS A705/1 Item 9/86/32. Disposal Seagull and Walrus Aircraft, Pegasus VI and 2M2 Engines, Spares and Associated Equipment. Air Board, 20.08.1948.
93. Letter to author 31.10.1995.
94. NAA ACT A705/1 Item 9/86/40. Disposal of Seagull and Walrus Aircraft and Spare Pegasus VI and 2M2 Engines. Minute 24, 3.12.1947.
95. X2705 was not issued and this serial must have been misquoted.
96. Copy of document reproduced in AHSA Newsletter 4.02.1988.
97. NAA ACT CRS A705/1 Item 9/86/40. *Op Cit.* Auction on Transfer Authority, 9.08.1948.

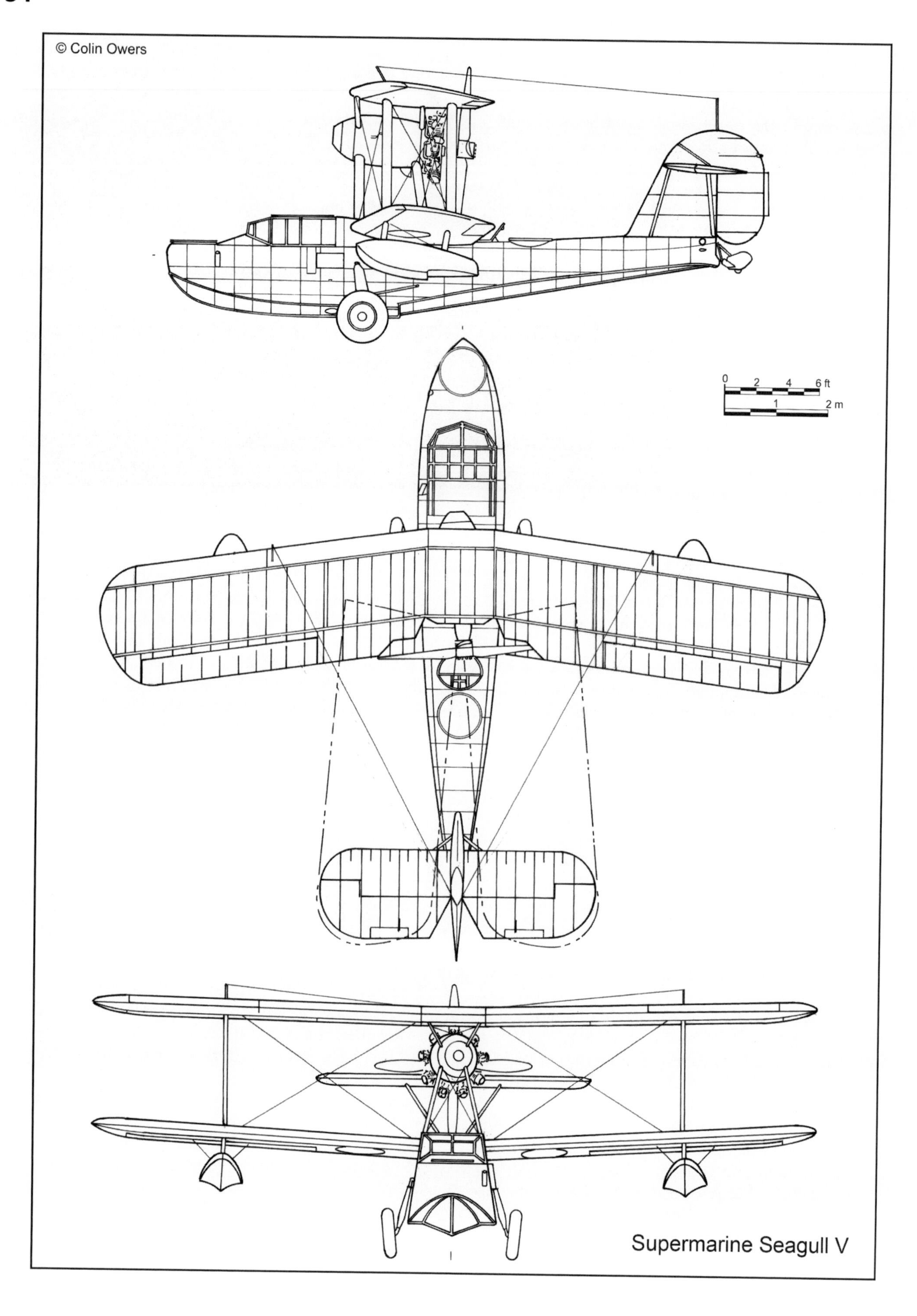


Supermarine Seagull V

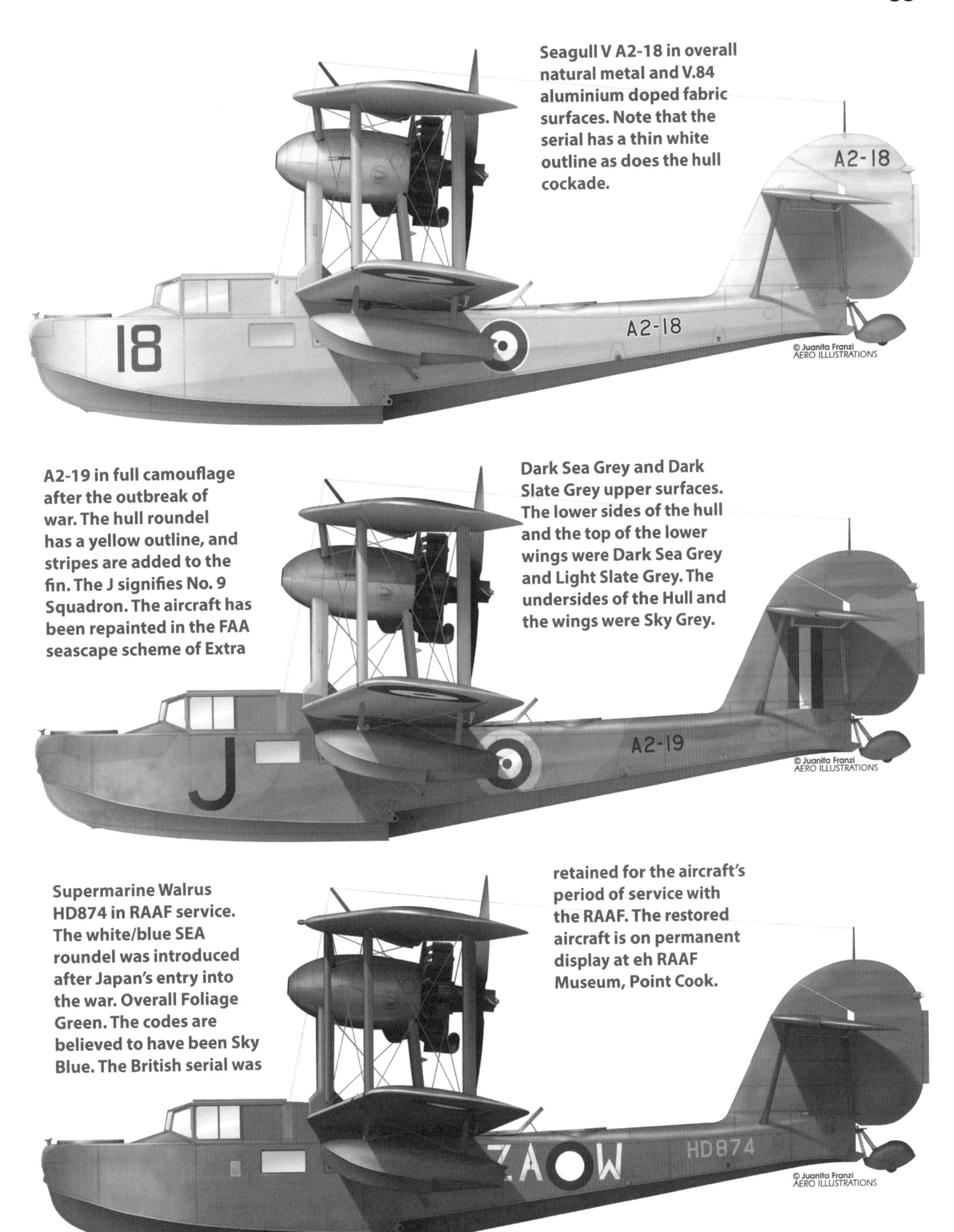


**Seagull V A2-18 in overall natural metal and V.84 aluminium doped fabric surfaces. Note that the serial has a thin white outline as does the hull cockade.**

**A2-19 in full camouflage after the outbreak of war. The hull roundel has a yellow outline, and stripes are added to the fin. The J signifies No. 9 Squadron. The aircraft has been repainted in the FAA seascape scheme of Extra Dark Sea Grey and Dark Slate Grey upper surfaces. The lower sides of the hull and the top of the lower wings were Dark Sea Grey and Light Slate Grey. The undersides of the Hull and the wings were Sky Grey.**

**Supermarine Walrus HD874 in RAAF service. The white/blue SEA roundel was introduced after Japan's entry into the war. Overall Foliage Green. The codes are believed to have been Sky Blue. The British serial was retained for the aircraft's period of service with the RAAF. The restored aircraft is on permanent display at eh RAAF Museum, Point Cook.**

**Above:** Why A2-1 has what appears to be a number 11 on the bow is unknown.

## Supermarine Seagull V – RAAF A2 Supermarine Walrus in RAAF Service Individual Aircraft Histories

### A2-1

25.06.35. First flight by G Pickering from Southampton on Water, UK. 26.06.35. At SBAC/RAF Hendon Display.
10.09.35. Embarked HMAS *Australia*.
9 to 12.09.35. Catapult trials on the Solent.
3.10.35 to 18.03.36. Engine stoppages in flight.
12.02.36. *Australia*. Damaged at Aboukir.
26.03.36. Alexandria. Pegasus 2.M.2 15533. While being hoisted in after an exercise split pin sheared dropping the aircraft to the gun deck. Extensive damage, returned to Supermarine for repair.
9.06.38. Embarked *Apollo*.
27.10.38. Southampton. Embarked *Hobart*.
15.11.38. *Hobart*. Damaged while hoisting in off Malta.
3.02.39. A4-18 taxied into A21.
7.06.41. 9 Sqn. *Manoora*.
12.09.41. Unserviceable due flying accident. Replaced by A211 on 13th. Disembarked at Archerfield.
6.07.42. Rathmines, received after repair by QANTAS.
22.07.42. Flt Lt McMahon. Parallel track cross over search with W2783 for possible submarine. Rathmines and return.
10.08.42. 9 Sqn. Rathmines.
24.08.42. P/Off Davis. Two inner anti-submarine patrol with W2783 for Force 'U'. Sighted a submarine but it submerged before aircraft could attack. Returned to Rathmines.
3.09.42. Rathmines. Night alighting accident, bounced and landed on port float due pilot's inexperience.
16.10.42. Manning River, NSW. Forced landing.
15.01.43. QANTAS, Rose Bay for overhaul.
30.08.44 to 29.09.44. No.3 Seagull Conversion Course.
12.11.44. 3 OTU. Williamtown, NSW. Sqn Ldr V.E. Townsend, AC1 W Hall. Cross-wind landing, starboard shock strut remained compressed causing ground loop, ran off runway into soft sand finishing in tail up position. Crash recovery crew takes machine to 5 OTU, Williamtown, NSW, delivering aircraft on 18th.
30.11.44. To QANTAS for repair.
19.01.45. Approved for conversion to components.
5.02.45. Received 2 CRD by road from QANTAS, Rose Bay.

### A2-2

18.10.35. Embarked HMAS *Sydney* in UK.
05.36. Served for a period in HMS *Glorious*.
20.05.36. Tailskid collapsed while taxying.
16.10.36. Search for missing launch *Mystery Star*.
17.10.36. Hawkesbury R, 8 ml from Richmond, NSW. Flt Lt C.W. Pearce, Lt Fogarty, RAN. Forced landing, engine failure. Replaced by A28. 23.
22.10.37. At 2 AD with engine removed.
16.12.37. 5 Sqn.
16.02.38. 5 Sqn. F/Off Hick, Lt Cdr Hall, TAC Upton, RAN. Accident at sea, 28 mls Gabo Is.
23 to 24.11.38. 1 FTS, Seaplane Sqn. To Benalla. F/Off I.S. Podger, Cpl J.A. O'Donnell, Cpl C.L. Taylor, LAC Smith, AC1 Sage. To act as ground W/T station for cadet cross country flights.
6.02.39. 1 FTS. F/Off I.S. Podger. Taxied into Moth A766.
(15.05.39). 1 FTS. Pegasus 16296.
13.07.39. Allotted 10 Sqn.

**Above:** A2-2 on the crane. The landing gear is in the down position and the engine is not in use.

15.02.40. STF (10 Sqn). Port Phillip Bay, Melbourne, Vic. Sqn Ldr D.A. Connelly, P/Off R.H. Thompson. Whilst doing take-off and alightings flames appeared near carburettor, burnt and sank. Crew rescued by paddle steamer *Weeroona*. W/off 19.02.40.

**A2-3**

3.12.35. Despatched *Warrangi*.
8.01.36. Received at 1 AD.
6.02.36. Erected and tested by Lt DA Connelly.
5.03.36. Flown from 1 AD to 1 FTS Seaplane Sqn. This was first of type to be erected in Australia.
26.03.36. Wing Cdr De La Rue, Cpl Grendon. Hull damaged while approaching slipway when wheels did not lock down.
9.04.36. F/Off Headlam. Flown to 1 AD for repair.
13.05.36. Flown from 1 AD to Point Cook on re-allotment to Seaplane Sqn.
27.05.36. 1 FTS, Seaplane Squadron. Point Cook. F/Off L.E. Burt. Structural failure of rudder hinges while taxying for take-off.
20 to 30.08.36. 1 FTS, Seaplane Sqn. Sqn Ldr A.E. Hempel, Sgt R.L. Peverell, Cpl G.L. Grendon. Left for Port Albert to assist A210 in search for the *Dorothea*, an overdue fishing boat. W/T fitted. Both aircraft suffered engine problems. Concluded boat sank or drifted beyond range aircraft and returned to Point Cook. Wing tip float damaged in alighting on Lake King. A210 sent float back after it reached Point Cook.
2.03.37. 1 FTS. Point Cook. Sgt C.E. Tuttleby, LAC W.D. Richmond, AC1 W.C.H. Kimpton. Port folding flap blew open hit prop.
30.03.38. 1 FTS. P/Off I.S. Podger, P/Off A.E. Cross. Accident in air, landing in Westernport Bay.
31.08.38. Flap damage in heavy seas.
11.10.38. 2 AD.
26.02.40. Embarked in *Manoora*.
1.03.40. First flight from *Manoora*.
(22.07.40). *Manoora*. Hull and other repairs required.
29.07.40. Unserviceable less than 1 month at 9 Sqn.
7.08.40. 2 AD for repair.
4.09.40. Test flown at QANTAS, Rose Bay.
10.09.40. STF. Sqn Ldr D.A. Connelly, Cpl Pope. Delivered to Rathmines from QANTAS, Rose Bay in exchange for A2-8.
6.11.40. Sqn Ldr D.A. Connelly. Engine test.
7.11.40. To 9 Sqn from ARS.
8.11.40. STF. Rathmines. Cdt R.B. Scutts, LAC C.E. Harwood. Forced landing due engine cutting out. Towed back Rathmines, engine restarted, no trouble since

**Above:** A2-5 at Rathmines.

experienced.
01.41. STF. Unserviceable at Rathmines undergoing 180 hourly and awaiting propeller.
1.11.41. Arrived 2 AD ex Rathmines.
6.07.42. QANTAS for overhaul.
11.10.42. 9 Sqn.
13.01.43. 9 Sqn. F/Off Woolcock, Sgt Birch. Landing accident. Starboard tyre blew out after touch down, damaged in ground loop. TFT 1,014:40 hrs.
28.04.43. In service.
14.06.43 to 24.06.43. Attached 8 Sqn, Townsville.
09.43 to 06.44. 2 FBRD. Overhaul.
07.44 to 11.44. 2 FBRD. Held for storage.
23.11.44. Base Torpedo Unit.
01.45. 2 FBRD for overhaul.
29.05.45. 2 CRD. Crash party left for Richmond to recover aircraft. 15.06.45. 3 OTU.
14.12.45. 2 FBRD for storage.
22.01.46. 3 OTU, Rathmines. TFT 1,433 hrs. Airframe requires new inner tube for tail wheel, complete fabric change, 4 new windows. Pegasus 2M2 P15535 requires complete overhaul as has been lying for approx. 3 months.
27.02.46. Offered to CDC for disposal.
25.04.46. Hailstorm damage, unserviceable.
1.10.47. Sold to Mr E McIllree for £35.
4.12.47. Issued to purchaser. Flown to Sydney. VH-BGP.
1.04.48. Arrived Papua New Guinea. Operated by Amphibious Airways. 16.06.54. Registration cancelled at owner's request; aircraft withdrawn from service.

**A2-4**

3.12.35. First flight.
21.02.36. Received 1 AD. Pegasus P.15531.
27.02.36. Work of erection begun.
18.03.36. Arrived 1 FTS Seaplane Sqn from 1 AD. To be operated by 101 Flt personnel.
1.04.36. F/Off Richards, Taylor. W/T Test.
20.04.36. 101 Flight redesignated 5 Sqn.
(22.05.36). 5 Sqn. Flown approx 100 hrs.
10.02.37 to 17.02.37. Jervis Bay. Participated in RAN exercise.
2.04.37. 5 Sqn. Flt Lt Athol Xaviere Richards. Casualty.
20.04.37. *Sydney*. Landed Richmond on way to Darwin to assist Anthropologist Dr D Thomson in survey of Arnhem Land.
10.06.37. Left Darwin for Richmond.
10.07.37. Hull pierced by jack.
15.07.37. 5 Sqn. Mallacoota. Accident, hull pierced by buoy.
22.08.37. Embarked *Sydney*. 15.03.38. 5 Sqn. *Sydney*. F/Off A.N. Hick. Catapult accident.
22.03.38. Jervis Bay, NSW. Immersed in sea for 18 hours.
29.03.38. 2 AD Richmond, for repairs. Pegasus 15531 recommended be converted due corrosion. (Note: engine must have been repaired as was recommended be converted to instructional engine on 20.07.40).
3.03.39. Richmond. Flt Lt D Connelly. Casualty, swung on landing.
8.08.39. 9 Sqn.
12.09.39. 10 Sqn, Rathmines.
14.09.39. Allotted to and collected by Rathmines, ex 9 Sqn. For use of CO Rathmines.
12.10.39. Taxied ashore Rathmines after temporary taxiway laid.
22.12.39. Rushcutters Bay, Sydney. Flt Lt Campbell. Roof hatch flew into propeller.
01.40. P/Off P.J. McMahon, Sgt T.A. Egerton. Collected from Rathmines and flown to 1 FTS, Point Cook.
13.02.40. 1 FTS, STF. P/Off P.J. McMahon. Landed without

**Above:** A2-6 displays the location of the serial number underneath the lower wings.

lowering u/carriage, had been operating from water.
19.02.40. Failure flap locking device, damage to propeller.
22.02.40. Allotted 2 AD for repair.
26.02.40. Sqn Ldr D.A. Connelly, Brown. Seaplane Conversion Course. 4.03.40. STF. Sgt T Brown, P/Off D Vernon, LAC G Jackson. Delivered to 2 AD.
11.07.40. Embarked on *Perth* at Farm Cove, Sydney.
24.09.40. 9 Sqn. *Perth*. Suffered damage to rudder, mainplanes and cockpit due to firing of port 4-in high Angle Guns without removing aircraft covers. (Flight records indicate that this may have happened to A218).
26.09.40. Landed for repairs, replaced by A217.
4.11.40. Serving with 9 Sqn.
3.12.40 to 9.12.40. Attached 1 Comm Flt, Laverton. Arrived on 3rd after being delayed by weather.
5 to 7, and 9.12.40. Drogue target towing for AA Regiment, Maribyrnong.
16.01.41. Repair and overhaul at 2AD.
21.01.41. 9 Sqn. Gunnamatta Bay in Port Hacking. P/Off G.M. Mason and three crew. Forced landing while engaged in towing target to air gunnery due failure of fitting which held flying wire.
10.02.41. 9 Sqn. Rathmines. Bounced during take-off, left wing stove in and became submerged.
11.09.41. Sqn Ldr D.A. Connelly. Rathmines to Rose Bay and return. 27.11.41. Arrived 2 AD for 180 hourly inspection.
12.41. To QANTAS for overhaul.
17.06.42. Arrived 2 AD from 9 Sqn and transferred to QANTAS, Rose Bay.
10.11.42. 9 Sqn.
6.02.43. Arrived 9 Sqn, Bowen, Qld, for anti-submarine patrol.
6.08.43. 9 Sqn Detached Flt, Cairns. Cairns, Qld. Sgt M.D. Smith and three crew. After transport flight to Mornington Is ground-looped, damaging port spar, aileron and float. TFT 1,213.05 hrs. Flown to Bowen for repair but could not be completed there. To 2 FBRD then QANTAS.
26.07.45. Received 3 OTU ex 2 FBRD.
09.45 to 22.01.46. At 3 OTU, Rathmines. Pegasus 2M2 16664.
14.12.45. 2 FBRD. Storage with Pegasus 2M2 16664.
3.02.46. 3 OTU. Flt Lt Rhode. To Rose Bay and return.
22.03.46. 2 AD Schofields, in storage.
25.04.46. Unserviceable due hailstorm damage at Schofields, registration VH-ALB reserved.
13.05.46. At Maintenance Sq, Rathmines. TFT 1,446.99 hrs. Fully serviceable.
3.10.46. Sold to Mc Illree Motors with engine 16664 for £600. Departed on 10.10.46.
13.09.50. Registration VH-ALB cancelled.

**Above:** A2-7 reportedly photographed shortly before its demise on 26 October 1939.

14.04.60. Registered VH-ALB.
27.01.70. Damaged in forced landing near Taree.
9.03.72. Registration cancelled at owner's request. Now on display at RAF Museum, Hendon, UK.

**A2-5**

11.01.36. Date of manufacture.
21.02.36. Received from overseas.
17.03.36. Received 1 AD. Pegasus P.15532.
3.04.36. Left Point Cook for Richmond. F/Off A.X. Richards. 101 Flt. 20.04.36. 5 Sqn. *Canberra.*
21.04.36 to 23.04.36. *Canberra.* Catapult trials in Port Jackson.
5.05.36. *Canberra.* Struck CMB target with port wingtip.
6.05.36. Jervis Bay. Forced landing, engine failed in flight.
4.07.36. Jervis Bay. At anchor when wind increased to 60 mph. Beached, rudder damaged by surf.
10.07.36. Embarked in *Canberra.*
3.09.36. *Canberra.* Mid Molle Is, Qld. F/Off A.X. Richards. Engine would not restart, recovered by launch in squall.
13.09.36. Disembarked to Richmond.
20.10.36. Flt Lt Pearce. Search for missing launch *Mystery Star.*
5.12.36. Embarked *Canberra.*
4.03.37. 5 Sqn. Hobart, Tas. F/Off A.X. Richards. Forced landing due engine failure.
28.07.37. *Australia.* Port Moresby, NG. F/Off W.N. Gibson. Tail skid collapsed on landing causing major damage to rear hull. Shipped back to Australia by SS *Montoro.* Repairs took nearly 3½ years.
6.01.40. 9 Sqn.
13.11.40. Sqn Ldr D.A. Connelly, Sgt Craig. From Richmond. To STF. 31.12.40. Allotted to *Manoora.* 2.01.41. Allotted from STF to 9 Sqn. 17.03.41. 9 Sqn. *Manoora.* Whitsunday Passage, Qld. Failure locking device starboard flap, sprung up whilst landing and fouled inner blades. 1.04.41. *Manoora.* Escorting SS *Katoomba* Rabaul to Sydney.
20.05.41. *Manoora.* Hull damaged while being hoisted in. Temporarily repaired on board.
2.06.41. Disembarked to Rathmines for repair.
18.06.41. At STF.
3.07.41. STF, Rathmines. Seaplane night training flight, failure locking device starboard flap, sprung up whilst landing and fouled inner blades. TFT 370.35 hrs.
2.08.41. Sqn Ldr D.A. Connelly. 'Final Check.'
22.09.41. To 9 Sqn ex STF.
22.11.41. *Manoora.* Replaced A29.
22 to 27.01.42. Dum-Dum Aerodrome, Bombay, India. Disembarked for overhaul and new engine. Pilot broke his arm and no flying until 05.42.
6.05.42. Rathmines. Disembarked to swing compass and re-embarked.
19.05.42. Port Vila, New Hebrides. Transferred to HMNZS *Leander*, replaced by Walrus W2755.
26.05.42. Embarked HMNZS *Leander.*
1.08.42. Received Melbourne ex-New Zealand.
18.08.42. To QANTAS for repair.

**Above:** The date when serials were added to the bow of the Seagull V boat amphibians is unknown.

28.10.43. 2 FBRD Rathmines. Repaired.
11.43 to 02.44. 2 FBRD. Under overhaul.
9.02.44. 8 CU informed that allotment of Walrus W2705 cancelled and A2-5 substituted. Immediately replied Seagull unsuitable this area and request reallotment of Walrus.
14.02.44. 8 CU. Townsville, Qld. Flt Sgt M.D. Smith and three crew. Undershot on alighting during ferry flight, powered to clear breakwater, touched down halfway across harbour, struck buoy, port float torn off, swung to starboard damaging both mainplanes and starboard float. TFT 567:20 hrs. To 13 ARD.
11.07.44. 9 Sqn. Bowen aerodrome, Qld. Flt Lt D.R. Howard, F/Off L.G. Woodcock. Hydraulic line burst during circuit training and wheels dropped but did not lock. U/carriage folded up during landing, skidded about 60 yards on the step; hull and port float damaged.
13 to 15.07.44. Airworthy, flight Bowen to Rathmines for repair.2 FBRD on 16th. On 20th allotted QANTAS, Rose Bay, for major hull repairs.
18.01.45. 2 FBRD. Operational fitment.
22.01.45. 3 OTU.
23.05.45. 3 OTU. Rathmines, NSW. Flt Lt L.G. Woolcock, plus two crew. Alighting attempt on smooth almost glassy sea, touch down with nose too low, water looped, tore both floats off and rolled onto its side. Both mainplanes wrecked and considerable damage done in order to prevent the aircraft sinking and in salvaging. TFT 684:30 hrs.
5.06.45. Received 2 CRD ex-3 OTU.
21.06.45. Approved convert to components.

### A2-6

13.05.36. Received 1 AD.
(22.05.36). 5 Sqn. Flown approx 100 hrs.
17.07 to 5.08.36. To Gippsland for photo survey.
20.08.36. To *Albatross* for hoisting and fitting into catapult trolley.
24.08.36. *Albatross*. First successful catapult launch.
(26.10.36). 5 Sqn. Buckling at rear in hull.
28.01.37. Embarked *Canberra*.
22.05.37. Wingtip damaged landing on wet airfield.
(30.08.37). 1 FTS. Complete overhaul recommended. TFT 324 hrs.
28.06.38. 5 Sqn.
(19.01.38). 2 AD. Extensive cracks in various parts frame.
13.07.38. Embarked *Canberra*.
20.07.38. 5 Sqn. *Canberra*. P/Off M.M. McInnes. Casualty.
(10.08.38). 5 Sqn. Navigator's and Wireless Operator's tables and wireless mounting collapsed during catapulting.
7.09.38. *Sydney*. Propeller damaged by starting handle.
9.09.38. 5 Sqn. *Sydney*. Rockhampton, Qld. F/Off T.M. Price, Lt Cdr Bacon, LAC Newton. Casualty.
6.10.38. To 2 AD for hull repairs.
4.11.38. F/Off K.C. Ekins, AC1 A.H. Hoffman, AC1 M.C. Houghton, AC1 J Fairway. Delivered to 1 FTS, Seaplane Sqn.
9.11.38. 1 FTS. Laverton. F/Off K.C. Eakins. Casualty, wingtip damaged.
28.04.39. 1 FTS. Point Cook. Damage caused by swinging

**Above:** The shooting of a Seagull V, here A2-9, leaving the catapult was a favourite photograph and appears in the collections of Seagull V crews. (Argus newspaper collection State Library of Victoria)

back of starboard wing.
30.06.39. 1 FTS. Coolalie Aerodrome. F/Off T.H. Davies. Forced landing.
1.07.39. 10 Sqn. Point Cook.
30.11.39. STF. Point Cook.
1.03.40. 9 Sqn.
13.05.40. STF. P/Off M.L. Judell. Engine failed on take-off at 400 ft due rubber from refuelling hose in petrol, successful alighting on water.
26.05.40. STF. P/Off D Vernon. Engine failed on take-off at 400 ft due rubber from refuelling hose in petrol, successful alighting on water. Pegasus II M2 15532 returned 2 AD for examination.
24.06.40. STF. Richmond. P/Off E.S. Yoeman. Swung on landing on aerodrome, extensive damage to port float and lower mainplane.
26.06.40. 2 AD Richmond, for repair.
16.01.41. Repair and overhaul at 2AD.
23.05.41. 9 Sqn.
7.06.41. STF. Point Cook.
12.06.41. Damaged due heavy landing in rough water.
14.07.41. 2 AD Richmond, for repair.
20.07.41. QANTAS, Rose Bay, to finish repairs.
9.09.41. 9 Sqn.
17.09.41. Returned to Rathmines.
7.10.41. Port float damaged due heavy landing.
3.01.42. Rathmines. U/carriage collapsed whilst beaching, damaged.
17.01.42. 9 Sqn. Rathmines, NSW. P/Off D Sanders, LAC H.W.F. Jacobs. Lake Macquarie. Damaged in heavy landing by pupil; port side buckled at pilot's seat.
29.01.42. QANTAS Rose Bay, for repair.
26.03.42. Sqn Ldr D.A. Connelly. Dual instruction.
12.06.42. Rathmines. P/Off Stacey. Three flights for inner anti-submarine patrol for Force 'V' operating from Nowra and Mascot.
6.07.42. QANTAS for repair.
28.04.43. 2 FBRD, Rathmines. Repairs completed during 05.43.
12.05.43. Received 9 Sqn Bowen, Qld.
29.08.43. Coral Sea. F/Off H Dowsley, Flt Sgt L Deacon, WO/AG Flt Sgt T.H.L. Beasley. Engine failure at sea.

**Above:** A RAAF Cadet poses with A2-10.

Landed at rear convoy in heavy seas and began to ship water. Salvaged as much equipment as possible; sunk by *Swan* gunfire. TFT 1520:40 hrs.
14.09.43. Officially w/off.

**A2-7**
13.05.36. Received 1 AD.
06.36. 5 Sqn.
15.08.36. Archerfield, Qld. Damaged due oleo leg failing while landing. To QANTAS, Archerfield, for repair.
17.08.36. Returned to Richmond.
24.08.36 to 10.36. 5 Sqn. Sqn Ldr L Lachal, Cpl Richardson, AC1 Barnes, AC1 Wilcox. Was to carry out survey of Portland Roads, Qld, but could not be carried out due weather.
15.12.36. Jervis Bay, ACT. Damaged when port wing hit water during landing.
28.01.37. Embarked *Sydney*.
23.02 to 28.03.37. 5 Sqn. Flt Lt Alexander. Pelagic fish survey.
17.07.37. Embarked *Sydney*.
3.08.37. Jervis Bay. P/Off A.N. Hicks. Damaged when rammed by crash-boat.
20.08.37. *Sydney*. Archerfield. Qld. P/Off A.N. Hick. U/carriage collapsed on landing. Starboard mainplanes smashed, hull buckled. To 2 AD for repair.
18.11.38. Transferred to 9 Sqn.
(21.01.39). 9 Sqn. Pegasus IIM.2 P15533. Engine support strut badly corroded.
31.01.39. Embarked *Hobart*. 9.02.39. 9 Sqn. Jervis Bay. F/Off F.M. Price. Casualty.
26.02.39. 9 Sqn, *Moresby*. Accident aboard ship.
2 to 5.05.39. *Hobart*.
9.07.39. Jervis Bay, ACT. Damaged when wave crushed wingtip and float.
10.07.39. Repaired onboard *Hobart*.
28.07.39. P/Off E.H. Beaumont. On landing run damaged when swung to right.
14.09.39. Transferred temporarily from 9 Sqn to 1 FTS.
17.09.39. Transferred to 10 Sqn.
3.10.39. Sqn Ldr D.A. Connelly, Lt Cdr Kennedy. To *Australia* and catapulted off.
26.10.39. 10 Sqn. Near Warburton, Vic. F/Off Magnus John May, AC1 Stanley George Bordiss, both with cuts & shock; AC1 Francis Reginald Holbe suffered broken thigh & shock. Forced landing on small piece of land on slopes of Yarra River. Airscrew disintegrated and took with it part of the starboard lower aileron. It appears that the pilot was engaged in a beat-up of the hospital where his girlfriend worked as a nurse.
31.05.40. Converted to components.
29.10.40. Pegasus IIM2 16294 handed to Stores Sqn by 2 AP.

**A2-8**
25.02.34(?). Date manufacture.
13.05.36. Received 1 AD.
(22.05.36). 5 Sqn. Flown approx 100 hrs.
24.08.36. To Queensland with A27 for photo survey of Portland Roads.

**Above:** Seagull A2-12 leads this line up of seven Seagull V amphibians. A2-11 is the second amphibian in line.

24.08.36 to 10.36. 5 Sqn. F/Off W Gibson, Cpl Tomkins, AC1 McLean, Cpl Cole. Survey of ortland Roads, Qld, could not be carried out due weather.
17.10.36 to 18.10.36. F/Off Gibson. Search for missing launch *Mystery Star.*
(20.11.36). Buckled hull, to be withdrawn from service at first opportunity.
1.02.38. F/Lt Garing. Damaged in heavy landing, crumpling of port wingtip float. To 2 AD for repair.
5.10.38. 1 FTS. Point Cook. F/Off K.C. Ekins, Cpl J Kearinden. Casualty, hull damaged on night flight.
28.10.38. F/Off K.C. Ekins. Delivered to 2 AD.
1.11.38. 5 Sqn. 2 AD store awaiting repair.
30.03.39. 2 AD.
13.02.40. 2 AD. F/Off Adler, E.J. Brunkhursh. Brakes failed, taxied into fire tender.
12.03.40. 9 Sqn.
5.04 to 1.05.40. Embarked *Westralia.*
7.04.40 to 8.05.40. F/Off Ekins, P.E. Carr, TAG Henzell, RAN. Sydney to Brisbane, Darwin: operations in Java Sea off Macassar.
10.04.40. Recce of Macassar Roads to identify if German ship *Scheer* present. Shadowed by twin-engine floatplane identified as Fokker.
11.04.40. 9 Sqn. F/Off K Ekins. Similar mission as above but without presence of floatplane. While being hoisted aboard forward tackle guy parted and aircraft swung into guard rail of ship.
23.04.40. Damaged repaired and test flown. Returned to Darwin and exchanged with A211.
1.05.40. Disembarked *Westralia.*
8.05.40. Darwin. Unserviceable.
27.05.40. Departed for 11 Sqn Port Moresby.
1.06.40. Arrived 11 Sqn.
9.07.40. 11 Sqn. Sqn Ldr P.G. Graham. Flown from Port Moresby to Rathmines reallocated to STF replacing A26.
20.07.40. Sqn Ldr Graham and crew together with A212 arrive Rathmines from Port Moresby via Thursday Is. Allotted to 9 Sqn.
31.07.40. Seaplane Training Flight. Richmond aerodrome. P/Off D Vernon (solo). On first solo, during landing run swing not corrected damaged port lower mainplane and float.
14.08.40. Test flown at 2 AD.
11.11.40. 9 Sqn.
24.11.40. Sqn Ldr D.A Connelly, Gillies. Mine search.
28.12.40. Flt Lt Glasscock. Outer anti-submarine patrol.
2.01.41. Loaned to STF by 9 Sqn.
11.04.41 to 14.04.41. At Rose Bay for HMS *Achilles* but not required and returned to base.
5.08.41. 2 AD for overhaul.
24.03.42. Sqn Ldr D.A. Connelly. Dual instruction.
25.03.42. Departed Rathmines for Sydney. To be transported by SS *Cagou* to join *Australia.*
30.03.42. Embarked *Australia.*
1.04.42. *Australia.* Catapulted at sea. To Vila, slick landing and picked up under way.
5.04.42. *Australia.* Landed at Uea Atoll.
13.04.42. *Australia.* Catapulted to carry out anti-submarine patrol of the approaches to Noumea where it landed to

**Above:** A2-13 is in camouflage with the hull roundel having a yellow outer ring, and with a thin fin stripe.

await the ship's arrival.
21.04.42. *Australia*. Left ship with message for Garden Island, Sydney. Moored overnight.
22.04.42. Carried out anti-submarine patrol for ship entering Sydney Harbour.
1.05.42. *Australia*. Catapulted for high angle shoot.
3.05.42. Photographic reconnaissance of Sanmarea and Fredrick Henry Reefs.
3.06.42. *Australia*. Catapulted to photograph Task Force 44.
5.06.42. Return to Rathmines. Anti-submarine patrol off Port Jackson whilst ship entered Sydney Harbour.
8.06.42. Replaced by W2783.
22.06.42. QANTAS, Rose Bay, for repair.
3.03.43. 2 FBRD for overhaul.
10.03.43. 3 OTU.
(7.04.43). Complaints re overhaul by QANTAS, Rose Bay.
9.04.43. 3 OTU. Rathmines, NSW. F/Off V.A. Hiles and two crew. Engine failure while drogue towing, insufficient time to close camera hatch before alighting; sank in 20 feet of water on alighting. TFT 47.45.
20.04.43 to 3.06.43. At 2 FBRD, Rathmines, for repair or overhaul.
10.07.43. Complete overhaul due to being submerged. TFT 47.35 hrs.
22.07.43. 3 OTU.
25.09.44. F/Off Bolton. No.3 Seaplane Conversion Course. Crosswinds and stalls.
13.02.45. Airframe to QANTAS for complete overhaul. Contract cancelled work stopped.
25.09.45 still at QANTAS. Issued 2 CRD in dismantled condition. Very little work had been carried out, nil on hull.
28.11.45. At 2 CRD, Richmond, NSW, less engine. TFT 510.20. Airframe completely dismantled, hull deteriorated throughout, requires complete overhaul and jig test.
17.12.45. Recommendation - convert.
22.03.46. 2 AD Schofields, in storage.
25.04.46. Damaged by hailstorm at Schofields.
28.05.47. Authorised by CDC for write off.
2.07.48. Issued to DAP ex-2 AD.
6.09.49. Action completed.

**A2-9**

19.05.36. Received 1 AD.
06.36. 9 Sqn.
25.09.36. 5 Sqn. Richmond, NSW. P/Off B.G. Braithwaite. Swung on landing, port float and wing damaged.
22.10.37. Flt Lt Pearce, AC1 Riazo, Wing Cdr A.T. Cole, AC1 McLean. Richmond to anchorage and return.
(22.11.37). 5 Sqn. Jervis Bay. Flt Lt C.W. Pearce. Starboard upper wing-tip crushed by crane, a/c was in normal stowage position.
26.01.38. Embarked *Canberra*.
07.38. 5 Sqn. Embarked *Sydney*.

**Above:** Fitting A2-14 up to the catapult on HMAS *Australia*.

26.07.38. 5 Sqn. *Sydney.* P/Off T.M.B. Price. Casualty.
17.03.39. Hangered at AN Airways.
21.08.39. 2 AD for overhaul.
4.09.40. STF. Sqn Ldr D.A. Connelly, Sgt Ostenfeld. Delivered from Richmond to Rathmines from 2 AD.
8.01.41. Rathmines. Failure locking device starboard flap, sprung up whilst landing and fouled inner blades.
14.04.41. 9 Sqn.
(15.04.41). From Rathmines to Rose Bay for embarkation in *Hobart*.
27.04.41. *Hobart*. Catapulted in the Hauraki Gulf to instruct F/Off McDonough in the slick method of landing and the towing method of recovery.
30.04.41. *Hobart*. Arrived Sydney, aircraft proceeded to Rathmines to replace stores.
30.05.41. *Hobart*. Hoisted out and flown in vicinity of Port Melbourne for W/T tuning.
1.07.41. 9 Sqn. Rathmines, NSW. P/Off A.V. McDonough and four crew. Forced landing due engine failure; port float damaged.
27.11.41. 9 Sqn. Illawarra. P/Off H.H. Rohde and two crew. Forced landing when gas starter adaptor blew off No.5 cylinder.
14.01.42. At Rathmines.
8.06.42. QANTAS rose Bay, for overhaul.
10.01.43. 9 Sqn.
8.02.43. 9 Sqn. Off Bowen, Qld. Lt Mc Whae, RN, Flt Lt D.J. Hocking, P/Off E.C.S. Seller. Took off to carry out dive bombing practice with 8½ lb practice bombs. All killed when aircraft dived into sea. Wreckage discovered some distance from target and distributed over a wide area. TFT 975.15.
23.02.43. Approval for conversion airframe and Pegasus VI P16673 to components.

**A2-10**

19.05.36. Received 1 AD.
(16.06.36). 2 Stn. Defective stringing and fabric on both upper mainplanes.
1.08.36. Issued 1 FTS.
19.08.36. 1 FTS, Seaplane Sqn. Flt Lt Garing, Sgt C.E. Tuttleby, LAC W.D. Richmond. Left for Port Albert to search for the *Dorothea*, an overdue fishing boat.
20 to 28.08.36. Joined by A23. Both amphibians suffered engine problems. Concluded boat sank or drifted beyond range aircraft and returned to Point Cook. Wing tip float dispatched to A23 at Metung.
14.10.36. 1 FTS. 200 yds south-east jetty Point Cook. P/Off Joseph Patrick Francis Xavier Godsell, AC1 (2078) Albert Henry Hoffman. Bad landing, capsized and sank due error training pilot.
25.11.36. Uneconomical to repair airframe and Pegasus 16293, conversion approved.

**A2-11**

19.05.36. Received 1 AD.
06.36. 5 Sqn.
16.10.36 to 18.10.36. F/Off Richards. Search for missing

**Above:** Nine Seagull V amphibians in flight. A2-20, A2-15, A2-21 identified.

launch *Mystery Star*.
19.10.36 to 1.12.36. 5 Sqn. F/Off A.X. Richards. Pelagic fish observation.
4.06.37. Type 'B' Drogue Target Towing winch fitted.
07.37 to 16.12.37. 5 Sqn.
27.09.37. *Canberra*. Took appendicitis case to Geraldton.
(12.10.37). *Australia*. Claim for fuel from HQ, RAF, Singapore.
27.01.38. Embarked *Australia*.
31.01.38. 5 Sqn. *Australia*. Flt Lt W.N. Gibson. Accident onboard.
15.02.38. 5 Sqn. *Australia*. Flt Lt W.N. Gibson. Accident when hooking on at sea off Cape Howe. Damaged.
2.08.38. 2 AD for repair.
3.08.39. 9 Sqn.
(14.10.39). 11 Sqn. Port Moresby, New Guinea.
04.40. Allotted *Westralia*.
14.11.40. 9 Sqn. *Westralia*. F/Off K C.H. Ekins. Collided with ship's side while being recovered by hoist, seriously damaging mainplanes, elevator, rudder and hull. Replaced by Walrus.
21.01.41. QANTAS Rose Bay, for repair.
25.08.41. 9 Sqn.
13.09.41. Embarked *Manoora* in place A21.
1.10.41. Rathmines. For repair.
31.01.42. 9 Sqn.
5.03.42. Lake Macquarie, NSW. Sgt T.F. Pickering (drowned), AC1 W.F. McConnell (injured). While approaching to land at Rathmines nosed in and turned over onto back. Beyond economic repair, convert to components.

### A2-12

23.04.36. Pegasus 16296. Shipped to Malta and embarked *Australia*. at Valetta to replace A21.
20.05.36 to 2.06.36. Engine failures in flight.
16.10.36 to 18.10.36. Flt Lt Alexander. Search for missing launch *Mystery Star*.
16.10.36 to 1.12.36. *Australia*. Flt Lt J Alexander, F/Off W.N. Gibson.
18.08.37. Embarked *Australia* to replace A25 damaged in New Guinea.
21.09.37. 5 Sqn. *Australia*. Jervis Bay. F/Off Gibson. Accident on catapult.
2.10.37. 5 Sqn. *Australia*. F/Off W.N. Gibson. Accident when being hoisted from catapult.
25.03.38. 2 AD for repair.
15.09.39. 9 Sqn.
(14.10.39). 11 Sqn. Port Moresby, New Guinea.
20.07.40. F/Off Hemsworth and crew together with A28

**Above:** A fine Kip Porteous photograph of A2-16 on a very wet aerodrome.

arrive Rathmines from Port Moresby via Thursday Is. Allotted to 9 Sqn.
5.08.40. Replaced A23 on board *Manoora.*
24.09.40. 9 Sqn. *Manoora.* F/Off P.J. McMahon, Sub Lt G.H. Jackson, TAG K Oxley. Hoisted into sea off Rottnest Is, took off in wake of ship, float struck swell causing it to collapse. Landed Pearce for repair.
2.10.40. Sqn Ldr D.A. Connelly co-opted by 9 Sqn to ferry Walrus L2319 to Pearce and bring back A212 which was allotted to STF. Left on 3rd with L2319.
(2.01.41). STF. Unserviceable Rathmines due 180 hourly awaiting propeller.
20.01.41. STF. Lake Macquarie. Sgt A.V. McDonough, AC1 B.M. O'Keefe. Damaged by drift wood when nearly airborne.
7.04.41. Allotted 2 AD for overhaul.
2.11.41. Point Cook, STF.
6.01.42. Seaplane Training Flight, Rathmines. Rathmines, NSW. P/Off A.C. Fleming, AC1 W.R. Farrell. Fire during take-off; all four mainplanes, tailplane and rudder burnt out.
30.03.42. Sqn Ldr D.A. Connelly. Dual instruction night.
13.04.42. Issued to HMNZS *Achilles* ex-Rathmines.
8.08.42. Allotted to 1 AD ex-New Zealand. 180 hourly inspection carried out.
21.09.42. 9 Sqn.
04.43 to 30.08.43. At 2 FBRD, Rathmines, for repair or overhaul.
(31.08.43). 2 FBRD. Owing to excessive corrosion tail section requires complete rebuild, plus sections of planning surface require replating. TFT 1119 hrs.
09.43. 2 FBRD. Being converted to component parts.
12.10.43. Approval for conversion to components.

**A2-13**
18.12.36. Received 2 AD.
17.03.37. 5 Sqn.
(7.04.37). Temporary stoppages in petrol system in flight.
(25.05.37). Received 2 AD.
16.12.37. 5 Sqn.
23.12.38. 9 Sqn.
15.11.39. 2 AD for overhaul.
2.10.40. QANTAS Rose Bay, to complete overhaul.
15.04.41. On *Westralia.*
17.09.41. Hull damaged by fire.
18.09.41. Repaired onboard *Westralia.*
20.09.41. 9 Sqn.
25.10.41. Point Cook, STF.
12.41. 9 Sqn.
25.03.42. Damaged.
26.03.42 Repaired onboard *Westralia.*
21.04.42. 9 Sqn.
1.06.42. Rathmines. P/Off Stacey. Extended search for enemy submarine.
12.06.42. P/Off Davis. Operating from Nowra and Mascot on inner anti-submarine patrols for Force 'V'. Could not land at Mascot due fog, after refuelling at Rose Bay holed its hull on slipway and could not proceed.
22.06.42. QANTAS Rose bay, for repair.
10.02.43. 9 Sqn.
1.04.43. 9 Sqn. Bowen, Qld. P/Off R.G. Bonyton and three crew. Forced landing in small paddock 3/4 ml from aerodrome due engine failure at 150 ft on takeoff. Hidden potholes port oleo u/c leg torn off, ground loop. Uneconomical to repair.
2.04.43. 12 SRU.
24.09.43. QANTAS Rose Bay, for repair. Beyond economic repair due deterioration due exposure since damaged.
20.12.43. To 2 FBRD ex-QANTAS for conversion.

**A2-14**
10.10.36. Date manufacture.
21.01.37. Received 2 AD. Defect, bilge pump full salt water.
01.37. 9 Sqn.

**Above:** A2-17 in formation with A2-16 taken from another Seagull V. (via P London)

16.07.37. 5 Sqn. Farm Cove, NSW. Accident.
9.08.37 to 12.08.37. *Australia.*
16.12.37. 5 Sqn.
21.12.37. 9 Sqn. F/Off H Birch, Flt Lt J Lerew (passenger). Inspection Myall River, Tanilba and Lake Macquarie for proposed RAAF bases.
24.02.38. 5 Sqn. Flt Lt C.W. Pearce. Forced landing Richmond golf course due engine stopping in flight.
2.07.38. Wing Cdr Hewitt. Inspection of Port Stephens area for RAAF bases.
23.12.38. 9 Sqn.
1939. 2 AD for overhaul.
6.03.40. 2 AD in storage.
27.03.40. STF. Sgt T Brown. Ferried from Richmond to Rathmines.
07.40. STF. Engine unserviceable due excessive oil consumption.
22.08.40. F/Off M.J. May. Formation flight with A21 and A219 over Newcastle on occasion of visit of Governor of NSW.
10.40. Damaged.
7.11.40. Allotted 2 AD for overhaul.
13.11.40. Sqn Ldr D.A. Connelly, Sgt Craig. To Richmond. Returned with A2-5.
3.07.41. On allotment from 2 AD to Rathmines.
28.07.41. Point Cook. Seaplane Training flight.
20.09.41. 9 Sqn. *Westralia.* Used in landing of Australian troops at Kupang Bay, Timor.
31.01.42. 9 Sqn.
31.01.42. Rathmines. Flt Lt Ekins. Outer anti-submarine patrol.
21.04.42. *Westralia.*
22.05.42. Landed, Rathmines.
26.05.42. 9 Sqn.
1.06.42. Rathmines. Flt Lt McMahon. Extended search for enemy submarine.
23.06.42. Flt Lt Laverack. Two flights on inner anti-submarine patrol for Force 'C'.
26.06.42. Flt Lt McMahon. Three patrols inner anti-submarine patrol Convey 'D' with A26 working in relays refuelling at Mascot, returned to Rathmines.
30.08.42. 9 Sqn.
09.42. Damaged.
22.09.42. 2 AD for repair.
25.10.42. QANTAS Rose Bay, to finish repairs
13.08.43. 2 FBRD. Complete overhaul at 1,007.00 hrs.
19.10.43. 9 Sqn. Archerfield, Qld. F/Off V.A. Lucas, Sgt N.A. Nahrung. Returned from Rathmines. Belly landed as u/carriage failed to come down into position; pilot made good landing aided by soft nature of ground following heavy rain; extensive repairs carried out. TFT 1,112 hrs.
22.10.43. 2 FBRD party carried out repairs. New mainplanes

**Above:** This appears to be a posed photograph of A2-18 at the end of the catapult as the propeller does not appear to be revolving. A2-18 served onboard HMAS *Sydney* from 1938 to 1940.

fitted, hull repaired.
7.11.43. Flown to Rathmines for repair and overhaul.
10.43. 2 FBRD. Repaired.
30.03.44. 3 OTU, Rathmines.
7.06.44. Damaged. Planning surfaces buckled whilst landing.
14.06.44. Further hull repairs, found unsatisfactory. Hull was changed, to QANTAS for complete overhaul.
25.09.45. At QANTAS, Rose Bay, Pegasus 33803. Work to be discontinued, allocate to 2 CRD for survey with view convert to components.
(12.12.45) to (21.05.47). At 2 CRD, Richmond, less engine. TFT 1,123.45 hours. Dismantled, unserviceable. Fuselage required complete overhaul and extensive metal repairs. Wings assessed as 50%, repairable.
22.12.45. Recommended for conversion by 2 CRD.
28.05.47. W/off authorised by CDC.
2.07.48. Issued to DAP Botany ex-2 AD.
6.09.49. DSD action completed.

**A2-15**

18.12.36. Received 2 AD.
4.05.37. Assembled 2 AD, issued 5 Sqn.
(22.07.37). 2 Station. Defect in fabric.
16.12.37. 5 Sqn.
(24.02.38). 5 Sqn. Corrosion bilge pump body.
28.03.38. 5 Sqn. F/Off A.N. Hick. Accident near Richmond.
29.03.38. 5 Sqn. Richmond. F/Off A.N. Hick. Accident.
28.11.38. 5 Sqn. Archerfield, Qld. F/Off Maxwell James Wiber, AC (2751) Eric Atholstone Everett, AC (2090) Albert Ernest Duncan Milner, and Police Constable Young. Search for missing woman along Albert R. Hit high tension lines, crashed, burst into flames. All killed.

**A2-16**

4.02.37. Received 2 AD.
6.10.37. 5 Sqn.
16.12.37. 5 Sqn.
16.05.38. Richmond. P/Off Douglas. Damaged in heavy landing.
19.05.38. 2 AD for repair.
(7.06.38). 5 Sqn. Defect in tail skid.
21.09.38. *Canberra.*
10.10.38. *Canberra.* Jervis Bay. F/Off J.N. Bell, Lt Cdr E Chapman, TAG Bowden, AC1 Endicott. Casualty while landing.
28.07.39. 9 Sqn.
21.10.39. 9 Sqn. F/Off Eakins. Depart Richmond for Laverton via Cootamundra. Returned on 28th.
(30.10.39). Campbellfield, Vic. F/Off K.C. Eakins. Forced landing.

**Right:** A2-19 on a typical grass aerodrome.

16.02.40. 9 Sqn. Watsons Bay, Sydney. Sqn Ldr S.A.C. Campbell. Engine trouble 20 miles to sea during towing practice, forced landing, No.5 cylinder almost detached from engine.
3.04.40. 9 Sqn. Lake Tuggerah. P/Off P.J. McMahon and two crew. Successful forced landing during target towing exercise due shortage of petrol.
21.06.40. 9 Sqn. 8 ml north Wangaratta, Vic. F/Off M.J. May and three crew. Pegasus 16662, gas-starter non-return valve blew out on No.7 cylinder. Anson flew spares to Benalla on 22nd.
29.06.40. 9 Sqn. Field at Napier, 4 ml east Lockhart, NSW. F/Off M.J. May and three crew. Owing to presence of fog at Wagga Wagga the pilot decided to land in a large paddock, starboard wing struck ground, bounced into air, swung around and came to rest in a collapsed condition. Extensive damage.
16.07.40. 2 AD for overhaul.
1940. QANTAS, Rose Bay, to complete overhaul.
16.01.41. Being overhauled Rose Bay.
10.12.41. Rathmines.
25.12.41. To *Canberra*.
18.05.42. Received 9 Sqn ex-*Canberra*. To Rathmines.
22.05.42. Rathmines, NSW. Accident, damaged beyond repair. Conversion of airframe and Pegasus P16666 recommended. Delivered to Engineering School, Ascot Vale, Vic, for training purposes.

**A2-17**
4.02.37. Received 2 AD.
6.10.37. 5 Sqn.
25.11.37. Richmond. Lt J Alexander. Accident.
16.12.37. 5 Sqn.
24.11.38. 5 Sqn. Richmond. F/Off M.M McInnes. Casualty.
7.12.38. *Canberra*. Wingtip hit side of ship.
2.02.39. 2 AD for repair.
23.02.39. 9 Sqn.
8.11.39. F/Off Eakins. Departed from Richmond for Brisbane on way to Darwin for drogue target co-operation with 12 Sqn.
12.02.40. 9 Sqn. Slipped off jack, float hit floor, correct lifting tackle not available. Hull and float damaged.
9.03.40. 9 Sqn. Approx 30 ml from Brunette Downs. F/Off K.C.H. Ekins and three crew. Became lost over difficult country, correctly landed before fuel exhausted.
(26.03.40). 9 Sqn. Engine cannot be located. Dismantled.
(28.03.40). 9 Sqn. Found to be unserviceable return to 2 AD for overhaul.
6.04.40. 9 Sqn. Embarked on *Perth*.
5.11.40. *Perth*. Landed Pearce, returned to ship.
14.12.40. At Rathmines.
11.01.41. Candia aerodrome, Crete. Machined-gunned while on ground, damage to rear spar and punctured fuel tank.
12.01.41. Walrus L2243 from HMS *Ajax* collided with and further damaged mainplanes.
13.01.41. Embarked in *Ajax* for Alexandria for repair. Walrus L2243 in exchange.
7.04.41. *Perth*.
28.04.41. Flt Lt Beaumont, Sub-Lt G.R. Brian, RN, Petty Officer D Bowden, RAN. Shot down over Crete by Junkers 88 bombers. Crew succeeded in escaping in rubber dingy and after several hours were picked up by HMS *Havoc*.

**A2-18**
8.03.37. Received 2 AD.
6.10.37. 5 Sqn.
16.12.37. 5 Sqn.
(5.06.38). 5 Sqn. Weakness in hull plate D7.
29.09.38. *Sydney*.

**Above:** A2-20's hull at Rathmines after return from New Guinea.

16.11.38. 5 Sqn. Saratoga, NSW. F/Off D.L.G. Douglas. Forced landing.
23.12.38. 9 Sqn.
28.07.39. *Sydney.*
5.04.40. 9 Sqn.
27.06.40. F/Off E.V. Beaumont. Conveys Gp Capt D.E.L Wilson to Rathmines.
12.07.40. Wing Cdr J.A.S. Brown, RAF, proceeds from Rathmines to Central Area and return.
1.08.40. 2 AD for overhaul.
2.01.41. Allotted from STF to 9 Sqn.
6.01.41. 9 Sqn.
20.01.41. From Rathmines to Sydney; embarked in *Hobart.*
27.01.41. *Hobart.* Catapulted and proceeded to RNZAF Station Auckland in order to swing compass. Returned *Hobart* in Auckland Harbour same day.
16.02.41. *Hobart.* Catapulted off Sydney and carried out gunnery, bombing and navigation exercises.
24.03.42. *Hobart.* Catapulted off Port Jackson, proceeded to Rose Bay for maintenance.
6.04.41. *Hobart.* Catapulted. P/Off McDonough Instructional flight. A224 from *Australia* crashed when catapult failed. Landed and saved Observer and TAG.
9.04.41. *Hobart.* Catapulted in Sydney Harbour. P/Off McDonough. Instructional flight.
10.04.41. Transferred to *Australia.*
15.04.41. Transferred from *Hobart* to *Australia.*
9.09.41. *Australia.* Indian Ocean. Crashed when alighting. Hull twisted and some frames buckled. Taken to Aden for repairs.
24.12.41. Status 'G' at Aden for repairs.

**A2-19**

8.03.37. Received 2 AD.
14.06.38. 5 Sqn.
28.08.38. 5 Sqn. F/Off M.J. Wilber. At Moresby.
(28.09.38). Air photos of Middleback Iron Ore Deposit, Whyalla, SA, required.
7.12.38. 5 Sqn. Flt Lt W.N. Gibson. Casualty during photographic survey duty.
23.12.38. 9 Sqn.
23.04.40. Rathmines. Trial mod of stern post.
2.07.40. CO proceeds from Rathmines to Central Area and return.
3.07.40. Wing Cdr J.A.S. Brown, RAF, proceeds from Rathmines to Central Area and return.
22.08.40. F/Off R.H. Thompson. Formation flight with A21 and A214 over Newcastle on occasion of visit of Governor of NSW.
28.12.40. Sqn Ldr Griffith. Outer anti-submarine patrol.
(3.06.41). Complete overhaul by maintenance personnel at Rathmines.
08.41. Damaged.
20.09.41. Rathmines, for repair.
16.02.42. 9 Sqn.
26.02.42. Flt Lt P.J. McMahon. Rathmines to Sydney to join HMNZS *Monowai* for passage to *Australia.*
2.03.42. Australia.
8.03.42. Damaged on take-off in heavy swell.
10.03.42. Anti-submarine patrol. Heavy landing rendering a/c unserviceable.
03.42. Landed Brisbane.
23.03.42. Shipped to Sydney via HMS *Athene.*

**Above:** A2-22 moving to a slipway at Rathmines seaplane station, 1940. Note the RAAF launches. The fin is fully covered by the red, white and blue tail stripes.

03.42. QANTAS Rose Bay, for repair.
30.12.42. 9 Sqn.
11.04.43. 1 Rescue and Communication Sqn.
4.07.43. F/Off Boney. Making base at Malawna (sic) Bay.
12.07.43. 1 R&CU. Ginger. F/Off Bonython. Makauna Mission, Malouna Bay. Rescued three survivors crashed B17.
16 and 18.07.43. 1 R&CU. Ginger. F/Off Bonython. To Trobriands. Hull to be patched.
23.07.43. 1 R&CU. Nil flying, 60 hourly.
28.07.43. 1 R&CU. Ginger. F/Off Bonython and crew. Three flights. To Cape Pierson to rescue Lt Morgan; to Milne Bay with appendicitis case; to Wedau.
11.08.43. Seagull to stand by, Beaufighter down. To Urasi Is with two US Army officers.
12.08.43. On search for missing aircraft.
9.09.43. 1 R&CU. F/Off Bonython. Arrived Kiriwina from Goodenough Is. Departed to look for Beaufighter down off the coast of New Britain.
11.09.43. 1 R&CU. P/Off R.G. Bonython, F/Off R.A. Kelley. Search for missing Beaufighter A19-132. Missing, no trace found.

**A2-20**
2.04.37. Received 2 AD.
1.04.38. 5 Sqn.
1.06.38. Damaged due tail touch-down first when landing.
06.38. 2 AD for repair.
1.11.38. 5 Sqn.
23.12.38. 9 Sqn.
14.03.39. 9 Sqn. Coffin Bay, SA. F/Off H.M. Birch. Forced alighting due worn threads on spark plug caused it to be blown out of cylinder. Engaged in Pelagic fish survey.
(12.04.39). 9 Sqn. Defect. Crack in hull plate.
24/25.05.39. 9 Sqn. Port Moresby, New Guinea. Flt Lt Gibson engaged in survey with Naval Detachment. Broke free moorings, sank in three feet water in high wind, port wing damaged, considerable hull damage.
8.06.39. Returned to Sydney for repair via SS *Macdhui*.
16.06.39. At 2 AD. Uneconomical to repair, convert, Pegasus 16668 not damaged.
16.09.39. Recommendation approved.
19.08.40. Instructional hull to be issued to QANTAS for repair as spare hull.
20.09.40. QANTAS Rose Bay. Hull for repair.
19.12.41. Work suspended due more important work.
1946. QANTAS holding as spare hull.

**A2-21**
30.04.37. Received 2 AD.

**Left:** A2-22 with the Rathmines' Seaplane Training Flight circa 1941. It is in camouflage, the separation of the two colours is just visible on the original. The lack of a roundel on the hull is noteworthy.

1.04.38. 5 Sqn.
20.05.38. 5 Sqn. Richmond. J.N. Bell. Failed to lower u/carriage. Repaired in unit by replacing two lower wings and floats, serviceable land operations only.
5.07.38. 5 Sqn. P/Off A.E. Cross. Engine failure in flight. Successfully restarted engine.
23.12.38. 9 Sqn.
23.02.39. 9 Sqn. Richmond. F/Off W.A. Aden. Casualty.
22.05.39. Chipping Norton. Casualty.
2.10.39. Allocated *Hobart.* Note: May be A2-23 for this reference.
13.10.39. Richmond to Farm Cove. Rendezvous with *Adelaide* for full calibre firing. Embarked in *Hobart* which immediately left for Darwin.
20.10.39. Catapulted to carry anti-submarine patrol ahead *Hobart* prior entering Darwin Harbour.
11.04.40. Ex-Pearce to *Sydney.*
21.06.40. 9 (FC) Sqn. *Sydney.* Flt Lt Thomas McBride Price. Attacked by RAF fighters, broke up on landing. P16675. Salvaged by 102 MU, FAA.
(7.11.40). Disposal of at Abu Sneir.

**A2-22**
24.05.37. Received 2 AD.
(22.06.37). 2 AD. Pegasus VI P.16670.
11.04.38. 5 Sqn.
1.12.38. 5 Sqn. Rockhampton, Qld. Blown over by wind.
23.12.38. 9 Sqn.
30.12.38. 2 Station.
8.09.39. Allotted to be flown from Mallacoota to Pearce for RAN use at Pearce.
5.04.40. *Sydney.* Embarked at Perth for delivery by 9 Sqn. Engine to be exchanged with A218.
7.04.40. 9 Sqn. Sqn Ldr S Campbell. Slight damage to wing float and aileron while taxying in gale. Later, pegged down but wind shifted and tipped onto one wing breaking lower starboard mainplane spars.
10.06.40. *Canberra.*
19.12.40. 9 Sqn. Laverton. Flt Lt P.O. Lavarack, Rear Admiral Grace, Lt Cdr Oldham. On landing the starboard float ran along the ground. No fault could be found with the undercarriage and it was attributed to an error of judgement by the pilot. To 1 AD for repair.
01.41. 1 AD. Repairs to centre section, mainplanes, floats. 180 hrs on engine.
23.01.41. At 1 AD. Bomb circuit mod.
2.03.41. Attached to Comm Flt, Laverton.
4 and 5.03.41. Two sorties each day for AA drogue practice.
3.03.41. 9 Sqn.
24.03.41. 2 AD for overhaul.
21.12.41. Arrived and departed Evans Head (1 BAGS) for Archerfield.
29.12.41. 9 Sqn.
27.12.41. *Canberra.*
28.12.41. Damaged, tipped onto port float during storm.
29.12.41. Repaired onboard *Canberra.*
23.01.42. Sqn Ldr D.A. Connelly. Dual instruction.
2.03.42. Rathmines.

**Above:** The crashed Seagull V in Singapore harbour.

**Above:** The Walrus had a permanent strut on the wing leading edge besides the engine to assist in wing folding and is readably seen on L2247 aboard HMAS *Australia* in 1940. The hull roundel has a yellow outer ring. The colours are thought to be Dark Sea Grey on upper surfaces and Sky Grey on lower surfaces. The fin stripes are carried onto the hull. (via H Lobb)

13.04.42. 9 Sqn.
26.06.42. Flt Lt McMahon. Inner anti-submarine patrol for Convoy 'SU' with W2768. Rathmines to Mascot to refuel and return.
1.07.42. Damaged.
21.07.42. P/Off Stacey. Two inner anti-submarine patrol for Convoy 'T' then replaced by Hudson which would then assume outer patrol.
23.07.42. P/Off Stacey. Two inner anti-submarine patrol with W2783 for Convoy 'U'.
30.07.42. P/Off Davis. Two inner anti-submarine patrols with W2783 for Force 'VV'.
9.08.42. P/Off Stacay. Inner anti-submarine patrol to escort Force 'D' to Newcastle Harbour.
14.02.43. 3 OTU Rathmines.
21.02.43. 3 OTU. Nowra, NSW. Sqn Ldr S.G. Stilling and two crew and one passenger. Ground loop during cross-wind landing; damage to port float and lower mainplane. TFT 1,110.05 hours.
9.04.43. At Rathmines.
8.05.44. QANTAS Rose Bay, for repair.
(13.11.44). Submitted for conversion.
20.11.44. Approval for conversion to components.
17.01.45. Received at 2 CRD by road from QANTAS.

**A2-23**
19.02.37. Received 2 AD.
(23.08.37). 2 Stn. P.16671(?).
12.07.39. Issued 9 Sqn.
12.10.39. *Hobart.*
31.10.39. 9 Sqn. *Hobart.* F/Off T.H. Davies. Damaged night landing exercise on rough sea, Singapore area. Recovered with great difficulty. Replaced by Walrus L2171.
8.05.40. Now lying at Seletar, Singapore.
(20.10.40). Convert to components.

**A2-24**
28.04.37. 1st Flight.
19.07.37. Received 2 AD.
20.09.39. 9 Sqn.
14.09.39. Allotted 9 Sqn from 2 AD in replacement of A27.
28.09.39. 9 Sqn. F/Off Courtney left Richmond for *Canberra.*
10.10.39. Sqn Ldr D.A. Connelly, Costello/Lavarack/Havyatt. Dual Catapult course *Australia.*
5.04.40. Issued to *Australia.*
08.40. During Norwegian campaign, foiled by low cloud in attempt to bomb Tromso, Norway.
24.08.40. Landed in UK for overhaul (possible at Saunders-Roe).
31.12.40. Embarked *Australia* after rebuild.
6.04.41. 9 Sqn. *Australia.* Lt J.J. Hoath, RN, (killed), P/Off R Clark, G.A.S. Stephenson both seriously injured. Catapult failure caused crash on launch. Aircraft not recovered.
6.09.41. W/off.

**WALRUS**
A total of 37 Walrus amphibians are reported as having been purchased, exchanged or operated on loan from the RAF and RN by the RAAF. The following aircraft are confirmed as having served with the RAAF.

**K8542**
26.06.40. On loan from FAA. Replaced A221 on *Sydney* after damage at Mersa Matruh.
23.09.40. Returned to FAA 103 MU, Aboukir. Replaced by L2177.

**K9516 (Probably X9516)**
23.11.42. To *Australia*
30.11.42. *Australia.* Anti-submarine patrol as ship departed Brisbane. Moreton Bay for spotting, tow sleeve target for AA shoot.
30.12.42. Unserviceable. To Townsville.
22.01.46. 2 FBRD, Rathmines. Pegasus VI 33818.

**Above:** L2318 has the blue and white roundels adopted after Japan's entry into the war.

**L2171**

4.11.39. Singapore. Ex-RAF Soletar Station to *Hobart* to replace A223.
28.12.39. *Hobart.* Catapulted to carry out inspection Lake Gaul.
03.40. Flown to Ratmalana aerodrome, Ceylon, where camouflage applied in accordance with Admiralty instructions.
7.03.40. 9 Sqn. Sqn Ldr Campbell. Bounced landing in heavy swell damaging port float.
7.04.40. 9 Sqn. F/Off T.H. Davies. Damage to port float.
6.06.40. At Aden. Due for 120 hourly, replaced by L2321.
23.11.40. *Hobart.* Returned to RAF. Replaced by L2321.

**L2177**

23.09.40. Ex-102 MU, FAA, to *Sydney* replacing K8542 at Aboukir, Egypt.
21.02.41. Under repair QANTAS, Rose Bay.
(29.09.41). Embarked *Sydney.*
19.11.41. *Sydney*. Lost in action with German armed merchant cruiser *Kormoran* off WA.
23.01.42. Approval to strike off records.

**L2231**

19.01.44. On loan from RN. Received 1 Transport and Movement office, Sydney ex-UK.
7.05.44. Received 8 CU.
18.05.44. 8 CU. Flt Lt (274003) B Hempenstall. Arrived Goodenough Island after ferry flight from Rathmines.
12.06.44. 8 CU. F/Off (407240) H.R. Hurlsthouse. Depart Goodenough for Momote detachment.
15.06.44. 8 CU. F/Off (407240) H.R. Hursthouse, W/O (415369) D.J. Watson, Flt Sgt W McCutcheon. Undercarriage collapsed on landing, unlikely to be repaired this area. TFT 479.55 hrs.
17.06.44. Mercantile (Code name of Momote airstrip on Admiralty Is). Undercarriage collapsed, extensive damage to hull.
19.06.44. 8 CU. X9516 depart for Momote to replace L2213.
30.06.44. Received 12 Repair and Service unit ex-8 CU.
16.07.44. Approval requested to convert as uneconomical to repair and difficulties in shipping airframe to mainland.
4.08.44. Approval given for conversion to components.

**L2222**

8.08.42. Received Rathmines ex-HMS *Leander* for 180 hourly inspection and recovering.

**Above:** This is believed to be X9510 when ready for disposal. Note the Commonwealth Mustang in the background. Colours believed to be overall Foliage Green.

1.06.42. Overhaul complete, to 9 Sqn.
10.06.42. Reallocated to RNZAF; became NZ151.
16.06.42. Shipped via SS *Rimutaka* to Wellington, NZ.

**L2243**
12.01.41. Collided with A217. Embarked on *Perth* in exchange for damaged A217.
7.04.41. Returned to FAA from *Perth*.

**L2247**
13.08.40. Loaned by FAA, replaced A224 on *Australia*.
25.09.40. Dakar, Senegal, north-west Africa. Flt LT G.K.I Clarke, Lt Cdr Fogarty, RN, C.K. Burnett. *Australia*. Shot down by three Vichy French Curtiss fighters during British naval bombardment of French Fleet. All killed. Pegasus VI 122869.

**L2293**
5.06.41. To *Perth* ex-HMS *Barham*.
(25.10.41). To *Canberra*.
17.12.41. Heavy landing, engine failure. Damaged.
24.12.41. At Rathmines for repair.
27.08.42. Issued *Westralia*.
21.09.42. 9 Sqn.
19.03.43. 6 CU, Batchelor, NT. Arrived from Rathmines on allotment this unit.
21.03.43. 6 CU. P/Off Lobwein, P/Off Brinkman. Trip to Bathurst Island Mission.
30.03.43. 6 CU. P/Off Lobwein, P/Off Brinkman. Depart for Darwin where they stood by for sea rescue work.
2.05.43. P/Off Lobwein. Trip to position in Timor Sea on sea rescue work.
3 to 4.05.43. P/Off Lobwein. To sea rescue work north of Darwin and return.
8.07.43. 6 CU. F/Off Lubwein. Return from 4 RSU.
15.06.44. Received QANTAS ex-8 CU.
21.09.44. At QANTAS, target towing equipment to be removed.
(13.11.44). Notified for conversion.
20.11.44. Approval for conversion to components.
31.05.45. Conversion completed.

**L2318**
30.03.39. Date manufacture.
5.07.40. Shipped to Australia via *Mangola*.
7.08.40. Received 2 AD ex-RAF Singapore. Airframe TFT 104.05 hr, P17981/125719 109.15 hrs.
30.10.40. 2 AP. Test flown, few minor adjustments necessary.
25.12.40. Allotted *Canberra,* replaced A222.
15.01.41. Extensively damaged on *Canberra*. To be repaired at Columbo.
27.12.41. Category 'G' at Columbo.

**L2319**
12.04.39. Date of manufacture.
5.07.40. Shipped to Australia via *Mangola*.
8.08.40. Received 2 AD ex-RAF Singapore. Airframe TFT 120.20 hrs; P17849/121989 131.05 hrs.
28.09.40. Allotted Pearce for *Manoora* as replacement for A212.
2.10.40. Sqn Ldr D.A. Connelly co-opted by 9 Sqn to ferry Walrus L2319 to Pearce and bring back A212 which was allotted to STF.
11.11.40. 9 Sqn. Fly Off P.J. McMahon, Sub Lt T.G.H.

Jackson, TAG K.W.E. Oxley. Lost during patrol and landed with 20 minutes petrol left. Ship located aircraft approx. 11 ml to starboard.
29.01.41. *Manoora*. Accident, damaged.
12.12.41. *Perth* proceeds to sea with aircraft aboard.
13.12.41. *Perth*. Catapulted for anti-submarine patrol.
27.02.42. Bantam Bay, north-west of Java. On *Perth*, assumed lost in action after battle with Japanese cruisers.
16.04.42. Officially w/off.

**L2321**
6.06.40. Erected at RAF Station Khomaksar. At Aden to *Hobart*.
19.06.40. *Hobart*. Catapulted to carry out bombing attack on Italian W/T station on Centre Peak Is. On completion of the attack the aircraft proceeded to Kamaran Is, refuelled and returned to Aden.
Due to damage inflicted by *Hobart* firing at hostile aircraft L2321 was disembarked onto the slipway at Obstruction Pier whenever the ship was in Aden. Re-embarked when ship proceeded to sea.
15.07.40. Search for Gloster Gladiator.
8.08.40. *Hobart*. Italian fighters attacked Berbera aerodrome. Catapulted to try and catch enemy refuelling at Zeila. No fighters but bombed and machine-gunned enemy positions.
7.09.40. Aden. Disembarked to RAF Station Khormaksar effect repairs to damage caused by guns firing at attacking Italian bombers.
1 to 12.10.40. Operated from Khormaksar carried out six reconnaissance flights.
12.10.40. Re-embarked *Hobart*.
19.10.40. From Colombo to RAF Station Trincomalee to carry out 40 hourly inspection.
23.11.40. On loan from FAA to replace L2171 on *Hobart*.
17.12.40. *Hobart*. Catapulted to search for armed raider.
28.12.40. *Hobart* arrived Freemantle. Landed at RAAF Pearce for transport by *Canberra* back to Colombo.
15.01.41. *Canberra*.
23.10.41. Returned to FAA.

**L2322**
18.11.40. On loan from FAA. Received by RAAF. Taken aboard *Westralia* in Ceylon.
3.12.40. *Westralia*. Damaged while taking off in heavy swell. Replaced by A211.
2.09.41. *Canberra*. Struck side of ship during recovery, extensive damage. Disembarked Fremantle for repair at Pearce.
16.10.41. Damaged by gun firing while wings spread on catapult.
25.10.41. *Canberra*. Taxied to Rose Bay and exchanged for L2293.
27.03.42. Ready for tests flight.
5.04.42. HMS *Leander*.
(17.07.42). Damaged. Report from RNZAF.
12.10.42. Received QANTAS ex-*Leander*.
(7.04.43). Complaints re overhaul by QANTAS, Rose Bay.
16.04.43. 9 Sqn. Bowen aerodrome. F/Off H Dowsley, P/Off D.R. Cooper. During night landing, after completing night alighting practice on water, overshot flare path, landed between last two flares, brakes would not stop, ran through boundary fence and came to rest in a ditch alongside the road. TFT 141.25 hrs.
12.08.44. 2 FBRD. Flt Lt Priest. Depart on ferry flight to 8 CU after repair.
22.02.45. Forced alighting Lake Wamberal, NSW, after engine failure.
06.45. 2 FBRD. Undergoing overhaul and modification.
22.06.45. Held on 2 FBRD Rathmines ledger but issued to RNAS Schofields, NSW. To be issued on loan to RN for air-sea rescue duties with British Pacific Fleet.
23.06.45. Returned to RN.

**L2327**
19.02.42. 9 Sqn. *Australia*. Assumed to be this aircraft as no other Seagull or Walrus was lost on this date. Crashed into ship's port quarter and burst into flames. Sub Lt Jackson, observer and F/Off E.J. Rowland, the air gunner, were picked up by boat from *Chicago*. The pilot, F/Off R.G. Rowan, was not seen. Pilot rendered unconscious when aircraft struck water due waist safety belt allowing his head to contact instrument panel, drowned. RAAF Type 1 Safety Harness to be fitted to Seagull V/Walrus aircraft as a result of this loss. See also W2768.

**P5664**
1.05.42. At QANTAS Rose Bay for erection.
13.12.42. 9 Sqn. Rathmines. Flt Lt Ekins. Inner anti-submarine patrol for Force 'VV' (HMAS *Westralia*). Returned with engine trouble, *Westralia* unattended for approx 25 minutes.
14.12.42. 9 Sqn. Rathmines. P/Off Ransom. Inner anti-submarine patrol with X9517 and X9520 for Force 'VT'.
26.06.44. 2 FBRD. Richmond, NSW. Flt Lt P.J. R Shields, Sgt Eastment, LAC C Mxx, LAC E.J. Gathercole. Engine stopped during landing and aircraft ground looped causing minor damage.
06.44 to 07.44. 2 FBRD. Undergoing repair.
29.07.44. 8 CU. Goodenough Is, New Guinea.
3.08.44. 8 CU. Depart Goodenough for detachment duty Momote.
5.10.44. 8 CU. P/Off (423071) N Agnew. Depart for Momote detachment. Agnew CCO detachment.
11.12.44. 8 CU. F/Off Gole, F/Off Hurlsthouse, 3 wounded AIF and 1 passenger. Madang to Awar and return.
15.02.45. 8 CU. F/Off (423031) N.M. Agnew, F/Off (423656) R.C. Crebbin. Dropped urgent supplies to Radar Detachment, Long Is.
17.02.45. 8 CU. F/Off (411310) R.M. Gole, Flt Sgt

(428722) K.G. Lennox. Carried supplies to Annenberg and evacuated two wounded NGIB personnel from Lake Vrabu to Madang.
22.02.45. F/Off (427458) A.C. Evans, Flt Sgt (28036) K.G. Horne. Carried our recce of Ramu and Sepik areas with Col Egan and staff of 35th Battalion.
28.02.45. 8 CU. F/Off (427458) A C Evans, Flt Sgt (428722) K G Lenox. Travel flight Moresby to Madang. Search for missing C47 on a coastal plain 10 ml north of Buna to Point Harvey and 30 miles seaward. Nil sightings.
10.04.45. 8 CU, Madang. F/Off (423031) Agnew, F/Off (43193) J.P. Brady. To Awar, personnel and supply drop. Took off from Lake Vrabu, forced to alight Ramu R due engine trouble. Aircraft successfully taxied up river through areas of known enemy activity to Annenberg. Catalina ferried out fitters and parts. Aircraft serviceable and returned Madang 12th.
25.09.45. At 1 FBMU, Pegasus 33341.
22.01.46 to 03.46. 2FBRD, Rathmines. TFT 684.45 hrs. Unserviceable. Held for storage.
22.08.47. Sold to E McIllree with Pegasus VI 33341 for £175. Became VH-BLD.

**P5715**
1.05.42. At QANTAS, Rose Bay for erection.
9.06.42. 9 Sqn. Rathmines. Flt Lt Laverack (one) and Flt Lt McMahon (two) Anti-submarine patrols for Force 'TT' Convoy C.P.1 proceeding Sydney to Brisbane.
11.06.42. To proceed to Amberley to be picked up by *Canberra*.
15.06.42. Embarked *Canberra*.
9.08.42. Damaged by Japanese gunfire during battle of Savo Is off Guadalcanal. Sunk with *Canberra* by USS *Ellett*.

**W1811**
No details available. Unlikely as recorded as crashing 20.08.42 at Lee-on-Solent killing all aboard while in RN service.

**W2705**
8.03.41. Date of manufacture.
15.05.42. At QANTAS Rose Bay, for erection.
6.08.42. 9 Sqn ex-QANTAS.
10.08.42. P/Off Davis. Two inner anti-submarine patrols with W2783 for Force 'VV'.
11.08.42. P/Off Davis. Three inner anti-submarine patrols with W2783 for Force 'SS'.
12.08.42. P/Off Davis. Inner anti-submarine patrols with W2783 for Force 'B'.
13.08.42. P/Off Stacy. Two inner anti-submarine patrols with W2783 for Force 'S'. Landed at Mascot.
14.08.42. P/Off Stacy. Two inner anti-submarine patrols with W2783 for Force 'S', then unserviceable due severly damaged undercarriage when landing at Moruya, NSW.
16.09.42. Damaged by gale while picketed.
11.10.42. Received at Townsville, flown to Challenger Bay for *Australia* to replace W2768.
16.11.42. *Australia*. Rose Bay. Flight test.
23.11.42. Replaced by L9516.
12.07.43. To 5 CU ex-9 Sqn.
15.07.43. Arrived 5 CU, Garbutt, to replace X9515. Ferried from Bowen. Sent to Horn Island to Torres Strait Defence Force.
21.07.43. F/Off Angove. Freight trip to Cloncurry, Inverleigh, Mornyton Is and return.
26.08.43. Flt Sgt Smith. Ferry aircraft to Bowen, on allotment to 1 RCS.
14.09.43. Flt Sgt Smith. From Kiriwina. After searching for missing Seagull A2-19; to replace lost aircraft.
27.10.43. 1 R&CU. Kiriwina Detachment. Rescued two members of Beaufighter A9-233 of 8 Sqn who had gone down into the sea.
11.43 to 02.44. 2 FBRD. Undergoing overhaul.
9.02.44. 8 CU informed that allotment of Walrus W2705 cancelled and A2-5 substituted. Immediately replied Seagull unsuitable this area and request reallotment of Walrus.
21.04.44. QANTAS for complete overhaul.
25.09.45. Airframe at QANTAS.
8.11.45 to 22.01.46. Airframe removed from QANTAS before completion & at 2 CRD for survey. TFT 553.45 hours. Rivets loose in hull.
13.12.45. Recommendation to convert.
28.05.47. Authorised by CDC for w/off.
2.07.48. Issued DAP, Botany ex-2 AD.
6.09.49. Action completed.

**W2707**
15.05.42. At QANTAS Rose Bay, for erection.
5.06.42. To 9 Sqn ex-QANTAS.
11.06.42. Rathmines. Flt Lt McMahon. Search and outer anti-submarine patrol.
16.06.42. Shipped to Wellington, NZ, via SS *Rimutaka* with L2222. Became NZ154.

**W2755**
1.05.42. At QANTAS, rose Bay for erection.
30.05.42. Issued *Manoora*.
(9.07.42). Damaged by fire on board *Manoora*.
29.09.42. 9 Sqn.
18.10.42. 9 Sqn. Rathmines. Flt Lt McMahon. Three inner anti-submarine patrols for Force 'SU'.
10.11.42. Arrived 1 FBRD on tour of possible landing places for flying boats en-route Rathmines.
18.01.43. Bowen. Exchanged with X9520 for *Australia*.
6.02.43. *Australia*. Catapulted, anti-submarine patrol for ship to enter Sydney Harbour.
(7.04.43). Damaged on catapult. Replaced by X9513. Probably refers to incident when *Australia's* crane tried to lift machine off catapult while it was still secured to the

catapult.
17.04.43. *Australia.* Forced alighting due engine failure. Recovered by ship.
4.01.44. To QANTAS for overhaul.
04.45. 2 FBRD. Operational fitment.
22.04.45. Received 6 CU.
14.08.45. 6 CU. F/Off J.H. Dening, LAC J.J. Godwin and two passengers. Cape Don (Darwin Area). Conveyed cinema film and supplies to Cape Don. On first attempt to take-off could not get up to flying speed. On second attempt bounced several times, throttle closed, port float struck swell hard and dug in and collapsed. Aircraft capsized and sank in minutes. Submerged in 40 ft of water. Four occupants escaped through one of the windows as the escape hatch jammed. Were picked up in a few minutes by a dingy lowered by a RAAF lugger. Aircraft a total loss. TFT 694.55 hrs.
30.08.45. Approved write-off.

**W2768**

1.05.42. At QANTAS, Rose Bay for erection.
15.05.42. Embarked *Canberra.*
16.06.42. P/Off Stacey. Inner anti-submarine patrol for convoy Force 'U'. With A26. Direct patrols from Rathmines; both to refuel at Mascot and one at Nowra where both were to remain overnight.
26.06.42. P/Off Davis. Inner anti-submarine patrol for Convoy 'SU' with A222. Rathmines to Mascot to refuel and return.
29.06.42. P/Off Davis. Inner anti-submarine patrol, escort Convoy 'U' from Newcastle.
30.06.42. Flown to Amberley, Qld, for *Australia.*
1.07.42. To *Australia.* ASV equipment fitted beforehand.
2.07.42. *Australia.* From ship to Amberley, Archerfield, then search for survivor of crash.
7.08.42. Damaged while being hoisted in.
6.10.42. *Australia.* South Pacific (just west of Fiji). F/Off E.J. Rowan, Sub Lt Jackson, unknown. Landing after an anti-submarine patrol the aircraft crashed head on into *Australia* 's port quarter, just above the waterline. It burst into flames and broke up. The pilot was killed but Jackson and the air gunner were rescued. Write off of airframe and Pegasus P3335.

**W2783**

1.05.42. At QANTAS, Rose Bay for erection.
1.07.42. *Australia.* Catapulted to carry out shadowing exercise, then to Archerfield. Replaced by W2763.
6.07.42. P/Off Davis. Inner anti-submarine patrol Convoy 'T'. Rathmines and return.
22.07.42. P/Off Davis. Parallel track cross over search with A21 for possible submarine. Rathmines and return.
23.07.42. P/Off Davis. Two inner anti-submarine patrol with A222 for Convoy 'U'; then to Mascot to be in readiness for RAT 36/24.
25.07.42. P/Off Stacey. Inner anti-submarine patrol for Force 'SS'. Unable to contact convoy owing to bad weather and poor visibility; landed at Mascot.
30.07.42. P/Off Stacey. Two inner anti-submarine patrols with A222 for Force 'VV'. Obliged to leave last patrol with engine trouble.
4.08.42. Flt Lt McMahon. Inner anti-submarine patrol with A21 for Force 'U'. Convoy returned to Port Jackson harbour.
10.08.42. Flt Lt Laverack. Two inner anti-submarine patrols with W2705 for Force 'VV'.
11.08.42. Flt Lt Laverack. Two inner anti-submarine patrols with W2705 for Force 'SS'.
12.08.42. P/Off Stacy. Inner anti-submarine patrols with W2705 for Force 'B'.
13.08.42. Flt Lt Laverack. Two inner anti-submarine patrols with W2705 for Force 'S'.
14.08.42. Flt Lt Laverack. From Rathmines to Moruya then inner anti-submarine patrols with W2705 for Force 'S'. On W2705 damaging undercarriage took up additional duty for total of four patrols before returning to Mallacoota.
23.08.42. F/Off Stacy. Inner anti-submarine patrol with A21 for Force 'E'.
24.08.42. F/Off Stacy. Two inner anti-submarine patrol with A21 for Force 'E'. Was shot at by Sydney anti-aircraft defences despite notification. Returned to Rathmines.
26.08.42. F/Off Stacy. Two inner anti-submarine patrol with A21 for Force 'D'.
27.08.42. P/Off Davis. Escorted vessels from Sydney and Newcastle to Brisbane with A21. Two inner anti-submarine patrols; returned to Rathmines.
19.10.42. Accident while taxying.
13.01.43. 9 Sqn. Bowen, Qld.
8.06.43. QANTAS for overhaul.
09.44. 2 FBRD. Under repair.
8.10.44. Arrived 8 CU on allotment.
01.45. 8 CU. F/Off (423656) R.C. Crebbin. Transported three AIF personnel and supplies to 30 Battn forward detachment Awar. Carried Medical Sergeant from Awar to Lake Vrabu where evacuated one stretcher patient (NGIB) private to Madang.
01.45. 8 CU. F/Off (423656) R.C. Crebbin, Flt Sgt (405198) E W Stubbin. To Annenberg, dropped message for Army. Landed Lake Vrabu and delivered supplies NGIB.
5.02.45. 8 CU. Long Is. F/Off (411310?) R.M. Gole, Flt Sgt (28036) K.G. Horn, Sqn Ldr G Gengos (passenger). Accident on take-off on non-operational communication flight on rough water. Planning on step when ran into swell which threw the aircraft into the air in partly stalled condition and fell onto oncoming wave. Hull damaged, beached aircraft and took off in placid waters next morning.
14.02.45. 8 CU. Allotted 1 FBRD for airframe repairs.
20.02.45. 8 CU. Departed for 1 FBRD.

2.03.45. 8 CU. Arrived Mascot. P/Off (423031) N.M. Agnew to return with X9510.
7.05.45. Approval to convert to components.

**W3085**
19.01.44. Received 1 TMO ex-UK. On loan from RN.
19.04.44. 2 FBRD.
30.06.44. 6 CU. F/Off Griggs. Flew first members of work party to Snake Bay to construct new strip. Journey to beach was in native dugout canoe which capsized, the crew receiving a ducking.
7.02.45. Left 6 CU, Batchelor, NT for Bowen, Qld.
18.06.45. At 1FBRD for repair. To be issued on loan to RN for air-sea rescue duties with British Pacific Fleet.
22.06.45. Delivered from 1 FBRD Lake Boga to Schofields; returned to FAA.

**W5664**
No details available.

**X9510**
20.10.42. Date manufacture.
19.10.42. Erection complete at Point Cook.
4.11.42. Depart Point Cook for Richmond with X9513 and X9514.
5.11.42. 9 Sqn.
28.04.43. 9 Sqn. F/Off D.R. Howard, Flt Sgt J.G. Beckenham, Sgt D.J. Beattie, Capt Ayreton (Army Intelligence), Capt Renshaw (Army doctor). Forced alighting 4 miles from Cap Is due to loss oil pressure, towed to Horne Is. TFT 189 hrs.
4.10.43. 9 Sqn. Flt Sgt S.T. Aistrope, Flt Sgt T.H. Robinson, Flt Sgt T.H. Beasley, Cpl T.W. Snape. Departed Bowen on travelling flight to Cairns when engine trouble caused forced alighting north Cape Bowling Green. TFT 425 hrs.
4.01.44. QANTAS for overhaul.
02.45. 2 FBRD. Operational fitment.
11.02.45. 8 CU complains that aircraft has been allotted from 2 FBRD but has not arrived.
2.03.45. P/Off (423031) N.M. Agnew arrived Mascot with W2783 to collect X9510 and ferry to Madang.
29.03.45. 8 CU. F/Off (423656) R.C. Crebbin. To Awar with supplies. Evacuate medical patient from Awar to Lake Vrabu.
4.04.45. 8 CU. F/Off (427458) A.C. Evans, W/O (417309) W H Lehmann and two fitters. Proceed Madang to Jacquinot Bay on detachment for the purposes of medical treatment.
6.04.45. 8 CU, Jacquinot Bay. F/Off (427458) A.C. Evans, W/O (417309) Lehmann. Evacuate four medical cases from Kalai. One stretcher and three sitting.
7.04.45. 8 CU, Jacquinot Bay. F/Off (427458) A.C. Evans, W/O (417309) Lehmann. Collide with Army barge damaging port lower mainplane wing tip. Aircraft returned Jacquinet Bay strip where repairs carried out by 18 RSU Detachment. Serviceable by 11th.
13.04.45. 8 CU, Jacquinot Bay. F/Off (427458) A.C. Evans, W/O (417309) Lehmann. Evacuated four medical cases from Tol. Owing to the swell loading had to be carried out from collapsible dingy.
13.04.45. 8 CU, Jacquinot Bay. F/Off (427458) A.C. Evans, W/O (417309) Lehmann. Search for missing patrol, located on beach six miles from their camp.
14.04.45. 8 CU, Jacquinot Bay. F/Off (427458) A.C. Evans, W/O (417309) Lehmann. Evacuated wounded from patrol located on 13th.
15.04.45. 8 CU, Jacquinot Bay. F/Off (427458) A.C. Evans, W/O (417309) Lehmann. Search for missing Beaufort in Waterfall Bay, nil sightings.
26.04.45. Collided with Army barge.
(19.05.45). To be modified as stretcher carrier in lieu X9516.
24.06.45. Sqn Ldr A.N. Pentland. W/O (426585) T.E. Hanley. To Awar to pick up four Jap POWs.
25.09.45. At 2 CRD, Pegasus 33327.
12.12.45. At 2 FBRD, Pegasus VI P.33327. Fuselage required rebuilding from bow to station 5 and from Station 18 aft to Station 21 due to kink in fuselage from keel to chine extending upwards.
15.12.45. Recommendation to convert.
01.46 to 03.46. 2 FBRD. Held for storage.
13.05.46. Maintenance Sqn, Rathmines. TFT 792.35. Unserviceable, dismantled for road transport.
23.08.48. Authorised for w/off.
2.03.49. At auction site Rathmines, sold for scrap.

**X9513**
19.10.42. Erection completed Point Cook.
4.11.42. Depart Point Cook for Richmond with X9510 and X9514.
7.12.42. 9 Sqn. Rathmines. F/Off Ransom. Inner anti-submarine patrol with X9514 for Force 'G'.
13.12.42. 9 Sqn. P/Off Ransom. Two inner anti-submarine patrol with P5664 for Force 'VV' (HMAS *Westralia*).
17.12.42. 9 Sqn. Rathmines. F/Off Mason. Inner anti-submarine patrol with X9517 for HMAS *Ping Wo* from Newcastle to Port Stephens.
7.03.44. 5 CU. Flt Sgt Aistrope. To Cooktown, Iron Range and Horn Is. To remain for air/sea rescue duties.
7.04.43. Sqn Ldr P.J. McMahon. To *Australia* off Dunk Is. Replaced W2755.
24.06.43. 9 Sqn.
7.03.44. 5 CU. Horn Island – Air Sea Rescue aircraft.
31.05.44. 5 CU. W/Off Aistrope. To Rose Bay on allotment to QANTAS for complete overhaul.
20.11.44. Approval to convert to components.
29.05.45. Issued to 2 CRD ex-QANTAS. Conversion completed.

### X9514

10.06.42. Date of manufacture.
19.10.42. At point Cook for erection.
23.10.42. Erection completed.
4.11.42. Depart Point Cook for Richmond with X9510 and X9513.
23.11.42. 9 Sqn. F/Off Rhode. Inner anti-submarine patrol for Force 'TT'. Nil visibility, returned to Rathmines. Later P/Off Hempenstall resumed duty and escorted convoy into Harbour.
7.12.42. 9 Sqn. Rathmines. F/Off Rhode. Inner anti-submarine patrol with X9513 for Force 'G'.
19.12.42. 9 Sqn. Flt Lt Mason. Inner anti-submarine patrol with X9520 for Force 'TS' from Port Stephens to Sydney.
13.01.43. 9 Sqn. Bowen, Qld.
30.06.43. Crashed landed at American Strip, Charters Towers, Qld.
5.08.43. Received at 1 RSU, Merauke. Damaged in collision with Kittyhawk A29-306.
15.07.44. Depart Bowen for QANTAS for overhaul.
25.09.45. Airframe at QANTAS.
4.10.45. At 2CRD. TFT 350.45. Received in dismantled condition with components partially overhauled.
22.01.46. Still at 2 CRD engineless.
28.05.47. Authorised by CDC for w/off.
2.07.48. Issued to DAP, Botany ex-2 AD.
6.09.49. Action completed.

### X9515

10.06.42. Date manufacture.
2.11.42. At Point Cook for erection.
14.11.42. Erection completed.
25.12.42. Arrived 5 CU, Garbutt, Qld. Starboard float damaged while taxying off runway.
31.12.42. 5 CU. F/Off Davis of 9 Sqn used aircraft for Special Naval duty.
4.01.43. 5 CU. F/Off Withell. To Horn Isle on special duty for Commander of Torres Straight Defence Force. Recalled next day.
25.01.43. 5 CU. F/Off Withell. To Bowen to pick up 22 Base Wing personnel. Became unserviceable at Bowen, returned in A2-19.
26.01.43. 5 CU. F/Off Withell. To Bowen in A2-19, picked up X9515 and returned.
27 to 30.01.43. 5 CU. F/Off Withell. To Dunk Is, Cairns, Cooktown, Stanley Is, Iron Range with NEI personnel.
7.04.43. 5 CU. F/Off Withell. To Cairns, Cooktown taking aircrew for Dragon A34-28 and return.
7.09.43. 6 CU. F/Off Gardner. Unsuccessful searches in Darwin area for Spitfire pilots.
17.09.43. F/Off Lobwein. To Darwin on standby for overdue aircraft, then onto Millingimbi on rescue duties. Picked up CO 59 OBU and co-operated with D.H.84 A34-52 rescuing crew of a Beaufighter which alighted on Arafura Sea. Passed instructions to NUNYAWL to search Blyth River for crew of Beaufighter forced down within 2 miles of the river. Returned Millingimbi. Returned to Batchelor at first light on 18th dropping supplies to bogged Hudson in vicinity of Tom Kinson River enroute. A34-52 found two Beaufighters and one crew.
30.09.43. Anson DJ322 force landed on beach west of Groote Eylandt. Crew picked up but port float damaged on take-off in rough sea. Landed Groote Eylandt, both floats removed and flew on to base.
6.01.44. 6 CU. F/Off Lobwein, Flt Sgt Hunter. To Snake Bay to pick up five escapees from enemy occupied island and return to Batchelor.
14.01.44. 6 CU. F/Off Lobwein, LAC Murgatroyd. As long-range Walrus was unserviceable, proceeded to Drysdale to attempt to rescue crew of our survey Dragon, A34-26, which landed on Maret Is 100 miles west of Drysdale in the Indian Ocean. On 15th Walrus took two fitters who stripped instrument panel, magnetoes and those parts likely to corrode. 15 lb of grease was smeared over wire wheels and engine and the aircraft tied down. Because of the load it was decided on the return to Drysdale to use as much of the fuel as possible before landing on that 'apology for a strip.'
06.45. 2 FBRD. Held for operational fitment next month.
7.06.45. F/Off Goll. Test flight at Bowen.
8.06.45. F/Off Goll. Departed Bowen for Cairns and Cooktown.
24.06.45. 8 CU, Madang. F/Off (427458) A.C. Evans, F/Off (43193) J.P. Brady. To Awar to pick up two Japanese POWs, carry out supply drops to forward Army personnel. Mysterious distress signals picked up in Blue Blvp area, search carried out, nil sightings.
8.07.45. 8 CU, Madang. F/Off (423031) N.M. Agnew. Attempt to rescue Lt Carter an American pilot of Combat Replacement Training Corps, who had bailed out of his P38 in vicinity of Karawari R, a tributary of the Sepik R, at present held by the enemy. Agnew landed on the Karawari which was only 40 yds wide and running at 4 to 5 knots carrying floating logs and debris. In spite of these extremely hazardous conditions, he successfully alighted and remained for approximately two hours while natives fetched Carter from his position deep in the kuani grass 200 yds from the landing point. Operation successful.
8.09.45. 8 CU, Madang. Flt Lt Payne, W/O (428722) K.G. Lennox. Army personnel and fresh fruit to Lake Vrabu and return.
25.09.45. At 8 CU, Pegasus 33392.
15.01.46. Received at 2 CRD, Richmond, from 8 CU. TFT 602.20 hrs. Pegasus VI 33392. Dismantled for road transport. Due extent corrosion recommended Category D Storage.
12.03.46. Convert to components.
23.08.48. Authorised for w/off.
2.03.49. At auction site Rathmines, sold for scrap.

**X9516**

19.10.42. At Point Cook for erection.
23.10.42. Erection completed.
15.11.42. Depart Point Cook for Richmond with X9517.
24.11.42. *Australia.*
1.01.43. *Australia.* Exchanged with X9529. Disembaraked in Townsville, Qld.
3.02.43. Departs Archerfield for Coffs Harbour.
11.43. 2 FBRD. Undergoing overhaul.
22.12.43. 8 CU.
25.02.44. 8 Comm Flt. Flt Sgt P.J. Briggs, Flt Sgt J.G. Laycock, Flt Sgt V.F. Peard, P/Off Smith. On alighting to deliver secret signal publication to HMAS *Stella Maris*, engine was cut to bring aircraft to rest approx 15 yards from ship which lost way, however barge continued and struck nose and port lower mainplane. TFT 173.25 hrs.
1.03.44. 26 RSU for repairs.
1.05.44. 8 CU. HD 864 returned Goodenough, will be replaced by X9516.
19.06.44. 8 CU. Depart for Momote to replace L2213.
3.08.44. QANTAS for overhaul, recovering and camouflaging.
12.44. 2 FBRD. For operational fitment.
23.12.44. 8 CU. F/Off (423656) R.C. Crebbin. Returned from mainland having ferried aircraft to unit.
6.01.45. 8 CU. F/Off (411310) Gole, F/Off Lehmuin(?). Brig Ferguson and two staff for Recce over Bosman Village which was being attacked by AIF.
21.01.45. 8 CU. F/Off (423656) R.C. Crebbin. Search for missing launch. Landed Awar then continued search and found launch.
23.01.45. 8 CU. F/Off (411310) R.M. Gole, Flt Sgt (28036) Horne, Flt Sgt (405198) E.W. Stubbin. Madang to Annenberg to pick up native police boy who required medical treatment; alight on Lake Vrabu. Successful pick up and night alighting to deliver patient.
3.02.45. 8 CU. F/Off (423656) R.C. Crebbin with Col Owen, USAF, as guide. To Awar where CRTC A20 (Boston) aircraft had crashed landed in centre of strip. Landed in restricted area of strip and picked up AIF patrol leaders and carried out search for parachuted A20 crew. Both members located and successfully rescued the following day.
5.02.45. 8 CU. F/Off (423656) R.C. Crebbin with Brig Major and Staff Captain of 8 Brigade HQ, carried out 'recce' of Sepik and Ramu Rivers. Landed Awar and advised forward AIF detachments results of 'recce.'
9.02.45. 8 CU. F/Off (427458) A.C. Evans. Flt Sgt (428722) K G Lenox. Conveyed three AIF personnel to Awar, then picked up officers of 30 Batallion and took them to point in estuary of the Rainu where AIF operation was in progress. Orders delivered and returned to Awar. From here two stretcher cases and two other wounded returned to Madang.
25.02.45. 8 CU. F/Off (411310) R.M. Gole, Flt Sgt (28036) K.G. Horne. Convey four RAAF personnel to Momate. The aircraft then carried out calibration flights with Radar Officers on instructions at Harangen Is and Buldranis Mission.
3.03.45. 8 CU. F/Off (427458) A.C. Evans, F/Off (43193) J.P. Brady. Proceed from Lake Vrabu to Awar on Army Co-op Recce. HD874 took personnel and tools to Lake Vrabu for unserviceable X9516. Made serviceable. Carried out supply drops in Ramu district.
28.05.45. 8 CU, Madang. F/Off (423656) R.C. Crebbin, Flt Sgt (405198) E.W. Stubbin. Transport GOC 1 Australian Army, Lt Gen Sturdee, one AIF Major, one AIF Corp to Wewak. Allotted off Capr Wom. AIF party taken ashore by Army ship. Aircraft proceeded to Tadji to await Sturdee's orders. Unserviceable due engine trouble. AIF evacuated by other air transport. Aircraft and crew return Madang on 31st.
25.09.45. At 2 FBRD, Pegasus 33818.
12.45. 2 FBRD. Undergoing overhaul.
8.05.44. 8 CU. To Ndrova Is to evacuate US Army Lieutenant wounded in action.
28.08.45. 8 CU, Madang. F/Off (427458) A.C. Evans, F/Off K.G. Smith. Departed on allotment to 2 FBRD.
01.46 to 03.46. 2 FBRD. Held for storage.
13.05.46. Maintenance Sq, Rathmines. TFT 495.25 hrs. Pegasus P.33818. Unserviceable, dismantled for road transport.
30.07.48. To be disposed by CDC by auction. Prior 13.12.48. Shipped to auction site.
2.03.49. At auction site Rathmines, sold for scrap. W/off.

**X9517**

2.11.42. At Point Cook for erection.
12.11.42. Erection completed.
15.11.42. Depart Point Cook for Richmond with X9516.
30.12.42. 9 Sqn. F/Off Hempenstall. Inner anti-submarine patrol with X9520 for Force 'VV' proceeding from Sydney to Port Stephens. Weather caused convoy to take shelter in Botany Bay, aircraft returned to Rathmines.
14.12.42. 9 Sqn. Rathmines. Flt Lt Mason. Inner anti-submarine patrol with X9520 and P5664 for Force 'VT'.
17.12.42. 9 Sqn. Rathmines. F/Off Rhode. Inner anti-submarine patrol with X9513 for HMAS *Ping Wo* from Newcastle to Port Stephens.
23.04.43. Starboard u/carriage leg collapsed on landing. Repaired on site & serviceable except for rough water alightings.
15.08.43. 9 Sqn Detachment, Cairns. F/Off H Dowsley, Sgt E.J. Thompson, Flt Sgt V.F. Peard. While returning to cairns after seaward patrol forced landing near Green Is due No.2 cylinder blew off in flight shattering airscrew. Picked up by Naval submarine Chaser and towed to Cairns. TFT 379.50.
(18.08.43). Awaiting new engine.
12.43 to 02.44. 2 FBRD. Undergoing overhaul.

25.09.45. At Qantas, Pegasus 33793.
22.01.46. Engineless at 2 CRD, Richmond. TFT 37.35.
2.07.48. Issued to DAP, Botany, ex-2 AD.
6.09.40. Action completed.

**X9520**

2.11.42. At Point Cook for erection.
10.11.42. Erection completed.
20.11.42. Depart Point Cook for Richmond.
30.12.42. 9 Sqn. Flt Lt Mason. Inner anti-submarine patrol with X9517 for Force 'VV' proceeding from Sydney to Port Stephens. Weather forced convoy to take shelter in Botany Bay, could not find convoy. Operation cancelled.
14.12.42. 9 Sqn. Rathmines. F/Off Rhodes. Inner anti-submarine patrol with X9517 and P5664 for Force 'VT'.
19.12.42. 9 Sqn. Flt Lt Rhode. Two inner anti-submarine patrol with X9514 for Force 'TS' from Port Stephens to Sydney. Alighted at Rose Bay.
3.01.43. Received at Townsville for *Australia*. Could not embark due weather.
8.01.43. Search for survivors on a raft.
11.01.43. *Australia.*
18.01.43. Palm Is. Spotting for gunnery practice. To Townsville then 9 Sqn Bowen to exchange with W2755.
3.03.43. F/Off Gardner and crew. Aircraft arrived and attached to 6 CU, Manbullo.
10.03.43. 6 CU. F/Off Gardner. Convey Wing Cdr Rooney to Bathurst Island Mission. Damaged port wheel on landing.
5 to 7.04.43. F/Off Gardener. 4 RSU, Pell Field, NT. Work in progress, repairs to float and fitting extra fuel tank.
7.04.43. 6 CU. Return from 4 RSU.
9.04.43. 6 CU. F/Off Gardner. Convey personnel to Millingimbi, Cape Wessell.
24.05.43. 6 CU. F/Off Fairbank. To Bynoe Harbour to pick up crew of Vultee Vengence.
29.05.43. 6 CU. F/Off Gardner. Departed for Millingambi for sea rescue work.
1.06.43. Returned 6 CU having completed duty.
20.06.43. 6 CU. F/Off Lobwein. Search Point Stephens area for reported parachutist.
6.07.43. 6 CU. F/Off Lobwein. To Peron Is to pick up F/Off Hinds, Spitfire pilot.
18 to 19.07.43. 6 CU. F/Off Gardner. To Cape Wessel to pick up sick patient and return.
20.09.43. 6 CU. F/Off Lobwein, Flt Sgt Hunter. Left with freight and passengers for Millingimbi but returned due to Hydraulic leak. Took off in afternoon for Cape Don. Alighted in open sea to evacuate appendicitis case to Batchelor.
6 to 13.12.43. 6 CU. F/Off K Gardner and Cpl V.W. Smith. To Cape Don with supplies. Remained overnight due heavy seas. ASI out of service. On take-off on 7th, port float detached and damaged front mainplane. Repairs on spot impossible. *Sapphire* arrived Thursday 9th. Temporary work carried out. Decided to tow aircraft to Darwin for mainplane change. Left on 10th. Due heavy seas unable to relieve Walrus crew until they anchored in lee Cape Hotham. Gale sprang up at 0245 on 11th. It was impossible to take-off Cpl Smith who was on board as 'anchor watch', and had to remain until Darwin was reached at 1930 hours. Landed Walrus on Mendle Beach on 12th h. On 13th ground party arrived fitted new wing, flown back to Batchelor.
20.12.43. 6 CU. Still completing repairs from above incident.
14.04.44. 6 CU. Batchelor, NT. F/Off G.P. Lobwein, Sgt G.H. Jones, Cpl R Thompson, LAC H.S. Steiger. Returned from Bathurst Is and during circuits engine cut out. Forced landed cross-wind with undercarriage retracted on rough portion of airfield, aircraft overturned, completely wrecked. Lobwein suffered severe shaking and slight injuries, Jones and three(?) passengers uninjured. TFT 250.25 hrs.
21.04.44. Issued 4 RSU ex-6 CU.
16.05.44. Approval for conversion to components.
07.44. 8 CRD. Crated by components and despatched to 2 FBRD for completion of conversion.

**X9559 Walrus Mk. II**

19.01.44. Received 1 TMO ex-UK.
18.06.44. 5 CU. Flt Lt D.P. Rose, Flt Sgt W Bernie, W/O H.S. Matthews, W/O D.G. Bell. Landed in strong cross wing, port float touched ground. Damage to rear spar beyond limits laid down. TFT 166.30 hrs.
06.44. Repaired at 2 FBRD.
13 to 16.06.44. 5 CU. Flt Sgt Bernie. To Princess Charlotte Bay to rescue Vultee Vengence crew.
18.06.44. 5 CU. F/Off Rosse. To Cooktown, aircraft damaged in landing. Spares flown to Cooktown.
26.06.44. Return to 5 CU.
26.08.44. Received 8 CU ex-9 Sqn.
22.07.44. 5 CU. Flt Lt Rose and crew. Test after engine change.
10.08.44. 5 CU. 'Ferry crew from Bowen collected this aircraft on allotment. Leaves two crews this unit without an aircraft to fly...this leaves us without the worry of amphibious aircraft now.'
15.08.44. L2322 exchanged.
25.10.44. 5 CU. Karasau Is. W/O J.M.T. Brown, P/Off W.B. Bernie. Conveyed Capt Evetson to Karasau Is off coast of New Guinea near Wewak to see if he could obtain any information from natives. Aircraft alighted near island. A covering Beaufort X9559 saw two men land, then ground fire, then the aircraft was seen on fire. Presumed they were PoWs. It was ascertained that the crew had asked a native in a canoe if there were any Japanese on the island and were told there were none. On landing they were shot from ambush. The Japanese then rowed out and shot the pilot who died of wounds. Aircraft burnt by enemy.
1.11.44. Approval for w/off.

**Z1804 Walrus Mk. II**

28.04.43. Received QANTAS, Rose Bay ex-UK. On loan from RN.
06.43. Repaired during month 1 FBRD.
22.06.43. F/Off Davis. From Bowen to *Australia* at Palm Is.
18.10.43. *Australia.* Hoisted out for anti-submarine exercise around Milne Bay.
8.11.43. *Australia.* Catapulted to take photographs of Task Force and proceed Samarai.
13.11.43. *Australia.* Flight from Port Purvis to Henderson Airfield, Guadalcanal.
20.11.43. *Australia.* Photographed islands vicinity Milne Bay.
21.11.43. *Australia.* Catapulted. Proceeded to Samarai with official dispatches and passengers.
27.11.43. *Australia* To Jenkins Bay with dispatches and passengers.
(12.43). Replaced by HD860.
8.03.44. 5 CU.
11.03.44. 5 CU. Sgt Bernie. Local practice water landings.
30.03.44. 5 CU. Sgt Bernie. To Merauke. To remain for use of 72 Wing HQ.
12.05.44. Flt Sgt Bernie. To Rose Bay, allotted to QANTAS for complete overhaul.
(27.06.45) Held on Rathmines ledger but issued to RNAS Schofields, NSW. On loan to FAA.
12.09.45. 2 FBRD.
8.10.45. Issued from 2 FBRD Rathmines to FAA on loan.
02.46. Returned to RN.
12.12.49. Official entry to clear ledger.

**Z1811 Walrus Mk. II**

19.01.44. Received 1 TMO ex-UK. On loan from RN.
06.44. Repaired AT 2 FBRD.
11.06.44. 6 CU. F/Off R.S. Strange. Ferried from Rathmines on allotment this unit.
25.08.44. 6 CU. Batchelor Strip. W/O M.L. Marsh. Ground looped towards end landing run due failure port brake. TFT 152.55 hrs.
17.05.45. 6 CU. W/Off Marsh. Ferry flight to Rose Bay, refuelled at Gorrie strip, on take-off unable to retract undercarriage, landed again, port leg collapsed causing ground loop. No further damage to machine.
07.45 to 11.45. 2 FBRD. Undergoing overhaul.
11.45. 2 FBRD. Storage.
25.09.45. 2 FBRD, Pegasus 33763.
(27.06.45). On loan to RN.
(12.12.45). At 2 FBRD, Rathmines.
17.12.45. To be loaned to FAA.
3.01.46. Issued from 2 FBRD Rathmines to FAA.
22.01.46. 2 FBRD, Rathmines. Pegasus 33363.
02.46. Returned to RN.
12.12.49. Official entry to clear ledger.

**HD812**

28.06.43. Received ex-UK, QANTAS Rose Bay.
08.43 to 10.43. 2 FBRD. Undergoing repair or overhaul.
31.08.43. 2 FBRD Rose Bay. Trial installation Mk. III IFF.
1.09.43. 9 Sqn. Kept for testing at Rathmines.
12.04.44. To *Australia.*
15.05.44. Disembarked Momote Strip, PNG, proceeded back to Bowen pending official advice regarding disposal.
07.45 to 08.45. 2 FBRD. Undergoing overhaul.
25.09.45 to 22.01.46. 2 FBRD, Rathmines. TFT 540.25 hrs. Pegasus 33403. Unserviceable, dismantled for road transport.
01.46 to 03.46. 2 FBRD. Held for storage.
13.05.46. With Maintenance Sqn.
28.05.47. Authorised by CDC for w/off.
2.03.49. At auction site Rathmines, sold for scrap.

**HD818**

28.06.43. Received QANTAS, Rose Bay.
08.43. 2 FBRD. Undergoing repair or overhaul.
9.09.43. Received 9 Sqn.
30.11.43. 9 Sqn. Wing Cdr E.B. Courtney, Sqn Ldr E.G. Forrest. During landing run after normal touch down aircraft developed violent turn to starboard which could not be stopped; port wing tip touched ground. Tail wheel developed shimmy before collapsing. TFT 114 hrs.
1.12.43. Horn Is. Collapse stern post.
17.04.44. To Milne Bay.
9.07.44. Left Milne Bay for Bowen.
3.08.44. From 9 Sqn to QANTAS for hull repairs.
(13.11.44). Notified for conversion. Approved on 20th.
3.04.45. 2 CRD. Received Seagull A2818 which consisted of one crate of parts less hull, wings and engine.
31.05.45. Conversion to components completed.

**HD860**

14.09.43. Received QANTAS, Rose Bay, ex-UK.
11.43. 2 FBRD. Undergoing overhaul.
19.12.43. To *Australia.*
15.01.44. Disembarked Rose Bay.
6.03.44. *Australia.*
15.04.44. Allotted to 9 Sqn, Milne Bay, PNG.
17.04.44. Replaced on *Australia* by HD812.
3.07.44. *Warrego.* Air Sea Rescue duties.
28.10.40. *Warrego.* Arrived Bowen. Leaving on 4th Nov. for repairs at QANTAS.
07.45 to 08.45. 2 FBRD. Undergoing overhaul.
08.45. 2 FBRD. Repair.
25.09.45 to 22.01.46. 2 FBRD, Rathmines. Airframe only, TFT 380.20 hrs. Dismantled for road transport.
02.46 to 03.46. 2 FBRD. Held for storage.
13.05.46. With Maintenance Sqn.
30.02.48. For public auction Rathmines.
2.03.49. At auction site Rathmines, sold for scrap.
19.03.49. W/off Rathmines.

**HD862**

14.09.43. Received QANTAS, Rose Bay ex-UK.
11.43 to 12.43. 2 FBRD. Undergoing overhaul.
27 and 29.05.45. 5 CU. Flt Lt Payne, F/Off Hage. Passenger flight from Garbutt to Bowen and return.
05.45. 5 CU. Being used in liaison work with the navy.
6.06.45. Landed Bowen from Garbutt delivered 'safe hand' bag to Chemical Research Unit.
18.06.45. At 5 CU to 2 FBRD.
21.06.45. 5 CU. Flt Lt Payne. Carried out ferry flight to Rathmines. Aircraft allotted to Rathmines.
06.45. 2 FBRD. Undergoing modification and held for operational fitment next month.
22.06.45. Held on Rathmines ledger but to be issued on loan to RN, Schofields, NSW, for air-sea rescue duties with British Pacific Fleet.

**HD864**

14.09.43. Received QANTAS Rose Bay ex-UK.
12.43. 2 FBRD. Undergoing overhaul.
3.02.44. 8 CU. F/Off (274003) B Hempenstall. Ferried aircraft to Goodenough.
6.04.44. 8 CU. F/Off (4072240) Hursthouse. Evacuate severly wounded American from Rambutyo Is.
10.04.44. 8 CU. During trip to Bat Is port tyre punctured; alighted Seeadler Harbour on return, changed tyre and flew back strip same afternoon.
1.05.44. 8 CU. Returned Goodenough will be replaced by X9516.
11.06.44. 8 CU. Kale Bay, Manus Is. Sgt J.G. Laycock, Gp Capt G.H. Steege, Colonel Murray, Major McCarthy. Struck 'nigger head' coral reef during take-off.
15.06.44. 8 CU. Return from Momote for repairs.
4.08.44. 8 Cu. F/Off (423656) R.C. Crebbin. Had been to Woodlark Is to evacuate a stretcher case and was returning to Goodenough Is via Milne Bay. Landed in strong cross wind, swung to port, float struck runway, tilted on nose damaging hull.
14.08.44. Damaged landing Wards Strip.
15.12.44. Approval for conversion to components.

**HD865**

14.09.43. Received QANTAS Rose Bay ex-UK.
12.43 to 01.44. 2 FBRD. Undergoing overhaul.
5.03.44. 8 CU. Flt Sgt (415367?) Watson, Flt Sgt (425377) Tait. Aircraft arrived at unit.
31.03.44. Saramo, Fergusson Isl, Papua New Guinea.. Flt Sgt (405746) J.G. Laycock (1st pilot), Flt Sgt (425377) D.C. Tait (2nd pilot), Flt Sgt (426138) W.P. McCutcheon; P/Off Smith of signals unit, passenger. On a 'Syko run.' Accident on take-off. Port wing dropped, float hit water, aircraft swung round, capsized and sank immediately. All crew managed to get out, the pilots through the hatch above their cockpit, the passengers through a window behind the cockpit. They hung onto a float for some time but it sank. Tait drifted away and was heard to call out he could not hold on any longer and he sank and drowned. Others were rescued by a native canoe.
24.04.44. Approval for w/off.

**HD874**

14.09.43. Received QANTAS Rose Bay ex-UK.
12.43. 2 FBRD. Undergoing overhaul.
17.12.43. Issued 9 Sqn.
21.06.44. Cairns, Qld. Emergency landing.
18.07.44. Issued to QANTAS for repair. Capable of flying to Rose Bay.
12.08.44. 2 FBRD. Flt Lt White. Depart on ferry flight to 8 CU after repair or operational fitment.
26.08.44. Joined 8 CU. Coded ZA-W.
16.10.44. 8 CU. Substitute for P5664 to be fitted as drogue tower.
14.11.44. 8 CU. To Sepik R area carrying Brig Gen Ferguson as passenger. Came under AA fire without damage. Mission successful.
14.11.44. 8 CU, Madang. F/Off (423656) R.C. Crebbin. Drogue towing exercise for co-operation with RAN.
2.03.45. F/Off (423656) R.C. Crebbin, Flt Lt Wright (of 41 Sqn). Recce Lake Vrabu and Ramu River to ascertain if suitable for PBM Mariner alighting.
3.03.45. 8 CU. F/Off (423656) R.C. Crebbin. Took personnel and tools to Lake Vrabu for unserviceable X9516. Made serviceable.
5.03.45. 8 CU. F/Off (411310) R.M. Gole, W/Off (417309) W.H. Lehmann. To Lake Vrabu in order to evacuate two AIF medical cases.
13.03.45. 8 CU. Allotted 1 FBRD for 240 hourly.
25.09.45 to 22.01.46. 1 FBRD, Lake Boga. TFT 480.25 hrs. Pegasus VI 33421. Airframe and engine serviceable, stored Category D.
15.08.47. Received Rathmines ex-Lake Boga.
27.08.47. Retain a/frame and engine for proposed Antarctic Expedition.
21.10.47. Issued to Dept of External Affairs for use by ANARE.
31.10.47. Issued to RAAF Antarctic Flight.
3.11.47. Issued to Antarctic Flight.
20-21.12.47. Wrecked in storm at Heard Is.
27.03.80. Recovered hull, now in RAAF Museum. (There is controversy that this is not the original hull of HD874 as it is a metal hull).
2022. Now on display in RAAF Museum, Point Cook.

# Chapter 21. The Supermarine Southampton

**Above:** A11-2 moored out. These Southampton flying boats were the largest aircraft operated by the RAAF pre-World War II. (AHMofWA P021479)

*Aircraft* magazine for 2 March 1936, recorded the return to Point Cook of Southampton flying boat A11-1 from *a mission which should have been completed in a few weeks had all gone well.* This mission commenced at 0730 hours on 26 June 1935, when the Southampton, piloted by Sqn Ldr Arthur E Hempel, took off with 600 gallons of petrol and full overseas equipment, *to make a reconnaissance of the route between Sydney and Darwin to determine the practicability of operating a regular air service between these points with large flying boats. The route the flying boat was to inspect was that proposed by British officials in connection with the future developments of Empire Air Mail Services.*[1] It was felt that such a survey was *necessary not only to ascertain the reasonable practicability of the route for flying boats, but also to determine the nature and extent of the ground organisation and facilities that will be required for the operation of such a route by flying boats of the type proposed by the British authorities.*[2]

In addition to Hempel, the crew comprised F/Off L.E. Burt (second pilot), Cpl P Neal (metal rigger), LAC J.A. O'Donnell (aero fitter) and LAC A.M.J. Clark (W/T operator and mechanic). The flight from Point Cook to Bowen followed the coastal route, and thence overland to Karumba on the Gulf of Carpentaria. From the Solitary Group of islands heavy rain and hail chipped both airscrews sufficiently to cause vibration. As the aircraft was flying blind at 150 feet a decision was made to land at Maclean on the Clarence River and to examine the airscrews while waiting for better weather. From Maclean they proceeded to Brisbane where the port airscrew was taken to QANTAS for balancing at their workshops. On 5 July while taking off from the Fitzroy River at Rockhampton, the tailplane was damaged when the wash threw a piece of driftwood against its leading edge stoving it in for a distance of four form ribs. A return was made to the anchorage and repairs effected with material carried on board. At Bowen they landed at 1310 hours and tied up to a RAAF mooring. Unfortunately, these moorings had been laid at the direction of the Portmaster, Marine Department, Brisbane, in a position other than that required without reference to RAAF HQ. The flying boat was moved closer to shore within the protection of the pier. Both airscrews were changed as the crew worked to get the aircraft ready for the 500 mile overland crossing on the next part of their journey.

The aircraft was filled with 600 gallons of fuel and loaded for a start at daybreak on the 13th. At 0750 Hempel attempted to take off from a glass-calm sea but the machine was unaccountably tail heavy and was unable to take off after 50 minutes of trying. When trying to take off solid water from the main step struck the inner front of the two 100-gallon auxiliary petrol tanks, rebounded on to the after part of the hull, tailplane and elevators, making the aircraft very tail heavy and flooding the rear cockpits.[3] The *effect is*

**Above:** An impression of a Felixstowe F.5 as it would have looked if taken into RAAF service. The serial series A11 was reserved for these flying boats. (RAAF official)

**Above:** Moving the huge packing crates containing the Southampton hulls through Melbourne was a major operation for the fledgling RAAF. A special 'jinker' was specifically constructed for the purpose of taking the flying boats from the wharf at Victoria Docks, Port Melbourne, to Point Cook. The 50 ft long and 13 ft high crates were put to good use as storage sheds. (via RAAF Museum)

*as of a heavy load at stern. It requires full strength to keep wheel forward with all load and crew forward of midships and when throttling back after an unsuccessful attempt the wheel cannot be held forward.*[4] On the new airscrews the timber had shrunk at the leading edge, the metal armouring having split in the excessive spray. The aircraft was returned to its moorings and the old airscrews replaced. After another unsuccessful attempt the next day under similar sea conditions the auxiliary tanks were removed and a successful take off was made in 42 seconds with a load on board equal to full auxiliary tanks. An additional 250 lbs were added and a take-off made in 68 seconds. As similar sea conditions could be expected along the route and some of these would be in uninhabited country it was decided to obtain smaller auxiliary tanks and if necessary, carry extra petrol in the hull. From Melbourne the Air Board could only suggest that the relative tail heaviness could be adjusted by draining the rear step or examining the saddle and mainplanes for incidence. 50-gallon auxiliary tanks were sent by passenger train arriving on the 22nd and the 'boat was ready to leave the next morning.

By the 24 July they had completed the reconnaissance as far north as the Mitchell River. On the 25th Papuan Concessions Ltd reported that the Short Scion seaplane piloted by Stuart A Campbell had not been heard of since leaving Daru, New Guinea, on the 23rd, and requested RAAF help. The company offered to pay all out-of-pocket expenses for the use of the Southampton. Campbell was with the RAF and took part in the Great Barrier Reef surveys of 1926, 1927 and 1928. He went to Antarctica with the Mawson expedition of 1929 and returned to Australia in 1930. He was reported as undertaking a survey of a vast unexplored area of the Fly River country on behalf of the Oroville Gold Dredging Co, a British mining syndicate.

Campbell was an ex-RAAF pilot and an old friend of Hempel. Accompanied by mechanic W Hellon, he had departed Sydney on 12 July reaching Daru on the 21st. On the 23rd they had left Daru for the Oroville base camp at Kiunga. The seaplane never reached its destination and was lost somewhere in the vast swamp of the Fly River country.

Hempel found the Scion moored to the jetty at the Madiri Plantation. On landing the tailplane was again

**Above:** The hull of S1158, probably just after it was removed from its crate. (via RAF Museum)

damaged. Campbell and Hellon were alive and well and surprised to see the flying boat. The Scion had flown due north from Daru and had been forced to alight on the Fly when one of the engines had stopped. On examination it proved to have a large hole in the crankcase and oil everywhere. They had no choice but to drift down the Fly. This proved to be frustratingly slow as winds often blew them back up the river against the slow current. Campbell estimated that they had landed about 60 miles from Madiri plantation. They had finally arrived after their third night on the river and had been just settling down to breakfast when they heard the roar of the Southampton overhead.[5]

Hempel flew to Daru and reported Campbell's situation and the *Vailala* sailed to tow the damaged Short back for repairs. When he arrived at Daru Campbell was surprised to see the Southampton still there. The flying boat had struck a reef in landing and while repairs were being undertaken to the hull it was discovered that one of the engines required replacing. When the new engine arrived and was installed, Hempel flew to Port Moresby at the request of the CCA, for the purpose of making a survey of the Papuan coast. Burt had

**Above & Below:** Still bearing its British serial S1158, A11-1 soon after being erected at Point Cook. (via AHMofWA P961646 & P961647)

been admitted to Moresby hospital on the 8th with malaria and was not discharged until the 12th. Hempel left for Thursday Island on 9 September; however, the new engine proved defective with the front roller race for the airscrew shaft showing excessive play after only 11 hours and they had to return to Moresby to await a new engine.

The Minister for Defence (Parkhill) waived the question of expenses for the Papuan adventure being recovered from Papuan Concessions Ltd as *Squadron Leader Hempel flew over difficult country which had not been previously explored by any member of the Royal Australian Air Force and on completion of the search the opportunity was taken of making a reconnaissance of the Fly River and its environs, and also of the southern coast of New Guinea.*[6] This was considered to be of value from a defence and civil aviation point of view and so the charges were waived.

The Southampton finally got away successfully on the 27th. Hempel's troubles were not over, for on returning to the Australian mainland he continued with the flight round the coast, but on the 30th he reported *that he had forced landed 3 miles south of Coen River, that the tailplane and port wing float had been damaged and that he was taxi-ing to Batavia River*

**Right:** *Like a half submerged whale*, S1158/A11-1 in the Torrens River, Port Adelaide, after encountering a freak squall. The machine was salvaged, the hull being undamaged. It was carried as deck cargo in a special cradle on the steamer *Saros*, from Port Adelaide to Melbourne, the engines and other parts being shipped in crates.

*(Cape York Peninsula) to examine the damage to the aircraft and engine.* An examination at the Mapoon Presbyterian Mission Station revealed the cause of the force landing to be a defective magneto. *The nearest telegraph station is at Moreton approximately 70 miles up river* and the Air Board had little information other than Hempel's first request for spares. These were arranged to be shipped by the SS *Taiping* which would then trans-ship them to a lugger at Thursday Island for the journey to the Mission Station.[7]

O'Donnell was sent to the Thursday Island hospital on the 15 October with tropical sores. He was flown back to Melbourne as unfit by F/Off Candy from 3 Squadron, who flew up LAC Sherwood in Demon A1-7 to replace O'Donnell.

On 22 November Hempel notified the Air Board that they were once more completely serviceable and that he proposed to continue with the original programme. On 4 December he had to beach the flying boat as the double bottom was again full of water. On the 21st the port engine cylinder head cracked at the valve feet, and he requested that another engine, two propellers, radiator, thermometer and motor generator be shipped to the boat at Geraldton where he proposed to beach the craft rather than Perth.

This delayed them until the 18 January. The rest of the flight to Perth, Albany, Ceduna, Port Lincoln, Adelaide and thence to Point Cook was almost uneventful. They were delayed on the 29th when strong headwinds of 20 knots prevented them from reaching Ceduna and forced them to shelter behind a sandbank in Israelite Bay.

The 'Specification for Organisation and Equipment of a Seaplane Airway' arrived after the flight was completed and this stated that seas of not more than 2½ feet from trough to crest *renders a site unsuitable*. Hempel wrote that it would have been advantageous to have had these specifications before he left on the journey, however he considered the requirement that a *large modern flying boat to require a sea of not more than 2½ feet* was unreasonable as the *Seagull and Southampton have operated in seas of 3 and 4-feet.*[8] Hempel's flight showed that the old flying boat was still capable of a credible performance.

Hempel actually thought that no place in Australia conformed to the specifications as the proposed Empire boats required *such a run of smooth, deep water into wind to take off, and so flat an approach to alight* that the most places were out of the question. Hudson Fysh of QANTAS, had tried to get Hempel to condemn the route as per the specification but state that it was suitable for flying boats.[9] In the event the British sent out their own expert, Major H.G. Brackley, air superintendent of Imperial Airways. Using a Short Singapore III flying boat borrowed from No. 205 Squadron, RAF, Brackley, accompanied by Hempel and A.R. McComb of the CAB, again covered the route back to Singapore. Hempel thought that the route did not even meet the revised specifications and refused to say otherwise. In the event the Empire Air Mail scheme went ahead despite the RAAF's objections to the use of flying boats. The CAS, Williams, had wanted multi-engine landplanes which would have more utility in time of war.

Australia with her thousands of miles of coastline had always appeared to be an ideal location to utilise the capabilities of the long-range flying boat. It was thought that for coastal reconnaissance the flying boat had many advantages over the landplane and in the event of a forced landing had a better chance of survival.

The Aeroplane Construction Committee had considered building large flying boats in Australia in 1918.[10] Post-Armistice various flying boats were looked at with the Felixstowe F.5, the last of the World War I series of these famous 'boats to be built, being considered for purchase. An early proposal was to establish No. 5 Squadron with F.5 flying boats, and the Shorts Company had notified the Air Board that it could provide six F.5 flying boats complete

**Above:** Metal hulled Southampton S1150 of the RAF Far East Flight. This aircraft carried two hull bands. S1149 carried a single band, while S1152 carried none. Local newspapers reported that a great crowd welcomed the *four British supermarine* (sic) *flying boats which left Adelaide at 7.15 a.m. alighted near St Kilda pier shortly after 2 p.m.* on Saturday 30 June 1928. (via AHMofWA P961585)

in every detail to Australian specifications including all the latest modifications for a cost of £37,020 net.[11] In 1921 it was planned to introduce the Short built F.5 into Australian service however financial restrictions led to the abandonment of this proposal. The serial designation 'A11' had been reserved for the flying boats when the Australian system was introduced. The initial requirement was seen as 18 large flying boats, but this was amended to eight.[12] As has been related in the history of the Seagull III, Williams, the CAS, was against the acquisition of flying boats because of the large cost of the special facilities required to operate them effectively.

In the proposal put forward by the Air Board for delegates to the 1926 Imperial Conference it was noted that the *recent flights of R.A.F. aeroplanes from Cairo to Cape Town and from Cairo to West Africa are of great value for the purpose of "showing the flag" and would welcome the extension of such flights by the R.A.F. towards Australia.*[13]

And so, in February 1927, when the Air Board considered the Estimates for the RAAF for 1927-1928, the Board was able to point out that the official reports of the Imperial Conference indicated that the Commonwealth Government had *undertaken to co-operate with the Imperial Government in the opening up of air routes and that experimental flights will be undertaken between Australia and Singapore by* (the) *R.A.A.F.* If this was so, then it appeared to the Board *that the Coast Reconnaissance Flight, which will be necessary eventually, should be formed as soon as possible to carry out these flights.*[14] In June the Air Board considered the purchase of large flying boats which *were intended for the development of inter-Empire Air Routes in co-operation with the R.A.F.* The Board noted that a sum of £66,000 had already been allocated for the purchase of two twin-engine flying boats, spare parts and a hangar to accommodate same. The best flying boat of this type was considered to be the Supermarine Southampton which was in use with the R.A.F. It was available in wooden and metal hulled versions. The price of a metal hull was about £4,000 more than a wooden one. Also, the *metal hull presents problems in regard to corrosion, etc. which are new.* The RAF Far East Flight was preparing to fly metal hulled Southamptons to Australia, *and knowledge in these matters (corrosion, etc.) will be obtained from* (this) *experience.* The RAAF had no experience with metal hulls but had mechanics who were *experienced and capable of handling and repairing wooden hulls.*[15] In a letter to Hugh Trenchard, Williams stated that apart from the above reasons of cost and experience with working with metal, another reason for the selection of the wooden hulls was that *we could not get delivery in time to co-ordinate with* the Far East Flight.[16] It was proposed to send the Australian flying boats to Singapore to accompany the British aircraft on the last part of their flight to Australia.

The engines of the Southampton were the Napier Lion Series V water cooled type, and while the Board had a policy of limiting the purchase of water-cooled engines as

**Above:** Supermarine Southampton S1152, one of the 'Flying Battleships' according to the press of the day, approaching the slipway at Point Cook. Note the crewman in the front cockpit with a grappling hook.

**Below:** On display at Point Cook S1149 is the object of the public's attention. S1149 had been placed on display between the large hangar and the landing jetty. The Melbourne *Argus* reported that the platform built over the boat enabled visitors at the top to see the cockpits, examine the controls and view the engines. *Two mechanics making final adjustments … and tuning up the engines added to the interest of the spectacle.* The weather showed the *graceful lines and clean silver and white of the boat relieved by the tri-colour circles and bars* of the national insignia. Photograph taken on weekend of 28/29 July 1928. The other two boats were kept in the Point Cook hanger.

**Above:** A11-1 now with its correct RAAF serial applied. The tailplane was the span of a light aircraft. (via RAAF Museum)

far as possible, the Lion was in service with the RAAF in the Seagull III and as such was considered acceptable. Air Board Order No.210 of 25 June 1927, was raised for two Supermarine Southampton flying boats with wooden hulls equipped with extra tanks, etc., the same as those fitted to the RAF Far East Flight boats.[17] The Board considered that these *machines will form the nucleus of what will probably become a Coastal Reconnaissance Flight*.[18]

The Southampton was Supermarine's replacement for the Felixstowe F5 in RAF service. Developed from the twin-engine Swan amphibian, the prototype Southampton flew on 10 March 1925. The timber hull of the Southampton Mk. I consisted of an inner body onto which was built the planning bottom. This double bottom ran from the bow to the rear step and was divided into ten watertight compartments. The inner hull was free from obstructions allowing a clear passage inside the hull from bow to stern and intercommunication between all cockpits. The Napier Lion engines were mounted independently of the Warren truss centre section bracing. This enabled an engine change to be undertaken without altering the wing structure. Gravity tanks were mounted on the upper wing, no fuel being carried in the hull.

The crew of five usually comprised a pilot and navigator, or alternatively two pilots, situated in the cockpits arranged in tandem about the centre portion of the hull, a gunner-bomber in the bow cockpits, and two gunners aft, one of which would also operate the wireless equipment. The two aft cockpits with Scarff rings mounted on a superstructure from the hull, were staggered, one being on the port side and one to starboard of the centreline of the hull. The crew members had excellent fields of view and fire for the front gunner, and the two rear gunners.

The bomb ger was operated from the front cockpit. Two 550-lb bombs, or an equivalent bomb load, could be carried under the bottom centre plane. When used for bombing one of the crew members was dispensed with and the W/T operator controlled both aft guns.

A special handling chassis was provided for beaching and launching the boat. It could be quickly attached to connecting points in the hull. This chassis was used with a tail trolley, the usual beach cradle being dispensed with.

The metal hulled Southampton Mk. II led to a reduction in weight of some 900 lb, 500 lb in the weight of the lighter duralumin hull and 400 lb in water soaked up by the wooden hull. Most RAF wooden hulled versions were given metal hulls. The type was used by Argentina, Japan, Turkey and Australia.

Two Southamptons with Napier Lion engines and tropical radiators were ordered on Indent No.210 at an estimated cost of £47,500.[19] The two flying boats were delivered to Melbourne as deck cargo on the SS *Ferndale* on 26 January 1928. They were kept in their cases for some time, F/Off F.A. Briggs conducting the first flight on 4 May.[20] These were preliminary trials with the official tests

**Above:** A11-1 on top of the slipway at Point Cook. Note that the fuel tanks under the upper wings are now painted a dark colour.

conducted on Friday the 18th with Briggs again as the pilot. These wooden hulled Southampton Mk. 1 flying boats bore RAF serials S1158 and S1159 when they were received in Australia, and they were operated with these serials for some considerable time. Given the serial prefix 'A11' in the Australian serial numbering system they were renumbered A11-1 and A11-2 respectively.

The proposed RAF Southampton cruise pointed out deficiencies in the slipway at Point Cook.

*The existing slipway was built in the early days...and the design was for light machines.*

*The weight of the flying boats now proposed will stress the structure to destruction...In addition the foreshore of this station is gradually silting up and where 3' of water existed at the slipway now only 9" of water exists at low water and it has been found impossible to raise seaplanes other than at high tide.*[21]

It was agreed to construct a new slipway and extend it 200 feet.

Another problem facing the RAAF was that it was very short of officers with big 'boat experience and *although one or two have had some experience of flying boats, none have had any such experience since the War.*[22] Approval was sought and granted to approach the RAF for the loan of a Flight Lieutenant with the necessary *flying boat experience preferably "Southampton" type.*[23] F/Off F.A. *Freddie* Briggs, who held a short service commission in the RAF, was selected. He resigned his RAF commission to take up an Australian commission, sailing before the British Government advised the Australian Government of this action through the Governor General.[24]

Before the flying boats were delivered the Minister approved, in October 1927, an experimental air service from Melbourne to Hobart to be operated by the two RAAF Southamptons.[25] The Prime Minister (Bruce) seemed keen on the idea and Williams did not immediately pour cold water on the proposal.[26] Indeed, the RAAF had considered that there was a possibility that a scheme of operating civil air routes by service aircraft could prove successful and thereby help *to lessen the cost of maintaining Air Forces in Australia.* This matter was to be placed on the agenda for the 1926 Imperial Conference as the Air Board *would like to have the views of Great Britain and the other Dominions*

**Right:** As part of the RAAF's efforts to encourage manufacturing of items of equipment, these fuel tanks for the Southampton were made at the MSB.

**Left:** The overload fuel tanks, that were carried under the lower wings of the Southampton, at the MSB.

*on this point.*[27] It has not been established if this was a ploy of Williams to gain support for the purchase of the coastal reconnaissance flying boats or whether the Air Board considered the matter had merit.

The RAAF prepared a proposal for a thrice weekly service between Point Cook and Ilfracombe on the Tamar via the Flinders Group of islands. It was proposed to inaugurate the service between 28 December and 29 February. The Air Board noted that the Southamptons *will have to leave Melbourne early in the new year for Singapore to co-operate with the R.A.F. Flight which propose arriving in Australia in June next.* The Board suggested that the service wait until the flying boats returned from Singapore.[28] It was then pointed out that the Southamptons were *boat seaplanes and can be operated from water only. They are designed for war, and these facts together with their characteristics in regard to fuel, speed, carrying capacity, etc. must be considered in connection with the work required of them.*[29] It would appear that the impracticality of operating warplanes as passenger transports was finally accepted and the idea for the service was abandoned around February 1928.

In the event the Southamptons did not leave Australia, however A11-1did fly to South Australia to meet the British boats. Wing-Commander Stanley J Goble and F/Off F Briggs and crew flew the 'boat, still bearing its British serial S1158, up to Adelaide on the Wednesday, 20 June 1928. The next day A11-1 was moored in the Torrens River, Port Adelaide, awaiting the RAF Far East Flight of metal hulled Southamptons when it was struck by a 30 second squall. *The squall struck the machine on the port quarter* recalled Cpl Douglas A Endean. *The whole machine appeared to lift bodily out of the water and then crashed on to the water again, the starboard wing striking the water first.*

*Both main spars of starboard wing snapped. I was by then standing on the gunner's platform and as the starboard wing hit the water, I was thrown out of the machine into the water.*

*The machine now commenced to roll over on its back in the direction of the broken wing and went over on its side, the tail commenced to lift out of the water simultaneously with a continuance of the roll which finally brought the machine on its vack* (sic) *with the tail up.*[30]

The RAAF officers had been preparing to embark in a

**Above:** S1158/A11-1 with the overload tanks under the bottom wings. (via AHMofWA P961625)

**Above:** Possibly S1158 in flight with overload tanks. (via AHMofWA P961644)

launch to go out to the flying boat when the wind struck. Endean swam to the Harbour Board's launch and was picked up. It was left for Wackett in his Widgeon II to escort the visitors into Adelaide. The Widgeon II did not alight on the river but left immediately for Albert Park aerodrome.

The Far East Flight, under Group Capt H.M. Cave-Browne-Cave, was the first-time aircraft of the RAF had flown to Australia. When the four flying boats arrived over Adelaide they saw *a peculiar object lying on the water, which resembled a half submerged whale. This turned out to be a RAAF Southampton I. ...It had been lifted out of the water and blown on its back by a sudden violent storm, known locally as a Willy-Willy, only two hours before our arrival.*[31] The helpless flying boat had been towed into shallow water and *was standing on her wings with the hull upside down at an angle of a little over 45 (degrees).* A diver had to be engaged to cut the mooring cable and free the machine from entangling ropes before towing it to shore near Torrens Island where it was made fast for the night. It was still upside down as the salvage crew were unable to obtain means to right it before night fell. The Harbour Board's 60-ton floating crane raised the machine on Sunday morning. It was then lowered onto the crane's pontoon and conveyed some three miles upstream to the Shell Company's wharf at Birkenhead. *Inspection on the wharf showed that the hull was absolutely undamaged and the engine to outward view not seriously affected by immersion to salt water. The wings were seriously damaged, the starboard wing being broken at the junction of the outer and inner bays at the time of the accident and the other wing probably being destroyed by water soakage. The tail unit is intact.* The aircraft was dismantled and crated for shipment back to

**Left & Above:** Working on the engine of a RAAF Southampton.

Point Cook for repair.[32] In February 1929, the Melbourne *Age* newspaper reported that the parts necessary to repair the boat had been ordered from the UK but had not yet been received. New wings and a centre section were necessary to refit the flying boat. The Air Board said the they were not concerned as the manufacturer was incorporating the *latest knowledge* into the required parts.

The RAF boats continued around the continent to Point Cook and from there across the Timor Sea to the Dutch East Indies, thence to Singapore. The Flight continued to eventually cover a distance of 24,000 nautical miles.

During Sir John Salmond's inspection of the RAAF in 1928, he was flown in A11-2 to Townsville, leaving Point Cook on 16 August with F/Off Briggs at the controls. While leaving Sydney the trailing wireless aerial was unreeled too quickly after taking off and the weight at the end of the aerial struck street lights in the suburb of Manly and damaged a Miss Brown's house. The Manly Council engineer stated that the damage could have been *extremely serious* if there had been high tension mains in the vicinity.[33] Although the crew professed to be ignorant of causing any damage it appears that the RAAF had to pay the Municipality of Manly £18.13.03 and Miss Brown £10 in compensation.[34] Wireless telegraphy had advanced little since the days of the 1914-1918 war and the aircrew of wireless equipped aircraft had to remember to wind their trailing aerials in before attempting a landing, or aerobatics!

In his report on the RAAF Salmond recommended the equipping of all coastal reconnaissance flights with flying boats. Williams again noted that *from the point of view of mobility, economy both in original establishment and in maintenance, ease of operation, performance and air endurance the same work can be done more efficiently and economically with multi-engined landplanes so long as units are based on the mainland of the Commonwealth, or at least near our vital centres.*

However, he did consider that Australia had *certain responsibilities* outside the mainland where the expenditure of large sums of money to make bases for landplanes would not be economical as flying boats could be operated at any time.[35] It was to be 1939 before the RAAF would acquire any more large flying boats and these Short Sunderlands would remain in the UK where their crews were engaged in accepting them for the RAAF when the 1939-1945 War broke out.

A combined exercise was conducted by the RAN and RAAF on 30 October 1929. As part of this exercise a Southampton was despatched to locate the 'enemy' vessels. There was no moon and clouds were down to 1,500 feet and if the ships had been blacked out a successful interception would not have been made. The flying boat flew over the 'hostile' fleet in order to identify the individual ships when it was caught by searchlights. It was unable to evade these lights as it was under instructions which prevented it seeking cloud cover. While held by the beams it was considered to be under fire from the fleet, however no searchlights had attempted to pick up the aircraft until it had passed over HMAS *Australia* when it would have been too late if it was engaged in a bombing attack. The beam from *Albatross* was not as strong s that from *Australia* and *Canberra,* but was well manned and was trained on the boat the whole time it was within range. The Southamptons, together with Wapiti and Moth biplanes, carried out mock attacks against the 'enemy' fleet. Despite the limitations of peace time conditions, it appears that the exercise was considered a success.[36]

A Combined Air & Sea Exercise was held on 30 October 1929. This exercise involved the Southampton A11-1 flown by Flt Lt Briggs with P/Off Dalton (2nd pilot); LAC Sims; AC1 Richmond, and F/Off Knox-Knight as Observer. The orders for the flight were to locate enemy forces and to identify the ships without being seen. Having forwarded this information, the Southampton was to bomb the enemy fleet. The following reconnaissance report was submitted for the flying boat (table next page).

On 17 April 1930, two Wapitis of 1 Squadron piloted by Flying Officers Andrew G Gerrand and Robert H *Bertie*

| Reconnaissance Report from Combined Air & Sea Exercise of 30 October 1929 | |
|---|---|
| **Time** | **Report** |
| 0415 | Left 1 FTS for Exercise 1. W/T tested and found satisfactory. |
| 0425 | My course is 150°, Speed 70 knots. Time of Receipt 0447. |
| 0427 | No enemy ships in sight over the arc enclosed between 145°and 160°, average visibility distance 3 miles. Time of Receipt 0450. |
| 0430 0435 | Sighted ship lights on Port bow. Four enemy cruisers, distance 20 miles at anchor. Time of Receipt 0455. Southampton attacked hostile fleet, but was caught by searchlights. |
| 0445 | Ships are Australia, Canberra, Albatross, Anzac. Time of Receipt 0502. |
| 0455 | Enemy 2 miles Frankston. This message was only received as far as Franks in Frankston when the W/T generator broke down at 0512. |
| 0530 | Machine landed. |
| Source: NAA A9376/1 Item Box 4 | |

Simms, left Point Cook for Tasmania to undertake a survey of forests for the Tasmanian State Forestry Department. They were given an escort by Supermarine Southampton A11-1 in case they had to ditch in the sea. They proceeded to Stanley where in a period of one month they photographed 300 square miles. On their return flight an *interception exercise was carried out by a "SOUTHAMPTON" Flying Boat to meet the "WAPITIS" at the north end of Flinders Island and escort them across Bass Strait.*[37] This was considered a valuable exercise and it became standard practice to escort landplanes with flying boats across Bass Straight.

The leader of the formation of landplanes was given the altitude and location of the point of interception as was the First Pilot of the Southampton, the remainder of the flying boat's crew were to solve the interception from the information supplied by the First Pilot. For example, an interception was to be carried out with three Wapitis and a Bulldog on 29 February 1932. The point of interception was to be *at 2500 feet or immediately beneath the clouds, whichever is the lowest, over Cape Franklin, the North Westerly point of Flinders Island.* Wapiti A5-10 carried a short-wave W/T and an R/T set. While air to ground reception was good, air to air (Southampton) was considered only fair. Nevertheless, a successful interception was carried out by the members of the Air Pilotage Course of the Seaplane Squadron, the flying boat and formation arriving over the appointed place at the correct time and correct height.[38] Other interceptions were conducted with the Navy and Seagull III amphibians.

After the 1934 annual training flight to Tasmania was carried out by Bulldogs and Wapitis, the Southampton escorting the flight from Cape Otway to King Island, Flt Lt Frank Wright pointed out that it was just as far over water from King Island to Smithon, and it was *necessary to cruise at not more than 1200 r.p.m. when accompanying the Southampton; this cruising speed is far from economical. Should strong headwinds be encountered the safe range of the Bulldog would be exceeded.* Wright suggested that both Southamptons patrol the central point on each of the two legs to and from King Island while the Bulldogs and Wapitis proceeded at their most economical speed and still retain the safety factor of the presence of the flying boat. It is not known if this idea was ever tried in practice.[39]

After escorting Wapitis across Bass Straight to Tasmania in April 1930, Southampton A11-1, carried out a series of flights from Strahan, Tasmania, to examine forests for commercial timber ventures. Strahan boasted an excellent mooring laid in Long Bay opposite the wharf, in a position sheltered from all winds. Forestry officials were carried and they concluded that an immense amount of time could be saved by aerial inspections. It was found that they could easily identify the various types of timber and also make a fairly accurate assessment as to whether it was of commercial use. Sqn Ldr Hepburn was in charge of the survey work.

Sqn Ldr Arthur Hempel concluded that a Gipsy Moth on floats would be suitable for such work in future as

(i) there was the complete absence of landing grounds and the country was unsuitable for forced landings.
(ii)there were sufficient rivers, lakes and sheltered harbours to operate a floatplane.
(iii) the type had a fair climbing speed and the manoeuvrability to examine narrow river valleys.
(iv) its low landing speed would help in the event of a forced landing and in such an event it would be easier to recover such a light aircraft.
(v) small capital cost involved.[40]

The failure of the Seagull III amphibians to achieve a satisfactory performance in exercises at Hobart in February 1931 led to the Navy requesting that the HMAS *Albatross* Flight *be augmented by at least one Southampton flying boat* for exercises with the Australian fleet.[41] Combined exercises with the New Zealand Squadron were planned but cancelled due to the New Zealand earthquake.

With the cancellation of the joint exercise the Air Board asked if a Southampton was still required and the Navy replied that it was for *air co-operation with gunnery and*

**Above:** *The cause – Port engine (Napier Lion) big end bearings jamd.* (P.E. Carr via RAN FAA Museum)

**Above:** *Shear legs for hauling out engines.* Note the depth of water. (P.E. Carr via RAN FAA Museum)

**Above:** *Bringing in the engines (About 1,000 lbs each).* Note the raft made up of Fairey IIID floats. (P.E. Carr via RAN FAA Museum)

**Above:** *Working party going out to the machine with landing chassis.* (P.E. Carr via RAN FAA Museum)

**Above:** *Building a corduroy track on the shore of the lake for tractor, transport and the hull when it came ashore. The team had to cut down saplings and lay them across the boggy ground in order to make a surface that would bear the weight of the tractor and its load. Although a poor photograph this gives some idea of the conditions of the site. (P.E. Carr via RAN FAA Museum)*

**Above:** *The hull with only bottom centre section & engine bed ashore and ready for jacking up on to trailer. (P.E. Carr via RAN FAA Museum)*

**Above:** *The hull on the trailer (about 3 tons.)* Note the planks laid to spread the load over the swampy ground. (P.E. Carr via RAN FAA Museum)

**Above:** *The Juggernaut* – an ancient kerosene tractor *starting the tow – about 30 miles to Lake Wellington (the first five miles through bush).* (P.E. Carr via RAN FAA Museum)

**Above:** The tractor has brought the dismantled machine out of the swamp. Now a truck would take over the job of towing. (P.E. Carr via RAN FAA Museum)

**Above:** Pulling down the overhanging branches of the trees on the road near Sale to allow the machine to pass. (P.E. Carr via RAN FAA Museum)

**Above:** The Southampton parked in front of the local pub after recovery. (P.E. Carr via RAN FAA Museum)

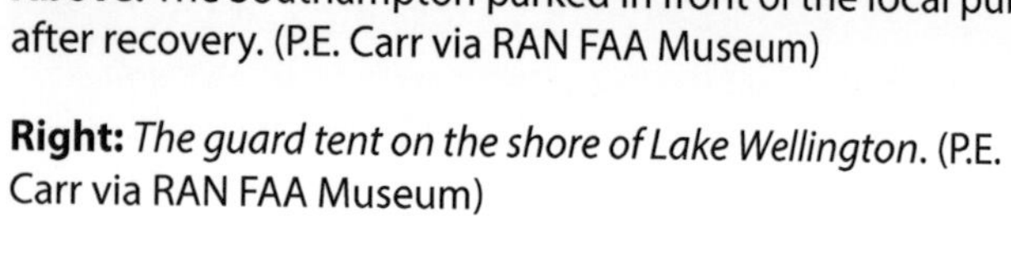

**Right:** *The guard tent on the shore of Lake Wellington.* (P.E. Carr via RAN FAA Museum)

**Above:** *Sammy Low's Ford Truck. The most useful motor vehicle.* (P.E. Carr via RAN FAA Museum)

**Left:** *Getting the upper mainplane in position.* Note the men lying on the upper wing centre section and the primitive supports erected for the wings. (P.E. Carr via RAN FAA Museum)

**Above:** *Working on the starboard main tank.* The engines and tailplane still have to be installed. The boat is mounted on its beaching gear. (P.E. Carr via RAN FAA Museum)

**Above:** *In the air again.* The work carried out was a tribute to the servicemen and their civilian helpers. (P.E. Carr via RAN FAA Museum)

*torpedo exercises.* The flying boat flew to Hobart and remained for over a week operating from *Albatross* as depot ship, however it was necessary for the Southampton to remain with the cruisers for a few days independent of maintenance by *Albatross*. Williams flew to Hobart in the flying boat to explain the situation re the replacements for the Seagull III amphibians with Admiral Evans. In the event the Seagulls were to be reconditioned.[42]

The long range of the Southampton enabled it to conduct searches for missing vessels. The Melbourne agents for the overdue collier *Christina Fraser* sought help from the RAAF in locating the ship on 28 June 1933, after it was last seen on the 25th, hove-to in raging seas. The agents had already charted the twin-engine amphibian flying boat Cutty Sark operated by G Jenkins, and a light aeroplane. In addition, the Hart Aircraft Co's Avro X made a deviation from its normal Tasmanian run to assist in the search.

A Southampton was detailed to assist and left Point Cook at daylight on the 29th. The six-man crew consisted of F/Off C.W. Pearce (pilot), Flt Lt P.E. Carr (second pilot and navigator), Cpl Kennedy, (motor boat coxswain), LACs Mc Cormick (carpenter rigger), O'Donnell (fitter aero), and Clarke (wireless operator). The advantage of the Southampton for long range patrols was its ability to carry the weight of *equipment capable of transmitting and receiving on short, long and commercial wavelengths.*[43] The A.T.2 Transmitter fitted enabled the flying boat to maintain *constant communication with Point Cook's A.R.3 receiver on 4000 Kc/s throughout the search...up to a maximum distance (of) 560 miles.*[44] The Southamptons were the only aircraft to have a specific wireless call sign. These were VMZAD and VMZAF for A11-1and A11-2, respectively.[45] The flying boat flew 26 hours 25 minutes over a period of four days before the search was called off. The CAS, Air Cdr S.J. Goble,

**Above:** RAF Short Rangoon K2809 of No. 203 Squadron on the water in Australia. Three Rangoons visited Australia from their base at Basra, Iraq, in September and October 1934, as part of the centenary celebrations of Melbourne. The Rangoon had a duralumin metal hull with metal used in the construction of the wing spars, and ribs. The wings were partly metal and partly fabric covered. These boats were a far advance on the wooden Southamptons still in use by the RAAF. (M Young Collection via R Alford)

described their work as *a really magnificent effort*. The crew had operated away from base alighting at Metung, Victoria, on the Gippsland Lakes, refuelling overnight and carrying on with the search the next day. This meant that all fuel had to be taken out to the flying boat in a launch and then pumped the 12 to 14 feet to the tanks.[46] Despite their work, the collier was never seen again and presumed to have been engulfed by a big sea.

A measure of the importance of the Southamptons for this type of work is reflected in a note which states that overhaul of A11-2 was begun without authority of RAAF HQ. The CAS was not notified as to the non-availability of the aircraft in the case of an emergency arising. The note concluded with a terse - *procedure to be tightened up*.[47]

During 1935 the RAF advised that a Southampton was at Singapore Island which was surplus to their requirements and it was offered to the RAAF. If not acceptable to the RAAF it was to be disposed of. No further record of the discussions on this subject has been found so the reasons for its rejection are unknown.[48] In 1936 the RAAF proposed the purchase of two Sikorsky amphibians from the USA. The type of Sikorsky and the reasoning behind the Air Board's desire to obtain these aircraft has not been found. The Board noted that while there were at present two Southamptons in service and a margin existed for one to be unserviceable, it *appears highly desirable, in order to avoid public criticism in regard to the capacity of the Air Force to undertake searches at sea* one Sikorsky be purchased now. Flying boats were third in the Government's priorities to upgrade the RAAF, however with the acquisition of new land planes capable of undertaking sea searches one amphibian would suffice for the present. This did not eventuate, the acquisition of Avro Ansons and the promise of the Bristol GP bomber/

**Above:** Flying boats required a lot of manpower to move in and out of the water. The forward beaching gear is still to be fitted to A11-2. (via RAAF Museum)

reconnaissance aircraft, as well as the problems which had arisen with the British over the selection of an American aircraft for training, probably combined to convince the Government that the acquisition of another American type was not warranted. The Southamptons remained the only long-range aircraft of the RAAF capable of maritime search and rescue until the arrival of Catalina amphibians after the Pacific War had broken out.[49]

The problems of operating these large flying boats are illustrated by an incident to A11-2. On 3 April 1934, Sqn Ldr A.E. Hempel with a crew of four flew to Twofold Bay where the Southampton was to be used as a *ground* W/T station at an advanced base during an exercise with His Majesty's Australian Squadron. On take-off both airscrews were damaged, the extent of which was not appreciated until after alighting at Twofold Bay. The exercise showed that

**Above:** The newly arrived S1158 at the Point Cook slipway. Note the men with the beaching gear. The walkways on the lower wing centre section are well shown here.

the technology of the time was not sufficiently advanced to allow for the use of the flying boat as an advanced W/T station. The next day saw the flying boat unable to take off due to a heavy swell, the tailplane and starboard airscrew being damaged in the attempt. Another attempt on the sixth saw the tailplane fabric again torn. After its repair and the offloading of 100 gallons of fuel, the next attempt was successful and the aircraft alighted at Metung. Leaving for Point Cook the next day the aircraft was over the sea under heavy rain clouds when the bearings in the starboard engine failed. The Southampton was at only 500 feet over a very rough sea with strong westerly winds. It was obvious to Hempel that the flying boat would have probably break-up if an attempt was made to alight on the open sea, however the nearest sheltered water was 10 miles distant. Hempel succeeded in alighting on Lake Reeve, the only suitable landing place. The lake is dry for the greater portion of the year and it was discovered that the water was only 12 inches deep over deep mud with a thin crust of shell and grass with logs and debris buried in the mud. The mud was such that when the thin crust was broken a 16 foot length of timber could be pushed straight down with no effort.

An examination determined against an attempt to fly the aircraft out, so it was decided to dismantle the flying boat and transport it over land to Lake Wellington. A salvage party consisting of a Leyland heavy tender and four-wheel trailer; Crossley light tender; Southampton cradle, launching chassis and tail truck; a spare Napier Lion engine; trestles, rigging, jacks, block and tackle, manila and steel wire ropes; two Fairey IIID floats; axes, etc, left Point Cook on the eighth and arrived the next day. The plan involved the haulage of the hull on its chassis one mile through the lake to the nearest point of hard ground at which point transport could be used. A track had to be cleared for 3 miles through timber to an unmade bush road which led to Lake Wellington.

While waiting for the arrival of the salvage party readily moveable parts such as the ailerons, tail unit and radiators were removed to the shore and the aircraft made ready for the dismantling of the engines and mainplanes. The launching chassis and tail trolley were attached to the aircraft and although the wheels sank into the mud, it assisted in keeping the aircraft upright. The engines were then removed by shear legs standing on mats of fence posts which carried the weight without sinking into the mud. Once raised from their mountings the engines were lowered onto the Fairey floats which carried the two engines within 200 yards of the light tender. The tender then drew the floats over the sand until they could be loaded by hand directly into the tender.

The wings were removed still boxed together and lowered onto the floats and brought to the beach by the same method. They were then dismantled and carried by hand to the heavy tender. An attempt to pull the hull to shore using an agricultural tractor failed due to its *antiquity* and condition. From the water's edge a corduroy road had to be constructed for 400 yards on the rushes just above the water edge and the

**Above:** A11-1 on its beaching gear with the large party of men required to handle these large boats in and out of the water from the slipway at Point Cook. Note that the main upper wing fuel tanks are a light colour at this time. (via RAAF Museum)

tractor travelled back and forwards on this track moving the hull in by increments equal to the length of the track. Once on the beach the aircraft rested entirely on its chassis. The top centre-section was removed and the hull with the lower centre section and engine mountings was towed to a clearing to be loaded onto a trailer. The Southampton's launching cradle was pulled by the tractor underneath the hull. The hull and cradle were then jacked up until the four-wheel trailer could be pulled underneath. The solid wheels of the trailer caused great anxiety on the soft ground and a long 6 inch square pole was lashed across the trailer to provide a point where the assemblage could be steadied in the event of a wheel sinking. While this gave some security, it meant that a wider track had to be carved from the bush. 12 axemen were in use at the same time because the width and height of the hull and centre-section meant that tree branches had to be trimmed even when on the main road.

The hull arrived at Clydebank on Lake Wellington on the evening of the 26th. The recovery party had covered 40 miles in three days, a truly magnificent effort. Erection presented no difficulty. A11-2 was launched on 12 May and after adjustments were made to the new engine, it returned to Point Cook on the 16th - 40 days after its forced alighting.[50]

Sgt D.J. Harkin and LAC Clark kept two W/T watches in the aircraft for three days after the forced landing. The entire short-wave equipment was then removed from A11-2 and set up in a fisherman's hut on the shore of the lake. Next day it was transported three miles to Gilder's farmhouse where it remained for 15 days. From there it went to a boarding house at Sale and finally was reinstalled in the aircraft at Lake Wellington three days before it was launched. W/T was maintained with Point Cook for the whole time and resulted in the Air Board noting the *excellent work* performed by the pair.[51]

The 1934 Royal Visit of HRH Prince Henry on HMS *Sussex* for the Melbourne Centenary Celebrations saw the RAF send three Short Rangoon flying boats of 203 Squadron based at Basra, Iraq, to Australia. The three (K2809, K3678 and S1433) made landfall at Darwin in late September.[52] They proceeded in leisurely fashion down the coast and were met off Port Melbourne by the RAAF Southamptons on 8 October. They also escorted *Sussex* into Port Melbourne on the 18th. The next day, on their escort flight to Geelong, Vic, one flying boat was ordered to carry a camera to secure oblique photographs of Mallacoota Inlet alighting site. The RAAF did not have the funds to miss any opportunity to achieve its objectives, Royal Visit or not!

On 19 November the two flying boats proceeded to Sydney where they were to repeat their royal escort. They were to alight on Sydney Harbour; however, they could not *land* in Farm Cove because of their size and special *arrangements had been made to transfer two R.A.A.F. moorings* to berths east of Garden Island.[53] In between these two escorts both aircraft had searched Bass Straight for the missing D.H.86 airliner, VH-URN, *Miss Hobart*, which had gone missing on 19 October during a flight to Tasmania. A seat was washed ashore on 18 November, no other wreckage or sign of the missing airliner or the pilot and his ten passengers was ever found.[54]

During 1938 it was planned to hold a series of

**Left:** Close-up of the nose of a Southampton showing the beaching gear. (via RAAF Museum)

pageants, however as the *Pier at Point Cook is undergoing reconstruction, and it is not anticipated that the work will be completed prior to JUNE. This will, in all probability prevent the SOUTHAMPTON from participating in Events. ...It may be possible to man-handle the SOUTHAMPTON into the water over the sand, but it is thought that the risk would be too great, as a change of weather would be liable to severely damage the aircraft.*[55] These two incidents highlight the problems of operating these large flying boats.

P.G. *Paddy* Heffernan had received his parachute training in 1932. He recalled that the *powers-that-be had decided that there would be no more free-fall jumps.* (See Chapter 8). The ALO advised that while the choice of free-fall or pull-off jumps was left to the individual in the RAF, pull-off jumps were considered advisable. The RAAF decided that all future training jumps were to be of the pull-off type. In this, the jumper stood on a small platform at the outer strut of the wings of a large aeroplane facing to the rear. He stood in this position during the take-off and until the correct height and location was reached. He then reversed his position so that he was facing the direction of travel and pulled his rip cord, the canopy pulling him off the platform as it deployed.[56]

The D.H.9a was not considered suitable for such use while the Southampton was, provided both wing tips were equally loaded while taking off. As Heffernan recalled, the *Southampton flying boat was the only suitable type of aircraft in the R.A.A.F. at the time.* After Supermarine confirmed that no alterations were required to the structure of the flying boat if Vimy type platforms were fitted, the aircraft was duly fitted with platforms for jumpers, 1 FTS reporting that the work had been completed on 2 July 1930.[57] Heffernan and Flt Lt Don Carroll won the ballot for the first jump. They boarded the Southampton, worked their way through the maze of struts and bracing wires to the jumping platforms where they waited while the flying boat climbed to position over Point Cook. *I think,* wrote Heffernan, *that this time was the worse part of the trip, because during take-off you could feel every movement of the wings and you felt sure that they were going to fall off. The Southampton was no fighter aircraft and it took us about twenty minutes to get to 1,800 feet...As we came over the southern boundary we got the signal to "Go"...we pulled our respective cords and the next thing we knew we were yanked off the platform and were floating in space.* The only regret that Heffernan had was that the descent was too short not giving him time to enjoy the sensation nor to try and control the chute. He brushed a tree, the canopy becoming entangled leaving him suspended some 10 feet from the ground.[58]

Trainees were given instruction on the correct maintenance, storage, folding, repair and dummy dropping of various parachutes. There were three types in use in the RAAF: the seat type, worn by pilots; the detachable type, used by observers; and the training type, for practice jumps. On completion of the course several of the personnel were permitted to make pull-off descents from a Southampton flying boat, using the special 28-foot training parachutes which they had inspected and folded personally.

At the 1935 course Heffernan, who was then in charge of instruction, decided to have another jump. The Southampton had been recently overhauled and managed to get to 2,500 feet. This time he did a free fall and felt the *opening shock was far less than being jerked off the platform.*[59]

Heffernan recalls the Southampton or *Swampton* as they

**Left:** Towing A11-2 from the launching ramp, circa 1929. (AHMofWA P030959)

**Above:** A11-2 was reconditioned in 1935 after a few years in storage and used for parachute training. The parachutist standing on the Vickers Vimy platform at the outer struts is facing rearwards. He had to hold this position until the machine had reached the correct altitude. (via P.G, Heffernan)

were known in the RAAF was a *quite useful old boat, mainly used for lost yachtsmen and the occasional aircraft that went missing in Bass Strait.*[60] It was a *kindly old tub, top speed of about 80 knots and in landing you flew them onto the water at about 65 knots. Depending on the wind, the take off could be up to a run of a mile.*[61] Despite this the type had an enviable record of service with the RAAF.

*The Southampton was a beautiful aeroplane to fly* recalled Air Commodore W *Bull* Garing. *It was a big aeroplane in those days. The people who built the hull were real experts, it was the top of wood craftsmanship. It had about a million screws in it; at least I didn't count them but that was what was continually repeated so I assumed it was right. The Napier Lion engines were not that reliable but again we got by with them. They were open exhausts and made a hell of a row (when heard) from the ground.*

This was used to advantage to arouse the ground crew

**Above:** He then turned around facing forward and still holding onto the strut he pulled the rip cord and the parachute deployed.

**Above & Below:** A dual jump from A11-2. The canopy deployed pulling the parachutist off the platform. Note the crewman in the front cockpit giving the order to release the parachute. (via W Garing)

**Above:** Flying boats were thought to be the best machines for long range transport in the 1920s to 1930s, but access could be a problem away from base. (via AHMof WA P961645)

when he had finished flying and was going to alight, as he used to bring the Southampton over the hangar. *We had to alight and catch a buoy at the end of the slipway. They would then attach ropes to it and pull it in attach the beaching gear and pull it in with a tractor. It had to go back in the hangar, we would never leave it moored out.*

*I found it a beautiful aeroplane, I could do anything with it. (At this time no one flew it at night) and I decided this was not good enough and as CO of the squadron I decided we were going to fly at night. To fly it at night it had two great big flares underneath the wings. Anyway, the first night I took off one engine cut out and I had to put it straight back on the water. It was a calm night there was no wind, so when I pressed the button which started the flares I looked down and could see the bottom of the ocean. There was no indication of where the water was. I got away with it twice that one night. Never had any more trouble with it, but that first night!*

*When we had glass calm sea conditions the hardest thing was to find the surface of the water. We used to roll up newspapers and we would fly along about half a mile or so dropping these papers over the side at regular intervals. Of course when you came around and came in you could see all these papers on top of the water.*[62]

This became standard practice at Point Cook.

In 1938, A11-2 was reconditioned and its use was *to be reserved for flying training and seamanship only* at 1 FTS and was *not to be flown outside Port Phillip Bay.*[63] Francis James recalled that the *Swampton* was of no operational use by this time and, though its engines boiled, it was kept flying *to give pilots practice in parachuting.*[64] Because of the harshness of the marine environment the Southampton was allowed 360 flying hours or one year in Category A, or 540 hours or two years in Category B before reconditioning. By comparison the equivalent hours for the Anson, which took over the maritime reconnaissance role, was allowed 720 hours and 1,080 flying hours in Categories A and B respectively. Capt V Hodgkinson commenced No.11 Seaplane Conversion Course in October 1939, and recorded that the Southampton was rarely used as it was *rather a bind to move in and out of the water.* He recalls that eventually the bottom of the hull collapsed and it was written off and burnt.[65] Officially its condition was such that its overhaul was considered too costly and the use to which it could be put if repaired was too limited to make this an economic proposition and the decision was made in April 1940 to convert it to produce. The five remaining Napier Lion engines were to be offered to technical colleges.[66] Alan Mitchell, a CAF officer with No. 21 Squadron, saw A11-1 dismantled with the uncovered wings showing their bare bones in June 1940. It cannot have

**Above:** W *Bull* Garing leading two Seagull V amphibians for a photographic session. (via W Garing)

**Above:** Five Saro London Mk. II flying boats from No. 204 Squadron, RAF, left their base in Plymouth Harbour on 2 December 1937, and flew to Australia to participate in the celebrations for Sydney's sesquicentenary in 1938. However, only four Londons reached Sydney on 25 January, one having been forced to alight in the Bay of Bengal and been towed to Burma. A replacement aircraft also had problems and did not arrive. One of the Londons preparing to moor judging by the crewman in the bow cockpit.

**Above & Below:** The flying boats flew in formation over Melbourne on 7 February when the starboard airscrew of K9686 flew to pieces. One part of the blade fell with such force it penetrated the iron roof of the Flinders Street railway station. and embedded itself nearly 3 feet into the platform. These two photographs were taken after the boat had been brought ashore for repair before the squadron could continue its flight.

survived long thereafter.[67]

Thus ended Australia's first attempt to utilise large flying boats. The Southampton had proved extremely tolerant of the conditions it operated under from the tropics to the southern reaches of Tasmania. Two flying boats could not effectively perform the function of coastal reconnaissance and in this their service must be judged as a failure, however they were the only long-range maritime aircraft operating in Australia until the acquisition of the Lockheed Hudson, the Avro Anson could by no stretch of the imagination be regarded as a suitable maritime reconnaissance aircraft.

**Above:** A11-2 taxying at speed. Note the parachute platform at the outer interplane strut.

## Specifications

Dimensions: Span 75 ft, Length 49 ft 8 in, Height 18 ft 7 in.
Weights: Empty 9.210 lb; Loaded 14,600 lbs.
Performance: Speed Max 108 mph; Cruising 82 mph. Range 930 mls.
Armament: Lewis guns on gun rings, one forward and two to rear of wings.

## End Notes

1. NAA ACT CRS A705/1 Item 205/2/631. Empire Air Mail - Survey of Route. Air Board, 6.081935.
2. *Ibid.* "Empire Air Mail Scheme; Survey of Route Darwin-Sydney", A/CCA to Air Board, 30.041935.
3. NAA ACT CRS A9376/1 Item 82. "Survey of Empire

**Above:** The crew can be seen at all positions in this photograph of S1158 taxying.

**Above:** Southampton A11-1 on the water. Note how a false background has been added to the photograph to make it appear to be in a more primitive area. (*Argus* Newspaper Collection. Victorian State Library.)

Air Routes (Darwin-Sydney section) and of Mooring Sites around Australian Coast by Southampton A.11-1 June 1935 to February, 1936" by H F De La Rue.

4. NAA ACT CRS A705/1 Item 205/2/631.*Op Cit.* Survey of Route Darwin-Sydney", FIS to Air Board, 16.071935.
5. Sinclair, J. *Wings of Gold*, Robert Brown and Assoc, Australia, 1978, P.242.
6. Quoted in Sinclair, J. P.242.
7. NNAA ACT CRS A705/1 Item 205/2/631. *Op Cit.* Minute; "Re Southampton Flying Boat". Telephone message from Melbourne, 10.10.1935.
8. *Ibid.* Hempel to Air Board, 21.01.36.
9. Gunn, J. *The Defeat of Distance - QANTAS 1919-1939*, UQP, Melbourne, 1985, Chapter 14.
10. NNAA ACT CRS A461/1 Item L314/1/1 PT.1. Aeroplane Construction In Australia.
11. NNAA ACT CRS A2 Item 1920/2258. Aviation - Flying Boats. Cable: Coates to PM Dept, 12.01.1920.
12. Air Board Agendum No.123. "Numbering of Aeroplanes, Seaplanes, etc.", 12.08.1921. The numbers of aircraft in this list were amended in pencil.
13. Imperial Conference 1926 - Air Matters. Air Board to Defence(?), 6.08.1926. Copy in *Third Brother* file, Air Power Studies Centre, Canberra.
14. NAA ACT CRS A664/1 Item 415/401/31. RAF Far Eastern Flight. Minute; "Estimates R.A.A.F. 1927/28", Air Board to Defence, 11.02.1927.
15. Air Board Agendum No.919. Approved 27.06.1927.
16. Williams to Trenchard, 31.12.1927. Williams Papers, copies held at Airpower Studies Centre, Canberra.
17. NAA ACT CRS A5954/1 Item 873/7. Manufacture of Aircraft in Australia - Formation of Commonwealth Aircraft Corporation 1935-37. Appendix "A", with Memo: "Deliveries of Aircraft from Orders placed in U.K.", CAS to Defence, 13.03.1936. Also Air Board Agendum No.919. *Op Cit.*
18. Air Board Agendum No.920. Meeting 23.06.1927.
19. NAA ACT CRS A2408/1 Item 199/3. Flying Boats. Letterbook entry No.50, 13.07.1927. Sir Richard Kingsland recalled that the RAAF had *two Southamptons, and they were massive wooden beasts. They were made of Mahogany. And Australia needed a decent sized flying boat, and Britain very kindly, having found that these could be built in metal, gave us their two wooden ones… - but they were very slow.* (Quoted in Knightly, J. "The Supermarine Southampton, Part 1", *Flightpath,* Vol.29, No. 4, 2018.) Kingsland was wrong. As related, Australia always paid her way. The only time the British gave anything away was the Imperial Gift of surplus material after WWI.
20. NAA ACT CRS A705 Item 69/2/257. Minute; Air

**Above:** Southampton with crew before it left for Bundaberg. A composite photograph of the Southampton A11-1 with crew in front of the seaplane. Note how the rear of the hull has been edited to produce an image for newspaper reproduction. (*Argus* Newspaper Collection. Victorian State Library.)

Board to Defence, 1.03.1928. Penciled note on original says "Not sent."; and *Flypast*, P.64.

21.Air Board Agendum No.911. Approved 27.06.1927.

22.Air Board Agenda No.917, 25.06.1927.

23.NAA ACT CRS A1606/1 Item D4/1. Co-Operation with Royal Air Force. Air Branch of Royal Navy. Dept of Defence to PM, 30.08.1927.

24. *Ibid.* PM to Governor General, 19.11.1927.

25.NAA ACT CRS A705/1 Item 4/10/32. Melbourne - Hobart Aerial Service. Air Board to Defence, 10.10.1927.

26. *Ibid.* Press cutting: *Sun*, 14.12.1927.

27.Imperial Conference 1926 - Air Matters. Air Board to Defence(?), 6.08.1926. Copy in *Third Brother* file, Air Power Studies Centre, Canberra.

28.NAA ACT CRS A705/1 Item 4/10/32. *Op Cit.* Minute: Air Board to Defence, 25.10.1927.

29. *Ibid.* Minute: "Melbourne - Tasmania Air Route." Air Board to Defence, 10.10.1927.

30.NAA Vic CRS MP116 Item Series 1. AAIC Minutes 1927-1936. Evidence of Cpl Doug A Endean. With Minutes 25.06.1928.

31.Livock, G E, *To the Ends of the Air*, HMSO, London, 1973.

32.NAA Vic CRS MP116 Item Series 1. AAIC Minutes 1928–1936. Report by Flt Lt Palstra to AAIC, 25.06.1928. With Minutes 25.06.1928.

33.Newspaper clipping via A Cookson.

34.NAA ACT CRS A2408 Item 109/4. Inspection Sir John Salmond. Letterbook entry No.103, 28.08.1928.

35.Minute: Report on the Royal Australian Air Force by Air Marshal Sir John Salmond, KCB, CMG, CVO, DSO, ADC. No date. Copy in *Third Brother* file, Air Power Studies Centre, Canberra.

36.NAA ACT CRS A9376/1 Item 45. Combined Land and Sea Exercise 30/10/29. No.1 FTS and Ships of RAN.

37.NAA ACT CRS A664/1 Item 464/401/676A. Estimates 1930-31. "Department of Defence: Summary of Activities April and May 1930. Air Operations."

38.NAA ACT CRS A9376/1 Item 57. "Report on Flight to Tasmania in connection with Tasmanian Air Pageants from 12/2/1932" by Flt Lt D.E.L. Wilson.

39.NAA ACT CRS A9376/1 Item 72. Training Flight to Tasmania - February-March 1934. Report by Flight Lieutenant FN Wright. Three Bulldogs - FTS. Report by

**Above:** A11-2 at the end of its life. Note the long-range tank to the rear. This photograph was taken at Pont Cook around June 1940 These beautiful machines are believed to have been burnt. (via Alan Mitchell)

Wright, 13.03.1934.
40.NAA ACT CRS A9376/1 Item 53. Letter, Wing Cmdr R Brown to Air Board, 20.06.1930.
41.NAA Vic CRS MP124/6 Item 415/201/660. Wireless message. RAS to Navy Office, 6.02.1931.
42.Jones, R. *Seagulls, Cruisers and Catapults*, Pelorus Publications, Tasmania, 1989, P.60.
43."Aerial Search For Missing Collier - Fine Performance by R.A.A.F. Southampton flying boat." *Aircraft*, 1.08.1933, P.13.
44.NAA ACT CRS A705 Item 150/1/101. RAAF Confidential Communication Orders 1933. "Signal Reports from Units, June 1933." 1 FTS Seaplane Squadron.
45.NAA ACT CRS A705/1 Item 150/1/80. R.A.A.F. Confidential Communication Orders.
46. *Aircraft*, 1.08.33. *Op Cit.*
47.NAA ACT CRS A2408/1 Item 199/5. L14 - Letter Book - Seaplanes Southampton. Entry No. 215 of 12.12.1935.
48.*Ibid.* Entry No.208 of 5.09.1935.
49.NAA ACT CRS A5954/1 Item 881/11. Aircraft Suitable for Search at Sea, 8.12.36.
50.1 FTS Unit Diary, RAAF Form A50; and *Flightpath*, P.64.
51.NAA ACT CRS A705/1 Item 208/1/79. Annual Training of W/T Operators And W/T Operator Mechanics (Permanent Force) 1934-35. AMP to CO, 1 FTS, 2.08.1934.
52.NAA ACT CRS A705 Item 34/3/139. Visit No.203 Sq (RAF) from Basra During Melbourne Celebrations 19334-335.
53.NAA ACT CRS A705/1 Item 34/3/315. Movement of Victorian Aircraft to Richmond, NSW in Connection with Air Escort To HRH at Sydney and Air Display, Richmond. Message; CSS to Naval Board, 14.11.1934.
54.1 FTS Unit Diary, RAAF Form A50.
55.NAA ACT CRS A705 Item 34/3/461. R.A.A.F. Displays April, 1938. Programme Of Events. Letter; "Air Display, 1938." CO, 1 FTS to Air Board, 1.02.1938.
56.Heffernan, P.G. "Parachuting For Beginners." *Stand To*, April–June, 1967.
57.NAA ACT CRS A2408 Item 208/9. Parachutes. Letterbook entries Nos.14, 35, and 46.
58. *Ibid.*
59. *Ibid.*
60.Letter to author, 14.09.1990.
61.Letter to author, 28.01.1991.
62.Tape recorded interview with Air Commodore W Garing, 1994.
63.NAA ACT CRS A2408 Item 9/11 Aircraft Southampton and Spares. Precis letter of 8.11.1938.
64.Interview with F James on 14.12.1987. Interview notes, RAAF Air Power Study Centre, Canberra.
65.Hodgkinson, V. "Water Wings", *Aeroplane Monthly*, Vol.10 No.4, April 1982, P.222.
66.Air Board Agendum No.2754, 3.04.1940. It has not proved possible to determine the fate of A11-1. A 1937 note refers to the disposal of Southamptons but it is not specific. The note mentions AFO 19/B/13. (NAA ACT CRS A2408/1 Item 199/5. L14 - Letter Book - Seaplanes - Southampton. Entry No.223 of 2.06.1937.)
67.Letter from A Mitchell to Editor *Wings*, 7.11.1998.

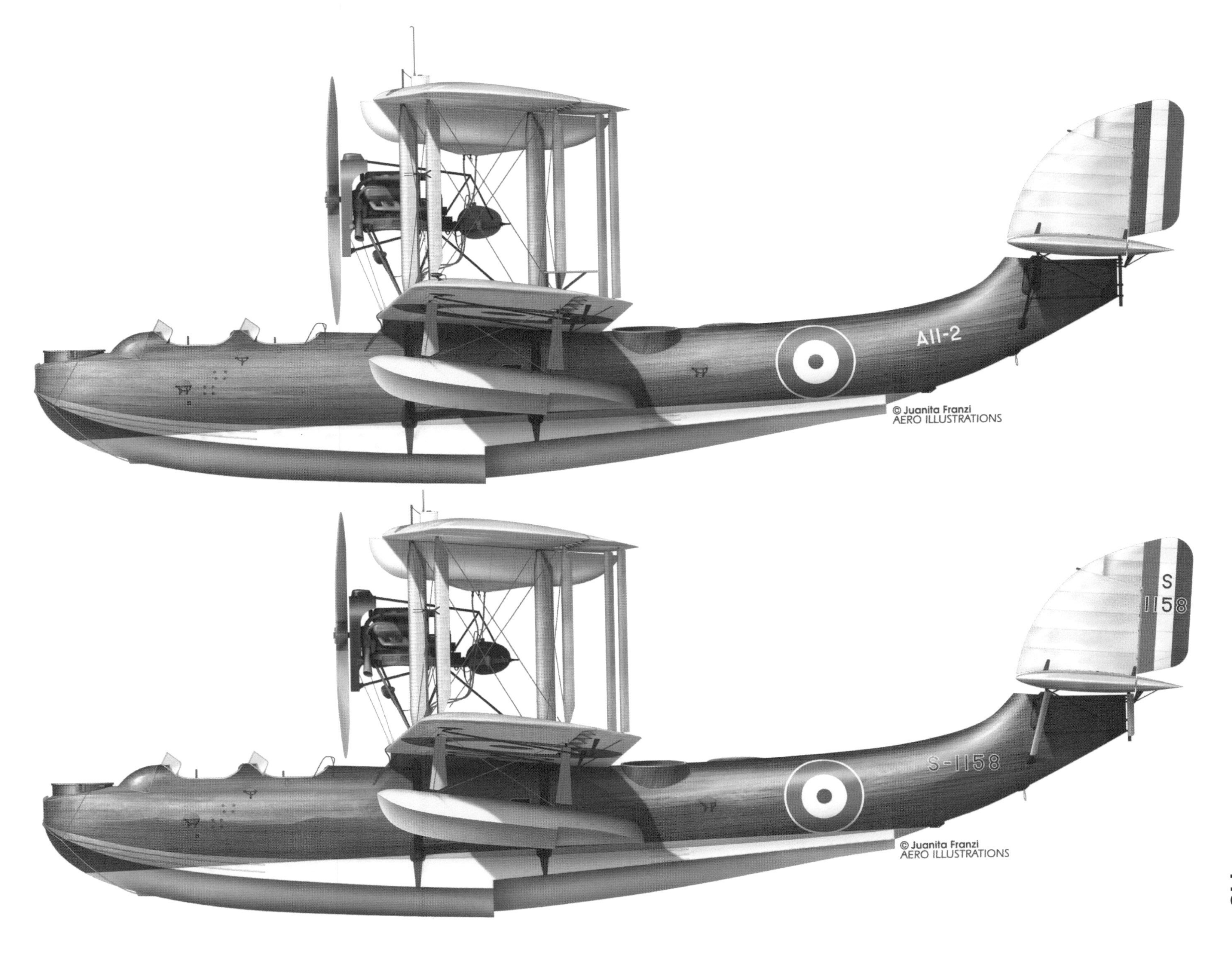
AII-2
© Juanita Franzi
AERO ILLUSTRATIONS
S
1158
S-1158
© Juanita Franzi
AERO ILLUSTRATIONS

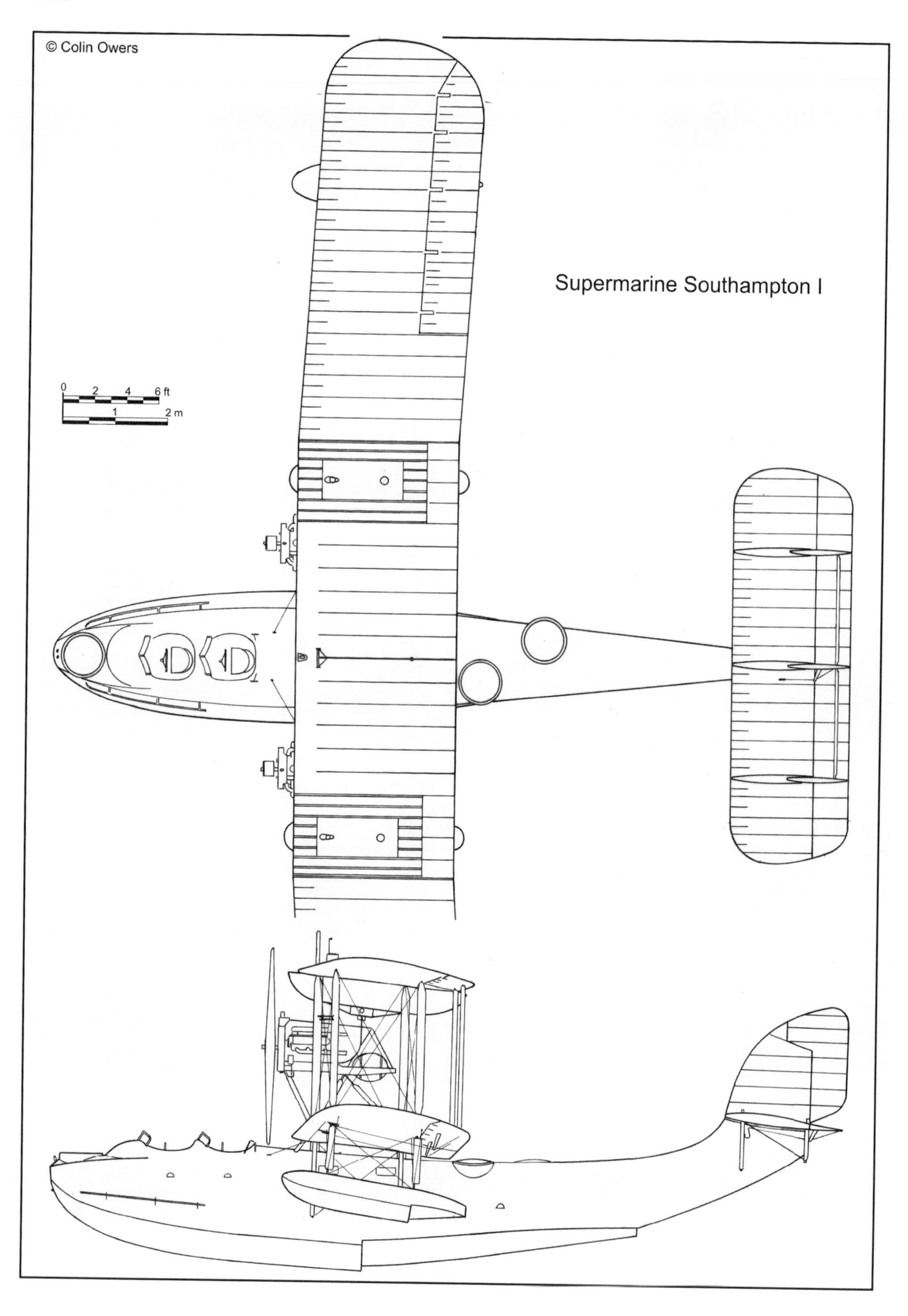
© Colin Owers
Supermarine Southampton I
0
2
4
6 ft
1
2 m

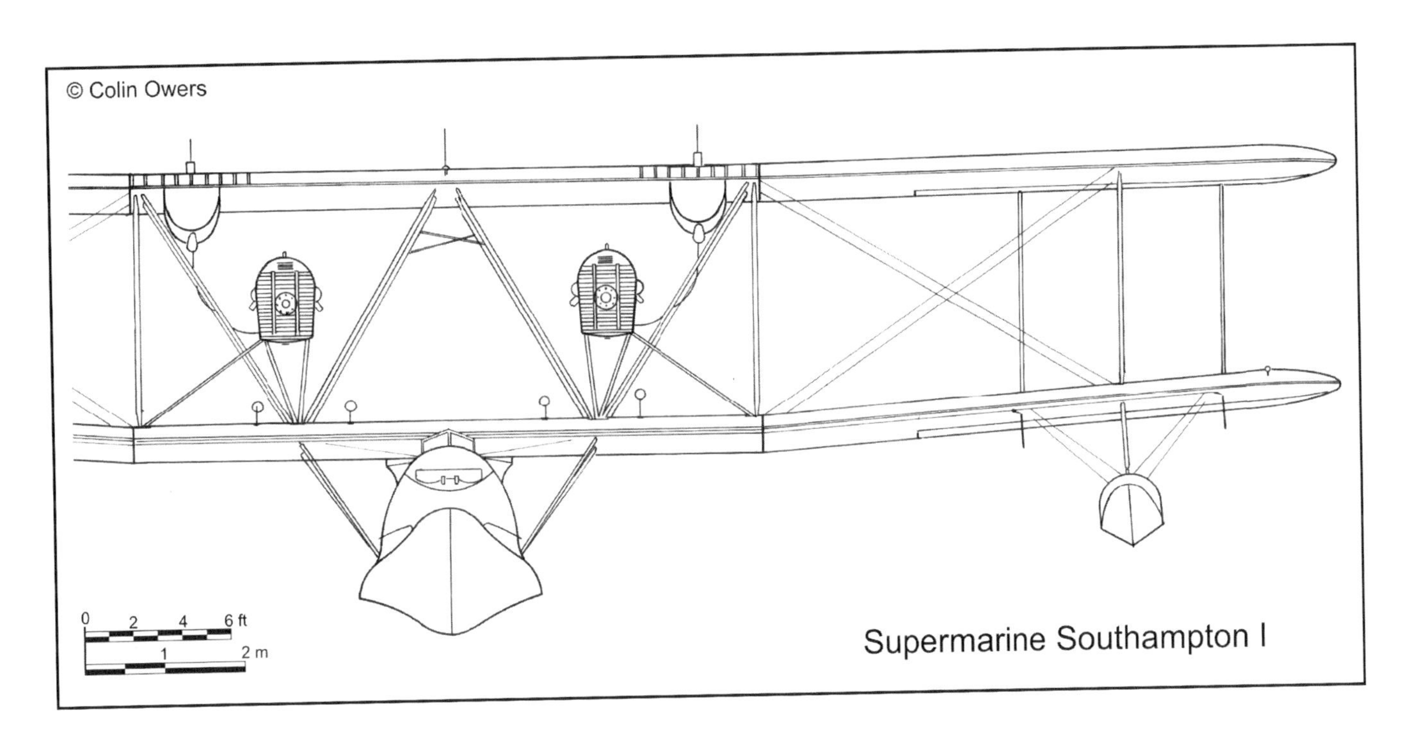
© Colin Owers
0 2 4 6 ft
1 2 m
Supermarine Southampton I

**Above:** One of the RAAF's Southamptons in flight. In the air ...

## Supermarine Southampton – RAAF A2 Individual Aircraft Histories

### A11-1

26.028. Arrived Australia as deck cargo on SS *Ferndale.*
22.06.28. 1 FTS. Adelaide, SA. Sunk by 'willy-willy'.
(29.11.28). 1 FTS. Inspection report on ailerons.
13.11.29. Sq Ldr R.J. Brownell, Fl Lt F.A. Briggs. Reconnaissance from Hobart, Tas. Survey of Port Davey as possible seaplane base.
19.11.29. Forced landing between Wamberal and Terrigal. Apparently due failure Napier Lion 51425.
30.10.29. Flt Lt Briggs, P/O Dalton, LAC Sims, AC1 Richmond, with F/Off Knox-Knight as observer. Exercise in Port Phillip Bay to locate 'enemy' fleet.
12 to 25.11.29. To Hobart, Sydney, Brisbane, Sydney, Melbourne.
14.11.29. Flt Lt Briggs, Sqn Ldr R Brownell. Engine test.
4.12.29. FTS. Cross country.
17.04.30 to 25.04.30. A.E. Hempel. Flight to Straham, Tas. Visit for Easter Monday Regatta and then reconnaissance of forest areas around Macquarie Harbour, Gordon River Valley, etc. Examination of coast and check of seaplane facilities.
(5.11.31). 1 FTS. *Rudder bars in first and second cockpits badly bent.*
12.02.32. Sqn Ldrd R.J. Brownell, Flt Lt Lachal. Point Cook to Reservoirs, Tasmania. Search for Wapiti lost in fog - found force landed at Bridport.
17.02.32. Hepburn Point, Oyster Bay, Tas. F/Off L.V. Lachal, R.J. Brownell and crew of 4. Hobart to Melbourne. Forced landing in Coles Bay due broken radiator pipe. Two flying boats from HMAS *Albatross* arrived on 18th and effected repairs. To leave on morrow.
20.02.32. Sqn Ldr R.J. Brownell, Flt Lt Lachal. Engine test.
(13.11.33). To be recovered.
(19.04.34). FTS. Radiator leaks at core.
9.08.34. Sqn Ldr Hempel, W Taylor. W/T Test.
14.08.34. Sqn Ldr A.E. Hempel, Lt Cmdr Kennedy, Flt Lt Carr, LAC O'Donnel, LAC Fitter and LAC Clark. Left for Metung, exercise with HMA Squadron. Gales led to exercises being postponed.
16.08.34. Left Metung for Launceston, Vic.
16 to 19.08.34. W/T Exercises with HMA Squadron and Point Cook.
20.08.34. Search and shadow exercise with HMA Squadron, return to Point Cook.
10.09.34. Flt Lt Lachal, W Taylor. W/T Test.
8.10.34. Sqn Ldr A.E. Hempel, Sgt Spooner, Sgt Symons, LAC O'Donnel, LAC Harpur and LAC Clark. Escort to RAF Rangoon flying boats to St Kilda for a state reception.
17.10.34. Left Point Cook for Geelong, Vic, escort duty in connection with the arrival of HRH Prince Henry on HMS *Sussex* on 18th.
20.10.34. Sqn Ldr A.E. Hempel, F/Off Pearce and crew Sgt Harkin, Cpl R Kennedy, AC Russell and AC Wilson. Left Point Cook on search for missing D.H.86 *Miss Hobart.*
21.10.34. F/Off C.W. Pearce, Sgt Cooper, crew LAC O'Donnell, LAC Heading and LAC Clarke. Another search, found wreckage 6 ml south-west Citadel Is thought to have come from missing D.H.86.
9.11.34. Sqn Ldr Hempel. Left for Geelong for Air Pageant at Laverton next day.
19.11.34. Sqn Ldr Hempel. Point Cook for Sydney for Royal escort to HMS *Sussex* on 22 and flypast Richmond, NSW

**Right & Following Page:** ...on the water the Southampton was always an impressive sight.

on 25th and 26th.
2 to 3.12.34. Left Sydney return to Point Cook, stayed overnight at Eden.
5.05.35. Flt Lt Lachal, W Taylor. Practice with A11-2 for King's Jubilee Review flypast then to Geelong overnight.
6.05.35. Flt Lt Lachal, W Taylor. Jubilee flypast led by Southamptons.
26.06.35. Sqn Ldr A.E. Hempel, P/Off Burt, crew Corp P Neale, LAC J.A. O'Donnel, LAC A.M.J. Clark. Left for Darwin, NT, on 'Round Australia Survey Flight.'
(5.02.36). Overhaul of tailplane ex-A11-1 report by 'M. Eng. of Seaplane Sqn.'
8.02.36. Return from 'Round Australia Survey Flight.' Unable to alight at Point Cook due weather, proceeded to Williamstown.
(4.06.36). 1 FTS. Report on airframe - inspection required.
12.36. Still in service.
(5.02.37). Reconditioning of fittings of A11-1, report on.
(19.11.37). 1 FTS.
It appears that it was converted, probably for spares for A11-2 and the rest destroyed.

**A11-2**

26.028. Arrived Australia as deck cargo on SS *Ferndale.*
(22.08.28). F/Off Briggs, AC1 H.W. Barry. Aerial weight caused damage to lights in Manly, NSW.
7.09.28. Return to Point Cook.
2.12.28. Forced landing off Cowes in Westernport.
21.02.29. Flt Lt Briggs, Sqn Ldr R Brownell. Melbourne to Hobart.
23.02.29. Flt Lt Briggs, Sqn Ldr R Brownell. Hobart to Sydney. (Non-stop. Aust. record flight).
31.07.29. Point Cook. D.A. Connelly. Bombing practice.
22.10.30. Point Cook. D.A. Connelly (2nd pilot).
15 to 20.03.33. Sqn Ldr R.J. Brownell (2nd pilot). Melbourne to Hobart, Sydney ("Record service 'endurance' flight"), Brisbane. Return Sydney on 24th.
16 to 19.02.34. Sqn Ldr A.E. Hempel, F/Off Garing, F/Off P.E. Carr and crew of three. Left Point Cook for Metung to carry out reconnaissance with HMA Squadron. Return flight on 19th, alighted Geelong as weather at Point Cook unsuitable.
22.02.34. Left Geelong for King Is to escort three Bulldogs and three Wapitis across Bass Straight, then return Point Cook via Geelong.
4.03.34. Flt Lt L.V. Lachal, F/Off W.H. Garing, and crew of 4. Point Cook to Flinders Is. Remained overnight Lady Barron Bay. Escort aircraft returning from Tasmania next day, however they had arrived over the mainland before Southampton tookff.
10.03.34. F/Off C.W. Pearce, Flt Lt P.E. Carr, F/Off W.H. Garing, F/Off Murdoch, Sgt Spooner, LAC A.M.J. Clark. Search Patrol in conjunction with HMA Squadron.
21.03.34. F/Off C.W. Pearce, Flt Lt P.E. Carr, F/Off W.H. Garing, F/Off Murdoch, Sgt Spooner, LAC A.M.J. Clark. Reconnaissance exercises with HMA Squadron off Cape Nelson.
3.04.34. Sqn Ldr A.E. Hempel, Sqn Ldr A Hepburn, Flt Lt P.E. Carr and crew of 3. Left Point Cook for Eden, NSW, for annual exercise. Returned on 6th, stayed overnight at Metung. On 7th forced landing due port engine failure on Reeve Lagoon, East Gippsland, Vic.
1.10.34. Sqn Ldr Hempel, W Taylor. W/T Test.
8.10.34. Flt Lt Lachal, Flt Lt Carr, Cpl Kelly, AC Heading, AC MacCormick. Escort to RAF Rangoon flying boats to St Kilda for a state reception.
17.10.34. Left Point Cook for Geelong, Vic, escort duty in connection with the arrival of HRH Prince Henry on HMS *Sussex* on 18th.
20.10.34. Flt Lt L.V. Lachall, F/Off Heffernan and crew Sgt Harkin, Cpl R Kennedy, AC Russell and AC Wilson. Left Point Cook on further search for missing D.H.86 *Miss Hobart*.
19.11.34. Flt Lt Lachal, W Taylor. Point Cook to Eden and

Sydney for Royal Escort.
22.11.34. Flt Lt Lachal, W Taylor. Royal Escort to HMS *Sussex*.
29.11.34. Flt Lt Lachal, W Taylor. Sydney to Batemans Bay, Eden, Metung; forced alighting because of weather. Return to Point Cook on 3 December due to being delayed by weather.
6.08.35. 'Pull-off' parachute drops.
9.08.35. Flt Lt Lachal. 'Pull-off' parachute drops.
16.09.35. Commenced a complete overhaul.
(3.10.35). Overhaul - OC FTS Workshop to supervise.
(12.12.35). FTS. Overhaul began without authority from HQ. Failure to notify CAS of u/s of aircraft - their non-availability in an emergency - procedure to be tightened up.
(4.06.36). 1 FTS. Report on airframe - inspection required.
(8.06.37). Overhaul.
(27.08.37). 1 FTS. Request to carry out modifications to crankcase drain plug.
22.09.38. Sqn Ldr L.V. Lachal, crew Gp Cpt F.W. F Lukie, Flt Lt W.H. Garing, Cpl J.A. O'Donnell, Cpl A.A. Whiffen. Test flight.
17.11.38. Parachute flights. Two participants were RNZAF members.
07.39. Transferred from Seaplane Sqn, 1 FTS, to 10 Sqn on formation.
09.39. 10 Sqn. Several parachute drops during month.
10.39. 10 Sqn. Two pull-off parachute practices were completed during month.
7.12.39. Sqn Ldr D.A. Connelly, Thurston/Wearne. Seaplane conversion course.
(5.04.40). Convert to components.

A report in the Melbourne *Age* newspaper of Thursday 25 June 1931, stated that a twin-engine Supermarine flying boat had been stranded in the Gellibrand River, at Princetown, since last Thursday. The crew was commanded by Sqn Ldr A.E. Hempel, and the machine had left Point Cook on Thursday for a navigation flight out to sea. *A heavy blow, with low cloud, came on and forced the pilots to take shelter* They alighted on the Gellibrand River but when the weather cleared, it was found that the tide had gone out and there was not enough water for the large flying boat to take-off. *A bar at the mouth of the river helped to keep the flying boat prisoner.* It was hoped to get the machine off on this date, the 25th. It has not been possible to identify which of the Southamptons this report relates to.

**Above & Facing Page:** The Southampton taking off with two of the new Seagull V amphibians, A2-2 and A2-6, for a photographic flight. Seagulls A2-6 and A2-2.

**Above:** A11-2 with the three forward cockpits occupied and a dingy at the rear for transporting personnel ashore.

**Above:** The Short Singapore III, K4581, that conducted the survey for the Empire Air Mai Route from Singapore to Sydney in 1936. The Singapore III was the latest in all metal biplane flying boats and the last biplane flying boat by the Short firm.

**Above:** S1159, alias A11-2, with beaching gear on the ramp at Point Cook.

**Above:** A11-2 was the subject of A magnificent close-up of a supermarine (sic) Southampton twin-engined flying boat in the air. The machine is fitted with 450 horse-power Napier "Lions" engines. The observer and the first and second pilots are plainly visible. The set was taken by photographer J.T. Harrison over Melbourne in February 1932.

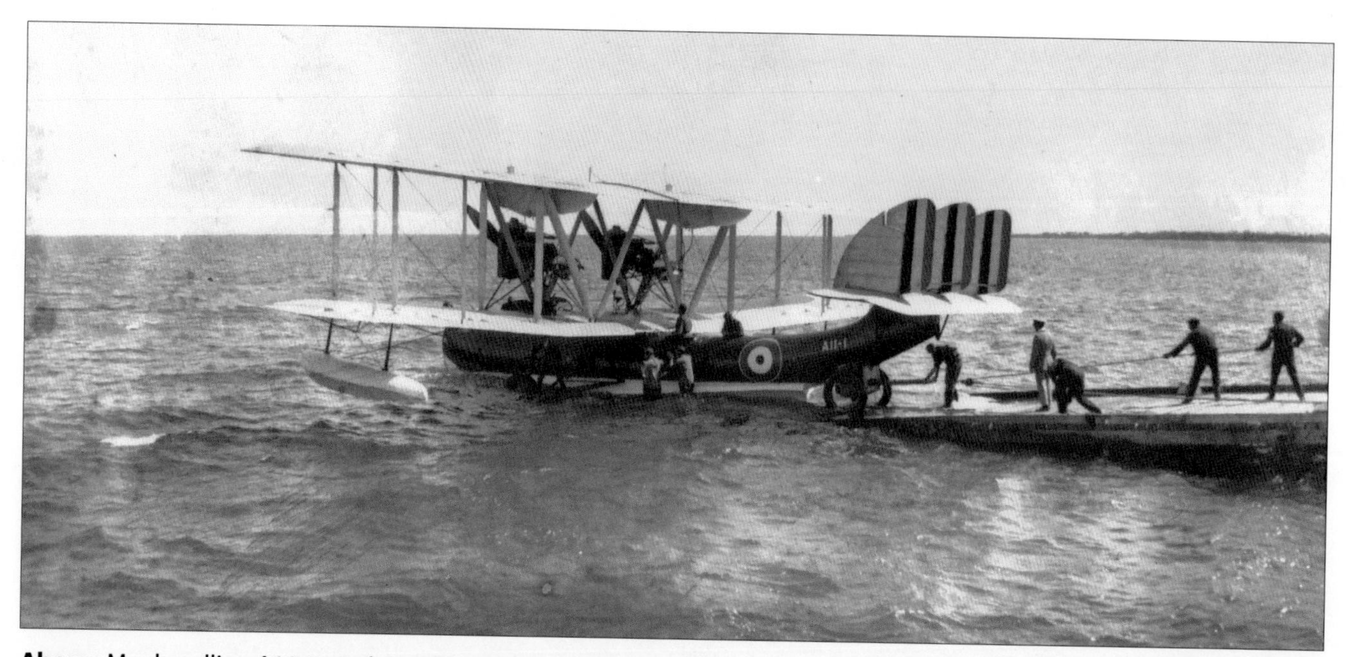

**Above:** Manhandling A11-1 on the ramp at Point Cook. Note the man with the wheeled trolley for the rear of the hull. Once in the water and buoyancy was obtained, the beaching gear would be removed, a time consuming process.

# Chapter 22. The Tugan/CAC L.J.W.7 Gannet

**Above & Following Page, Above:** MTugan LJW.7 Gannet VH-UVU was completed in February 1936. It was sold to W.A.S.P. Airlines the following month. It survived until 1945 and, apparently, was not impressed in World War II. It is shown as first delivered to W.A.S.P. Airlines, the fuselage is reported as being coloured blue, and later appeared with the additional fins to the tailplane. (via AHMof WA P021520)

After leaving the RAAF (see Chapter 24) Lawrence Wackett went to the Cockatoo Island Dockyard where he undertook aircraft construction and repair work. This was the subject of much criticism by the local aircraft industry who stated that Wackett was subsidised by the Government and private enterprise could not compete with the prices offered by the Dockyard.[1] While at the Dockyard Wackett designed and built the L.J.W.6 Codock, a small twin-engine airliner, for Sir Charles Kingsford Smith. Sir Charles first flew the Codock on 6 March 1934, at Mascot.[2] The Codock was not a success, in particular it experienced a good deal of engine trouble.

Wackett designed an improved version, the L.J.W.7, and he apparently 'sold' this design to the RAAF in late 1934,[3] as the Contract Board was informed in February 1935 that the Minister's approval had been obtained for Order No.16055 for one monoplane.[4] Wackett informed the Board *that he was joining up with the Tugan Aircraft Ltd, Sydney, which had purchased the drawings and rights of manufacture...and this was the only company which was in a position to undertake the work as the design was not available to other parties.* The Board agreed and decided not to call tenders but to communicate with Tugan Aircraft Ltd to work out contract details.[5] Contract No.3124[6] was raised and the Minister proudly announced that *in pursuance of the policy of local manufacture of aircraft, an order* had been placed for the construction of a locally designed Gannet.[7]

Tugan Aircraft Ltd was set up in the defunct General Aircraft facilities at Mascot. The name Tugan came from combining the two partners' names, Leo Turl and Frank Gannon. The partnership progressed slowly with repair work until J.C. Carpenter, a well-known Sydney commercial pilot, entered the scene and floated the partnership into a £10,000 company. The L.J.W.7 was the company's first aircraft and was promoted as having being derived from the Codock, which had *been fully certified and demonstrated its ability to fly with full load on one engine*[8]*...General improvements have been made which give better streamlining, larger cabin space, and lighter weight* due to the use of high-grade steel tube. The lighter structural weight coupled with the increased strength led to an increase in gross load to 5,000 lb.[9]

The Gannet was externally similar to the Codock and was a twin-engine high wing cabin monoplane. The cantilevered wing was of wooden Fokker-type construction with ply covering. The fuselage was constructed of welded steel tube with fabric covering. The landing gear incorporated oil operated oleo legs with axle and radius rods. Power was supplied by closely cowled Gipsy VI engines mounted in front of the leading edge of the wing close to the fuselage centreline.[10] Tugan also had the Australian agency for the Menasco engine and offered the Gannet with the Menasco B.6.S. as an alternative.

Three Gannet monoplanes were laid down as the initial production line. The first of these aircraft was for the RAAF and was *more than half completed* in July 1935. The second was for Western and Provincial Airlines Ltd (WASP) and was *almost at the same stage of progress.*[11] The first completed Gannet was test flown at Mascot by J Chapman on 12 October 1935, and was delivered to WASP with the civil registration VH-UUZ.

**Above & Above Right:** The wooden wing, engine cowls and wheel covers for Gannet monoplanes under construction at Tugan Aircraft Ltd.

The RAAF specification provided for the following variations from the standard commercial version of the monoplane:

1. Provision of Dual Control.
2. Adaptation of all seats to take parachutes.
3. Installation of several extra instruments, a small table, camera port, special electrical appliances for night flying including landing light and special tail light, the latter requiring modification to the rudder.
4. Provision of sun blinds and windscreen wiper.[12]

The RAAF was to supply instruments and engines for the aircraft, two Gipsy VI engines being approved for the aircraft on 1 May 1935.[13] The Contract Board noted that *this machine is not a purely service one and its acceptance is subject to it obtaining an Australian Certificate of Airworthiness.*[14]

As noted above the RAAF machine was apparently the second Gannet completed although the Air Board order was the first placed with Tugan. It was *proposed to use this aircraft for transport and advanced air training,* however, as will be detailed hereunder, the aircraft was immediately used for the aerial survey of Northern Australia.[15] It appears that the Gannet and De Havilland Rapide (See Chapter 11) were to be tested to determine which was the better aircraft for Australian conditions.

The RAAF Gannet, A4-1, was ready for final inspection on 6 November. (The A4 designation was to be allocated to the Avro Anson and the Gannets were re-serialled creating confusion in documents. The serial in use at the time is given here.) Wackett had agreed to give the RAAF pilot selected to fly the acceptance trials *some dual instruction in the civil type L.J.W.7 when that machine is being tested for its airworthiness certificate. He* (Wackett) *has already engaged the pilot who flies the Codock to do this test as well as our own and has constructed a set*

**Above:** The A4-1 the first RAAF Gannet in pristine condition. Note the open engine cowls. It was soon realised that the machine had been incorrectly serialled as the 'A4' prefix was reserved for the Avro Anson. The Rockhampton *Evening News* reported on 25 November 1936, that tomorrow the *Gannet reconnaissance plane ordered by the Commonwealth Government for the Air Board will be test-flown and 'handed over at Mascot, where it has been built. The Gannet…is ready to spread its silver wings, which are dignified with the - red, white and blue Air Force insignia.*
*In the six high-backed wicker chairs in the cabin, the Chief of the Air Staff, and even, it is thought, the Minister for Defence, Will be able to cruise over - the continent in cushioned comfort, at 130 miles an hour.…Trap-doors are provided In the floor for aerial camera, and there are special fitting for radio gear. The new Gannet will be maintained at the Point Cook base.* (via P.G. Heffernan)

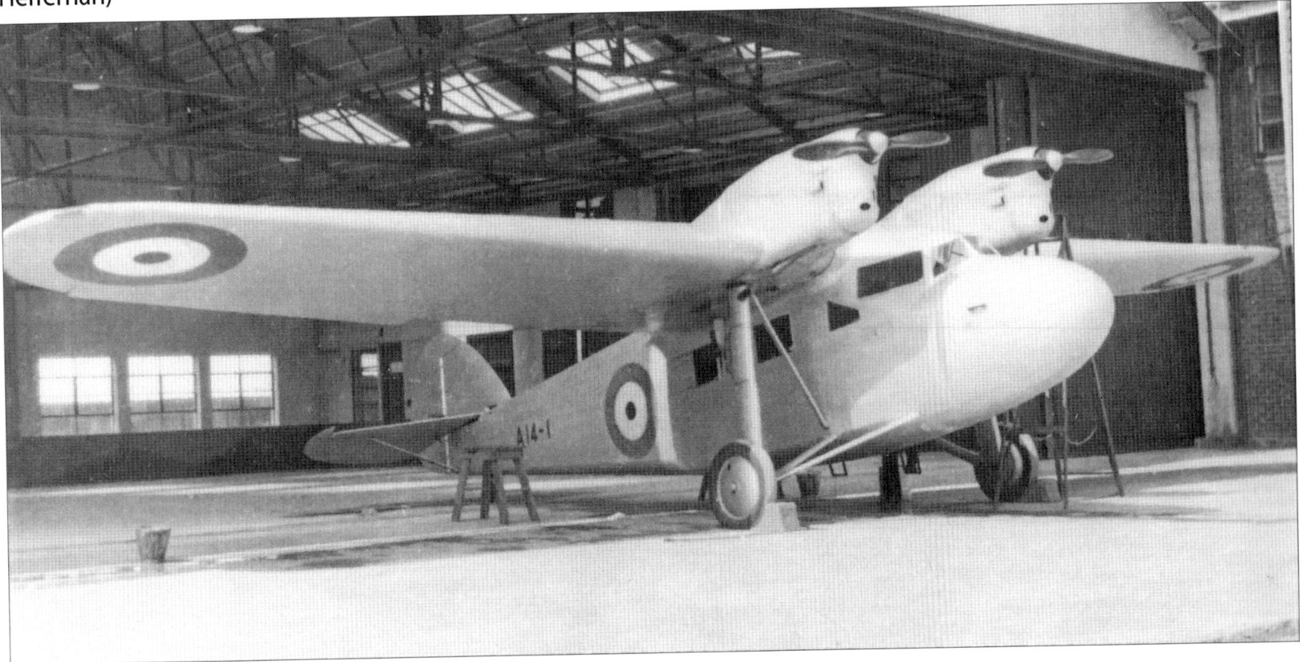


**Above:** The same aircraft as above after it received its correct serial, A14-1. Note the spinners on the airscrews. According to The *Sydney Morning Herald* of 26 November 1936, this monoplane, the second Gannet constructed, made its first flight the previous day, with J Chapman as the pilot. It was later taken over by the Air Board with Flt Lt Fleming then flying the aircraft with Chapman and Gp-Capts Cole and Harrison as passengers, to Richmond. (via J Hopton)

**Above:** The A14-2 appears to be on a civilian airfield.

*of dual. There will be no charge, of course, for such instruction.*[16] Flt Lt Fleming of 3 Squadron was selected as the pilot for the test programme.

As noted above, the RAAF specifications included the requirement for a Certificate of Airworthiness as well as the following:
Maximum speed - Not less than 150 miles per hour.
Maximum take-off run -- Not greater than 250 yards.
Initial climb -- Not less than 1000 feet per minute.
Absolute ceiling - Not less than 16,000 feet.
Ceiling on one engine (on descent) -- Not less than 5,000 ft.
Landing without brakes -- Not more than 500 yards.[17]

A4-1 underwent testing at RAAF Station Richmond. The aircraft performed in excess of the requirements on five points; absolute ceiling, take off run, landing run with and without brakes; and ceiling on one engine. The rate of climb figure was 920 ft/min, but this was considered within ordinary guarantee figures and the *aircraft was therefore considered to substantially conform to specification requirements.*[18]

The tests were carried out in unfavourable atmospheric conditions. *Electric storms accompanied by mass movements of air were almost daily occurrences, and flying on many occasions was carried out in rain or climbs interrupted to avoid heavy rain storms*, and it was suggested that other testing be carried out away from Richmond.[19] In the meantime the aircraft was formally accepted *in accordance with the Contract* on 20 December,[20] the CAS noting that *the aircraft has done extraordinarily well.*[21] Williams must have been heartened by the success of the Gannet after his unstinting support of Wackett over many years and through many trials and tribulations.

Fleming reported that all items relating to the cockpit layout were satisfactory or reasonable. The controls were effective although aileron control disappeared at stalling speed. The Gannet handled well in banks with no evidence of any tendency to spin. The view from the cockpit was not very good in making S-turn approaches to land and in taxying there was no view aft. He suggested more ventilation for the passenger cabin and as *this aircraft, as a Service machine, will rarely be filled to capacity with passengers, serious consideration should be given to providing extra tankage. The construction of the mainplane lends itself to the fitting of extra tanks with the minimum of trouble.*[22]

During testing it was found that the airscrews provided by the RAAF were unsuitable and they were replaced with ones designed by Tugan and these, *with minor alterations gave satisfactory results.* In addition, the accumulators provided could not give sufficient power to operate the hand-starting device and special unspillable batteries had to be procured instead.[23]

A4-1 was flown to Laverton by Fleming on 8 December 1935. It was reported that the Gannet would be subject to extended service trials and that the name Gannet would be dropped in the RAAF as *someone recalled the feathered Gannets reputation as a sea bird that dives head on into the sea.*[24] This proved not to be the case and the name continued to be used, the aircraft being designated *Gannet (L.J.W.7)* on the maintenance schedules for the type.[25] In official documents it was usually referred to as the Gannet. The monoplane was soon renumbered A14-1 as it was realised that the serial prefix 'A4' had been allocated to the Avro Anson bombers on order.

Between 3 February and 20 March 1936, A14-1 was allocated to 1 AD for testing. In order to answer questions posed by the CAS, Wing Cdr G Jones flew the monoplane on 3 March for the purpose of comparing it with the De Havilland Rapide. Jones reported that: -
(a) When turning the view from the pilot's seat of the

**Above:** A14-3 at Laverton shows the extra fins added to the tailplane to improve directional control. It bears the CAC logo on the fin. (via A Whetthers)

L.J.W.7 was much inferior to that of the Rapide.

(b) At top speed the L.J.W.7 was nearly 20 mph slower than the Rapide assuming that the instruments were correct.

(c) The L.W.J.7 took off and landed in a much smaller space.

(d) It had a much steeper gliding angle than the Rapide.

(e) The monoplane appeared to be directionally unstable. If permitted to swing in either direction it gave the impression that it would continue and develop into a flat spin. After the swing was allowed to develop for about three seconds the rudder was just powerful enough to check it. When going into a turn the same tendency was evident. When the aircraft was well into a turn powerful top rudder was required to keep the nose up and prevent the aircraft going into a steep spiral.[26]

The DTS (E Wackett) considered this report and concluded that the directional instability referred to was not a cause for concern and *that if an aircraft of this class flies reasonably with normal attention from the pilot (that is what he is there for, anyhow), both engine on and off, it is satisfactory.*[27] The AMS noted that he had discussed this problem with the designer and that Wackett had explained *that this was caused by the two engines set closely together and (having) a single fin and rudder. He said that future machines would have a double finned tailplane to overcome this.*[28] The AMS then asked if it was proposed to order any more of this type.

Williams, as usual, followed the progress of Wackett's latest creation with great interest. Despite his friendship with Wackett, he had no illusions as to accepting an aircraft which did not meet its specifications and noted the above discussion with the statement that *if we are to have locally made aircraft we must get into the habit of thoroughly testing out a type before it goes into service.*

*The point now is do pilots and technical services consider any modifications should be carried out before this aircraft goes into general use?* Williams did not propose to order additional Gannet monoplanes at this time.[29]

Further trials included small photographic flights in NSW and Victoria, and one to Tasmania. This latter flight was 1 Squadron's annual training flight to the island state and was used to test the suitability of a cabin monoplane for aerial photography. A4-1, with Flt Lt A.M. Charlesworth as pilot, covered an area from Western Junction to Campbelltown, an area of 600 square miles in 24 hours 24 minutes flying time, and *the suitability of the cabin machine for photography was proven.*[30]

A14-1 was then attached to the North Australian Survey Flight replacing the Wapiti biplanes previously in use. The RAAF had formed two Flights to carry out aerial photography for mapping the remote regions of Australia's north. The Flight from 1 Squadron was in charge of Flt Lt A.G. Carr and used A14-1, while that from 3 Squadron used a Rapide. A14-1 left Laverton for Cloncurry on 14 April 1936, however the Rapide had a forced landing (See Chapter 11), and the Gannet was involved in the search operations until it was grounded at Wave Hill on the 17th with engine damage, thus seriously delaying the mapping programme. The continuing breakages of valve springs on the Gipsy VI engines was a matter for concern. The monoplane did not arrive at Cloncurry until the 28th and photography was not commenced until 8 May.

**Above:** A14-3 before departing to Singapore. The CAS, R Williams, is holding the pith helmet. Daily newspapers carried the following story: *In the first plane built in the new factory of the Commonwealth Aircraft Corporation at Fisherman's Bend, Air Vice-Marshal R. Williams left Laverton today on the first stage of his flight to attend the official opening of the Singapore Base Graving Dock on February 14. The plane is an R.A.A.F. Gannet high wing monoplane. It will be the first Australian designed and Australian built plane to be flown beyond the Commonwealth and its territories. When it reaches Singapore, it will be at the farthest point that any RAAF. plane has reached from its base.*
*The Gannet monoplane was designed by Wing-Commander L.J. Wackett, the Australian aeroplane designer. It was delivered to the R.A.A.F. only last week.* (via RAAF Museum)

The Gannet *was engaged upon work not connected with the survey as from the 29th June.*[31] In July it was returned to the manufacturers for overhaul and minor modifications which included changes to the fin and rudder to overcome the directional instability referred to above, and two 23 gallon petrol tanks installed in the wings *to give the aircraft greater range for certain photographic survey work about to be carried out in the Croydon-Normanton area, Western Queensland.*[32] The modified Gannet was now similar to the *New Gannets coming forward* from the factory.[33] It then returned to the Survey Flight being based at Cloncurry until 28 September when it was back at Laverton. A14-1 was also used for VIP transportation and general communication duties.

Following the loss of Rapide A3-2, the Minister directed that survey aircraft be equipped with W/T equipment and a Ground Receiving Station be set up to keep a listening watch on such aircraft. A14-1 received a T.22 transmitter by early June. Testing revealed slight problems which were quickly overcome with transmissions being made on the 1200 m wave length.[34]

The Chairman of Directors of Tugan Aircraft Ltd (Carpenter) wrote to the Minister for Defence (Parkhill) in May 1936 requesting more Defence Department work. Carpenter wrote that he was continually reading of the intention to establish an aircraft manufacturing industry, but Tugan was manufacturing aircraft. Construction work on *No.4 "Gannet" monoplane...* (was) *nearing completion* and Tugan wanted to be *favoured with an order for a few more aeroplanes of the type."*[35] The Air Board had ordered the first machine of this type *from drawings only, - the order from W.A.S.P. Airlines followed later* and was upset by the tone of Carpenter's letter. The Board pointed out that as the Gannet

**Above:** Another view of A14-3 on a grass field with Anson A4-35 alongside.

**Right:** *Gannet – Soft Ground, Laverton 1935 or 1938.* The Gannet standing on its nose is thought to be A14-1, however the serial cannot be read on the original photograph. (via P.G. Heffernan)

was a commercial type it had limited use in the R.A.A.F. *No demand exists for additional aeroplanes of this type in the near future.*[36]

However, in August consideration was given to the purchase of a second Gannet, the Air Board notifying Carr that *Your opinion* (of) *this type covering handling qualities maintenance and suitability for use* (for) *photo survey* was urgently required.[37] This action was the probably the result of the crash of Rapide A3-2 and its withdrawal from service while it was rebuilt.

Carr replied that *Since the incorporation of the modified fin the handling qualities of the aircraft have improved considerably. The tendency to yaw has almost completely disappeared, but the aircraft will not fly "feet off" owing to the consistent tendency to swing to the right.* He thought that offsetting the fin would correct this problem. The rudder modifications had made it more positive in action and better control was maintained in a turn than formerly. *From a maintenance point of view the aircraft is ideal.* The Gipsy VI engines were reported to be very satisfactory indicating that the earlier problems had been overcome. Carr considered that the maintenance inspection periods could be increased from 10 and 20 hours to 15 and 30 hours respectively. Access to the engines was considered difficult due to their height above ground level.

As to suitability for photographic survey work, Carr noted that this *aircraft is, at first, harder to fly for photography than a "Wapiti" but with a little practice the pilot can become proficient.* It was *quite suitable for photographic work...The camera operator is able to attend to, and adjust, the camera more easily as has far more room in which to work.* He considered that the aircraft needed to *have at least an extra 100 H.P.* to improve take-off and climb performance. The rate of climb was 12,000 feet in 45 minutes. Before the weather became hot and the extra fuel tanks were fitted this altitude was reached in 35 minutes. Carr also criticised the electric wiring which was not to RAAF standards and suggested that an engine driven generator be fitted. If dual control was to be fitted then the second pilot's seat would have to be relocated as it was *practically useless* as fitted. The camera could be better fitted as far forward as possible behind the pilot's seat to enable

**Above:** A14-2 on the airfield at Alice Springs in 1937, being serviced by the local 'Vacum Aviation Services.' (via K Porteous)
**Left:** Pilot's view of the Gannet's cockpit. (via G Booth)

the operator to sit behind the camera and communicate with the pilot. Also, the *small tacks used in fastening the ply wood coverings on to the inner wooden members are inclined to vibrate out after a considerable amount of flying*, but this was not considered a serious problem.[38]

Tugan offered the second Gannet at a price of £5,710 which was considerably higher than the £3,090 paid for the first one. The Contract Board noted that A14-1 was *the first of its type built and the Company was particularly anxious that the type should be used in the R.A.A.F. This resulted in the suppliers quoting at a cut price.* Also, the Department had provided engines and airscrews for the first machine and when these were allowed for the price was considered fair. *The L.J.W.7 has already been constructed and only requires modification before being delivered.*[39] Order No.22185 for A14-2, a Gannet Mk.II, was placed on 10 November.[40] The Gannet Mk.II differed in that it had controllable pitch propellers and Gipsy Six Series II engines together with a Sperry (blind flying) panel fitted. The Mk.I had fixed pitch propellers and Gipsy Six Series I or Menasco B6S engines.[41] The aircraft of the second batch of three had detail changes from those of the first batch. The window area was increased, the generator was placed in the nose rather than under the starboard wing strut, the luggage door was relocated to the port side and the cabin door was redesigned. In fact, the door locations on RAAF Gannets seems to have varied considerably, A14-3 having a one on the port and two on the starboard side. The RAAF Gannet was noted as being different from the commercial type and these alterations are presumed to be associated with the fittings required for aerial photographic work. Documents indicate that some of the alterations recommended by Carr were incorporated into the new aircraft.

The Gannets was to continue survey work the following year, one being attached to the Western Detachment under Flt Lt W.L. Hely, and undertaking photographic work in Western Australia and the Northern Territory. A14-1 was attached to the Eastern Air Detachment under F/Off D McLean for the work in Queensland.[42] It would appear that the aircraft were actually on charge to the Training Depot, Laverton.[43]

The Eastern Detachment left Melbourne for Cairns towards the end of April. The landing ground constructed at the Lockhart Mission proved unsuitable and photography of the Portland Roads district had to be abandoned.[44] On 20 June after a photographic flight in the Herberton region when 150 square miles were photographed, McLean landed A14-1 at Cairns, Queensland, when the *Aircraft tipped on to* (its) *nose in soft sand, whilst taxying at low speed at finish of landing run.*[45] The airframe suffered major damage with the *lower half of nose crushed to* (the) *bulkhead.*[46] Wing Cmdr P.G. Heffernan noted that it was very easy to tip the Gannet on its nose.[47] The Gannet was unserviceable until a rigger from Laverton arrived and repairs commenced on the 26th

**Above:** A typical bush landing ground with the RAAF Survey Flight Gannet surrounded by locals. Circa 1938. (AHMofWA P000092.)

**Above:** Kip Porteous photograph of A14-4 on the hardstand. Note the wind-driven generator mounted in the nose of the monoplane to power the wireless equipment. (via K Porteous)

after obtaining suitable materials for the job. Repairs were completed and A14-1 test flown on 1 July. The only problem caused by the heat and rain was cracking of the dope around the lap joints in the plywood on top of and along the trailing edge of the mainplanes. This was overcome by doping strips of fabric along these joints and re-doping the upper surface of the mainplanes.[48]

The Western Detachment had left Melbourne on 19 May for Western Australia but its Gannet, A14-2, was diverted to search for RAAF Rapide A3-2, which had made another forced landing near Lake Mackay. This diversion prevented photography from commencing until the middle of June. Even so, the report to 30 June recorded that photographic work completed included the *key-strips and some photography in the Tanami-Granites district; the key-strips of the West Kimberley areas; and the photography of the Baker River and Granite Range area (West Kimberley).*[49] After it completed its survey work the aircraft was traded to the Commonwealth Aircraft Corporation (CAC) which had taken over Tugan's assets in November 1936. It was to enter the civil register as VH-UXE and ended up in New Guinea where it was apparently destroyed by enemy action during the 1939-45 war.

On 20 March 1937, Flt Lt Lerew test flew modified Gannet VH-UYE (c/n TA 57) in order to ascertain whether it was worth having modifications to the tailplane embodied in the RAAF Gannets. He found that stability in the yawing plane greatly improved, the *aircraft would maintain a steady*

**Left:** *How we arrived at Low.* The wheel collapsed on this Gannet, possibly A14-4, and the incident of 10 May 1942. (via RAAF Museum)

*course for two or three minutes "feet off." Turns at rate 4 could be easily maintained in either direction, the rate of turn being controlled by the "stick" rather than by partial rudder as in unmodified type.* However, both machines tested tended to fly left wing low (due probably to alteration in fin camber) and Lerew suggested that this tendency be corrected before giving consideration to the modification of the RAAF Gannets.[50]

The Air Board wanted to be assured *from a further test, that the tendency to fly "left-wing-low" has been corrected without adverse effect in other respects.*[51] CAC replied that this fault had been noted by previous pilots but was considered as very slight. *However, the wing is provided with a means of overcoming this fault and an adjustment has been made* and a further test could be made any time after the 24 May 1937.[52] Lerew conducted tests on VH-UYE on 10 June, and reported that this tendency had been eliminated. The aircraft still *possesses a definite tendency to "wallow". The movement is a combination of rolling and pitching, and is gradual; increasing in amplitude until a "stall" or an excessive diving speed is reached. This is increased by moving three people (the approximate equivalent of the weight of wireless, camera and operator, as required by this service) aft.* However, the stability was much better than the unmodified version.[53] The DTS (E Wackett) considered that the modification was advantageous, and the CAS agreed and asked for it to be arranged at the first opportunity.[54]

A Gannet had suffered a fractured front tailplane spar in 1937 and the report on the incident stated that there was *no evidence to suggest that the failure of the spar was due to faulty material or to faulty workmanship*, and was blamed on fatigue stress, *due possibly to tail plane vibration of a mechanical or aerodynamic origin.*[55] This may have been the reason why the RAAF desired to have *precise information as to the design of the vertical and horizontal tail surfaces now fitted* to their Gannet aircraft, in order to determine whether it was desirable *to fit these aeroplanes with the modified (2 auxiliary fins) tail unit and rubber mountings.*[56]. However, a report by a CAB aeronautical engineer on the tail mountings of the Gannet recorded his *complete disagreement with the principle of attaching the tail planes of these aeroplanes to their fuselages by means of elastic connections.* It was pointed out that the damaging vibrations of the tail plane were thought to have an aerodynamic origin and *consequently the amplitude of the vibration of the tail plane is likely to be increased by allowing greater freedom at the fuselage attachments.* This modification was referred to as one more questionable feature in a design which already had a number of such features.[57] A note to this Minute states that it was not considered justified *condemning this arrangement* as the rubber mounting was so rigid it did not involve any degree of appreciable increase in the amplitude of oscillation of the tailplane. Despite this acquiescence, it can be seen that Wackett was still pursuing his own path despite what the official view was. There were fatigue failures in the welds of the tailplane, and these modifications may have been related to this. (See Chapter 11 for details of problems with A14-2's tailplane.)

In October 1937, A14-1 and A14-2 were to be modified and reconditioned and a quotation for the work was requested from CAC. As an alternative CAC submitted a proposal wherein they offered to supply two new Mark II Gannets at £6,900 each and accept the two worn Gannets as part payment to the amount of £7,700. This offer was accepted by the Board and the old aircraft were duly handed over to CAC.[58] These two new Gannets were A14-3 and A14-4 as in March 1938, a Gannet *now completed as per contract for photography and wireless* was offered by CAC at £6,000 to *replace the crashed Rapide* A3-2, which had been written off on 3 February. The Minister approved this purchase on 19 April and A14-5 was noted as having been bought complete as per Order 31281 on the 29 August.[59] Confirmation that this was a separate contract from the purchase of A14-3 and A14-4 is the statement that the price was compared favourably with that previously paid of £6,900. Additional modifications were required to A14-5 to bring it to the standard required for survey work at an extra cost of £113.14.0.[60]

A14-5 survived until 15 June 1942, when it crashed into Mount Russell after take-off from Canberra aerodrome. The pilot, Flt Lt Bruce William Graham suffered a fractured ankle, the nursing orderly broke a shoulder blade, but the rest of the crew, a radio operator and an aircraft mechanic, were

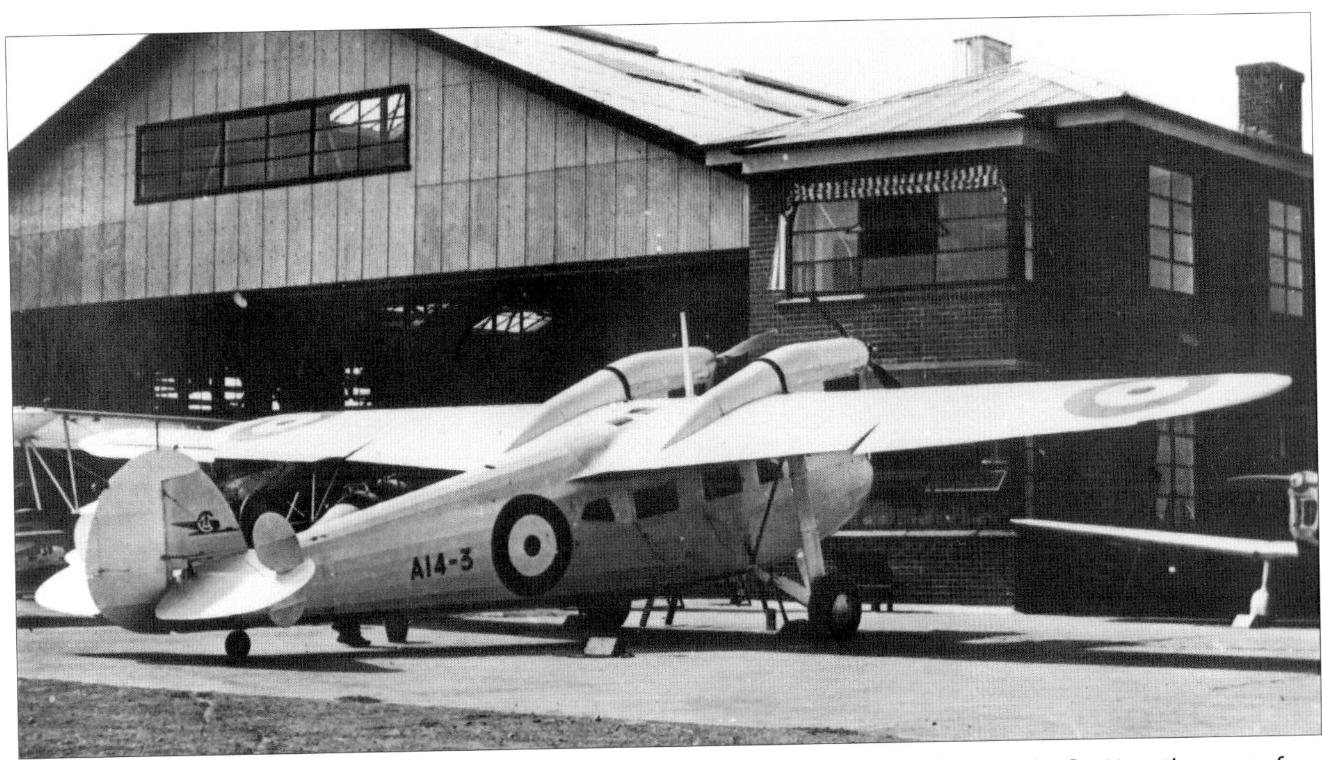


**Above:** A14-3 on the hard stand displays the added fins on the tailplane and the CAC logo on the fin. Note the nose of the solitary RAAF Miles Magister trainer to the right.

unhurt and discharged from hospital after observation. The remains were converted to components.

A14-4 was VH-UZW according to Department of Civil Aviation files and was disposed of to the RAAF on 24 March 1938. This was the eighth Gannet constructed (c/n TA 59), CAC asking for an urgent airworthiness certification on 3 November 1937, at which time it had a total flight time of 1 hour 40 minutes. The Certificate of Airworthiness and Certificate of Registration were issued on 4 November for a seven-seat configuration.[61]

VH-UYF (c/n TA 58) is recorded as having been sold to the Air Board but no date is given. The DCA noted that *the tare weight allows for the carrying of 4 passengers only with full tanks, whereas seating for five passengers is provided.* It has not proved possible to identify the RAAF serial of this machine.[62]

Considerable detail has been presented on the origins of A14-3 and A14-4 as previously it has been stated that A14-3 was VH-UYE which had been completed on 30 March 1937. VH-UYE was the first Australian designed and built aircraft to fly overseas on a charter when it was hired to fly a group of journalists from Sydney to Rabaul, New Britain, to report on a violent volcanic eruption in May 1935. As the aircraft offered by CAC were 'new' aircraft then it seems unlikely that the RAAF would have accepted a reconditioned civil machine as a 'new'" aircraft, particularly considering the price paid for the machine. If VH-UYE was the not the Gannet purchased by the RAAF, then the mystery of which Gannet became A14-3 remains.

A14-3 was brought on charge at 1 AD on 3 February 1938. It was allocated to the Communication and Survey Flight at 1 Training Depot. On 6 February it left Laverton en route for Singapore for the official opening of the King George VI dry dock with the CAS, Williams, on board. Williams explains in his autobiography that he felt that the only reason an air force officer was selected for what was purely a naval occasion was that the Government had put off

**Above:** VH-UVY after it came to rest on a bunker at the Gosford golf course. The pilot, H.F. Boston, mechanic T.C. Connor and solitary passenger, R.H. Gibbs, were all unhurt. Gibbs was on his was to Sydney to enter hospital and completed the trip by train, along with the mail on board. In heavy weather the pilot could not locate Mascot aerodrome. Boston reportedly said *we were not in any real danger and there was no big smash. We made a perfect landing but we got bunkered!*

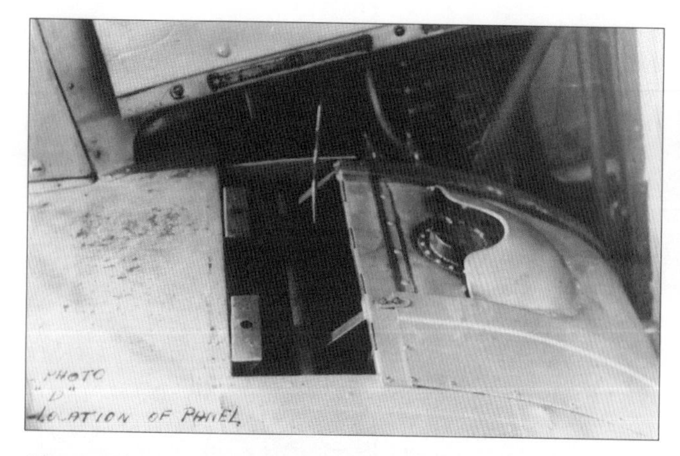


**Above:** The location of the panel of A14-6 that almost caused the loss of the aircraft. (NAA A705/1 Item 32/10/2696)

**Above:** The same panel on A14-7. (NAA A705/1 Item 32/10/2696)

**Left:** AC1 George Booth in full flying gear, 2 AAU, Canberra, April 1942. (via G Booth)

**Above:** A Gannett undergoing maintenance in the North Queensland Airways Hangar. Note that although the machine is in the hangar, the windscreen is covered to protect the machine from the sun. The North Queensland Airways Ltd was in service from 7 May 1936, to 25 October 1938, when it was taken over by Air Lines of Australia after a series of fatal crashes. (via AHMofWA P031870)

making a decision as to who to send that in the end it was too late for anyone to reach Singapore except possibly in a service aircraft.

The Gannet was flown by Sqn Ldr Allan Leslie Walters with Corporals Taylor (radio operator) and Connelly (Fitter/rigger) as crew. Walters was an Army officer who had transferred to the RAAF in 1928. He would leave the RAAF with the rank of Air Cdr. The RAAF Gannet had a radio fitted *with high-tension supply derived from a wind-driven generator mounted in the nose above the landing light.*[63] They arrived on schedule on 12 February. The ceremonies went off as only the Imperial British could conduct them and the crew left on the 16th for Palembang in Sumatra. Approaching the coastline north of Palembang they obtained radio bearings from the Dutch operators and the height of the low cloud which covered the mainland. This information seemed to allow for a safe altitude under the cloud and so Walters descended below the cloud to find himself over water and below trees on both sides of the aircraft - they were over a river! Walters quickly regained height and they were able to find an opening in the clouds and make their way to a safe landing.[64]

The rest of the return trip was uneventful until the last day when they encountered cloud over Victoria. Australia did not have the facilities of the Dutch and Walters was forced to fly

**Above:** George Booth, in more casual attire, poses with another form of transport, with an ambulance Gannet as a backdrop. (via G Booth)

**Above:** The crews of the two Gannets pose at Mildura, NSW, on their way to the Batchelor, just south of Darwin, NT. The leisurely journey was completed by the two crews, each comprising a pilot, W/T operator and mechanic. (via G Booth)

**Right:** Rex Curphy was the only other W/T operator in the crews. His pose here shows the Gannet's nose mounted landing lights, generator and the side hatch. (via G Booth)

**Left & Below:** A14-5 continues the habit of Gannet's standing on their nose, however the large Red Cross insignia applied on the fuselage to wing join is well shown here. (via G Booth)

a compass course eventually coming though the cloud over the ocean south of Lorne. They came home to Point Cook from a direction from which they were not expected, *not quite skimming the water.*[65]

A14-3 carried out survey work from March to October 1938, and carried Sir Herbert Gepp to Central Australia to inspect the work being done by the Survey Flight. However, the aircraft was forced to remain at Alice Springs while an engine was removed from A14-5 and flown out in an Anson.[66] A14-3 and A14-4 were modified *for survey and service operations* around September 1938, such modifications including the *installation of (a) Long Range Fuel Tank (100 miles).*[67] A14-3 continued to carry out survey work in Northern Australia and in NSW, being allocated to the Southern Queensland Survey Detachment on 18 June 1940. The following May the port undercarriage was torn off in a landing accident at Bairnsdale, Vic. Following temporary repairs, it was flown to Butler Air Transport at Mascot for repair.[68]

When the Practice and Communication Flight at 1 AD

**Above:** Typical outback strip with 44-gallon petrol drums. All fuelling was done with hand pumps, a long tiring process in the hot Australian outback. The dark camouflage led to fast deterioration of the fabric and a request was made to dope the Gannets in V.84 aluminium. (via G Booth)

**Right:** A crewman poses with one of the ambulance Gannets. The red crosses on the fuselage and on top of the fuselage were marked in a white circle. Those underneath the wings were marked directly onto the wing under-surface colour. (via G Booth)

was made an independent Communications and Survey Flight in early 1937, its aircraft comprised an Anson and three Gannets.[69] A report by the CO of the new Flight in March 1939 indicated that the Gannet was unsuitable for the purpose of air photography and recommended the provision of Anson aircraft for this task.[70] The Survey Flight was made a separate unit in October 1939 with the following allotment of aircraft:- Ansons A4-45 and A4-46, and Gannets A14-3, A14-4 and A14-5.[71] The outbreak of war had led to the retention of the Gannets in their photographic role until they were required as aerial ambulances. (Tugan Aircraft had provided details of proposals to convert the Gannet to a technical supply carrier and to ambulance configuration as early as December 1935).[72]

As has been noted above A14-1 was turned over to CAC in April 1938, and the Corporation applied for a C of A and Certificate of Registration on 7 November after the aircraft had *been rebuilt*. Modifications included the tailplane and elevator spar; rudder trim tab, strengthening one pair of fuselage members to allow an increase in all up weight from 5,400 lb to 5,550 lb.[73] It became VH-ACD and was retained by CAC until 25 June 1940, when it was impressed as A14-6.

CAC Offered the Air Board a Gannet Mk. II with Gipsy VI engines and constant speed airscrews and all extras and fittings etc., for £6,500 on 16 September 1938.[74] This offer was not taken up and CAC apparently stored the remaining Gannets, the exact number completed or semi-completed has not been determined. On the declaration of war CAC offered the RAAF two Gannets for immediate use.[75] These two were probably A14-1 and VH-UVY (c/n TA 55). As noted, the former was impressed as A14-6, and was allotted to the Survey Flight, Laverton, shortly before this unit moved to Canberra.

VH-UVY was impressed as A14-7 and received at 1 AD on 25 June 1940.[76] This latter aircraft's C of A had expired on 24 November 1938, and had not been renewed, the monoplane apparently being another of those stored at CAC's Fishermen's Bend facility until acquisition by the RAAF. Powered by Menasco BS.6 engines VH-UVY was designated as an L.J.W.7A. These engines gave continuous trouble and the aircraft remained virtually unserviceable until 13 July 1941, when they were replaced by Gipsy VI engines.[77] A14-7 carried out survey work in the Northern Territory and Western Australia until converted to an ambulance aircraft.

On 30 July 1940, P/Off R.R.H. Winter, together with LAC Martin, was flying A14-6 from Canberra when, after

**Above:** A14-8 with A14-6 in full red cross camouflage on Daily Waters outback airstrip in 1942. The Ambulance Gannets were fitted with two stretchers and a special chair for sitting patients. (via G Booth)

**Above:** A despondent George Booth on the overturned A14-6. (via G Booth)

**Above:** A I Phil Bronk (left) and Sgt Frank Smallhorn, pose with the sad remains of A14-6. (via G booth)

completing his photographic runs and descending from 12,000 to 9,000 feet at an airspeed of 130 mph, *a loud crack was heard followed by severe shuddering and loss of rudder control.* The shuddering became worse and at 6,000 feet Winter ordered Martin to abandon the aircraft *as the chances of landing seemed remote.* Fortunately, Winter was able to steer by means of the motors and carried out a successful landing at Canberra.[78] An examination revealed that the cause of the loss of control was the failure of the joint of the two portions of the inspection panel which was located in the top surface of the main plane, between the engine nacelle and the fuselage. The rear half of the panel, which stood proud of the front half, was lifted by the slipstream and folded backwards. The panel did not detach from the aircraft but flapped in the slip stream causing turbulence in the air flow with consequent partial loss of rudder control accompanied by severe buffeting. The joints on these panels differed on individual aircraft. On A14-4 the panel slid into a grooved joint over the second half of the panel; on A14-6 the joint was a lap type; while on A14-7 the joint was of the latest hinged type, and as this was considered the most satisfactory, the defective panel on A14-6 was replaced by one of these later types.[79]

**Above:** Sgt Gordon Dix (Left) and AC1 George Booth pose with their Gannet A14-6 as a backdrop, Kathrine, NT, May 1942. *Tall, elegant, and quietly spoken, he inspired confidence.* By the time they crossed Australia, Gordon and George were firm friends.

**Above:** The remains of A14-6 at Elcho Island mission where they were removed to after the war. George wrote that he had contacted the missionary who found the Gannet where *by an educated guess we had located it. Motors and airframe were salvaged only a month or two after we left the plane even though in the meantime the whole swamp went up in flames.* (G Booth)

Late in 1940 plans were made to convert Gannets to ambulance aircraft. Two of the five Gannets of the Survey Flight were examined at Canberra on 15 January 1941, and a provisional location selected for the trial installation. Each aircraft would be fitted with two moveable stretchers, medical lockers and a collapsible seat, being able to carry the pilot, W/T operator, two stretcher cases and either a sitting-up case or a medical orderly. It was expected that the installation would require little modification to the aircraft. *The rearmost seat must be removed, and the wireless operator's seat moved forward and tilted slightly to provide additional room.* It will also be necessary to provide a fold-back type seat for the medical attendant. *The attachment fittings for the stretcher would remain permanently in the aircraft so that the support frames for the stretchers could be installed at short notice. The attachment fittings will not interfere with the use of the aircraft in normal survey work.* It was noted that individual Gannets had doors on different sides and the installation would have to be suitable for all of the aircraft.[80] The ambulance aircraft were to be camouflaged in the standard earth brown and foliage green scheme with aluminium under surfaces. No ambulance markings were to be applied as the conversion was an emergency measure, however photographs show that red crosses were painted onto the aircraft.[81] Towards the end of 1941 the conversion programme suddenly became extremely urgent, probably as a result of Japan's expanding military threat. *In view of the present situation and the scarcity of ambulance aircraft it would be appreciated if the matter of equipping the remaining Gannets for Ambulance duty be expedited...and the matter...be treated as one of extreme urgency and priority be invoked for necessary material.*[82]

A14-3 was at Mascot on 30 January 1942, for a complete overhaul following the Bairnsdale accident which damaged *the centre fuselage, under-carriage attachments, undercarriage axle and legs and the nose of the fuselage,*[83] *and the conversion of...*(this)*...aeroplane and its return to service, is a vitally urgent matter*. The holdup with the repairs was its undercarriage, and it was planned to fit modified Anson wheels to bring it back into service.[84]

The modified Gannets were to be allocated to 2 Air Ambulance Unit (AAU) based at Canberra, ACT, under the control of the Medical Directorate. This unit was formed on 1 March 1942, and was to receive its operational nucleus of aircraft by the conversion of the Survey Flight's Gannet aircraft, one by one, to air ambulances. A14-5, A14-6 and A14-7 were reported as being available by 15 March and A14-4 by the 20th. A14-7 was at Pearce, Western Australia, and the fittings were fabricated in Canberra and sent to Pearce for *the installation to be carried out as soon as possible.*[85]

As the Survey Flight was reduced to a nucleus without aircraft the pilots and part of the maintenance staff were transferred to 2 AAU. On 12 March, A14-5 and A14-7 under the command of P/Off Ingham and Sgt Dix respectively, left Canberra for Daly Waters. They had no sooner reached their destination when they were recalled as the hospital at Daly Waters was not ready for occupation. The strength of the Unit at the end of its first month of operations was:

A14-3 Unserviceable. At Mascot, complete.
A14-4 Unserviceable. At Laverton, complete.
A14-5 Unserviceable. At Daly Waters, temporarily repaired after nose over.
A14-6 Unserviceable. At Canberra, undergoing 180 hourly inspection.
A14-7 Serviceable. At Daly Waters.[86]

It was decided to move the Detachment to Batchelor, south of Darwin, until further notice. A14-3 and A14-6 flying to Bachelor in April 1942, where a base of operations for ambulance aircraft was established. The detachment began to carry out operations including civilian work such as that of the 17 May when three leper cases were moved from Katherine to Mt Isa by A14-3.

On 19 May A14-6, with a three-man crew consisting of Sgt Frank Smallhorn (pilot); AC1 George Booth (W/T operator) and Cpl Phillip Bronk (Nursing Orderly), left for Groote Eylandt to pick up an airman who was suffering from dysentery. After four hours flying the crew were lost due to the low cloud base and terrain over which they flew. The whole area looked like a maze of swamps, mangroves, islands, none of which were recognisable from their maps. Although he still had fuel Smallhorn elected to make a landing before the fuel situation became critical. The crew tried to find a beach but none was visible, however a well grassed plain appeared to offer a good landing ground. A touch and go seemed to confirm that they would be landing on soft but safe ground. George Booth wrote that when the wheels stopped spinning, they could see a covering of thick grey slime. Smallhorn decided to go ahead for a soft landing. George was aware that making such a landing with fixed undercarriage was asking for trouble but he felt *anger rather than fear* as it would be a *a stupid bloody way to go.* Shortly after touch down the plane began to bump and rock with increasing violence. The crew, with the exception of the pilot who was strapped in, were flung about the cabin, until suddenly *the poor old plane* dug her nose in and flipped over onto her back. Booth and Bronk were catapulted into the rear section of the fuselage but other than being severely shaken were unhurt. Fortunately, Smallhorn also was not seriously hurt.

Despite his parachute and harness, Phil Bronck beat George to the broken window and became wedged in the frame. They were conscious that the aircraft could still catch fire and Smallhorn, who was already outside, tried to pull him through, while George was pulling him back inside the fuselage. Bronck realised the problem and let himself be pulled inside and took off his parachute, then they all had vacated the aircraft. Smallhorn had a small gash on his forehead, but George and Bronck were unharmed, the bruises would appear later.

The Gannet *lay there on her back, the front bulk-head smashed in, her body broken, her propellers smashed her wheels pointing skywards as if in mute supplication.*[87] They had landed in the middle of a vast swamp the entire surface of which was covered in reeds about three feet high. What followed was an epic in survival.

Four Hudson aircraft were despatched to search for the missing aircraft the day after A14-6 went missing but found nothing, the aerial search being called off on the 27th. The three survivors decided that as rescue had not arrived after 10 days they would attempt to walk to the coast. On day 20 of their ordeal they met friendly Aborigines and the worst part of their journey was over. The Aboriginals cared for the exhausted half-starved crew and eventually took them to Millingimbi Mission where they were able to contact the RAAF.[88]

Smallhorn was to have two more force landings and then achieved his ambition to get away from being a *bloody chauffer in a geriatric plane* and went onto Beaufighters. He was returning to Williamtown on a cross country training flight on 7 November 1944, when he was caught in foul weather. No trace of the aircraft was ever found, Frank's body was recovered from the ocean two weeks later. He was just 23 years of age.

The Unit's Gannets continued to be depleted, A14-5 being lost when it crashed into Mount Russell as related above. At one time the Unit operated Ryan trainer A50-10 as a communication aircraft until it was written off in an accident which claimed the lives of two of the Unit's pilots.

In early 1944, a Detachment comprising A14-4 and A14-7 was set up at Corunna Downs under command of Flt Lt Byfield. The Detachment did excellent work but the limitations of the Gannets were becoming more apparent. For the period 14 to 31 May 1944, there was no flying as the only job offering was to carry a patient to Perth, a distance too long for the Gannet and a C.47 was given a special run for this patient.

A14-4 continued to give good service until 25 August 1944. The aircraft had arrived at 76 OBU at about 1730 hours the previous day. They were to complete their present trip to fly to Broome to pick up a patient that Dr Sangster wanted to get to Perth. By the time the aircraft reached Perth it would be due for its 180 hourly inspection that had to be carried out at Perth. In response to an urgent call to attend a critical case on Argyle Downs Station, WA, the crew discussed the situation and agreed to go to Argyle Downs. They would fly to 73 OBU where they asked for the other Gannet to be made ready for them.

They left the following morning at 0530, the strip being lighted by a double flare path composed of kerosene flares running the full length of the strip. Sometime later a LAC reported hearing an aircraft then an explosion. It was at first thought that this might have been Beaufort A9-340 that had taken off just prior to the departure of the Gannet. After daybreak, Anson W1544 took off to retrace the Gannet's flight path. It returned within a short time and reported that they had seen the wreckage in the water near the shore, almost in line with the end of the strip.

Pilot F/Off Gordon Edward Dix, with Sgt Norman Catton as W/O, and passenger Sqn Ldr Dr John Clive Sangster, were all killed approximately 50 yards off shore about one mile from the landing ground at Exmouth Gulf. The aircraft apparently dived into water about six feet deep. The forward portion and main planes were totally smashed into small pieces. The Aircraft Accident Data Card recorded that the cause of the accident was held to be *the pilot's lack of experience of night flying. F/O Dix had only 6 hours 15 min total night flying as first pilot, of which only 20 minutes was on Gannet A/c. The 20 minutes was the only night flying as first pilot in 2½ years.* The bodies were recovered and taken to the American base where they were places in a refrigerator room until burial arrangements could be made. The Gannet was totally wrecked, salvageable parts being sent to 4 Central Recovery Depot.[89]

The Court of Inquiry into the accident found that although there was insufficient evidence to determine the cause of the accident, it was considered that Dix had committed an error of judgement in taking-off at night. As a result of this accident, all pilots of 2 AAU were restricted to day flying until such a time as they:

Shall receive instrument flying instruction and were to be checked as competent. This was to cover 'blind' take-off is possible.

Were to receive instruction in night flying and be checked as competent. They had to have ten hours as first pilot (night) before doing any cross-country trips carrying passengers.

Pilots had to do a minimum of five night take-offs and landings per month to stay competent.

No explanation as to a cause for the accident was ever discovered, however the incident to A14-6 related above was paralleled by A14-3 on 4 November 1944.F/Off Kennedy had just taken off from Kalgoorlie when at 1,500 feet the port motor cowl blew loose, ripped away from the front fasteners and buckled causing the aircraft to lose speed and dive steeply. Kennedy was able to make a safe landing back at the aerodrome.[90] It is not known if the cowlings of A14-4 were examined for similar damage.

A14-7 had been exposed to the weather since its arrival at Corunna Downs and the heat of August and September saw the fabric deteriorate and the plywood warp making it unfit to fly. As a result of this and similar incidents the OC, 2 AAU, requested that camouflage be deleted from ambulance aircraft not in front line operations as V.84 aluminium dope reflected the sun's rays prolonging life of the airframe. On 25 September, it was decided to wind up the affairs of the Detachment and close it.

A14-3 was proceeding from 2 AAU Archerfield, to the detachment at Corunna Downs on 11 November 1944, when it was forced to land with the port engine unserviceable at 71 Advanced Operational Base which had been established at Carnarvon. It was to remain here until the necessary repairs were effected. On 1 December a second party arrived from 17 Repair and Salvage Unit (RSU), Pearce, with another Gipsy 6 Mk.I engine from A14-7. One engine from this aircraft had already been sent but as A14-3 was equipped with Gipsy 6 Mk.II engines, both engines had to be changed to the Mk.I variety to bring the aircraft into a serviceable condition. The complete engine change was finished by the 3rd and a test flight on the 4th was abandoned as the instruments were unserviceable. Another test flight on the 7th produced the same result. A14-3 finally departed to 17 RSU, Pearce, on the 9th. It was probably due to frustration over this incident that F/Off N Kennedy was to submit a report wherein he stated that *the Gannet was not a suitable type of aircraft for ambulance work in hot climates.*[91]

Two Gannets were offered for sale by tender closing on 20 February 1945. At that time, they were in Western Australia. It has not proved possible to identify these two machines but it seems that they must have been A14-3 and A14-7. A14-7 was the longest serving Gannet being declared unserviceable on 10 September 1944. Allotted to 17 RSU it was finally approved, along with A14-3. to be converted to components on 21 February 1946.[92] Newspaper reports in July stated that hundreds of aircraft would be reduced to scrap including Spitfires, Hurricanes, Beaufighters, Beauforts, Boomerangs, Oxfords, Fairey Battles and Gannets. All saleable parts were to be removed from the planes and the metal will be sold as scrap. The refusal of the Civil Aviation Department to licence the planes was based on the fact that they were built for a short life and would be dangerous to operated and that they are practically impossible to convert to civilian use without wasting money and time.

George Booth was a teacher at a single teacher school in rural NSW, when he enlisted in the RAAF in 1941. His experiences in A14-6 are described above. His personal account of his days flying in Gannets – *33 Days* (Greenhouse Publications Pty Ltd, Vic, 1988) - is one of the few accounts of the Gannet's operations in the war. George was introduced to the Gannet ambulances at 2 AAU at Canberra, in late March 1942. In the hangar marked with a large red cross *stood four or five unlovely aircraft. Gannets! (I learnt later). They were the quaintest, clumsiest aircraft I had ever seen! They bulged in all the wrong places, something like an ancient seaplane with legs stuck on as an afterthought. Surely, I thought, some leftovers from World War 1.*[93]

The Gannet's flying characteristics also came in for comment from its pilots. P.G. *Paddy* Heffernan recalled that the Gannet *had no single engine performance.* He *managed to do some five hours on it and was terrified all the time.* Frank Neale, an ex-RFC pilot of some renown is reported to have made this famous remark about the Gannet. He said *When I prised this thing off the ground, I realised that I had done the wrong thing.* According to Heffernan this was a *very apt summary of the general low regard in which the Gannet was held.*[94] Despite this at least one person remembered the

Gannet as *a very suitable aircraft for aerial survey. Its high wing provided the camera operator with good visibility; it also provided a safety factor in landing in cross winds and on small airstrips.* These are the recollections of G.A. Everingham who was in charge of the North Australia Survey Flight's photographic section at Cloncurry in 1939.[95] The type performed well in the survey and ambulance role and deserves to be remembered as a brave attempt to build a commuter airliner in Australia. It is unfortunate that its Fokker style of construction was obsolescent by the time the Gannet was conceived. By then Australia was to operate the latest US built twin-engine all metal airliners of stressed skin monocoque construction; if the Gannet had been constructed ten years earlier the story may well have been different.

### Specifications

Dimensions: Span 52 ft, Length 34 ft 6 in, Height 11 ft 6 in.
Weights: Empty 3,400 lbs; Loaded 5,550 lbs.
Performance: Speed Max 150 mph. Cruising 130 mph.
Range 500 mls.

## End Notes

1. NAA ACT CRS A458/1 Item AG20/1. Cockatoo Island Dockyard Construction of Aeroplanes. A Murray Jones, the General Manager of De Havilland Australia wrote that *he was against the manufacture of spare parts or "Moth" planes for private concerns at prices which do not permit his company to compete.* Notes for Cabinet re Cockatoo Island Dockyard; Competition with Private Enterprise. It would appear that the Defence Department (RAAF) kept the Cockatoo activity subsidised by giving it work to carry out and it would thus be another instance of Williams promoting and protecting Wackett in his activities.
2. The L.J.W. numbers are thought to represent Wackett's design sequence, the letters being his initials, thus the L.J.W.6 would be his sixth design. However there appear to be more designs than numbers and the true sequence of Wackett's work has yet to be determined.
3. NAA ACT CRS A2408 Item 121/1 LANDPLANES. Letterbook entry No.430 of 27.11.1934 records an offer by Wackett of a L.J.W.7 monoplane with Gipsy engines for £4,750.
4. *Ibid.* Letterbook entry No.444, 7.05.1935.
5. Contract Board Agendum No.149 and 324. 12.02.1935 and 2.04.1935 respectively.
6. NAA ACT CRS A2408 Item 121/1. *Op Cit.* Letterbook entry No.446, 2.07.1935.
7. NAA ACT CRS A664/1 Item 474/401/1183. Estimates of Expenditure 1935/36. "Department of Defence, Estimate of Expenditure 1935-36, Explanatory Statement Prepared by Direction of the Minister for Defence."
8. Wg Cdr P.G. Heffernan noted on the draft chapter an emphatic 'NO' to the statement that the Gannet could fly with full load on one engine.
9. "Development of N.S.W. Aircraft Company". *Aircraft.* 1.11.1934, P.15.
10. *Ibid.*
11. NAA ACT CRS A5954 Item 873/1. Aircraft Manufacture in Australia File No.1 July 1935 - November 1935. Letter from Tugan to the Minister (Parkhill), 07.1935.
12. Contract Board Agendum No.324.
13. Air Board Agendum No. 1736. The approval for the construction of the L.J.W.7 was apparently not considered by the Board. Meeting 30.04.1935. *Aircraft* magazine for 1.06.1935, announced that the Air Board had ordered the first machine.
14. Contract Board Agendum No.324.
15. NAA ACT CRS A664/1 Item 474/401/1183. *Op Cit.* "Department of Defence, Estimate of Expenditure 1935-36, Explanatory Statement Prepared by Direction of the Minister for Defence."
16. NAA ACT CRS A705 Item 9/13/24. Gannet Aircraft Specification Test. Minute: "Test of L.J.W.7 Monoplane". AMS to DTS, 27.09.1935.
17. *Ibid.* Minute: "Test of L.J.W. Monoplane", DTS to AMS, 24.09.1935.
18. *Ibid.* Minute: "L.J.W. Monoplane", DTS to AMS, 19.12.1935.
19. *Ibid.*
20. *Ibid.* Note by AMS to Minute.
21. *Ibid.* CAS to AMS, 23.12.1935.
22. *Ibid.* "Appendix to specification Tests L.J.W.7 Monoplane - Pilot's Observations."
23. Contract Board Agendum No.8, 3.01.1936.
24. *Aircraft*, 1 January 1936.
25. NAA ACT CRS A705/1 Item 9/13/18. L.J.W.7 GANNET MAINTENANCE SCHEDULE.
26. *Ibid.* Minute; "L.J.W.7 Monoplane." DofT to AMS, 3.03.1936.
27. *Ibid.* Minute: "L.J.W.7 Monoplane." DTS to AMS, 13.03.1936.
28. *Ibid.* AMS to CAS, 16.03.1936.
29. *Ibid.* CAS to AMS, 19.03.1936.
30. No.1 Squadron Unit Diary. RAAF Form A50.
31. NAA ACT CRS A1/1 Item 38/1432. "Report of the Committee to Direct and Control the Aerial Geological and Geophysical Survey of North Australia for the period ended 30th June 1936", P.18.
32. Contract Board Agendum No.742, 1.07.1936.
33. NAA ACT CRS A705/1 Item 9/13/24. *Op Cit.* Minute: "L.J.W.7 Monoplane". DTS to AMS, 20.05.1936.
34. 1 Squadron Unit Diary. RAAF Form A50.
35. NAA Vic CRS MP115 Item 8/102/91. Construction of Gannet Aircraft in Australia by Tugan Aircraft Coy. Letter: Tugan to Parkhill, 5.05.1936.
36. *Ibid.* Minute: "Tugan Aircraft Ltd." Air Board to CAB, 5.06.1936.
37. NAA ACT CRS A705/1 Item 19/13/24. *Op Cit.* Telegram; Air Board to Carr, Cloncurry, 24.08.1936.

38. *Ibid.* Letter: Carr to Air Board, 24.08.1936.
39. Contract Board Agendum No.1340, 10.11.1936.
40. NAA ACT CRS A705/1 Item 19/13/24. *Op Cit.* Minute; "Purchase of L.J.W. Aircraft - NO. A.14-2." DOI to DE, 10.11.1936.
41. *Man And Aerial Machines* No.31, Sept-Oct 1992, P.58. Research by J Hopton.
42. NAA ACT CRS A431/1 Item 46/2219. Aerial Geophysical And Geophysical Survey N.T. Pt.2. "Report of the Committee Appointed to Direct and Control the Aerial, Geological and Geophysical Survey of North Australia for the Period Ended 30th June, 1937", P.14.
43. NAA Vic CRS MP187/3/0 Item WOB1. RAAF Preliminary Reports on Flying Accidents And Forced Landings 24.4.1936 to 25.5.1939.
44. NAA ACT CRS A431/1 Item 46/2219. *Op Cit.* "Report of the Committee Appointed to Direct and Control the Aerial, Geological and Geophysical Survey of Northern Australia for the Period Ended 30th June, 1937".
45. This seems to have been a fault of the design as the Codock, and civil Gannet VH-UVU suffered similar accidents which were blamed on soft ground.
46. NAA Vic MP187/3.
47. Notes to draft chapter, 4.09.1991.
48. NAA ACT CRS A9376 Item 91. RAAF Report on the Operation of the Western Air Detachment Training Depot 1937, and North Australia Survey Flight Report on North Queensland Survey By Flying Officer D Mclean September 1937.
49. NAA ACT CRS A431/1 Item 46/2219. *Op Cit.* "Report of the Committee Appointed to Direct and Control the Aerial, Geological and Geophysical Survey of Northern Australia for the Period Ended 30th June, 1937".
50. NAA ACT CRS A705/1 Item 9/13/24. *Op Cit.* Minute: "Test of Modified Gannet at Mascot on 20.04.1937." Lerew to DTS, 30.04.1937.
51. *bid.* Letter: Air Board to CAC, 7.05.1937.
52. *Ibid.* Letter; CAC to Air Board, 19.05.1937.
53. *Ibid.* Minute: "Test of Modified Gannet - 10.6.1937." Lerew to DTS, 6.07.1937.
54. *Ibid.* Notes to Minute.
55. NAA Vic CRS MP1118/2 Item 69/2/729. Report No.M37-241 of 18.08.1937 and accompanying letter of 26.08.1937.
56. NAA Vic CRS MP115/1 Item 8/101/849. L.J.W.7 and 7A. Letter, CAB to CAC, 13.05.1938.
57. *Ibid.* Minute: "Gannet Aeroplanes - Tail Plane Attachments." Superintendent of Aircraft from H A Wills, 8.07.1938.
58. Contract Board Agendum No.2139, 24.02.1938; and Agendum No.2364, 6.04.1938. Status Cards for A14-3 and A14-4 state that they were both obtained under Order No. A.30974.
59. NAA ACT CRS A2408/1 Item 9/13. Gannet and Spares. Letterbook entries Nos.1 and 7. Contract Board Agendum No.3267 of 10.08.1938.
60. Contract Board Agendum No.3258 and No.3267, 10.08.1938. Also AA ACT CRS A2409 Item 9/13. *Op Cit.* Letterbook entry No.1, 21.03.1938.
61. NAA Vic CRS 113/1/0 Item VH-UZW. CAC to DCA, 14.10.1938.
62. NAA Vic CRS MP113/1/0 Item VH-UYF. Minute: "L.J.W.7 Aircraft VH-UYF", 11.08.1937.
63. "Royal Australian Air Force Activities". *Aircraft,* 1.03.1938, P.24.
64. Williams, R. *These Are Facts,* P.231.
65. *Ibid.* P.233.
66. NAA ACT CRS A2408 Item 9/13. *Op Cit.* Letterbook entry No.11, 17.10.1938.
67. *Ibid.* Letterbook entries Nos. 5 and 8.
68. Alford, R. *Tugan/C.A.C Gannet Aircraft History Sheet Summary*, 1989. Private research.
69. NAA ACT CRS A705/1 Item 153/2/142. Communication and Survey Flight Formation and Policy. Minute: "Communications and Survey Flight", Air Board to CAS. No date, noted 21.04.1937.
70. NAA ACT CRS A2408 Item 9/13. *Op Cit.* Letterbook entry No.19, 15.03.1939.
71. NAA ACT CRS A2408 Item 9/2. Allotment of Aircraft. Letterbook entry No.151 for 19.10.1939.
72. NAA ACT CRS A2408 Item 121/1. LANDPLANES. Letterbook entry No.477, 20.12.1935.
73. NAA Vic MP115/1 Item 8/101/849. *Op Cit.* CAC to ?, "L.J.W.7 Aircraft", 7.11.1938.
74. This is consistent with the price offered to civil operators as the Tugan Aircraft Ltd, Mascot, brochure, which had the CAC logo printed on the front, offered the Gannet at £5,500 delivered at Mascot with Gipsy VI engines, or £6,500 with Gipsy VI Series II engines and variable pitch airscrews. Sperry instruments, etc., were extra. No date was given in the document.
75. NAA ACT CRS A2408 Item 9/13. *Op Cit.* Letterbook entry No.32 of 20.09.1939.
76. The Status Cards for A14-7 show it as having previously been A14-1, however the Menasaco engines confirm its identity as VH-UVY.
77. *Brief History of the L.J.W.7 (A4) "GANNET" Aircraft*, RAAF Historical Section Manuscript.
78. NAA ACT CRS A705/1 Item 32/10/2696. Accident To Gannet A14-6 and Lac Martin. Pilot Officer Winter. 30.07.1940.
79. *Ibid.* "Defect Experienced in Inspection panel Top Main Plane Gannet Aircraft A 14-6." RAAF HQ, Central Area to Air Board, 29.08.1940.
80. NAA ACT CRS A705/1 Item 9/16/138. Conversion of Aircraft for Ambulance Duties Gannet. Minute No.6, 22.01.1941.
81. *Ibid.* Minute No.32, 3.07.1941.
82. *Ibid.* Minute No.45. DMS to DTS (TS1 (c), 8.12.1941.
83. Letter: "Repairs to Gannet A14-3." Area Technical

Officer to DPD, 31.01.1942.

84. NAA ACT CRS A705/1 Item 9/16/138. *Op Cit.* Memorandum. "Gannet A14/3 - Conversion to Air Ambulance". DPD to ATO, NSW, 27.02.1942.
85. *Ibid.* Message: Survey Flight Canberra, Southern Area, to Pearce, Western Area. Probably 9.02.1942.
86. AWM 64, File 2/1. Operations Record Book, No.2 Air Ambulance Unit 1942-1946. RAAF Form A.50.
87. Booth, G. *33 Days*. Greenhouse Publications, Elwood, Vic, Australia, 1988, P.19.
88. The full story is told in George Booth's *33 Days*. Greenhouse Publications, Elwood, Vic, Australia. 1988.
89. AWM 64 File 2/1. *Op Cit.*
90. *Ibid.*
91. NAA ACT CRS A9186/18 Item 546. Advanced Operational Base Carnarvon. RAAF Form A50.
92. *Tugan/CAC Gannet Aircraft History Sheets. Op Cit.*
93. Booth, G. *Op Cit.* P.6.
94. Letter to author. 14.04.1990.
95. Quoted by D Vincent in his draft chapter, "RAAF Survey Flight", of his RAAF Lockheed Hudson history.

Three view drawing from *Aircraft* magazine.

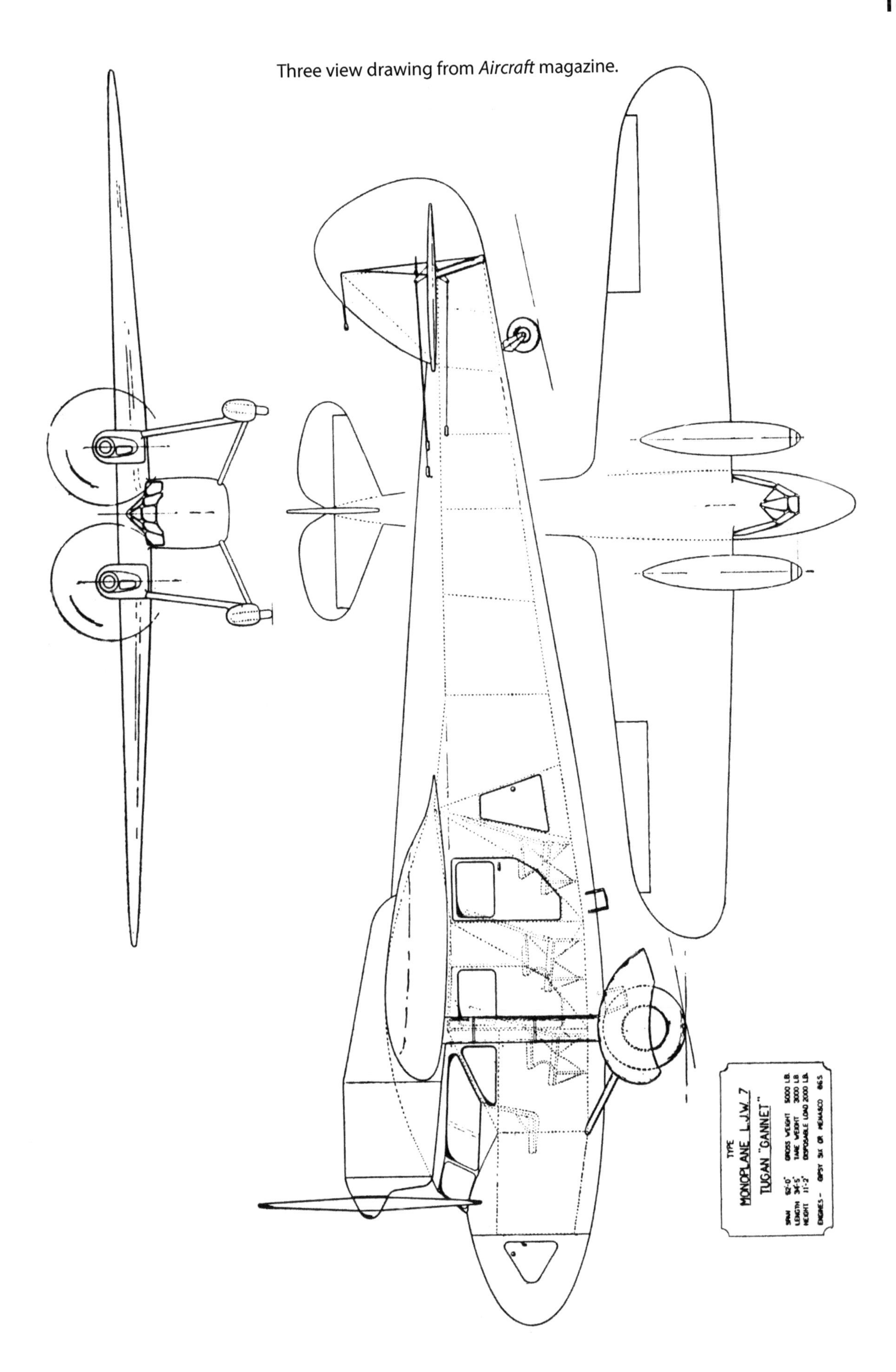

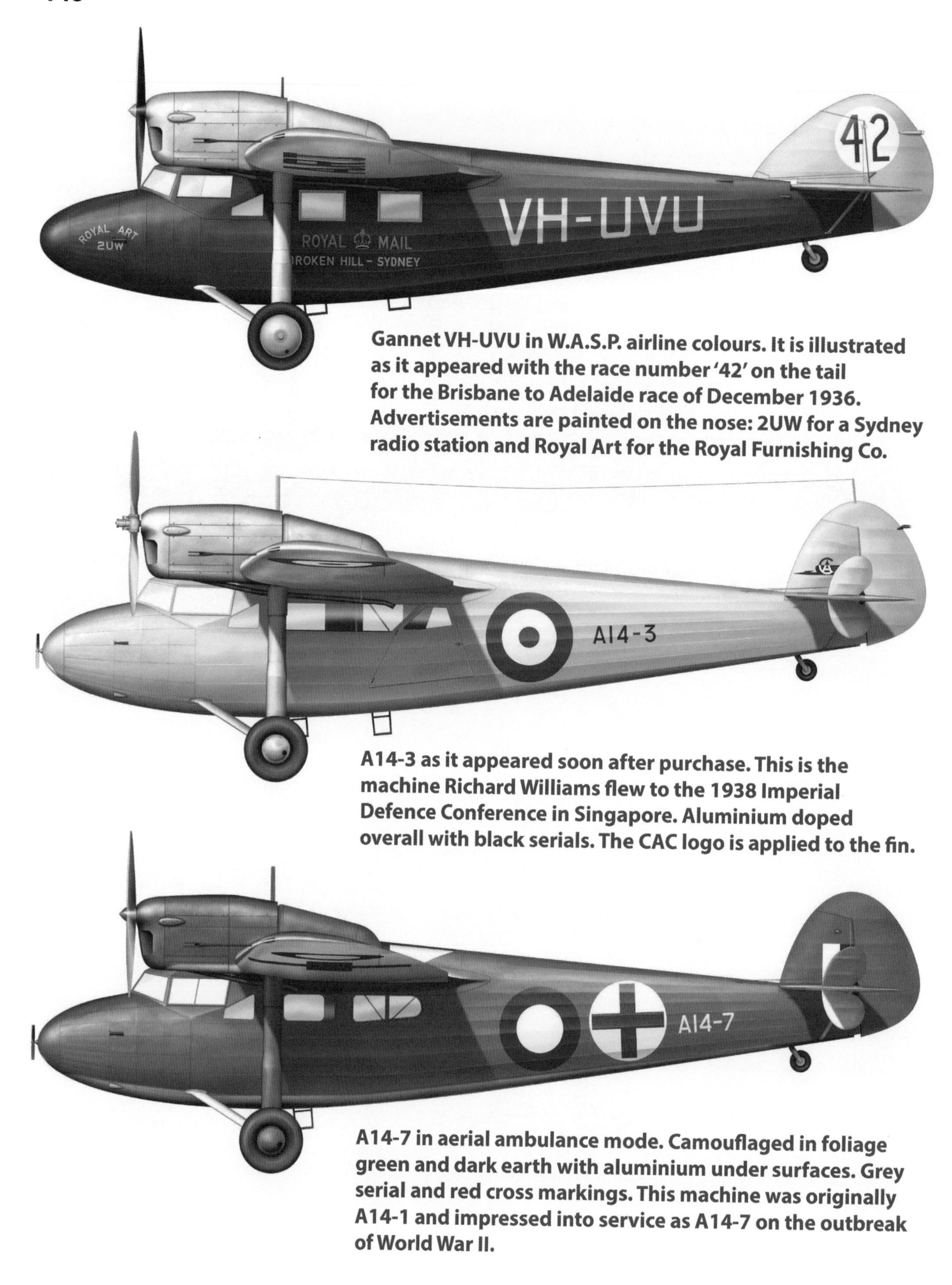


**Gannet VH-UVU in W.A.S.P. airline colours. It is illustrated as it appeared with the race number '42' on the tail for the Brisbane to Adelaide race of December 1936. Advertisements are painted on the nose: 2UW for a Sydney radio station and Royal Art for the Royal Furnishing Co.**

**A14-3 as it appeared soon after purchase. This is the machine Richard Williams flew to the 1938 Imperial Defence Conference in Singapore. Aluminium doped overall with black serials. The CAC logo is applied to the fin.**

**A14-7 in aerial ambulance mode. Camouflaged in foliage green and dark earth with aluminium under surfaces. Grey serial and red cross markings. This machine was originally A14-1 and impressed into service as A14-7 on the outbreak of World War II.**

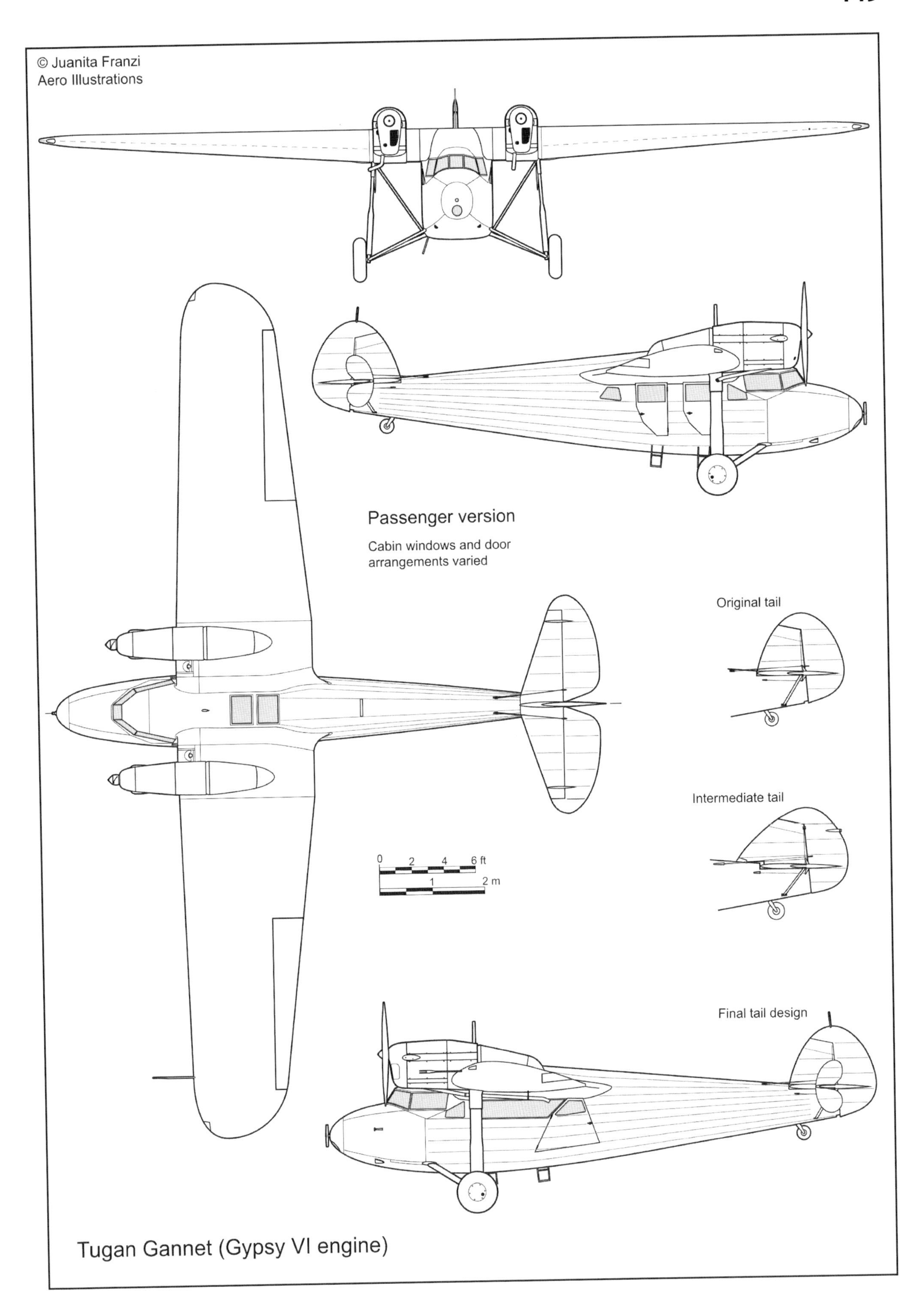
© Juanita Franzi
Aero Illustrations
Passenger version
Cabin windows and door arrangements varied
Original tail
Intermediate tail
0 2 4 6 ft
1 2 m
Final tail design
Tugan Gannet (Gypsy VI engine)

Above: A14-1 running up its engines. Note the original tailplane arrangement. The Tasmanian *Examiner* for 4 February 1936, reported that the LJW7 is the military version of the twin-engined high-wing Tugan Gannet monoplane, manufactured by the *Tugan Aircraft Company, of Mascot, Sydney. The machine is specially fitted for the photographic survey of about 600 square miles of country to the south of Launceston. This survey may be commenced this morning if weather conditions are suitable.*

## Tugan/CAC Gannet – RAAF A4 Individual Aircraft Histories

### A4-1/A14-1/A14-6

(6.11.35). Ready for final inspection. Received by RAAF 14.11.35.

25.11.35. Flt Lt J.R. Fleming. Taken over by RAAF at Mascot and flown to Richmond for service trials.

26.11.35. Flt Lt J.R. Fleming, Wing Cdr A.T. Cole plus three. Local flight trial. Recorded as A4-1.

11 & 12.35. 3 Sqn. Richmond. Flt Lt J.R. Fleming. Service trails.

3.12.35. To Tugan, Mascot, for modification.

7.12.35. Return to 3 Sqn and further trials.

8.12.35. Flt Lt J'R' Fleming. Richmond to 1 AD, Laverton.

18.12.35. 1 AD. Sqn Ldr A.W. Murphy, F/Off Lightfoot. Practice flight. Recorded as A4-1.

3.02.36. On charge 1 AD. Flight trials to 20.03.36.

3 to 26.02.36. 1 Sqn. Flt Lt A.M. Charlesworth, Cpl J.F. Kelly, LAC W.R. Burns. Trials of A4-1 as to suitability as a photo aircraft during Sqn's annual training flight to Tasmania.

20.03.36. 1 AD. Lt V.E. Hancock, Lt I.J. Lightfoot, AC1 W Miles. To carry out survey of range sites.

14.04.36 to 06.36. 1 Sqn. Flt Lt A.G. Carr. Recorded as A14-1. With North Australian Survey Flight. Left Laverton for Cloncurry, diverted to search for missing Rapide, engine failure, forced landing at Wave Hill, arrived Cloncurry 28.04.36.

29.06.36. Flt Lt A.G. Carr and three crew. Flew from Darwin to Cloncurry to survey Darwin water scheme.

2.07.36. Reconnaissance flight of several areas with Dr Woolnough, Mr Fleetwood and Mr Mulholland.

4.07.36. Photography completed.

8.07.36. Returned to Tugan for major modifications and overhaul.

25.07.36. Mr Graham of Tugan tested aircraft.

29.07.36. Flt Lt Carr. return to Cloncurry.

1.08.36. Reconnaissance of Daly and Fitzmaurice Rivers.

14 to 17.08.36. From Cloncurry to new base at Croydon, photos of Golden Gate, Stanhills, Mt Elliot and Lockness areas completed, returned to Cloncurry.

21.08.36. Cloncurry to Pine Creek for photography.

23.08.36. Pine Creek to Darwin to pick up Minister of Commerce on his return from Singapore, and fly him to Cloncurry where a Demon carried him to Cootamundra.

25.08.36. Return to Pine Creek to complete photography of area.

1 and 8.09.36. Trips from Pine Creek to Darwin to forward exposed film to Cloncurry by air mail for development.

10.09.36. To Darwin to report to CGS.

11.09.36. Reconnaissance for Major General Lavarack and Col White. Remained at Darwin until part to repair tailskid arrived on 14th.

15.09.36. Darwin to Tennants Creek via Daly Waters.

19.09.36. Photography completed by 18th, returned to Cloncurry.

26 to 27.09.36. Cloncurry to Laverton.

28.09.36. Reallotment and Returned from 1 Sqn to 1 AD for overhaul and installation T37 and R74 W/T sets.

10.10.36. 1 AD. Lt A.G. Carr, LAC W Miles. Left for Seymour to pick up Governor General, Lord Gowrie, and

**Above:** A14-2 alongside an Avro Anson.

staff officer for trip to Newstead. Return to Laverton.
16.10.36. 1 AD. F/Off J.M. Lerew, AC1 J.M. McBride, AC1 P.E. Dines. Left Laverton for Sydney to conduct search for missing journalists.
7.12.36. 1 AD. Sqn Ldr A.W. Murphy, Group Cpt Wrigley, F/Off Lerew. Test flight.
15.12.36. 1 AD. F/Off J.M. Lerew, F/Off Blake, Sgt Eckert. Guided ground party to crash of A12-7.
23.02.37 to 9.03.37. Laverton to Western Junction, Tas, and return. From 1 AD attached to 1 Sqn. F/Off D McLean from 21 Sqn selected as pilot.
10 to 11.03.37. 1 AD. F/Off Lerew. Air reconnaissance of Armament Training sites. Laverton to Menindee, Bourke, Cootamundra and return.
15.03.37 to 7.04.37. 1 Sqn (on loan from 1 AD). P/Off David John Macpherson. Mt Gambier to carry out survey for CSIR.
23.04.37. 1 AD. F/Off D McLean. Left Laverton to carry out photo operations in connection with Northern Australian geological and geophysical survey.
20.06.37. F/Off D McLean; LAC Everingham. Landing accident Cairns while operating with North Queensland Survey Flight. Tipped on nose in soft sand. Crushed nose. Unserviceable until 1.07.37. According *to The Daily Telegraph* of 21.06.1937, *After landing in a tricky wind, it bounded off the edge of the runway, ran into loose sand for 100 yards, became bogged, and slowly tipped on its nose.*
04.38. Taken over from RAAF by CAC.
(7.11.38). Now completely rebuilt. Became VH-ACD.
25.06.40. Received at 1 AD, impressed by RAAF from CAC. New serial A14-6.
1.07.40. Received RAAF Canberra. Survey Flt.
30.07.40. Forced landing.
30.07.40. Survey Flt. Canberra, ACT. P/Off R.R.H. Winter, LAC Martin. Loud crack was followed by loss of rudder control, at 6,000 ft. Panel on starboard engine came loose and made aircraft almost uncontrollable at 3,000 ft over Lake George. Martin ordered to bail out as chance of landing seemed remote: Winter successfully landed on Canberra 'drome using engines for directional control.
22.08.40. Survey Flt. Canberra. P/Off R.R.H. Winter; Flt Sgt P Stirling (529). Successful forced landing due failure port engine.
3.08.41. Received at Pearce Station from Survey Flt.
30.08.41. Received at Survey Flt from Pearce.
11.41. Survey Flt. Unserviceable.
24.12.41. Converted to ambulance.
27.01.42. Sgt Ingham. Arrived 1 ATS, Cressy, Vic, to photograph Military survey area.
02.42. Survey Flt. Unserviceable.
1.03.42. 2 AAU formed at Canberra. Gannets of Survey Flt transferred to 2 AAU after conversion to air ambulance.
8.03.42. Allotted 2 AAU from Survey Flt after conversion to air ambulance at Canberra.
10.03.42. Allotted from Survey Flt to 2 AAU.
14.03.42. At Canberra being fitted out as ambulance.
31.03.42. Canberra. Unserviceable undergoing 180 hourly inspection.
21 to 25.04.42. Sgt G.E. Dix. To Daly Waters with A14-3.
19.05.42. Sgt Francis Edward Smallhorn, Cpl *Phil* Bronk,

**Above:** A14-3 with the addition fins added to the horizontal tailplane. The CAC logo is carried on the fin. (AHMofWA P021511)

AC1 George Booth. Crashed during flight from Batchelor to Groote Eyrelandt. Crew walk to safety.
23.06.42. Written off.
14.01.43. Official date conversion to components.

**A14-2**

20.08.36. Completed.
10.11.36. Order No.22185 placed for Gannet.
27.11.36. Received 2 AD from Tugan at Mascot.
2.12.36. Lt Rae. Flown to Laverton from Sydney. Received 1 AD.
18 to 20.12.36. 1 AD. Lt Carr. Transport AVM Williams and passengers to Adelaide Centenary celebrations and return.
1.01.37. CofA issued as VH-UXE.
3.02.37. 1 AD. F/Off J.M. Lerew, Cpl G.H. Harford, Cpl AM Clarke. Sent to Tasmania to search for missing Demon A1-8.
7.02.37. 1 AD. F/Off McLean. Left Western Junction for Laverton. Handed over to 1 Sqn for photographic duties in Tasmania.
1.03.37. 1 AD. Lt J.M. Lerew. Inspection of proposed Armament Training Camp sites.
23.03.37. 1 AD. Lt J.M. Lerew, Sgt Buckley, AC1 Dines. Search for A12-8 in Port Phillip Bay.
7 to 21.04.37. 1 AD. Lt J.M. Lerew, Taylor. Took Wing Cdr tour of probable sites for RAAF aerodromes. Laverton to Narromine, Charleville, Longreach, Camooweal, Daly Waters, Darwin and return via Daly Waters, Camooweal, Cloncurry, Longreach, Roma, Brisbane, Mascot, Richmond, Canberra to Laverton.
11.04.37. Flt Lt J.M. Lerew, Taylor. D/F calibration.
19 to 21.05.37. Lt W.L. Hely, AC1 A.E. Moore, LAC W Taylor. Left Laverton for Western and Central Australian geological and geophysical survey. Laverton to Nhill, Murray Bridge, Adelaide, Port Pirie, Farina.
21.05.37 to 4.06.37. Flt Lt W.L. Hely, LAC.W. Taylor. Search for missing Rapide A3-2. Farina to Oodnadatta, Alice Springs, The Granites. 23rd. D/F test for lost Rapide. Granites to Tanami and return. To Lake McKay. Tanami to The Granites. 25th giving directions to ground party. 26th dropping water to Rapide. 27th to 29th giving directions to ground party. 31st The Granites to Lake MacKay and return with Rapide.
2 and 3.06.37. Flt Lt Hely, LAC W Taylor. Contact with ground party.
5.06.37 to 08.37. Western and Central Australian geological and geophysical survey.
12.07.37. Hit tin of sand on take-off from Onslow. Landed OK at Port Hedland. Tyre 'a mess.'
29.07.37 to 4.08.37. Flt Lt Hely, LAC W Taylor. Pt Hedland to Derby, Halls Ck, The Granites, Alice Springs. Changed to Rapide A32 on 23rd.
(22.08.37). Due to cracks discovered in tailplane, replaced

**Above:** A14-4 with the addition fins added to the horizontal tailplane. The CAC logo is carried on the fin. (AHMofWA P021511)

at Alice Springs by Rapide. Temporary repairs made and returned to Laverton.
Traded-in to CAC.
7.07.38. Registered as VH-UXE.
25.07.38. CofA renewed.
6.02.39. Stephens Aviation Ltd, Wau, New Guinea.
(2.01.42). Offered to RAAF by Stephens Aviation.
03.42. Destroyed by enemy action.

**A14-3**
3.02.38. Delivered to 1 AD. Engines 4035, 4036.
5.02.38. Sqn Ldr Allan Leslie Walters, LAC W Taylor. Generator test; W/T test.
6 to 23.02.38. Sqn Ldr A.L. Walters, Cpl W.T. Taylor, Cpl K Connolly. Laverton to Singapore, arriving on 12th. Transport CAS to opening of Dry Dock. Laverton to Richmond, Brisbane, Charleville, Longreach, Cloncurry, Camooweal, Daly Waters, Pine Creek, Darwin, Koepang, Rambang, Sourabaya, Batavia, Palambang, Singapore. Left on return flight on 16th. Singapore to Palembang, Batavia, Bandoing, Sourabaya, Rambang, Koepang, Derby, Port Hedland, Carnarvon, Perth, Kalgoolie, Forrest, Ceduna, Adelaide, Laverton.
03.38 to 10.38. Northern Australian Survey Flt.
18.07.38. Laverton. Flt Lt A.D. Charlton. Casualty.
(21.07.38). Gipsy 4036 temporarily allotted to 1 AD from Training Depot for urgent repair work.
(5.09.38). To CAC for installation of Long Range Fuel System (1,000 miles).
(11.10.38). RAAF Laverton. Gipsy 4036, 4036.
11.10.38. Training Depot, Laverton. 10 ml N-W Alice Springs. Flt Lt A.G. Carr, Sir H Gepp, Mr P.B. Nye, LAC H.J. Tarrant, LAC J McBride. Forced landing due starboard engine, No. 4035, cutting out, oil pressure dropped, damage negligible.
25.10.38. Engine 4035 replaced by 4146.
(18.11.39). Gipsy VI II No. 4035 - Failed in flight, oil pressure dropped.
(3.05.39). W/T tests carried out.
4.07.39. Laverton. Sgt Bender. Became bogged and tilted on nose.
11.09.39. F/Off C.J. Sharpe. After landing and taxying down wind, wheels bogged on marked section of drome, tilting aircraft on nose.
18.09.39. Awaiting exhaust pipe, serviceable on 15th.
4.10.39. Allotted from C&SF to newly formed Survey Flt.
18.12.39. Tail plane Unserviceable.
7.02.40. Survey Flt. F/Off C.J. Sharpe. Mishap to u/carriage on landing, port wingtip and port oleo damaged.
24.06.40. Survey Flt. Serviceable.
8.07.40 to 15.07.40. Survey Flt, Canberra. Unserviceable.
18.07.40. Attached to Southern Qld survey detachment.
14.10.40. Survey Flt. Serviceable.
27.01.41 to 7.04.41. Unserviceable.

**Above:** The Gannet was a valiant attempt to produce an indigenous airliner, however by the time it came into service its Fokker type of construction had been overtaken by all-metal aircraft.

04.41. Service Flt.
20.05.41. Bairnsdale. Hit fence at end landing run. Port undercarriage torn off. Damaged port wing and nose. Temporarily repaired and issued to Butler Air Transport on 21.06.41 for a complete airframe and engine overhaul.
19.06.41. Sqn Ldr L.W. Law. Left Canberra for Butler, Mascot, for repairs.
07.41 to 12.41. Survey Flt. Unserviceable. At Mascot for complete overhaul.
(12.41). To be converted into ambulance.
30.01.42. Still at Butler Air Transport, Mascot.
(27.02.42). Conversion to ambulance urgent. Held up due to problems with obtaining u/carriage; to fit Anson wheels.
1.03.42. 2 AAU formed at Canberra. Gannets of Survey Flt transferred to 2 AAU after conversion to air ambulance.
23.03.42. At Butler Air Transport, Mascot. Allotted to 2 AAU after complete overhaul.
1.04.42. Mascot. Flt Lt Loxton test flew and took delivery after overhaul. To 2 AAU, Canberra.
6.04.42. Received 2 AAU.
21 to 25.04.42. Sgt Smallhorn. To Daly Waters with A14-6.
8.05.42. Detachment to be stationed at Batchelor.
15.05.42. Cylinder head gasket port engine blew out on flight from Batchelor to Katherine where damage repaired by next day.
17.05.42. Katherine to Mt Isa. Three civilian leper cases.
3.08.42. Sgt G.E. Dix. Batchelor for Millingimbi and return.
6.08.42. P/Off Ingham. Batchelor for Millingimbi, crash at Millingimbi when u/carriage collapsed on landing. Port u/carriage broken, wing tip damaged, wing damaged above u/carriage, probable internal damage. Lower fuselage damaged.
30.09.42. Millingimbi. Still Unserviceable. (RSU, Batchelor for repairs.)
8.10.42. Allotted 1 RSU.
19.11.42 1 RSU. Completed, ready for delivery.
2.12.42. Allotted 2 AAU from 1 RSU.
22.12.42. To Canberra.
31.12.42 Canberra. Unserviceable. 180 hourly inspection.
15.04.43. Sgt Smallhorn. Deliver to 3 AD for repair.
30.04.43. At Marshalls, Mascot for repair.
13.05.43. Allotted 3 AD from 2 AAU.
10.06.43. 3 AD. Inspection and rigging check completed.
15.07.43. Issued 2 AAU from 3 AD.
17.07.43. Received 2 AAU from 3 AD.
7.10.43. Received Marshall Airways from 2 AAU for repairs.
7.04.44. Received 2 AP from Marshalls.
13.04.44. Received 2 AAU from 2 AP.
31.08.44. Unserviceable, brake drums being machined.
19.10.44. W/O Miller, F/Off Kennedy. Conversion to type. Kennedy then flew a/c from Archerfield to Kingaroy.
31.10.44. F/Off Kennedy. En route to Corunna Downs, faulty compass. Precautionary landing at Rathgar Station, Parragundi.
1.11.44. Petrol taken out to a/c, then flown back to Bourke and then to Broken Hill.
4.11.44. F/Off Kennedy. On take-off from Kalgoorlie at 1500 ft the cowl on the port motor blew loose. Lost sped and dived steeply, safe landing. New cowl made by 4 AD.
11.11.44. 2 AAU. F/Off N Kennedy, F/Sgt J.B. Hooke. From Archerfield to Guildford, Geraldton, Carnarvon. On landing at 71 OBU Carnarvon cylinder head blown on port engine. Engine changed but all Sperry instruments unserviceable. Still unserviceable at Carnarvon on 30th.

22.11.44. At 71 OBU, Carnarvon, engines to be changed.
1.12.44. Second party from 17 RSU arrives with another Gipsy 6 Mk. I from A14-7. A14-3 had Mk. II engines and so complete engine change needed to make serviceable.
3.12.44. Engine change completed.
5.12.44. 17 RSU Team arrive at 71 OBU to carry out engine change.
4 and 7.12.44. Test flight. Instruments unserviceable.
9.12.44. Depart for 17 RSU Pearce.
13.12.44. 2 AAU. F/Off N.H. Kennedy. delivered to 17 RSU, Pearce, for 60 hourly.
16.12.44. Received 17 RSU from 2 AAU for 60 hourly and repairs.
1.01.45. 17 RSU awaiting allotment.
(16.01.45). Report for disposal of aircraft by Commonwealth Disposal Commission.
18.01.45. Received 2 AD from 17 RSU for storage.
9.02.45. Received 1 AOBSS for storage.
21.02.46. Converted to components.
24.07.46. Destroyed by burning.

**A14-4**

8.07.37. Test as VH-UYF.
4.11.37. Trial flight, Mascot, NSW. CofA and CofR as VH-UZW, c/n TA 59.
24.03.38. To 1 AD, Laverton. Gipsy VI Mk.II Nos. 4042 and 4045. Allotted TDL.
12.04.38. Hangared by Vacum Oil at Broken Hill.
12 to 14.04.38. Flt Lt McLean, LAC W Taylor. Laverton to Broken Hill, Alice Springs, Newcastle Waters, Darwin.
12.04.38. Hangared by Vacum Oil at Broken Hill.
(14.04.38). RAAF Laverton. Log books fwd.
18 and 20.04.38. Flt Lt McLean, LAC W Taylor. Survey of Melville Is.
20.04.38. Flt Lt McLean, LAC W Taylor. Photographic N.T. coast.
22 to 23.04.38. Flt Lt McLean, LAC W Taylor. Darwin to Newcastle Waters, Camooweal, Cloncurry.
4.05.38. Flt Lt McLean, LAC W Taylor. Cloncurry to Burketown.7.05.38. Flt Lt McLean, LAC W Taylor. Reco Lawn Hill.
8.05.38. Flt Lt McLean, LAC W Taylor. Reco Border strip.
9.05.38. Flt Lt McLean, LAC W Taylor. Burketown to Cloncurry.
14.05.38. Flt Lt McLean, LAC W Taylor. Cloncurry to Burketown.14.05.38. Flt Lt McLean, LAC W Taylor. Photographic Border strip.
15 and 16.05.38. Flt Lt McLean, LAC W Taylor. Photographic Lawn Hill.
16.05.38. Flt Lt McLean, LAC W Taylor. Burketown to Cloncurry.
23 to 24.05.38. Flt Lt McLean, LAC W Taylor. Cloncurry to Burnette Down, Daly Waters, Wave Hill, Derby.
26 and 27.05.38. Flt Lt McLean, LAC W Taylor. Photographic Yampi sound.
28.05.38. Flt Lt McLean, LAC W Taylor. Derby to Halls Creek, Daly Waters.
5.06.38. Flt Lt McLean, LAC W Taylor. Photographic McArthur River area.
6.06.38. Flt Lt McLean, LAC W Taylor. Daly Waters to Katherine and Photography.
8.06.38. Flt Lt McLean, LAC W Taylor. Photography Cullen area.
9.06.38. Flt Lt McLean, LAC W Taylor. 'Key strips Yeralba and Sth Alligator.'
10.06.38. Flt Lt McLean, LAC W Taylor. Photography Fergusson River.
11.06.38. Flt Lt McLean, LAC W Taylor. Reconnaissance Howley Ck Area.
13 to 17.06.38. Flt Lt McLean, LAC W Taylor. Katherine to Daly Waters, Camooweal, Cloncurry, Burnett Downs(?), (?), Daly Waters.
18.06.38. Flt Lt McLean, LAC W Taylor. Photographic McArthur River then Daly Waters to Kathrine.
19.06.38. Flt Lt McLean, LAC W Taylor. Photographic Brocks Ck.
20.06.38. Flt Lt McLean, LAC W Taylor. Reconnaissance flight.
21.06.38. Flt Lt McLean, LAC W Taylor. Photography Sth Alligator River.
26.06.38. Flt Lt McLean, LAC W Taylor. Photography Ferguson River.
27.06.38. Flt Lt McLean, LAC W Taylor. Photography Yeurabla area.
28 and 30.06.38. Flt Lt McLean, LAC W Taylor. Photography Ferguson River area.
30.06.38. Flt Lt McLean, LAC W Taylor. Katherine to Daly Waters.
1.07.38. Flt Lt McLean, LAC W Taylor. Daly Waters to Cloncurry.
11 to 12.07.38. Flt Lt McLean, LAC W Taylor. Cloncurry to Longreach, Charlville, Bourke, Laverton.
19.09.38. To de Havilland for inspection of airscrews. 1030 hrs.
25.09.38. Allotted TDL.
(6.10.38). Aircraft at Richmond. To be given 120 hr inspection in lieu of 250 hr when 25 hr extension of 250 expires.
20.02.39. At TDL, serviceable.
(3.05.39). W/T tests carried out.
4.10.39. Allotted from C&SF to newly formed Survey Flt.
29.01.40. F/Off Burden. Arrived Richmond from Scone, NSW.
8.07.40. Survey Flt, Canberra. Unserviceable until 30.09.40.
8.02.41. Survey Flt. Gipsy VI Mk. II Nos.4042 and 4045 to De Havilland.
10.04.41. Survey Flt. Still awaiting engines.
23.06.41. F/Off H.A. Gamble. Arrived Canberra from Benalla on completion survey.

26.06.41. Sqn Ldr L.W. Law. Left for Townsville on photo survey.
10.11.41. Flt Lt Gamble and three crew. Arrived 6 EFTS, Tamworth, for photographic duties.
22.12.41. To Canberra for conversion to air ambulance.
14.01.42. Received 1 AD from Survey Fl for overhaul.
16.01.42. Issued 1 AD from Canberra.
1.03.42. 2 AAU formed at Canberra. Gannets of Survey Flt transferred to 2 AAU after conversion to air ambulance.
14.03.42. At 1 AD undergoing a complete overhaul. Ambulance fittings already installed.
25.03.42. Allotted 2 AAU from 1 AD when serviceable.
9.04.42. Issued Canberra from 1 AD.
13.04.42. Received 2 AAU from 1 AD.
30.04.42. Canberra. Serviceable.
10.05.42. Force landing after starboard engine cut out. Hit stone on landing in paddock, skidded and went over on nose when starboard wheel collapsed. Longerons twisted, nose damaged.
18.05.42. At 1 AD for repairs.
31.05.42. Laverton. Unserviceable, repairs to airframe, modified to ambulance aircraft.
22.06.42. Allotted and issued to 2 AAU from 1 AD. Repaired, flown Laverton to Canberra.
23 to 30.06.42. 2 AAU. P/Off Thorley. Flew to Charters Towers and Townsville. Patients collected and flown to Brisbane and Sydney.
7 to 18.07.42. 2 AAU. P/Off Thorley. Canberra to Charters Towers and return.
20.07.42. Unserviceable at 2 AAU.
31.07.42. Bankstown. Unserviceable.
31.08.42. 2 AAU, Canberra. Serviceable.
21.09.42. Unserviceable at 2 AAU.
22.09.42. 2 AAU. Sgt G.E. Dix. Canberra to Wagga Wagga to Mascot.
24 to 25.09.42. Sgt G.E. Dix. Canberra to Archerfield to collect 2 patients for transport to Mascot.
25 to 26.09.42. Lt Loxton. To Archerfield to transport 3 patients to Mascot. Sgt G.E. Dix. Returned to Canberra.
27.09.42. F/Sgt G.E. Dix and two crew. Canberra to Narromine to Mascot with two patients.
30.09.42. Canberra. Serviceable.
2.10.42. Sgt G.E. Dix. Detached to Archerfield, attached to 4 Communications Flt.
10.10.42. Sgt G.E. Dix. Archerfield for Maryborough, returned due to bad weather.
26.10.42. 2 AAU. Unserviceable at Archerfield.
31.10.42. Archerfield. Unserviceable, repairs to airframe after hail storm damage.
8.11.42. Sgt Smallhorn. Archerfield for Maryborough and return.
15.11.42. Sgt Smallhorn. Archerfield to Sydney. Landed at Coffs Harbour due to bad weather. Patient to Sydney by train. Returned next day.
20.11.42. Sgt Smallhorn. Archerfield for Melbourne with two patients. Forced landing beach at Terrigal owing to petrol blockage, patient moved to Sydney. Take off Terrigal to Mascot on 22nd. Return to Canberra on 26th.
28.11.42. Sgt Smallhorn. To Archerfield to carry out detached duties.
30.11.42. Canberra. Unserviceable.
7.01.43. Left Sydney forced to land Coffs Harbour due bad weather. Next day left Coffs Harbour but had to return, engine seized.
25.02.43. Sgt Smallhorn and crew. Depart Archerfield for Kingaroy and Maryborough and return with two patients.
(4.03.43). Reported as *very old and difficult to maintain in an airworthy condition*.
3.04.43. Allotted Ansett, Mascot, for complete overhaul.
5.04.43. F/Off Thorley. Ferried a/c to Mascot.
13.04.43. Received Ansett from 2 AAU.
4.12.43. Allotted 2 AAU from 2 AP on receipt from Ansett.
31.12.43. Allotted from 2 AP to 2 AAU on receipt from Ansett, Mascot, after completion repairs.
28.02.44. Issued and received 2 AP from Ansett.
6.03.44. Issued 2 AAU from 2 AP.
7.03.44. Received 2 AAU from 2 AP.
31.03.44. F/Off G.E. Dix. Kingaroy. Load test.
1.04.44. F/Off G.E. Dix. Kingaroy to Corunna Downs for duty with detachment.
9.04.44. F/Off G.E. Dix arrives to take over detachment.
12 to 13.05.44. F/Off G.E. Dix. Left Corunna Downs for Yanrey. Did not find Yanrey and landed on edge salt lake about 90 miles south Exmouth because of fuel shortage. Douglas arrived afternoon with fuel. Flew to Yanrey next day, collected 2 patients and returned Corunna Downs.
25.05.44. Landed 74 OBU, Yanrey, to convey LAC Reynolds who had been badly burnt in Transport Section to Guilford.
3 to 9.06.44. Flt Lt Byfield. Ambulance flights each day.
2.07.44. Reported lost between Onslow and Potshot. Landed North-West Cape.
18 to 21.07.44. Flt Lt Byefield. Arrived from Corunna Downs with MO to inspect camp and evacuate Sgt Kirby to Port Headland hospital. Ambulance flight.
31.07.44. Corunna Downs. Serviceable. Has been held back to conserve hours as 180 hourly has to be done at Perth.
25.08.44. F/Off G.E. Dix (401423); Sgt Norman Catton; Sqn Ldr J.C. Sangster (medical branch), W/O N Cotton. Crashed into sea in Exmouth Gulf, 1 mile off Landine Strip. All killed.
26.08.44. Many pieces of wreckage scattered on seabed. USN assisting with recovery.
31.08.44. Corunna Downs. Unserviceable, crashed awaiting salvage, not yet written off.
7.09.44. To 4 CRD for conversion.
21.09.44. Approval to convert.

**A14-5**

10.37. Completed as VH-UZW.

13.08.38. To RAAF.
23.08.38. Received 1 AD and allotted to Survey Flt, Laverton. Gipsy VI Mk. II Nos. 4145 and 4146.
23.09.38. Allotted TDL.
(14.10.38). One engine to be removed and flown to Alice Springs to be installed in A14-3.
28.11.38. Engine 4146 replaced by 4189.
(3.05.39). W/T tests carried out.
4.10.39. Allotted from C&SF to newly formed Survey Flt.
24.06.40. Survey Flt. Serviceable.
7.10.40. Survey Flt. Unserviceable.
11.11.40. Survey Flt. Serviceable.
04.41. Survey Flt. Serviceable.
21.04.41. Airframe to be overhauled while engines are overhauled at 1 AD.
23.04.41. To be flown to Ansett at Essendon this day for overhaul.
05.41 & 06. Survey Flt. Serviceable.
07.41. Survey Flt. Unserviceable.
(13.05.41). Ambulance, overhaul and modification.
7.08.41. Sqn Ldr Law, Sqn Ldr Borland. Prototype of improved ambulance installation completed by Ansett Airways Ltd flight tested. Law to fly back to Canberra today.
9.08.41. Received Survey Flt from Ansett.
(13.12.41). Authorisation of extension of flying hours.
01.42 & 02.42. Survey Flt. Unserviceable.
1.03.42. 2 AAU formed at Canberra, Gannets of Survey Flt transferred to 2 AAU after conversion to air ambulance.
10.03.42. Allotted to 2 AAU.
12.03.42. P/Off Ingham. Left Canberra for Daly Waters with A14-7. Wait at Mildura after forced landing of A14-7.
14 to 16.03.42. Mildura to Daly Waters.
23.03.42. Issued and received from Survey Flt by 2 AAU.
28.03.42. Daly Waters. Ingham? Tipped on nose on landing. Can be temporarily repaired.
31.03.42. Daly Waters. Unserviceable, temporary repairs after nose over.
6.04.42. Daly Waters. Return to Canberra.
7.04.42. Oodnadatta. Unserviceable due blown head gasket, extensive damage, engine requires replacement.
18.04.42. Arrived Canberra.
30.05.42. Modified as ambulance aircraft.
8 to 14.06.42. P/Off Thorley. To Charters Towers and return to Canberra.
15.06.42. 2 AAU. Mt Russell, ACT. Flt Lt Bruce William Graham (fractured ankle), Sgt Reginald Charles Kupsch (4369), Sgt John Paul Craig (19736) (medical orderly) (Fractured shoulder blade), Sgt Glenn Gullifer Smith (408530) W/T. Crashed ½ ml from Canberra aerodrome on take-off, port motor failed. Not repairable.
3.07.42. Convert to components.

**A14-6**

See A14-1.

**A14-7**

25.06.40. Received 1 AD from CAC. Engines Menasco Nos 6048 and 6049.
3.07.40. Allotted to Survey Flt, Canberra. Unserviceable due engines.
8.07.40. Survey Flt. Serviceable.
13.07.40. Menasco engines replaced with Gipsy VI engines.
16.07.40. To Darwin for survey work.
30.07.40. Survey Flt, Canberra. P/Off R.R.H. Winter, LAC Martin. Forced landing due inspection cowl on port engine becoming loose. Martin ordered to bail out. Winter made successful landing.
18.11.40. Survey Flt. Canberra aerodrome. Flt Lt L.W. Law, Cpl N.A. Boddington (1974), AC1 R.C. Caswell (33121). Port engine failure caused by partial failure of supercharger, successfully forced landed on aerodrome. Engine required complete overhaul.
(26.08.41). Modification of engine bays.
31.08.41. Received at Pearce, WA, from Survey Flt.
2.02.42. Proceed to Survey Flt, Canberra for replacement.
9.02.42. At Pearce, WA.
1.03.42. 2 AAU formed at Canberra, Gannets of Survey Flt transferred to 2 AAU after conversion to air ambulance.
12.03.42. Sgt G.E. Dix. Left Canberra for Daly Waters with A14-5. Successful force landing in paddock 5 ml from Mildura aerodrome.
13.03.42. Successful take off for Mildura aerodrome.
14 to 16.03.42. Left Mildura and proceeded to Daly Waters with A145.
23.03.42. Issued and received by 2 AAU from Survey Flt.
31.03.42. Daly Waters. Serviceable.
6 to 10.04.42. Daly Waters to Canberra.
30.05.42. Modified as ambulance aircraft.
19.08.42. Sgt Smallhorn. Canberra for Batchelor to return the crew of A14-3 to base.
24.09.42. Lt Loxton. Canberra for Archerfield. Precautionary landing at Camden with engine trouble. Proceeded to Mascot to hand aircraft over to de Havilland for repair.
30.09.42. Mascot. Unserviceable, repairs to engine.
8.10.42. Allotted to De Havilland from 2 AAU for engine change.
10.11.42. Allotted 2 AAU from De Havilland via 2 AD.
23.11.42. Issued 2 AAU from 2 AD.
28.11.42. Smallhorn. To Archerfield on detachment.
19.10.42. Archerfield. Damaged in hail storm.
31.12.42. Archerfield. Unserviceable due hail damage.
22.02.43. F/Off Thorley. Arrived Archerfield direct from Mascot.
(4.03.43). Reported as *very old and difficult to maintain in an airworthy condition. Airframe has a very limited further serviceable life.*
9.04.43. Lt C.S. Hill. Ferry flight to Mascot.

13.04.43. Allotted and received Marshall Airways for repair. Issued next day.
29.09.43. Received 2 AP from Marshalls, allotted 2 AAU.
3.10.43. Issued 2 AAU from 2 AP.
9.10.43. Mascot to Amberley for final check and to be returned to its unit.
10.10.43. Aircraft now at Amberley for repairs.
11.10.43. Received 3 AD from 2 AP for repair.
9.11.43. Issued and delivered to 2 AAU.
10.11.43. F/Off N.H. Byfield. To Archerfield with 3 patients.
5.05.44. Allotted to MacRobertson Miller Airlines for 180 hourly.
7.05.44. Received 2 AAU on completion.
8.05.44. F/Off N.H. Byfield. Returned to Corunna Downs from Maylands after 180 hourly inspection.
12.05.44. F/Off N.H. Byfield. After A14-4 force landed, flew to 74 OBU Yanrey in its place. Stayed overnight departed for Corunna next day.
09.44. Exposure taken toll of fabric and plywood. Unfit to fly. Lt Minchin flew a/c to Pearce for inspection.
1.11.44. Pearce. At 17 RSU, Pearce, awaiting instructions.
27.11.44. Issued to 17 RSU for repair.
1.12.44. Allotted 17 RSU. Gipsy 6 Mk. I engines sent to 71 OBU, Carnarvon, for A143.
6.12.44. Received 17 RSU from 2 AAU.
1.01 to 1.07.45. 17 RSU. Awaiting instructions.
1.04.45. 17 RSU. Waiting for engines.
1.11.45. 17 RSU. Storage.
21.02.46. To be converted to components.
5.03.46. Received 14 ARD from 17 RSU.

# Chapter 23. The Vickers F.B.27 Vimy

**Above:** The Vickers Vimy G-EAOU or 'God 'El All of Us', after arrival in Australia.

On the demobilisation of the AFC in France and Egypt after the end of hostilities in 1918, the Australian Government contemplating the establishment of a Commonwealth Air Force and General Birdwood recommended that the future air force should have four squadrons as follows:

1. Sopwith Snipe fighter squadron.
2. Bristol Fighter two-seater reconnaissance squadron.
3. De Havilland D.H.9a day bomber squadron.
4. Vickers Vimy long distance and night bomber squadron.

This appears to be the first time the Vimy was proposed for the Australian air force.[1]

The Australian Prime Minister, the Rt Hon W.M. *Billy* Hughes was in Paris for the Peace Conference which ended World War I, when he was approached by Australian aviators who were desirous of attempting to fly a Handley Page biplane from London to Australia. This idea fired Hughes's imagination and he sent a cablegram to the Defence Department suggesting that a prize of £10,000 be offered for the first successful flight from London to Australia by Australian aviators. This cable was the start of what has been called the greatest air race.

Capt Ross Smith MC, DFC, AFC, and his brother, Lt Keith Smith, late of the AFC, approached Vickers Ltd for the use of a Vimy bomber in the proposed race.1 The Vimy was a twin engined biplane bomber which had first flown in November 1917 and more than 1,000 were on order until the Armistice resulted in wholesale cancellation of military orders. The war ended before the type could be used operationally. Squadron deliveries commenced in July 1919, the type serving until 1924, although some soldiered on as parachute trainers. A civil version was developed as the Vernon and it was also very successful. The Vimy biplane supplied to the Smith brothers was a standard machine, serial F8630, powered by two 360-hp Rolls Royce Eagle VIII engines with all military equipment removed.

In June 1919 Vickers had approached Hughes and offered to set up and operate an aircraft factory and run an aerial service in Australia.[2] Vickers proposed to build 10 Rolls Royce Vimy bombers; five Commercial Vimys; 20 Viking amphibians; and three Valentine flying boats.[3] There appears to be some connection between this offer and the proposal set out by Brigadier-General T.A. Blamey, the Chief of Staff, for the formation of the proposed Australian air force. Blamey's plan was for four squadrons comprising 24 Sopwith Snipe fighters, 24 Bristol Fighters for corps reconnaissance duty, 18 De Havilland D.H.9a bombers, and 10 Vickers Vimy long-distance or night bombers. There was to be 100% spares in aircraft. Blamey noted that *None of the machines which have been recommended are available as gift machines.* The gift machines are of types of which the Air Ministry has a surplus.[4] Vickers may have seen the race as an opportunity for them to become established in Australia and made the Vimy, now bearing the civil registration G-EAOU, available to the Smith brothers to prove its usefulness in long distance flights.

G-EAOU left the United Kingdom in November 1919 with the Smith boys and mechanics Sergeants W.H. Shiers and J.M. Bennett as crew. They covered the 11,130 miles in just under 136 flying hours, landing at Port Darwin on

**Left:** The Smith brothers made a film of their journey and the cameraman in the front cockpit continues filming after their triumphant flight across Australia.

10 December.[5] At Darwin they were met by Wrigley and Murphy of the AAC. (See Chapter 16).

The AWM had been quick to ask for permanent control of the Vimy, a telegram being sent to the Prime Minister suggesting that Ross Smith be asked *to give Australian War Museum first opportunity of ultimately acquiring aeroplane and equipment for nation.*[6] Hughes followed up this request and Vickers instructed Smith to hand the aeroplane over to the Commonwealth as a gift. The aircraft was formally handed over on 19 March 1920.

Ross Smith wanted to make a flight to Adelaide, his home-town, however Vickers refused permission for the flight. The Prime Minister, Hughes, gave permission for a flight over Melbourne to Adelaide and return to Point Cook. It was not until after the Vimy had departed that a cable was received from Vickers Ltd stating that they were of the opinion that it was inadvisable to fly the aircraft until the engines had been thoroughly overhauled by Rolls Royce. Concern was expressed that the repairs done to the engines during the flight across Australia were not effected by the makers and *the whole value of the flight would be lost should there be any accident now.*[7]

The Vimy was placed on show at the Royal Exhibition Building in Melbourne along with the captured and Allied aircraft returned from Europe and the Middle East for the proposed Australian war museums. The AWM had again asked for permanent possession of the Vimy in July 1920, however it had been decided to have the machine *Thoroughly overhauled by the mechanics of...*(the Department of Defence) *and all necessary action to be taken to make the machine safe for future use.*[8] This action was to make the machine fit again for flying and it was to be handed back to the Department of Defence for this purpose.[9]

The announcement of the Imperial Gift of aircraft to the Dominions saw the Australian proposals for the composition of the proposed air force changed. The only aircraft wanted in addition to the 100 Gift machines were four Vimy bombers. It has been suggested that it may have been intended to use G-EAOU as the nucleus of the four plane long-range bomber squadron proposed in 1919.[10] A Defence document addressing the task of preparing the aircraft for flight noted that the machine was suffering from exposure and would require a complete overhaul and re-trueing before being flown. The port engine had been overhauled at the CFS and was in good order but the starboard was not. The epicyclic gear case was broken and had been patched in Adelaide simply to get the aircraft back to Melbourne.[11] Defence suggested that this machine should not be flown again, but the *PM directs that all necessary action be taken to put machine in good order for flying as soon as possible.*[12] Thus it would appear that the proposed use of the Vimy by the AAC was Hughes' idea. Unfortunately, no hint of what he proposed to do with the machine has been found.

In September the Vimy was reported as being readied for flight, however by the end of January 1921 the aircraft was stored dismantled at Point Cook.[13] The Vimy was recorded as being taken on charge by 1 FTS, AAF from CFS, AAC, on 31 March 1921.[14] Although the serial designation 'A5'

**Above:** There were no airfields worthy of the name when the Vimy arrived. This is a typical example of an outback landing ground.

**Above:** The Vimy was welcomed by crowds wherever it landed. This was the first time most of these people had seen an aeroplane. (AHMofWA P017350)

was reserved for the Vickers Vimy it appears that G-EAOU was never given an 'A' number and was referred to by its civil registration.

The aircraft was apparently never flown again and was finally handed over to the AWM. The Vimy was displayed at Canberra in the Memorial's Aeroplane Hall until after the Second World War when it was given to the RAAF for storage, its place eventually being taken by the Avro Lancaster W4783 – 'G for George.'

A fund was established to raise a suitable building to house the Vimy in Adelaide. In November 1957 the aircraft was trucked to Adelaide by the RAAF. Fire gutted one of the trucks completely destroying two mainplanes, two propellers and one engine cowling. In order to have the aircraft ready in time for the official opening of the memorial, only a 'mock-up' restoration was carried out.[15] The aircraft has been on display at Adelaide's West Beach airport ever since. Although stored in a glass fronted hangar it has suffered from age and

**Above:** The Vimy was powered by two Rolls Royce engines and would have been an exceptional bomber if the First World War had continued. As it was, the type served the RAF in the Middle East for many years.

exposure to sunlight and is in a deteriorating condition in need of restoration at the time of writing. A new climate-controlled building was proposed in 2019, and the aircraft was moved to a new enclosure at the main terminal in 2022.

### Specifications

Dimensions: Span 67 ft 2 in. Length 43 ft 6½ in. Chord 10 ft 6 in. Gap 10 ft. Height 15 ft 3 in.
Areas: Wings: Upper 686 ft2, Lower 644 ft2, Total 1,220 ft2.
Performance: Speed 100 mph.
Armament: Provision was made for a load of eighteen 112-lb and two 230-lb bombs. Radio and navigation flares were also carried.

## End Notes

1 Correspondence RE: Types of Aeroplanes to be taken to Australia by Australian Flying Corps. Cable: Gen Birdwood to Defence, Melbourne, 27.01.1919. Copy in Alan Fraser Collection.
2 NAA ACT CRS A461/1 Item L314/1/1 Pt.1. Aeroplane Construction in Australia. Letter: SBAC to Prime Minister, 26.06.1919.
3 Ibid. Copy Cable; Vickers to Prime Minister.
4 NAA Vic MP367 (Box10) Item A415/1/1214. Aviation Gift - Aeroplanes, Etc. Secret "Note on Australian Air Service". T Blamey, 21.06.1919.
5 This epic flight is outside the scope of this work and readers are referred to Grenfell Price's "The Skies Remember" and N Eustis's "The Greatest Air Race", both published by Angus and Robertson.
6 NAA ACT CRS A2/1 Item 1920/2299. Aviation - Disposal of Sir Ross Smith's Machine. Gullett to PM, 8.12.1919.
7 NAA ACT CRS A2 Item 1920/2299. Op Cit. Vickers to PM, 19.03.1920.
8 Ibid. PM Dept to Defence, 23.04.1920.
9 NAA ACT CRS A2 Item 1919/2299. Op Cit. PM Dept to AWM, 17.07.1920.
10 See Coulthard-Clark, C. *The Third Brother*, P.163.
11 NAA CRS A2 Item 1920/2299. Op Cit. "Vickers Vimy Aeroplane". Defence to PM, 10.05.1920.
12 Ibid. Memo to letter of 10.05.20.
13 Ibid. Minute: Disposal of Sir Ross Smith's Aeroplane, 29.01.1921.
14 Daily Routine Orders, CFS, Laverton and Point Cook. 3.09.20 to 3.08.23. Copy in RAAF Museum, Point Cook.
15 NAA ACT CRS A705/1 Item 129/1/92. Transfer of Vickers Vimy Aircraft from RAAF Canberra to Adelaide for Air Memorial to the late Sir Ross and Sir Keith Smith. Minute; "Repairs to the Vickers Vimy Aircraft". To AMTS, 18.12.1957.

**Above:** The exhibition of the aircraft sent to Australia by the British Government under the Imperial Gift scheme, the German aircraft returned for display in the proposed War Museum and the Imperial Gift aircraft was held in the Melbourne in 1920. The Vimy was also displayed alongside the Deperdussin monoplane of the AFC Point Cook flying school. These two aircraft are the only ones to survive to the present day, the Vimy in Adelaide and the Deperdussin in the Australian War Memorial's collection.

**Right:** The Vickers Vimy in Aeroplane Hall of the AWM. Surrounding the Vimy from the left may be seen the tail of the Parer and MacIntosh D.H.9, Albatros D.Va 5390/17, S.E.5a A2-4, Pfalz D.XII 2600/18, Avro 504K and the Deperdussin monoplane taxi trainer used at Point Cook during World War I. See Chapter 13 for a view of the Fairey IIID on display with some of the same aircraft. (AWM)

**This Page:** The Vickers Vimy on display at Adelaide's airport. It has been moved from its old hangar to the new enclosure at the main terminal. (via P Bravo)

**This Page:** The Vickers Vimy on display at Adelaide's airport. It has been moved from its old hangar to the new enclosure at the main terminal. (via P Bravo)

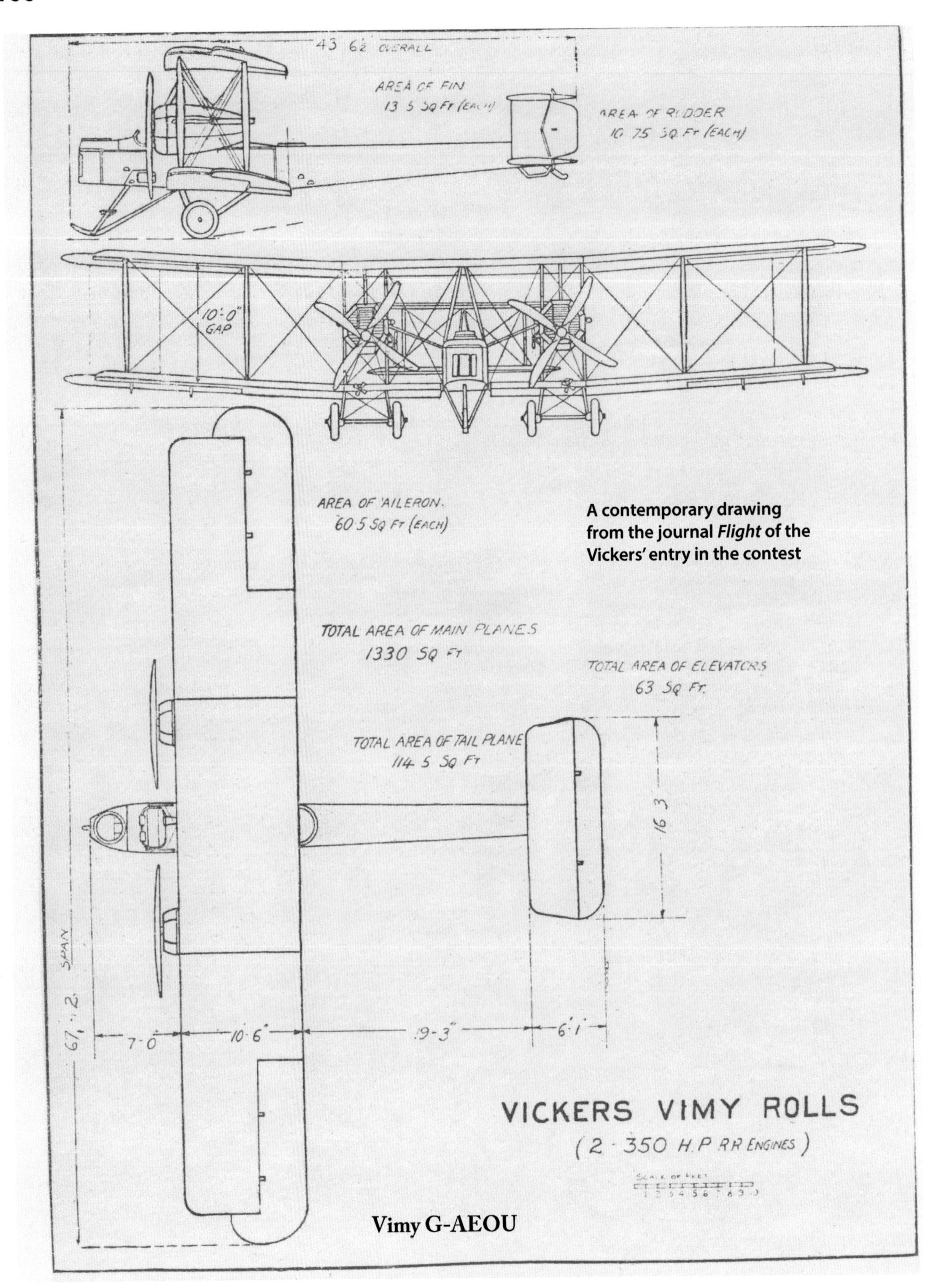


A contemporary drawing from the journal *Flight* of the Vickers' entry in the contest

Vimy G-AEOU

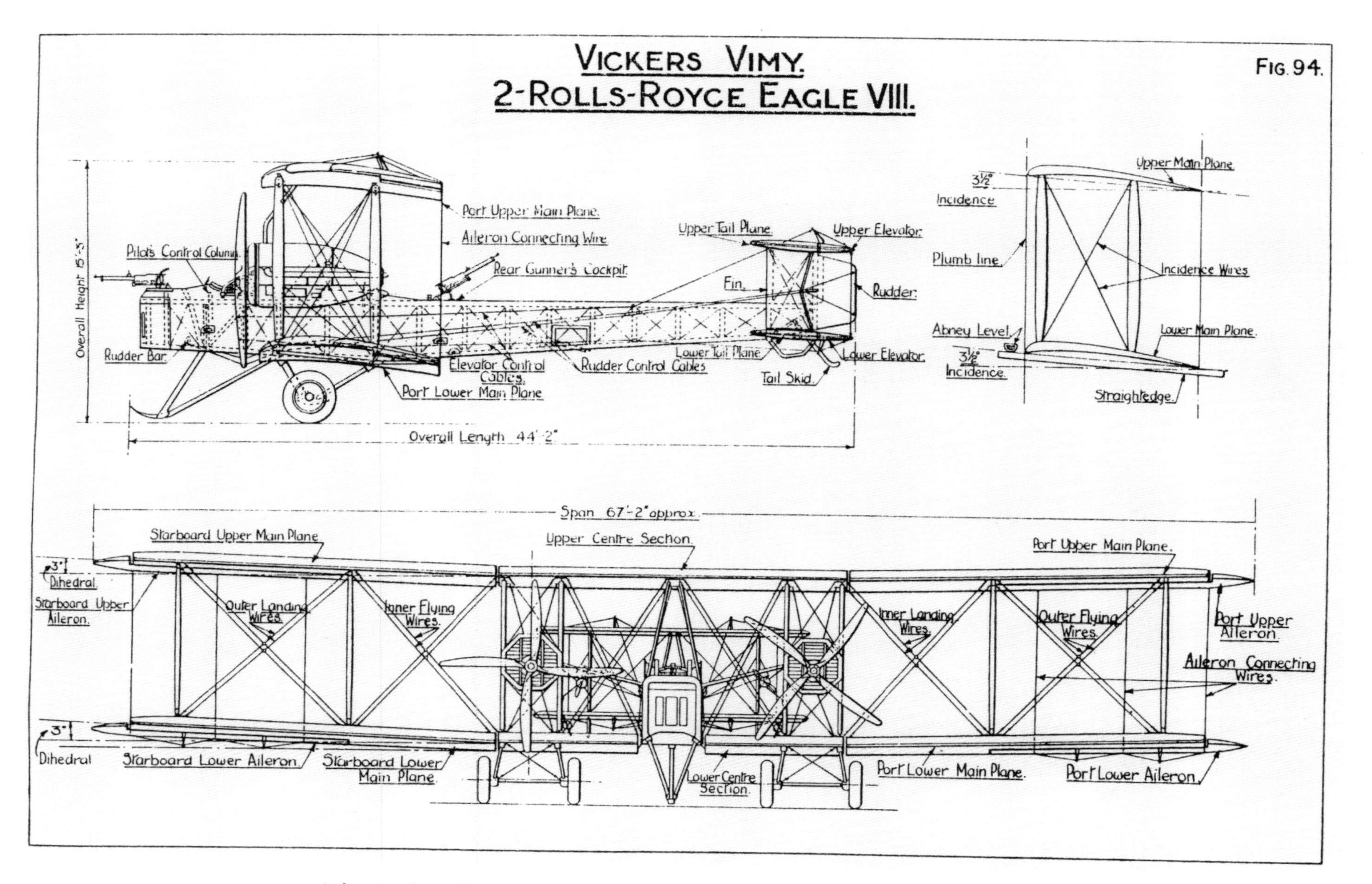


A drawing from the manual for the Vickers Vimy bomber showing the military version of the type. Being a new type then entering RAF service, it is no wonder that it was thought that G-EAOU could be the leader of a long-range bombing force for Australia.

# Chapter 24. Wackett (RAAF Experimental Section) Widgeon

**Above:** The Widgeon I outside the tent at Botany Bay before its first attempt at flight. Note the out of sequence registration G-AEKB.

At about 3.10 pm on 6 January 1930, the amphibian Widgeon II took off from Point Cook with Flt Lt Fredrick Albert Briggs as pilot, and Captain, the Honourable Hugh R. Grosvenor, ADC to the Governor of South Australia, and LAC D.C. Ewen as passengers. About an hour later the aircraft was seen to enter a *vertical dive at about between 400 and 500 feet from the water. It was apparently oscillating about its longitudinal axis...it continued this motion until it struck the water and entirely disappeared* in about 30 feet of water.[1] A rescue was immediately organised and two Moth trainers flew over the wreckage. Seagull A9-3 was in the workshops and even if serviceable could not have been used due to the rough sea condition. F/Off F.J.B. Wright followed the drift of wreckage which led him to *a large black piece of the hull of the Widgeon. Clinging on this piece of wreckage was a man...I could say with a fair amount of certainty that the man was neither Briggs nor Grosvenor. I circled around the man, who was lying in the water with both arms on top of the piece of wreckage* until about 5.20 pm when he slowly sank back into the water.[2] Wight tried to direct a rescue boat to the survivor, but he had disappeared.

The tragedy gained headlines in the press and the story was repeated in newspapers across Australia. The South Australian *Border Watch* reported on 9 January, as follows:

*Wrecked almost beyond recognition, with the propeller and both wings so broken that hardly a square yard of material was left, and with the hull in pieces, the Widgeon II. was recovered in 32 ft. of water, one and a half miles from Point, Cook yesterday morning. After the amphibian had been investigated by a diver, the wreck was secured by cable and hauled up by the derrick punt. It was taken to Williamstown and transported thence by motor truck to-Point Cook.*

*The Royal Australian Air Force enquiry board began its enquiries yesterday, but. cannot make its findings public before the coroner has given his finding. The coroner cannot hold an inquest until, the bodies are recovered. Air Force experts are unwilling to express opinions about the cause of the smash pending an official reason, but it is thought likely that there was a structural breakage. If the engine had merely failed, it is said, the dive would not have been so sudden. After the. recovery of the machine, Police, and Air Force patrols began to search the coast. Diver K.J. Martin, made an extensive search of the sea floor, where the amphibian crashed, in case the bodies had not come to the surface, but nothing was' found. At Dawn on Tuesday the Harbour Trust*

**Above & Below:** Construction of the Widgeon I's hull. The diagonal strips of planking to the hull are well seen. The hull sides had vertical and diagonal planking. (via National Archives of Australia)

*launch... accompanied by a hopper barge and towing a punt, left Williamstown to begin the salvage of the plane.*

*Two Point Cook airmen searching, on Tuesday night could not locate the wreck, and early yesterday morning Flight-Lieut. E. J. Wackett; (brother of the designer of the wrecked machine), and Flying-Office Wight were aloft, scouring; the water for the plane. Wackett was the first to sight the wreck at the bottom of the bay. The outline of the machine was clearly visible to him from a good height soon after the arrival of the Harbour Trust vessel. Diver C. Fox was immediately lowered into the: water. He returned in a few minutes and reported that the plane had been completely wrecked, with its nose buried in the sand. There was no sign of the bodies. It was impossible; however, for him, to move among the: tangled mass of wreckage: to make a thorough search. He descended again, and made a rope fast to the wrecked. machine; and the machine was then lifted. The greater portion of the plane was hauled out of the water and made fast to the punt.*

*The hull had been smashed, to pieces; the wings were crumpled and there was scarcely a square yard of fabric that was not tattered and torn. Evidently, the machine had struck the bottom with terrific force. It is believed that the three airmen were not strapped in the plane at- the time of the crash, and that they were killed instantly and the bodies washed away.*

The Widgeon was salvaged the next day and brought ashore, it was a total wreck. The bodies of the crew were never recovered.

Thus ended the association of the RAAF and the Wackett Widgeon, the first aircraft designed by Sqn Ldr L Wackett and built by the RAAF Experimental Section, Randwick. It was not the end of the Widgeon story as controversy over its design and safety continued throughout the investigation into the crash and brought into question Wackett's competence as an aircraft designer.

The Widgeon was designed by Wackett on behalf of the Civil Aviation Branch in 1923. Wackett states that he sold the Controller the idea of constructing a small flying boat which might be of service along the coast.[3] If successful the design could be used for commercial passenger service in Australia. The resultant flying boat was of tractor layout powered by a 240-hp Siddeley Puma engine with seating for four in double seats. Two passengers were accommodated immediately over the centre of gravity, abaft of which was a large compartment for luggage and mail. Special care was taken to enable passengers to be embarked without difficulty from the front or rear of the main planes, bracing wires or other obstacles being avoided in the design of the centre-section.

The hull was built up on formers which were later removed and five main spruce longitudinals - four longerons and a keel - were substituted. The two layers of hull planking were of $^{1}/_{8}$ in Queensland maple separated by a layer of varnished fabric and fastened by boat builders copper nails

**Above:** The Hull of Widgeon I complete with registration G-AEKB with the upper wing centre-section in place and engine being installed.

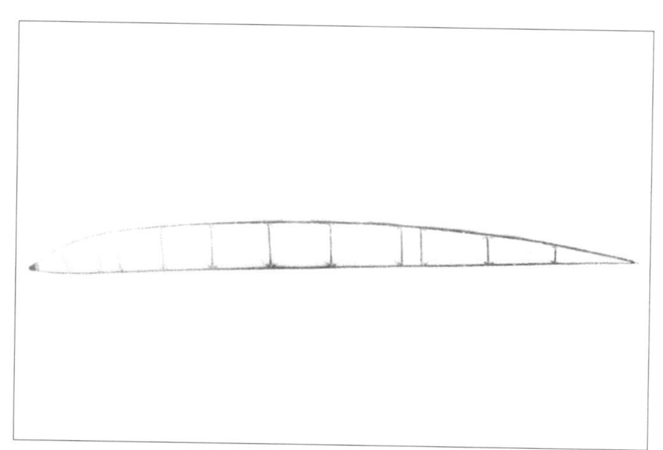

**This Page:** Constructing the wings of the Widgeon I. (via National Archives of Australia)

and brass screws, no glue being used in the construction. The hull bottom being of double-diagonal planks.

The main planes were designed to fold forwards to minimise stowage space. The wings were built up on two solid spruce spars. The leading edges were rolled sheet brass with a piano wire trailing edge. Wing and tailplane ribs were of hard drawn 30-gauge brass, being rustless, strong and easily worked. The fabric was not stitched to the ribs but was pulled into the rib channel and retained by a wire passing through eyelets. Upper and lower flanges were of channel section with light tubes forming the struts, the whole being soldered together. One unusual feature of the design was that the rear hull fairing was a 10 foot 6 inch dingy. This was designed to be used in an emergency or where normal boat transport was not available.[4] The Supermarine Company complained to the Australian authorities in the UK that the Widgeon was a copy of their earlier designs. This allegation was sent to Wackett but no reply was recorded.[5]

There was controversy from the start of construction as to why the Government was building a flying boat and that this would have been better left to private enterprise. The Widgeon was launched at La Perouse on the shores of Botany Bay on 7 July 1925. During taxi trials it hit a sandbank but no damage was caused to the hull. Botany Bay was not an ideal location for trials because of rough seas.

Wackett attempted to take to the air, with Brinsmead and two mechanics as passengers, on 8 July 1925. Later Wackett was to admit that he lost attention as the flying boat hit a large swell which lifted the aircraft into the air to a height of three feet and it then dove at 30 knots into the sea. The force of the impact stove in the bow swamping the cockpit and left the aircraft floating with its nose submerged and the four occupants floundering in the waters of Botany Bay. Wackett recalled that he was trapped by the controls and almost lost

**Above:** Fitting the wings to the hull of the Widgeon I. The rear hull decking is in place. This was a small dingy. (via National Archives of Australia)

**Above:** The rear hull decking of the Widgeon I was a small dingy. The idea was to provide access to shore in remote locations. (via National Archives of Australia)

**Above:** The Widgeon I outside the tent at Botany Bay before its first attempt at flight. Note the out of sequence registration G-AEKB.

his life as he got clear just as he was losing consciousness.[6] It was unfortunate that a large crowd of dignitaries including the CAS as well as various reporters, photographers and cinemaphotographers had gathered for the historic event.

The resultant mishap was sensational news and press reports showed photographs of the aircraft with its nose and lower wings covered by the sea. *Australian Aero-Submarining* was the title of an article in the British Journal *The Aeroplane*, on the attempted flight.[7] The only sane voice came from the December 1925, issue of *Aircraft* magazine which complained that the Widgeon had been *publicly condemned without a trial.*[8] The article went on to say that most newspaper readers would believe that the Widgeon was a failure whereas it had not as yet flown. The flying boat had been recovered and returned to Randwick for repairs.

Brinsmead, the Director General of Civil Aviation, came to Wackett's defence and was reported in newspapers such as the following from *The Sun* (Sydney) of 10 July 1925:

*To suggest that Squadron-Leader Wackett's Widgeon is an experimental failure' is to confess that Australia is totally incapable of designing and manufacturing aeroplanes suited to her special requirements.*

*I was on board, the Widgeon on her trial flight, and I for one will never support such a suggestion.*

*A lot of rot is being talked about the Widgeon. It is being suggested that she is nose-heavy, that her tail is too short, that her engine is too far forward, and a host of other things. It might be information for some of the experts who are saying these things to learn that there is nothing whatever experimental in the design of the Widgeon's hull, and nothing experimental about the position in which her engine is placed. The experimental features are in her wings, where delicate adjustments of the utmost technicality have been made.*

*I was in the' seaplane when she came to grief in Botany Bay, and I have the greatest confidence in her. Squadron-Leader Wackett is equally confident, and as he is easily the most brilliant man we have in Australia in aerodynamics, I see no reason to fear other opinions.*

Because of this adverse publicity Wackett vowed to keep the news of any future trials secret and *give her a trial flight without any fuss or publicity.*[9] This he did on 3 December with three passengers.

Flt Lt I.E. McIntyre tested the flying boat on 7 April and reported that the Widgeon I had a *very good performance and...* (met) *all the requirements of a small single engined flying boat.* The machine could be flown *hands and feet off the controls* and there was an *entire absence of longitudinal change of trim due to throttling the engine.* It was outstandingly easy to land, the take-off was easy without any porpoising and the flying qualities were considered *exceptionally good for a single engined flying boat.*[10]

Arrangements were made with the CCA for the Widgeon I to carry out trials as to its suitability as a training machine for the RAAF Seaplane Flight. The Widgeon I was to be transferred to Point Cook where *Its first use will be as a machine for the training of pilots for "Seagulls". With this end*

**Above:** Widgeon I prior to launching.

*in view it is desired that you go into the matter of fitting the machine with a wheel undercarriage so that it may be used as an amphibian.*[11]

The Puma engine was replaced by a 300-hp Nimbus supplied by the Civil Aviation Branch. Williams wanted a Rolls Royce Eagle VIII fitted before 101 Flight carried out any RAAF tests. In the event the RAAF took over the Nimbus and ordered a replacement for the CAB. The Nimbus was mounted six inches further forward, the wing dihedral was increased from 3½° to 5°, the elevators and rudder were almost doubled in area, the bow lengthened, and the fuel feed and control systems were redesigned. An amphibian undercarriage was also fitted.

The now amphibious Widgeon I was requested to take part in the escort of HMS *Renown* when it visited Sydney in March/April 1927. The RAAF would greet visiting warships. A flight, usually of Seagull III would meet the visitor out of sight of land and escort them to port. This was usually, of necessity, the Seagull III amphibians. On this occasion the Widgeon and three Seagulls were to meet the *Renown as soon after daylight as possible and escort her as long as possible.* On 14 April the Widgeon and one Seagull was to carry a W/T and one of HMA ships would listen-in for signals *in case of emergency.* This latter flight proved eventful as Wackett, accompanied by Flt Lt McIntyre, flew into very unsettled weather which ultimately caused them to alight at Rose Bay in torrential rain. The Widgeon I was left at its moorings while a *storm raged for three days.*[12] On the 15th McIntyre had attempted to fly back but had to land at once due to excessive water on the engine. The next day Wackett attempted to fly off but *just when turning on the water to take off, a squall nearly blew the machine over sideways and a wing tip was crushed owing to hydrostatic pressure when immersed. The weather was cyclonic continuously.* The machine was removed by road to Randwick following a *strenuous effort* on the Sunday. Wackett commented that much had been learned from these incidents which would be incorporated in improvements and also applied to Widgeon II.[13]

After test at 1 FTS, Widgeon I was assessed as being *eminently suitable as an instructional type with a modified windscreen to keep* (the) *crew dry.*[14] The biplane was kept in use at 1 FTS for a period of two years for preliminary flying boat training. Although Wackett asserted that *many pilots flew the aircraft during training courses in subsequent years*[15] it has been reported as being little used.[16] A.T. Cole recording a 10 minute instructional flight on it on 25 July 1927, the only mention of the type in his log book. Commander Frank G Crowther, RAN, has recorded how he and Geoffrey A Hall attended the 4th Course at 1 FTS in 1926. He remembered that *Our course, numbering 24 in all, consisted of 2 Naval Officers, 4 Army Officers, 1 New Zealand Army officer, 1 Air Force officer, 12 cadets and 4 N.C,O.'s. This was the largest course undertaken by the R.A.A.F. since it was formed. six of the Cadets were for the R.A.F. The* ab initio *training was carried out in Avro 504K aircraft and the more advanced training in S.E.5a, D.H.9a's. In our case Hall and I only flew D.H.9's and then went on to Fairey IIID seaplanes. We also did a lot of dual on Wackett's Widgeon 1, but were never allowed to fly it solo, as*

**Above:** The result of *Australian Aero-Submarining*. Wackett was lucky he was not drowned when he became trapped in the cockpit.

*it was somewhat unstable and required an experienced pilot to understand some of it's habits. Shortly after we had used it, it was condemned and broken up.*[17]

The popular Sydney *Smith's Weekly* newspaper, in an article about Point Cook titled 'Where a Crash is part of the Day's Work,' reported that the Widgeon I, *now housed in the hangars at Point Cook* was *used by thrill-seeking officers for taxiing round the bay, and at times is requisitioned by fishing parties.* The article stated that the cost of the machine was £65,000 and no doubt the tone was deliberate to create controversy, still it gives an idea of how the Widgeon was viewed by some.

In October 1929 it was reported as being in *such a condition that it requires extensive overhaul and reconditioning before any further use can be made of it.*[18] As it was not considered economical to repair the aircraft it was recommended that it be reduced to produce and the Nimbus engine, that had only 113 hours, be disposed of. The Widgeon I was reported as having been burnt on 11 December and the Nimbus engine was given back to the CAB.

It is not known if the Widgeon I was ever given RAAF markings; photographs suggest that it retained its civil registration during its time at Point Cook.[19] It is interesting to compare its service with that of the Widgeon II when one considers that *at the time of the construction of the Widgeon I, no non-corrosive materials were available, and full precautions were not possible. In Widgeon II. all metal fittings are of non-corrosive metal, and so are all bolts and nuts. The steel tubes are protected internally and externally.*[20]

Wackett now proposed that he develop a *service type Widgeon.*[21] Thus Widgeon II was a purely military machine even though it was described as having *originated from a desire on the part of the Controller of Civil Aviation to benefit from the experience gained in the construction and operation of Widgeon I.* As early as July 1927 it was being promoted as being the aircraft for the seaplane carrier HMAS *Albatross* if it was successful in its tests.[22] The Widgeon II was apparently paid for from the CAB vote. It is thought that the CAS, Williams, was instrumental in allowing Wackett to pursue his dream of constructing aircraft in Australia.

The Widgeon II was designed with a Jaguar IV engine *to operate over long distances.*[23] Different materials were used in the construction of the Widgeon II; the hull and spars were of Tasmanian blackwood, the hull had a skin of Queensland beech which showed a considerable resistance to water absorption, and the struts were of hoop pine, the propeller was constructed of laminations of Queensland maple. Australian timbers were used exclusively throughout. Water rudders and bilge pumps were of non-corrodible Monel metal and stainless steel. The landing wheels were Monel metal and fitted with Australian Dunlop balloon tyres. An un-sinkable three man dingy was also incorporated into the design. The amphibian was painted in battleship-grey pyroxalin lacquer and carried RAAF roundels but no A-number.

The flying characteristics of Widgeon II were the subject of an intensive cross examination during the AAIC investigation of its crash. Early trials had revealed that *Once in the air, the amphibian has a very much better turn of speed than the "Seagull", but is not so controllable coming out of turns.*[24] Wackett considered that the amphibian did not possess any unusual characteristics when in a bank. It used to fall away to starboard when stalled but the fitting of slots rectified this. A considerable amount of questioning of witnesses was directed towards the operation of the retractable undercarriage. It appeared that it was possible to foul the controls when dual controls were fitted. It was extremely difficult to lower the undercarriage according to Sqn Ldr A.E. Hempel. He considered that the aircraft did not show any dangerous

**Above:** Widgeon I on the water.

**Above & Facing Page:** G-AEKB after conversion to an amphibian and wearing a new colour scheme.

tendencies in the air. He noted that *you came out of a steep dive quicker in a normal flying boat by shutting the engine off as this makes the nose come up and tail down* the tendency was there in Widgeon II but not to the same extent as in a Seagull III.[25] The Committee concluded that while there were several theories which could explain why the amphibian went into a dive and failed to recover, there was insufficient evidence to *justify the Committee in selecting any one of them as the cause of the accident*. At the time of the accident the aircraft was fitted with dual control and the wheels were two-fifths down.[26]

The AAIC noted that the amphibian had been *designed, constructed and tested by the same individual, whose experience as a designer was limited.*[27] It was suggested that the drawings of the Widgeon II be checked in England as

evidence cast *considerable doubt* as to whether the design of the Widgeon *was carried out in accordance with ordinary engineering standards of safety.*[28] The enquiry was also not satisfied that the testing of the amphibian had been *carried out satisfactorily.*[29] The Air Board disagreed considering that the expense of an investigation into the design of the Widgeon II was a waste of money, but agreed to have the design calculations of the Warrigal II, which was nearing completion, checked by a competent person before that aircraft was flown.

Controversy had arisen earlier between the CAB and Wackett over the use of Monel metal in the construction of the amphibian. Chief Aircraft Inspector Howard was acquainted with the fact that Monel metal was not approved by the Air Ministry for *highly stressed aircraft fittings* and questioned its use in the Widgeon II.[30] Wackett's terse reply

**Above & Below:** The Widgeon I at Point Cook. Widgeon I is believed to have retained its civil markings while in RAAF service.

**Above:** The Nimbus powered Widgeon I hydroplaning prior to take-off.

**Below:** Manhandling the Widgeon I in the shallows.

**Above:** In its late colour scheme, G-AEKB is most probably at Point Cook where this photograph was taken. Note the Avro 504 trainer in the background.

to the CCA displays his overbearing nature in the worse light. *Before replying to the report re Monel Metal* he wrote, *I require to know the name of the author, and, to have a statement, if possible, of what experience he has had in the manipulation and use of the high grades of Monel Metal now available ...Under no circumstances shall I reply to an anonymous report.*[31] Wackett virtually considered the aircraft produced at Randwick as his own personal property. He had refused to let the CO of the Seaplane Squadron, Sqn Ldr V.R. Scriven, fly the Widgeon after Scriven had journeyed to Sydney on the orders of the CAS to test fly the aircraft.

The Australian ALO cabled the information that Monel metal was *not considered suitable* for aircraft construction, its best characteristic being its non-corrosive qualities, however stainless steel was considered to offer better weight and strength features and it was recommended that stainless steel replace any Monel metal as it became necessary during maintenance.[32] A further cable noted that the Air Ministry advised that *Monel Metal only suitable lightly stressed parts or fittings and where non-corrosive quality essential...now not used in any British aircraft.*[33]

When this disquieting news was forwarded to Wackett he replied in a four page letter that Monel metal had been used in the drive shaft of the *Miss America V* speedboat which had broken the world's speed record. He had studied the matter thoroughly and *consider MONEL METAL an efficient material for aircraft.*

*It is not surprising that the Air Ministry cannot give it much of a recommendation. Their cable clearly indicates clearly what I guessed, viz., they have had too little experience in its use to express a definite opinion and give only a guarded one based on their own experience...*

*It is my duty as an experimenter to use it on its merits and on my results and not on hearsay or unsupported opinions of inexperienced and prejudiced individuals.*[34]

The following day Wackett sent another blast to the CCA wherein he noted that the latter's telegram *alleging that the use of Monel Metal constituted a patent cause of failure in the air is not a criticism of Monel Metal but of my own ability as a designer.*[35]

The Widgeon II was moved to Mascot during February 1928, and on the 17th was *now completely assembled Mascot. Preliminary taxi test yesterday.*[36] Wackett now proposed to carry out full flight tests as soon as weather permitted. This put the CCA in a difficult position and he asked for an opinion as to whether there were any *weakness...of monel fittings which only affect safety adversely after, say, some hundreds of hours flight*...(and) *that no further action is essential to delay test flights of Widgeon II?*[37]

Follett, the Superintendent of Aircraft, replied that even if it could be shown that a weakness could be attributed to any particular component it was impossible from the data available to tender any opinion as to the period of safe life. He concluded that *to take any action to delay test could only reasonably follow as a natural corollary to non-acceptance of the designer's assumptions and conclusions as to the suitability and characteristics of monel metal.*[38]

Brinsmead gave permission for the test which took place on 21 February, Wackett telegraphing the Air Board that the initial flight was *very satisfactory. Now ready*

**Above:** Widgeon II without any markings, probably on the occasion of its roll-out.

**Above & Above Right:** The new Widgeon II in its hangar at Mascot. (NLA 163214941 & 163268956)

*any demonstration.*[39] Brinsmead noted after a telephone discussion with the CAS that Williams agreed with him that *it is somewhat optimistic to believe the Widgeon can be deemed ready for* any demonstration *after a test of 5 minutes*. The Air Board had not given any instructions as to what trials were to be carried out as the aircraft had been built to the order of the CAB. Brinsmead wanted a full set of tests to British specifications carried out, but in the event, they were never

**Above:** Manhandling the Widgeon II back into its hangar. (Victorian State Library)

carried out.

Wackett's faith in Monel metal was verified after the crash of the Widgeon II. Various parts of the aircraft were sent to the MSB for testing and the report on rudder controls noted that *the monel metal is untarnished.*[40] The parts checked by the MSB were *in no way responsible for the crash.*[41] Further, the Air Board reported that checks had shown that Wackett had worked to higher factors of safety than those set by the British authorities.

In March 1928, Williams requested the CCA to *make "Widgeon II" available to the R.A.A.F. during May and June of this year* for the purpose of meeting the RAF Far Eastern Flight of four metal-hulled Supermarine Southampton flying boats in Singapore.[42] The British Government had decided to station a flying boat detachment at Singapore and that this Far East Flight would make a goodwill flight to Australia.

Wackett, P/Off H.C. Owen and AC W.K. Thompkins were to leave Sydney on 30 April. The Widgeon II flew from Sydney to Darwin where the amphibian's performance was severely affected by the tropical heat that it could not take off from Darwin harbour with full load. The wireless was removed to reduce weight but the aircraft would only take off with one man on board. After two unsuccessful attempts it finally took off after careening *over the water at enormous speed for about a quarter of a mile before it rose.*[43] Thompkins and his wireless were sent back to Sydney by sea. The lack of a metal propeller caused problems with tip erosion caused by water spray. This occurred even when the water was quite smooth. Wackett wrote that with the finest materials and excellent workmanship, it was barely possible to produce blades which would stand up to a half-dozen take-offs. *I was always afraid of a broken propeller and the consequences would have been disastrous.*[44] This was undoubtably the reason that the Widgeon II did not leave Australia but waited for the RAF flying boats at Darwin. Wackett stated that he operated from land wherever possible to reduce tip erosion, and also, he could take-off with more fuel this way. It appears that it is more probable that it was the only way he could be sure that he would take to the air in these tropical conditions.

Problems were experienced with the Monel wheels which were damaged by rocks on the primitive landing grounds. When Darwin was reached Wackett found serious cracks in the wheel rims and these had to be repaired at once. He had brought a supply of Monel metal with him as it was unprocurable anywhere *en route*. Finding a garage with oxy-acetylene equipment he fitted patches over the cracks, riveted them, then brazed them with Tobin bronze. He had to repair the wheels three times during the trip and concluded that the gauge used to construct the rims was not thick enough for the rough fields then in use. When he returned to Sydney, he

**Right & Below:** Widgeon II at Darwin awaiting the RAF Far Eastern Flight. The machine operated from land wherever it could, confirming the CAS, Richard Williams' views on the utility of amphibians over seaplanes. (AHMofWA P891420 & P891421)

had new wheels constructed of a heavier gauge Monel metal and had no more trouble with cracking.[45]

Newspapers of the day covered aerial events in detail and published details of Wackett's trip. Wackett was reported as covered 550 miles from Darwin to Wyndham, and arriving at Broome on 22 May 1928, after making 90 mph from Wyndham to Broome. He waited here for the RAF flying boats here. The RAF contingent arriving at Broome on 1 June

Because of his superior speed he would take-off an half an hour after the Southamptons and gradually overtake them. He would then fly onto the next refuelling stop and continue the procedure. The flying boats flew to Port Headland, Carnarvon, Perth, Albany, Israelite Bay and Murat Bay where the Widgeon II left the Flight and returned to Sydney, the first Australian designed aircraft to have made a round-Australia flight.

The RAF Flight continued on their leisurely cruise, visiting all capital cities on the coast, reaching Darwin on 30 August and returning to Singapore by 15 September. The cruise had been a remarkable success.

This long cross-country flight immediately after the preliminary tests meant that Wackett had no opportunity to undertake a series of performance trials. Wackett now proceeded with a series of modifications to the aircraft. These included an *all metal rear cabin, extra beam and buoyancy to hull, automatic wing slots, water rudder, special aligning and folding arrangements, exhaust ring manifold, and higher lifting wheel undercarriage.*[46] This produced an immediate reaction from the CAB as to who authorised the modifications and who was going to pay for them!

During the search for the *Southern Cross*, (see Chapter 8), the Widgeon II was put forward as an idea aircraft for such a venture. It appears that Williams favoured the use of the Widgeon II participating in the search. The amphibian was in the workshops undergoing modifications with a view to carrying out trials in HMAS *Albatross*, and Brinsmead thought that the aircraft would *have a much better prospect of a successful journey if the time intervening is employed in tightening up the organisation for the journey and testing out the modifications recently installed.* In the event the aircraft did not take a part in this search nor that for the ill-fated *Kookaburra*.[47]

In June 1929, Wackett reported that the *aircraft has now been developed as far as practicable, in its present form.* All improvements suggested by the flight to Darwin had been successfully incorporated into the design, and in addition those modifications necessary for the aircraft to be carried by the seaplane carrier HMAS *Albatross*. These consisted of increasing the buoyancy at the bow; raising and moving the engine forward; fitting slots and hoisting gear; arranging for the wings to fold; removal of the dingy and fitting a metal cabin top; modifying the axles and fitting improved fins with an extra rib *to stiffen it up*.[48] He considered that the

**Above & Facing Page, Above:** Widgeon II at Point Cook. (AHMofWA P950475 & RAAF Museum)

most important was in the amphibian's water performance. *Added buoyancy has made the aircraft entirely different, than previously, and it is now possible to take off the water with the full load, carried previously only from land aerodromes.* These modifications resulted in a decrease in cruising speed from 90 to 85 mph at full load. Wackett wanted to fit a geared Jaguar engine as the *improvement of performance with a geared engine would be remarkable.*[49]

The Widgeon II taken aboard *Albatross* for an Island Cruise but was only hoisted out at Rabaul on the 16th and 18th July. It was not flown again during the cruise. Four pilots of 101 Flight flew the amphibian while it was attached to *Albatross* and while agreeing that it was fast, climbed well, was manoeuvrable with a superior performance to that of the Fairey IIID and Seagull III, and was remarkably easy to maintain, the hull characteristics were such that hydrodynamically it *does not appear to be good in any respect taking off but lands with little shock.* The machine buried its bow on opening the throttle, dangerously obscuring the pilot's view for an appreciable number of seconds until the bow rose. Under favourable conditions the take-off run was twice as long as a Seagull which rendered the aircraft impossible in heavy seas. In summary it was *considered that the aerodynamic structure of "Widgeon II" mounted on a hull with the characteristics of a Seagull would provide a machine of considerable value.*[50] The RAN was not taken with the Widgeon II considering that it would take too long to develop the amphibian for use in *Albatross.* Also, it was thought that nine Fairey IIIF floatplanes could be purchased for the price of six Widgeons.

When the report on the flight trials of the amphibian were finally received by the CAB it was noted that the *essence of the report...definitely suggests that it is neither sufficiently airworthy nor seaworthy to justify a Certificate of Airworthiness for any private use. Without such certificate the machine will be valueless outside the service.*[51] The Air Board indicated willingness to accept the machine and 1 FTS was instructed on 18 October 1929, to conduct tests on the amphibian to determine its suitability for training purposes.

*On 21st October* Albatross *arrived at Port Arlington with L.J. Wackett's recently designed Widgeon II amphibian which had been tested for naval cooperation but not recommended as a replacement for Seagull amphibians. Joe* Hewitt was assigned to fly it from the ship to Point Cook.

*Widgeon II had a tendency to bury its nose in the sea on the pilot opening up his engine for take off. I found this disconcerting on my first flight with Corporal Clarke as my passenger. I was forced to alight in Corio Bay while Clarke checked the engine and petrol supply. He discovered an airlock. I returned to* Albatross, *had the engine checked and tested on deck. I then took off the following morning in a disturbed sea. After it lifted off, which required some effort in the rough sea, I flew to Point Cook, landed on the aerodrome and taxied to the tarmac to hand it over to the Seaplane Squadron. Flight Lieutenant Briggs, an experienced*

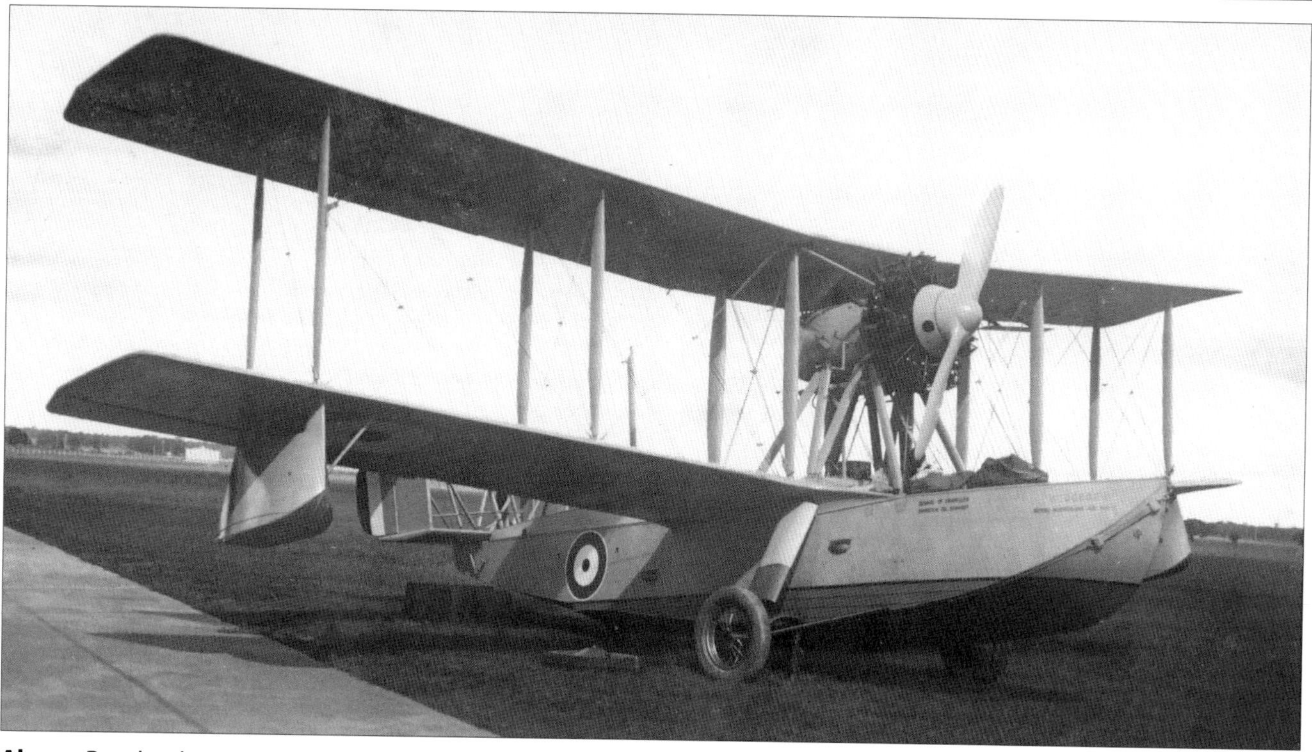

**Above:** Resplendent in RAAF colours the amphibian has its name 'Widgeon II' on the bow above 'Royal Australian Air Force.' Note the 'Beware of Propeller' warning. The hull bottom would have been coated with a bitumen waterproofing anti-fouling paint. (AHMofWA P961601)

*flying boat pilot from the R.A.F. and now in the R.A.A.F. asked me as I got out how I liked the Widgeon II. I said "You can have it".*[52]

Tests were carried out by Briggs, and Sqn Ldr V.R. Scriven, AFC, RAF. Briggs undertook five flights in December. His report was unfavourable citing a lengthy take off on land and on water; water conditions had to be favourable to ensure a take-off; the pilot's view was restricted on flattening out on landing; the aircraft tended to 'porpoise' before settling down in the water; it was hard to taxi and impossible to steer on a set course coming into the slipway down wind. He considered it unsuitable as an instructional

**Left & Below:** Widgeon II at Point Cook.

machine and suitable only for experienced pilots; it was not suitable for Naval co-operation work, air pilotage, navigation or bombing instruction. Briggs summed up by stating that it *was not clear to what purpose this aircraft could be put.*[53] Both concluded that after *very careful consideration...that the Widgeon II was entirely unsuitable for any service purpose. We agreed that it would be quite useless for carrying out flying instruction owing to the restricted view ahead when landing and to the difficulty in getting the machine off the water.*[54]

Briggs told Scriven that Wackett did not agree with their opinion and that he *proposed to carry out additional tests.*[55]

The Auditor-General's Report for the year ending 30 June 1930, was scathing in its criticism of the activities of the Experimental Section. The Report repeated Sqn Ldr Hepburn's allegation that the *outstanding possibility was that the machine was aerodynamically inefficient.*[56] It noted that the testing of the Widgeon was never satisfactorily carried out despite the Air Board requesting such testing as far back as the beginning of 1928. It questioned whether the design was carried out in accordance with standard engineering safety procedures. Naturally questions were asked in Parliament. The Air Board denied the allegations. Widgeon I was reported as having been used for instructional purposes, while Widgeon II was *constructed for the Civil Aviation Branch but the Air Board did not recommend its construction.*[57] As can be seen, the Board was using semantics to cover its involvement as Wackett had indicated from the beginning that it was a military aircraft. In early 1931 a similar series of questions was asked, this time including Warrigal I.

The crash of Widgeon II ended any chance that Wackett might have continued to develop the design. An approach had been made in 1927 to have the Cockatoo Dockyards in Sydney build the Widgeon for sale to private companies but had come to nothing. By now Wackett was immersed in the design and testing of the Warrigal biplane for the RAAF, and involved in another controversy, this time arguing with his fellow RAAF officers.

## Specifications

Widgeon I Puma engine.
Dimensions: Span 39 ft 3 in; Length 29 ft 9¼ in; Length Folded 34 ft 6 in; Height 13 ft 9½ in on wheels, 13 ft 5 in off wheels. Area mainplanes 424.32 $ft^2$
Weights: Puma engine: Empty 2,900 lb including water in radiator; Flying weight 3,959 lb.
Performance: Endurance: 3 hrs.

**Above:** Photographs of the Widgeon II in flight are rare.

**Above:** Widgeon II on the deck of HMAS *Albatross.*

**Above:** The Widgeon II is hauled out in New Guinea waters. This was the only time the amphibian was taken on a cruise. (RAAF Museum)

**Widgeon I with Nimbus engine**
Dimensions: Span 39 ft 3 in; Length 29 ft 9¼ in; Length Folded 34 ft 6 in; Height 13 ft 9½ in on wheels, 13 ft 5 in off wheels. Area mainplanes 424.32 $ft^2$
Weights: Empty 2,940 lb including water in radiator; Flying weight 4,250 lb.
Performance: Speed Max100 mph; Cruise 87 mph.
Endurance: 3 hrs.

**Widgeon II**
Dimensions: Span 43 ft 4 ins. Length 30 ft 3 in; Height 13 ft 2 in.
Weights: Empty 4,000 lbs: Loaded 6,600 lbs.
Performance: Speed Max 120 mph.

## End Notes:

1 NAA ACT CRS A705/1 Item 32/10/1094. Court of Enquiry. Crash of Widgeon II, Point Cook. 6.01.1930. Testimony of Flight Sergeant N.H. Clutterbuck.
2 *Ibid.* Testimony of Flying Officer Wight.
3 Wackett, L.J. *Aircraft Pioneer*, Angus and Robertson, Sydney, 1972, P.90.
4 Connolly, J.V. "The History of Aeronautical Engineering in Australia", *The Aeroplane*, 28 September 1938, P.382; and "Australian Experimental Aircraft", *The Aeroplane*, 14.01.1925, P.34.
5 NAA ACT CRS A2408/1 Item 199/3. Flying Boats. Letterbook entry No.26, 15.04.1926.
6 Wackett, LJ. *Op Cit*. P.92.
7 *The Aeroplane*, 2.09.1925, P.294. This is typical of

**Above & Below:** A mud splattered Widgeon II with the race number '20' carried on the fin and under the lower wings for the 1928 Aerial Derby. The wingtip floats were removed and the machine was flown as a 'land plane' for the Derby. Note the RAAF flag on the interplane struts. The RAAF also entered two de Havilland D.H.9a biplanes in the race, flown by F/Off Mulroney, who came in first, and Sqn Ldr Jones, who came in second. The Widgeon came in third.

**Above & Below:** Widgeon II being refuelled is the object of the attention of the locals. Note the 4-gallon tins used at the time. (AHMofWA P001234 & P001233)

**Above:** Widgeon II under public inspection (AHMofWA P971585)

**Above:** Widgeon II moored out at Darwin.

**Above:** Widgeon II at Darwin, NT. The Widgeon II was the first Australian designed and built aeroplane to make a round Australia flight.

**Right:** Setting out a mooring mast for the Widgeon II.

**Above:** The care taken with the Widgeon II is illustrated by the way the hull upper surface colours was separated from the bottom anti-fouling paint by a neat paint line. Unfortunately, the colours used on the machine are unknown.

**Above:** RAAF personnel and a local posing with the Widgeon II give a good idea of its size. (AHMofWA P017297)

C.G. Grey's editorial style when it came to Australia trying to free itself of the dominion of British aircraft manufacturers.

8 "Concerning The Widgeon". *Aircraft*, 1 December 1925, P.194.

9 "The Widgeon Flies." *Aircraft*, 1 January 1926, P.260.

10 NAA ACT CRS A705/1 Item 199/3/88. Reports on Widgeon. (Boat Seaplane). Summary of Trials of G-AEKB. 12.04.1926.

11 *Ibid.*

12 *Ibid.* Wackett to Air Board. 19.04.1927.

13 *Ibid.*

14 *Ibid.* CO, 1 FTS Report, 5.08.1927.

15 Wackett, L.J.. *Op Cit.* P.94.

16 See Coulthard Clark, *The Third Brother*, Allen & Unwin, 1991. P.264.

17 Crowther, FG. *Experiences of a Fleet Air Arm Pilot 1926-1930.* Manuscript in Australian Naval Aviation Museum, Nowra, NSW.

18 Air Board Agenda No.1343. "Disposal of Widgeon I. and Nimbus engine." Meeting of 9.10.1929.

19 The aircraft appeared with the registration G-AEKB which was said to stand for E.K. Bowen, the Minister of Defence at the time. Apparently it was allocated the registration G-AUKB but this was never taken up. (Cookson, B. *The Historic Civil Aircraft Register of Australia (Pre War) G-AUAA to VH-UZZ,* Austairdata, Qld, 1996.)

20 NAA ACT CRS A705/1 Item 199/3/88. Wackett to Air Board. "Widgeon I", 17.10.1927.

21 *Ibid.* Letter from CAS to OC, Randwick Experimental Station, 12.06.1926.

22 "New Lease of Life - Increased Activity in Air Force." *Herald*, 25.07.1927.

23 NAA ACT CRS A705/1 Item 32/10/1094. *Op Cit.* "Air Accidents Investigation Committee Report No.71."

24 *Ibid.* Minute: "Widgeon II". Squadron Leader Scriven, CO Seaplane Squadron, to CO, 1 FTS. 12.12.1929.

25 *Ibid.* Evidence of Hempel.

26 *Ibid.* "AAIC Report No.71". 29.01.1930.

27 *Ibid.*

28 *Ibid.* Confidential Minute; President, Court of Enquiry to AMP. 17.01.1930.

29 *Ibid.*

30 NAA ACT CRS A705/1 Item 44/4/31. "Widgeon II Construction". Memorandum to CO, Experimental Section from CCA, 9.01.1928.

31 *Ibid.* Wackett to CCA, 21.12.1927.

32 *Ibid.* Wireless message; Austair to Air Board, 16.12.1927.

33 *Ibid.* Cable. Liaison to Air Board, 6.01.1928.

34 *Ibid.* Wackett to CCA, 30.01.1928.

35 *Ibid.* Wackett to CCA, 31.01.1928.

36 *Ibid.* Wireless message. Experimental Section to Air Board, 17.02.1928.

37 *Ibid.* Note by H.C. Brinsmead, 17.02.1928.

38 *Ibid.* Follett to CCA, 18.0219.28.

39 *Ibid.* Telegram. Wackett to Air Board, 21.02.1928.

40 NAA ACT CRS A705/1 Item 32/10/970. WIDGEON II Reports. Report of 23.01.1930.

41 *Ibid.* Minute: "Accident to Widgeon II." DAI to Air Board, 3.02.1930.

42 NAA ACT CRS A705/1 Item 44/4/31. *Op Cit.* Minute, CAS to CCA, 24.03.1928.

43 Newspaper cutting in Wackett scrapbook, un-named and undated. Australian National Library MS4858.

44 Wackett, LJ. *Op Cit.* P.97.

45 *Ibid.* P.99-101.

46 NAA ACT CRS A705/1 Item 44/4/31. *Op Cit.* Minute: Air Board to CCA. "Flight Trials of "Widgeon" II", 25.01.1929.

47 NAA ACT CRS A705/1 Item 153/1/456. Search For Southern Cross. Use Of Widgeon II. Minute: CCA, 3.04.1929.

48 NAA ACT CRS A705/1 Item 32/10/1094. *Op Cit.* Testimony of Wing Cmdr Wackett.

49 NAA ACT CRS A705/1 Item 44/4/31. "Widgeon II. Amphibian". Copy memo from Wackett, 10.06.1929.

50 *Ibid.* "Report on Widgeon II" by Flight Lieutenant F.G. Crowther, 4.09.1929.

51 *Ibid.* Minute: Widgeon II. Superintendent of Aircraft to CCA, 14.10.1929.

52 Hewitt, J. *The Black One.* Langate Publishing, Vic, 1984, P.126.

53 NAA ACT CRS A705/1 Item 32/10/1094. *Op Cit.* Minute; "Report On "Widgeon" II", 11.12.1929.

54 *Ibid.* Testimony of Squadron Leader V.R. Scriven.

55 *Ibid.*

56 NAA ACT CRS A705/1 Item 8/5/48. Extract from Auditor-General's Report for the Year Ending 30th June, 1930.

57 *Ibid.* House of Representatives, Questions for this Day, Monday 4 August, 1930.

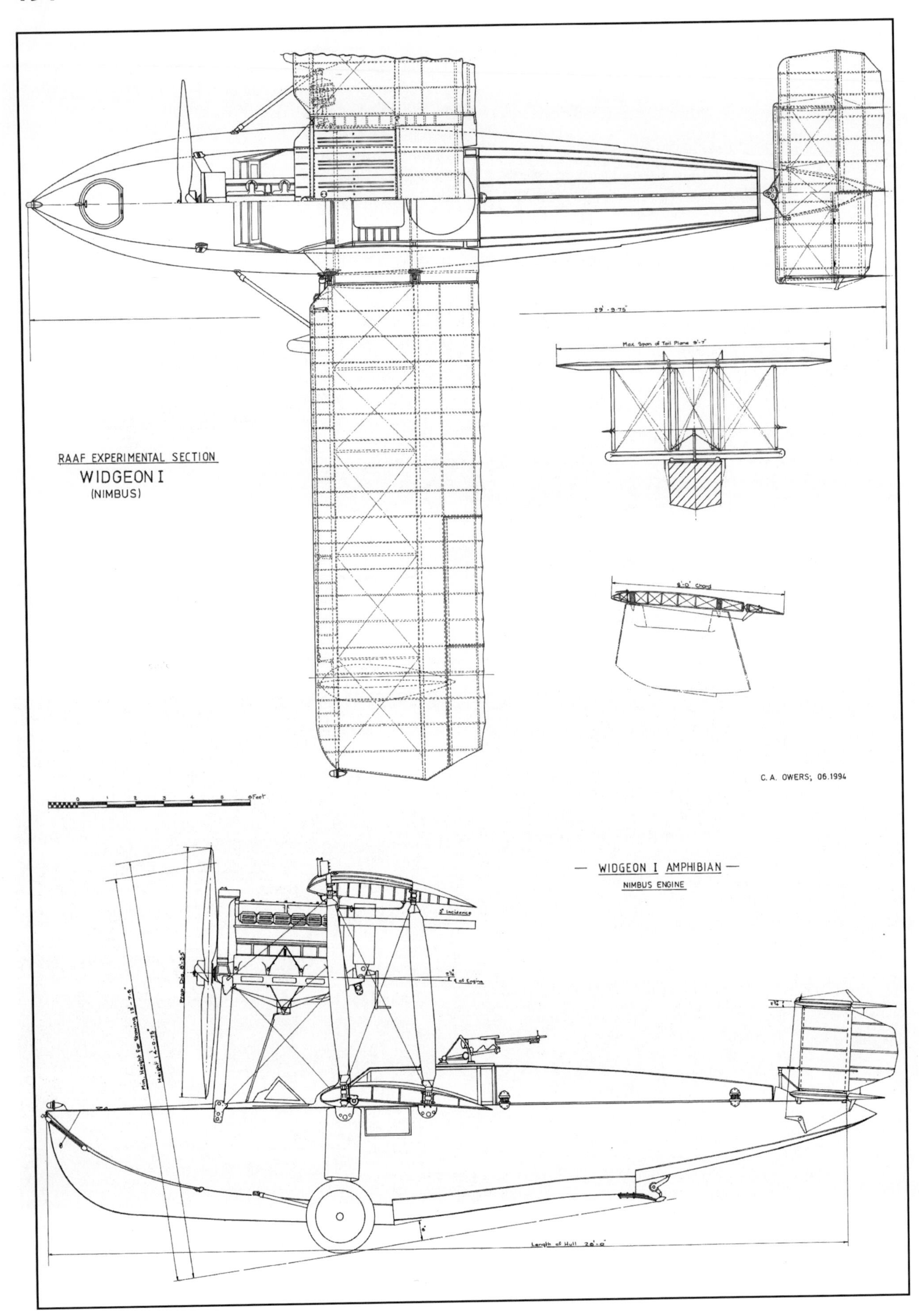

RAAF EXPERIMENTAL SECTION
WIDGEON I
(NIMBUS)
29' · 9·75"
Max. Span of Tail Plane 9'-7"
8'-0" Chord
C. A. OWERS; 06.1994
0 1 2 3 4 5 6 Feet
— WIDGEON I AMPHIBIAN —
NIMBUS ENGINE
5° Incidence
℄ of Engine
Prop. Dia. 8'-3.5"
Min. Height for Stowing 13'-7.6"
Height 14'-0.75"
Length of Hull 28'-0"

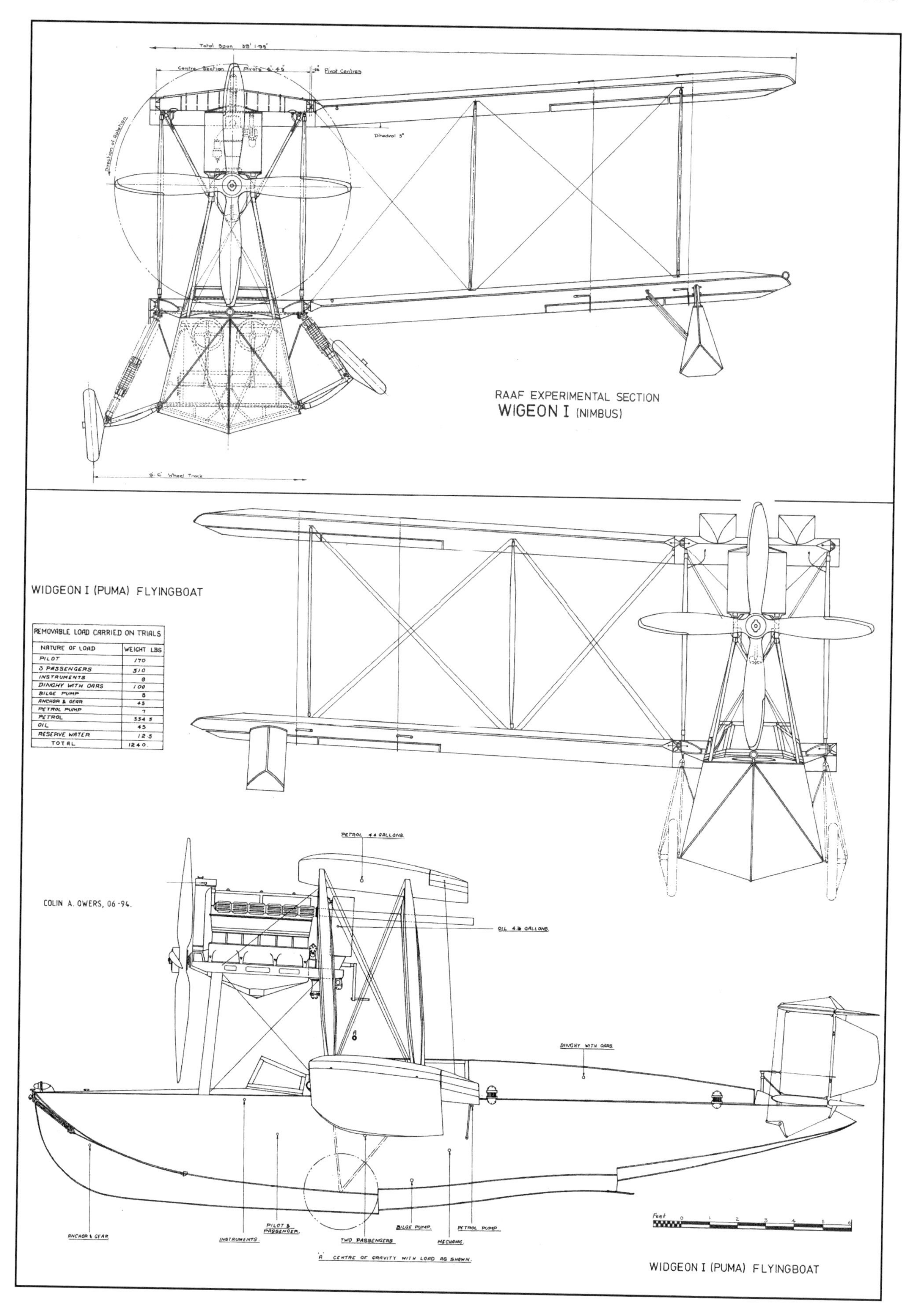


| REMOVABLE LOAD CARRIED ON TRIALS | |
|---|---|
| NATURE OF LOAD | WEIGHT LBS |
| PILOT | 170 |
| 3 PASSENGERS | 510 |
| INSTRUMENTS | 8 |
| DINGHY WITH OARS | 100 |
| BILGE PUMP | 8 |
| ANCHOR & GEAR | 45 |
| PETROL PUMP | 7 |
| PETROL | 334 5 |
| OIL | 45 |
| RESERVE WATER | 12·5 |
| TOTAL | 1240. |

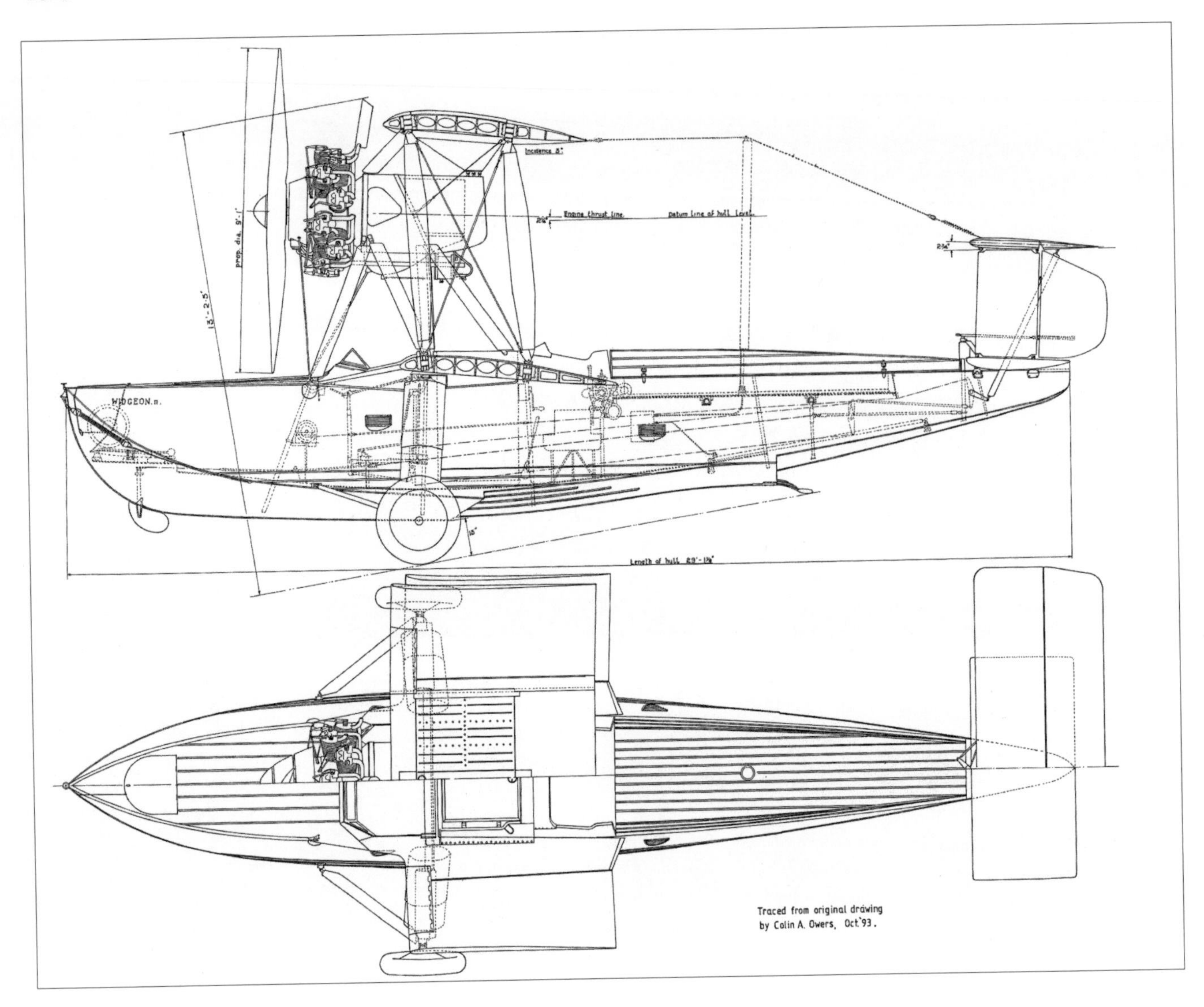
Incidence 5°
2½°
Engine thrust line.
Datum line of hull Level.
prop. dia. 9'-1"
13'-2.5"
WIDGEON.II.
Length of hull 29'-1⅛"
Traced from original drawing
by Colin A. Owers, Oct.'93.

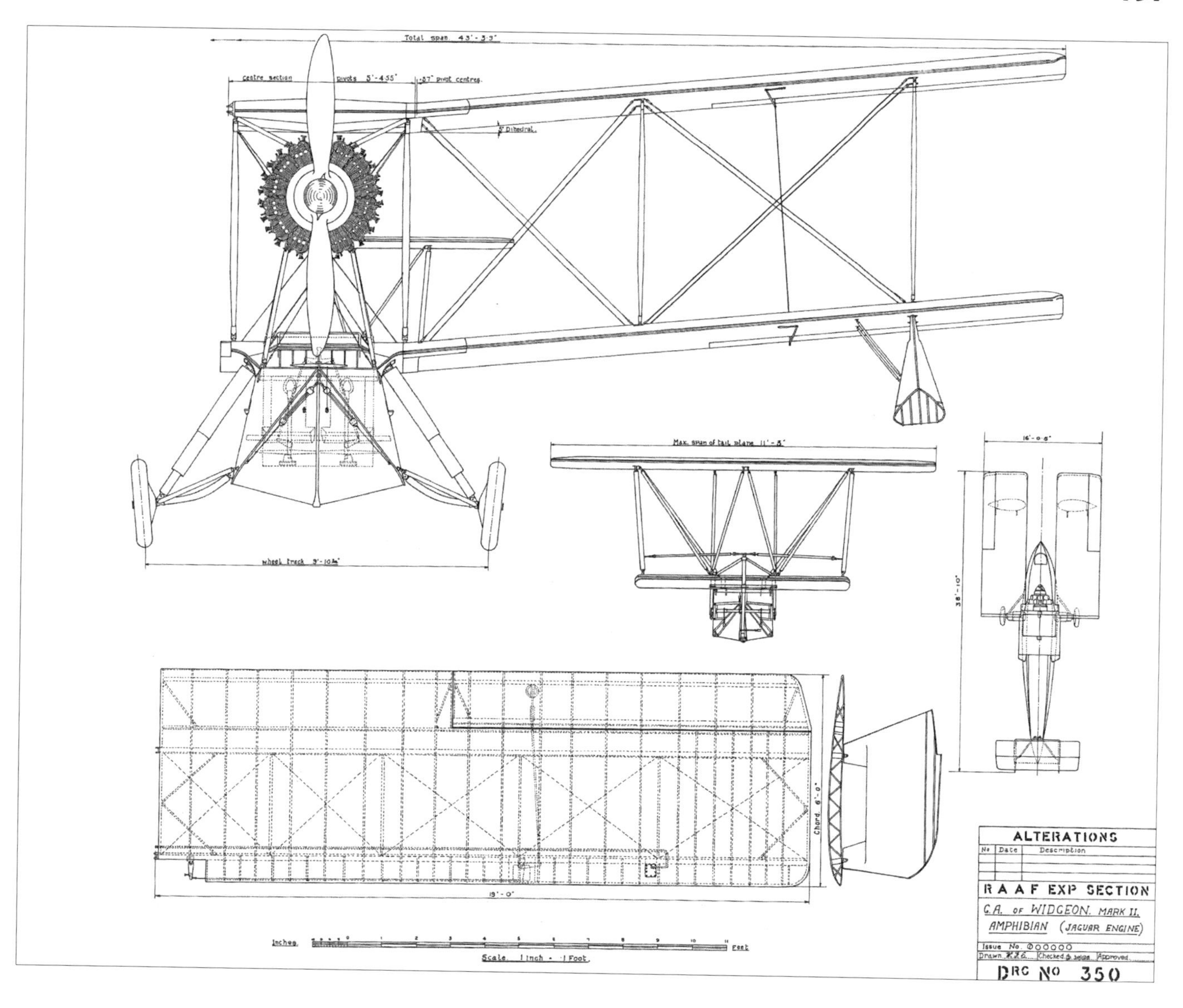

Total span 43'-3.9"
centre section
pivots 3'-4.55"
.87" pivot centres.
Max. span of tail plane 11'-3"
16'-0.6"
wheel track 9'-10¾"
38'-10"
Chord 6'-0"
19'-0"
Inches
Feet
Scale 1 Inch - 1 Foot
ALTERATIONS
No Date Description
R A A F EXP SECTION
G.A. OF WIDGEON. MARK II.
AMPHIBIAN (JAGUAR ENGINE)
Issue No.
Drawn
Checked
Approved
DRG No 350

**The Widgeon I as first launched. Fabric surfaces were aluminium doped. The hull was finished with marine varnish. The civil registration is thought to bbe blue with white outline.**

**Widgeon II as delivered to the RAAF. Standard RAAF practice was followed with the national makings. Presumed to be grey overall with dark anti-fouling paint to the hull bottom, separated by a thin black line. Widgeon II was applied to the bow in raised letters (presumed brass). Below this was the words Royal Australian Air Force in what appears to be gold lettering with black/red outlining. On the hull, in line with the airscrew, was the legend Beware of the Propeller and Voorzich Tig. The latter is thought to be an incorrect of the Dutch Voorzichtig Schroef (Caution Propeller).**

# Chapter 25. The Wackett (RAAF Experimental Section) Warrigal

**Left & Below:** The Warrigal I was a crude looking machine with a lot of external controls from the engine and under the tailplane. (RAAF Museum)

In January 1926 Williams considered the question of a replacement for the Avro 504K for the preliminary training of pilots. He thought that the De Havilland Moth would not...meet all our requirements in this respect, and wanted a machine capable of carrying out all branches of a pilot's training, including gunnery, photography, wireless, bombing, etc. The machine would have to be fitted with a stationary engine and he had the Armstrong Siddeley Lynx radial in mind. His ideas were as follows:

1. Machine to have flying characteristics equal to the Avro.
2. Seats to be arranged similar to those of the Bristol Fighter.
3. Instructor's seat to be the rear one.
4. Dual control to instructor's seat to be removable.
5. One or two Vickers guns in front seat.
6. Scarff Ring on back seat.
7. Arrangements to be made for fitting bomb-sight, wireless apparatus and camera.
8. Personnel both to be equipped with seat-type parachutes.
9. Engine to be fitted in mounting which is detachable from the machine and which will be removable with it when engine is overhauled.
10. Long exhaust pipes to be fitted.
11. Adjustable tail-plane.
12. Tail-plane, rudder and fin constructed to interfere as little as possible with fire of rear gun.
13. Oleo type land undercarriage.

14. Twin float undercarriage to fit same fittings.
15. Machine to be standardised as far as possible so far as parts are concerned, and to be made up of as few parts as possible.
16. Rigging to be fixed as far as possible.
17. Wings to fold.
18. Damaged parts to be replaced as easily as possible.
19. Machine to require as small crates as possible for transport by road or rail.

*Williams thought that a "MOCK-UP" could be made at the Experimental Section and all officers concerned given an opportunity of examining it.*[1]

In response to this Minute, Sqn Ldr Adrian *King* Cole, the Director of Personnel and Training (DPT), replied that such a training machine could act *as a stepping stone to the heavier present day service type. Initial training to be carried out...in a lighter machine, possibly a Moth.* He further suggested that one of the forward guns be of the *Cinema type* and that wing tip flare brackets, navigation lights and the *necessary fuselage fittings for high flying practice be fitted.*[2]

On the same date, 15 February, Wackett advised that the work of producing a mock-up *of the seating positions and location of equipment...will be ready for inspection by officers, adept in training requirements, at a very early date.* Wackett had already discussed the proposed trainer with Williams during his *most recent visit to Head Quarters*, and enclosed a draft copy of the specification for the design and construction of *a new Training Aeroplane for the R.A.A.F.* with his letter.[3] Even considering the relative simplicity of design at this time, from these dates it would appear that Wackett had already completed the preliminary work on the design of the trainer and that Williams wrote the Minute to fit in with Wackett's proposal. Wackett suggested that the type be named Warrigal *which is a typically Australian name.*[4]

Williams had the list of his suggestions circulated to flying instructors at 1 FTS in order to obtain from them *any information which is the result of their experience in training pupils and in maintaining aircraft for that work, in order that it may be made use of in the design of the present machine if possible.* Additional items added to the list included rod control; interchangeable wings; fuel for 3 hours at full power and engine to be a 180-hp Armstrong Siddeley Lynx.[5]

A meeting was held on 14 April at RAAF Headquarters with the DPT, Sqn Ldr Cole; and the OCs of No. 1 FTS, the flying squadron and Workshops, Flt Lts De La Rue, Brownell and Jones, respectively and also Flt Lt Mustard. While agreeing with most of the suggestions they requested that *with the introduction of parachutes* a simpler form of intercommunication be introduced between pupil and pilot to *reduce the number of gadjets* (sic) *impeding the pilot* in the event of an emergency departure from the cockpits. Other suggestions included the incorporation of a prone bombing position in the design, and the Vickers gun to be mounted on the fuselage side with the sights on the centre line. The meeting was unanimous that *training would be greatly assisted if such a machine...were available.*[6] The Director of Operations and Intelligence noted that if the *O.C. Experimental Section thinks it possible and provided the finished article has flying characteristics equally as good as the Avro 504K it seems most desirable to build the proposed new trainer.*[7]

Williams proposed that a landplane for preliminary instruction in flying be built by the Experimental Section, noting that it possessed the following features as compared with present equipment:

(a). Fitted with a radial engine with detachable mounting, which would be less expensive to maintain and requiring fewer hours for overhaul, and fewer overhauls.
(b). Fitted with folding wings to save hangar space.
(c). The fuselage to be in two pieces to facilitate handling and repair.
(d). To be fitted with oleo undercarriage to minimize minor crashes.
(e). To be fitted for a float undercarriage for seaplane training.
(f). To be fitted for training in gunnery, bombing, wireless and photography to save the use of more expensive service types from early training in these subjects.
(g). To have interchangeable parts as far as possible to save expense in stores and spares.

*It is considered to be thoroughly practical and should mean a considerable saving in the cost of preliminary training, it should considerably improve that training and result in a big saving in service types of aircraft.*[8] What Williams does not say is that far from being a simple type with broad application, the specification now covered all RAAF applications from fighting to training, indeed the machine which would emerge was stated to be capable of conversion to a single seat scout, 'scout' being synonymous with fighter from First World War usage.[9]

The Minister's sanction was obtained *for the development of a Training machine to take* (the) *place of the Avro and for the purchase of an 180-hp Lynx radial engine.*[10] By the end of November many of the components were well in hand towards completion but no actual assembly of the fuselage had been commenced.

*As the work is likely to be delayed by the building of "Widgeon" Mark II, and the manufacture of a considerable quantity of spares for No.1 A.D., it appears unlikely that the 'Warregul'* (sic) *will be completed in less than 4 to 6 months.*[11]

This and similar references led to Wackett writing a terse note stating that it was 'Warrigal' not 'Warregul' as it *would be as well to settle this small point definitely.*[12] As will be seen the name continued to receive various spellings in documents and the Press.

The Wackett Warrigal was a small two-bay biplane. The wings were constructed around spars of Australian Blackwood with metal ribs made from brass strips manufactured at the MSB, Maribyrnong. The imported Armstrong Siddeley Lynx radial engine was mounted on a locally cast stainless steel and phosphor bronze mount

**Left & Below:** An elaborate but crude arrangement was set up for the christening of the Warrigal I by Mrs Williams who succeeded in breaking the requisite bottle of champagne on the airscrew boss on the last day of January 1929. (via Mrs J Stewart & RAAF Museum)

well forward of the cockpit, separated by a large empty compartment which would take most of the shock and breakage of a crash tending to keep the instructor's and pupil's seats intact. The fuselage was constructed in four easily detachable modules which could be removed if damaged and a new section inserted. The forward section was oval and covered with two thicknesses of diagonal planking while the rear rectangular sections were covered with blackwood three-ply. Wings, including ailerons, were interchangeable. It was reported that the Warrigal was remarkable in the construction of the fuselage *which may be altered speedily to take engines of different type and horse-power. The plane may also be altered from a two-seater to a single-seater scout.*[13] There is no mention of this latter capability in surviving documents. Wheels were constructed of monel metal. A 70-gallon tank was mounted in the fuselage. A wind driven pump raised fuel to the 40-gallon gravity tank built into the upper centre section.

Williams had hopes that if the Warrigal was successful *and fitted with a 'Jupiter' engine,* (it) *might eventually become our army co-op machine. In the meantime I suggest that the Army Co-op Flight of No.3 Squadron be equipped with the Armstrong Siddeley "ATLAS".* As the Eagle VIII engines in the RAAF's possession could not be fitted in the three Fairey IIIF floatplanes being considered for purchase, Williams recommended that the funds marked for the Faireys be transferred to the purchase of six Atlas biplanes.[14] (See Chapter 26).

The Air Board had issued Specifications A.C.34, A.C.35, A.C.36 and A.C.37 for a two-seat general training aircraft Warragull, two-seat general Army co-operation landplane

or seaplane, two-seat Army co-operation landplane, and two-seat light bomber, respectively, the previous year. The story now takes on an international flavour as in February 1927, A V Roe and Co Ltd (Avro) wrote to the Australian Minister of Defence (N Howse) that their representative, H.E. Broadsmith, was proceeding to Australia. The object of Broadsmith's visit was to discuss the above specifications for re-equipping the RAAF. Because of his earlier involvement with the Australian aircraft industry (See Chapter 1), Broadsmith was the considered the best man for the job of pushing the sale of Avro military aircraft to the Australian government.

The Larkin Aircraft Supply Co (LASCO) had been approached by the Department of Defence with the suggestion that they bring these specifications to the notice

**Above:** Warrigal I at Point Cook. (via AHMofWA P961604)

of aircraft manufacturers in the UK and LASCO had contacted Avro.[15] The most likely sales prospect seemed to be the replacement of the RAAF's standard trainer, the rotary engine Avro 504K, by a stationary engine aircraft.

The British Air Ministry had issued Technical Order No.128/25 in 1925 which directed that all new RAF Avro 504 aeroplanes were to be of the 504N type and all 504K trainer were to be converted to 504N standard when reconditioned. In essence the 504N differed from the 504K as follows:

a). tail adjusting gear was fitted to the 504N.
b). minor alterations to the tail including an additional tail strut.
c). steerable tail skid.
d). oleo undercarriage.
e). the mainplanes were altered in that the centre-section and outer roots were cut away to improve vision. Tapered ailerons were fitted.
f). two petrol tanks were carried under the top wing.
g). new oil tank.
h). a new fireproof bulkhead.
i). replacement of the rotary engine by a stationary engine.

The Air Board noted that the Avro 504N Lynx was recognised as an *improvement on the original Avro 504N training machine with rotary engine*. It was anticipated that it would be the RAF trainer of the future.

Despite this, in April 1927 the Air Board recorded that the RAAF still had considerable numbers of the 504K which were *comparatively efficient for training* and the Service could not afford to scrap these at the present time. It can be seen that this statement is at odds with the views which were expressed to the investigating committee and those recorded by Williams. Moreover, there were the two machines being constructed at Randwick to Wackett's designs, which, if successful, would prove a satisfactory replacement for the Avro. These were being built to the same specifications as those which had aroused Avro's interest.

Avro put forward two proposals to meet Specification No. A.C.34 'Warragull.'[16] These were:

(a) The 504N in a modified form.
(b) An entirely new design.

Proposal (a) was for a machine which was virtually the 504N. The Air Board wanted folding wings, an axle-less type of undercarriage and interior bomb stowage and the Avro proposal detailed why the 504N, which did not offer any of these features, would still be a good buy. Nevertheless, Avro was engaged in the preparation of an alternative design which would *cover every requirement of your specification*, this would be submitted later.[17] Two months later Avro proposed converting the existing RAAF 504K machines to *504N Warregul* standard. This conversion was represented as being easily carried out. The wings, body and tail unit could be used for the 504N. Alternatively, a quantity of 504N machines was then under construction and it was stated that it would be possible to give almost immediate delivery to these modified to meet the 'Warregul' specifications. Avro pointed out that

**Left:** Pulling the airscrew on the Lynx engine required the efforts of two men.

the same cockpit unit could be fitted to all the machines to meet the specifications and *in the case of the AC 36 having a smaller span, a shorter length of body is fitted aft of the observer's cockpit, and the same tail unit used.*[18]

A licence for the manufacture of Avro designs would only be granted on the understanding that the aircraft would be used solely by the RAAF and not sold to private or commercial users. On 7 June, Broadsmith wrote to Williams informing him that arrangements were well in hand for the local production of any of the three types. Four days later the Air Board replied that the Government could not commit itself to the support of any firm which would ensure that firm a monopoly on Government orders. Broadsmith immediately wrote that he fully realised this and had no idea that his letter had conveyed this impression. He concluded with the interesting remark that with regards to the construction of other aircraft *we have, for some time past, been negotiating with other British Aircraft Constructors, with a view to being in a position to offer local construction of any type of aircraft you may decide to obtain.* In essence, Broadsmith was proposing the establishment of a Government Aircraft Factory. This idea had been the subject of debate and was opposed by Harrison, the Director of Technical Services. In August 1925, he had submitted a Minute suggesting a Government Aircraft Factory which would, because of Australia's small requirements, absorb all aircraft work, was a bad idea because the necessary base to expand in war would not be there. He considered that the placing of small orders with private firms for aeroplane parts in peace time was useful as it educated these firms in service requirements.[19] It can be seen that Broadsmith's proposed factory would become the only plant capable of manufacturing military and eventually civil aircraft in Australia because of the small size of the Australian market and the power of the British interests behind it.

Herbert Joseph Larkin, DFC, Croix de Guerre, had built an aircraft factory in 1927 on Coode Island, Vic, probably the most modern and best equipped facility in the southern hemisphere at this time. There LASCO constructed one D.H.50A, and the Shackleton designed Lascoter, Lascondor monoplanes and Lark glider. The business was liquidated by February 1932. Larkin engaged in a number of questionable campaigns and was sued for defamation on one occasion. His attitude did not endear him to officialdom. Following the failure of his Australian business he returned to the UK settling in the Channel Islands, dying in 1972.

Broadsmith offered the Type 590 Avro Warrigal Mark I to be manufactured in Australia by LASCO. A full-sized wood and canvas mock-up was constructed *to suit your specification A.C.3520* and was offered in the Army co-operation with a wing span of 45 ft or as a light bomber with a span of 37 ft, the same drawings being submitted for both. The Avro Type 590 was a two-seat two-bay, conventional biplane featuring folding wings, split oleo undercarriage with the portly fuselage connected to the bottom wing by means of a keel. A land undercarriage or floats could be fitted. Power was to be supplied by a 450-hp Bristol Jupiter VI radial engine. As a light bomber it could carry four 112-lb bombs.

The other design offered was a smaller two-seat single-bay Army co-operation landplane or floatplane powered by an Airdisco Nimbus engine. It was virtually a smaller version of the Type 590 with inline engine. This design could carry 12 light bombs.

LASCO tendered for 20 Avro 'Warragul' aircraft on 15 June 1927.[21] It is not clear if this was the A.C.35 specification or another of the designs called for, however Broadsmith recorded that LASCSO tendered for local production of the 504N on 8 June. The *full scale "mock-up" fuselage designed by Messrs A.V. Roe & Co. Ltd* had been forwarded to Victoria Barracks, Melbourne for inspection about July and Larkin wrote in August asking what the situation was with regard to local construction of this aircraft.[22] Larkin's financial position was probably vulnerable as he had recently taken possession of his new factory on Coode Island at a cost of £20,000.[23]

The 504N was offered to fill the trainer role and Broadsmith was successful in gaining a tentative order for this trainer, the Air Board recommending the purchase of twelve 504N biplanes, six machines to be purchased from Avro in the UK for £1,911 each; six machines to be built locally at an estimated cost of £2,350 each; and spares and engines to the value of £4,434 to give a total estimate of

**Above:** Warrigal I. The location thought to be at Point Cook.

£30,000. Importation of six trainers was recommended as *they were required for the next flying training course commencing in December, 1927.* The 504N was a standard machine and could be supplied by that date. Locally built machines could not be obtained for nine to ten months and thus would not be available for the next two courses.[24] The Air Board had stated that apart from building six Avro 504N trainers locally, it did not recommend a new training machine at the present time as the Wackett Warrigal was being developed and *if it proves successful it will supersede the Avros as the standard initial training machine* in the RAAF.

On 15 August, Williams was advised that the Minister had not yet approved the Avro proposals *pending advise from England cost drawings royalties enable Department tender locally.*[25] Two months later the Minister wanted to know what was being done re the local manufacture of Avros. One suspects that Larkin was again at work lobbying behind the scenes. The Air Ministry was approached with the request that they ascertain from Avros if they would be willing to supply six sets of works drawings to the Department for the use of the successful tenderer for manufacture in Australia. Avro did not want the design let to public tender as they *wished to exercise some technical supervision in order that the Avro standard of excellence may be maintained* and the Minister's insistence on public tenders would mean the cancellation of the arrangements with LASCO and *deprive us* (Avro) *of the opportunity to exercise control.*

The Minister continued to ask for information regarding what arrangements had been made for local construction and the Air Liaison Office (ALO) in London, (Wing Cdr Anderson), advised that there were tentative arrangements between Avro and LASCO. The De Havilland Moth now appears in these discussions as a potential replacement for the 504K. (See Chapter 9).

The idea of using a light aeroplane in the training role became generally known as Broadsmith wrote Williams that he understood from their discussions that the decision with respect to the order for the 504N was definite, however Williams procrastinated and replied that *it has now been decided to try a certain number of these machines* (De Havilland Moths) *before deciding what our training machine for the future will be.*[26] Williams had already advised the Minister of *the possibility of using light planes with improved engines for preliminary flying training as this would result in a considerable savings as the cost per machine would be a little more than half that of those originally proposed.*[27]

Broadsmith detailed his version of events in Melbourne. He noted that at that time Williams stated that he did not wish to purchase drawings and favoured making his own arrangements for local manufacture. It was Williams who had suggested that it should be possible for Larkin to come to a mutual arrangement with the Avro Co whereby the purchase of designs would be covered thus saving the Department the initial expense of purchasing a design. On journeying from Australia Broadsmith left his ship at Marseilles and within five days of leaving Melbourne had arranged matters with his principals and cabled Larkin an arrangement whereby they would manufacture the 504N in Australia. In the meantime, the ALO asked for the cost of purchasing drawings and calling for public tenders. All Broadsmith's negotiations with Larkin had been on the understanding that *you did not intend to take such action.* He also noted that *at all times it was open to you to purchase designs and call for public tender and this was still the case.* (This is the direct opposite of the ALO's advice). In conclusion Broadsmith asked that before deciding on 'Light Planes' for

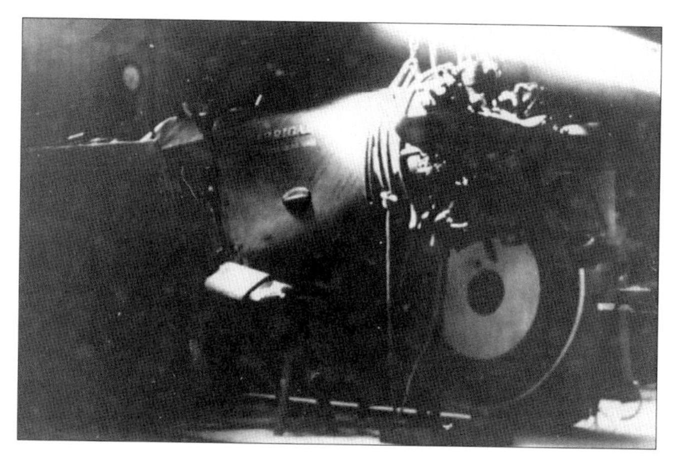

**Above:** The remains of the Warrigal I awaiting disposal. (via RAAF Museum)

**Above:** Photographs of the Warrigal II are rare. This is the landplane version. It was a much neater looking biplane than Warrigal I. (via AHMofWA P021484)

**Above:** This photograph of the Warrigal II comes from Wackett's own scrapbook. (National Library of Australia MS4858)

training the RAAF should at least try the 504N Lynx or the Avro Gosport 'Mongoose.' If price was the consideration then the Gosport 'Mongoose' was the ideal machine. Williams agreed with these recollections; however, he stated that it was a decision of the Minister to allow for the public tendering for the contract.[28] He noted that while he quite understood Broadsmith's point of view, *it would be foolish for us to go on with a machine costing about £2,000 if one of about half that price might do the job.*[29] Nowhere does it appear that the Minister was told that Avro had no objections to the calling of public tenders for the 504N. In fact the reverse is recorded as noted above.

The problem of a replacement for the ageing 504K trainers was becoming acute. No. 1 Flying Training School wrote in November 1927, that if the position was not improved then it could not do further flying instruction. Its establishment was 18 in service with 18 in reserve, whereas it had only 10 in service with nil reserves.[30] It was at this time that a problem involving faulty Avro mainplanes came to the fore and this would have increased pressure for a replacement to be selected quickly. 71 reconditioned Avro 504K mainplanes were accepted by the Inspection Branch and some had flown from 100 to 200 hours before they were condemned by the RAAF for having plugged holes in the spars. On 25 January, 1928, the Defence Department announced that the De Havilland Moth would be purchased for Australia together with drawings and manufacturing rights.

Larkin again contacted the Air Board in February 1928,

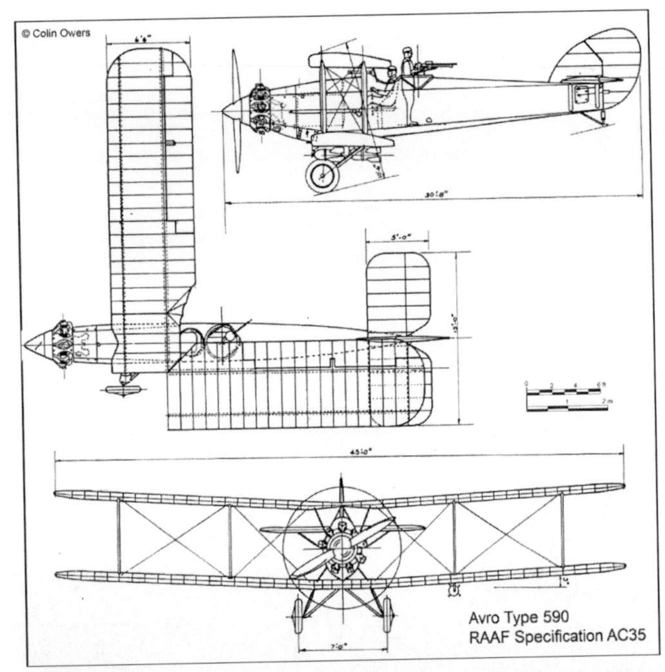


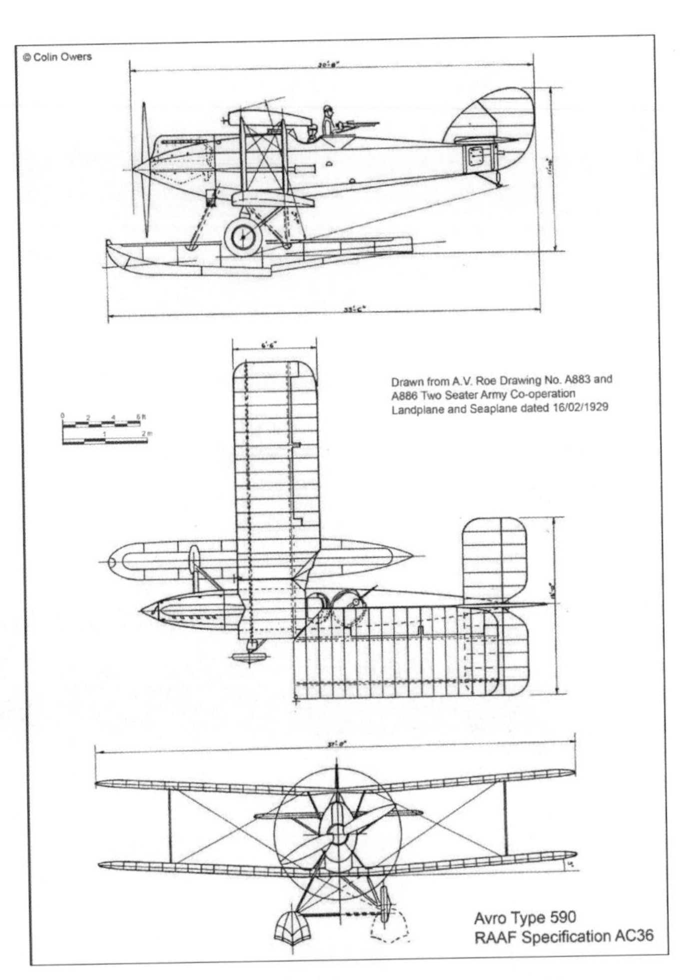


**Above:** Avro three-view Drawing of the long wing version of the Type 590 Warrigal.
**Right:** Avro three-view drawing of the short span version of the Avro Type 590 with in-line engine showing the alternative land and float undercarriage.
**Below:** Sketch of the long wing version on floats with bombs showing the alternative uses of the design.
**Below Right:** Sketch of the Type 590 in the Army co-operation role with in-line engine.

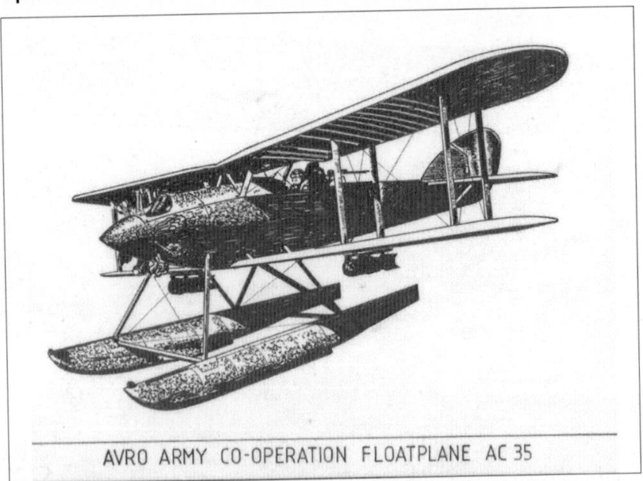
AVRO ARMY CO-OPERATION FLOATPLANE AC 35

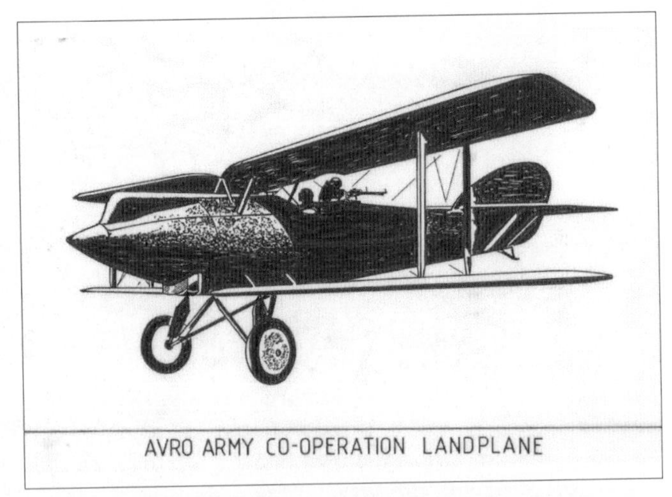
AVRO ARMY CO-OPERATION LANDPLANE

asking if the RAAF was still interested in the Army co-operation and light bombing aircraft as *we are now in a position to quote for the local construction of machines of this type.* Larkin also asked what the situation was with the Warrigal trainer being developed at the Experimental Section as he had been advised that if it was successful, it would be manufactured locally and he was interested in tendering for such production.[31]

The A.C.35 mock-up was still at No.1 Air Depot in May 1928, the Air Board requesting the company to remove it on the 15th of the month. No documentation has been found to explain why the other Avro proposals were not adopted. Meantime, Wackett soldiered on at the Experimental Section. It would be 20 August 1928, before Wackett would advise that the trainer was complete and is stripped for painting.[32]

In November the Warrigal was transported to RAAF Richmond from where it made its first flight on 4 December. The biplane was flown on 14 test flights on the Tuesday and Wednesday by Wackett, Kenneck(?), Simms, the CAS and Shortridge.[33] The official handing over ceremony was conducted on 31 January 1929, at No. 1 FTS, Point Cook, with Mrs Ettie Williams, wife of the CAS, performing the christening. She was taken into the air for a flight in the Warrigal I by Wackett immediately afterwards. Williams recorded that he would not have allowed this had he *not had complete confidence in Wackett both technically and as a pilot who did not do silly things in the air.*[34] Sqn Ldr William D Bostock then gave an aerial display in the new biplane.

An exhaustive series of trials were undertaken by Flt Lt Douglas E.L. Wilson and checked by Sqn Ldr Bostock. The ease with which routine inspections and engine maintenance could be carried out was the subject of favourable comment. The adjustment control for trimming the tail plane was considered too coarse for *nice trimming of the aeroplane.* In normal flight the Warrigal I responded well to control movements, but the aileron control was out of harmony with the rudder and elevator and was too heavy for comfort. There was a marked tendency to swing to the right when taking off and the machine was rather sluggish when leaving the ground. Landing was easy except for a decided swing to the right which was always apparent immediately on contact with the ground. The machine was easy to taxi with no tendency to swing even in a strong cross wind.

Owing to the lack of sensitiveness in the aileron control, flying in disturbed air was distinctly uncomfortable. This was considered unacceptable in a training machine which had to instil a *spirit of confidence in a pupil.* The pilot's view was satisfactory but restricted upwards. The observer had a satisfactory view in all directions except immediately downwards.

The gun mounting for the Vickers was not considered satisfactory on account of access to the feed block. Otherwise the machine was considered suitable for gun training with the Vickers and Lewis. It was not considered suitable for bombing training as the bomb-sight was not mounted in an effective position and the sighting hole in the fuselage floor was thought to be too small. Prone bombing could not be carried out in a *restful position.*

Warrigal I showed peculiar spinning characteristics. When attempting to spin to the left from a straight stall, the machine dropped the right wing on stalling and commenced to turn to the right. The pilot reversed controls to conform to a right-hand spin and held the machine into the spin for two turns. The machine did not recover from the spin until full engine was used with full opposite rudder and stick full forward. The biplane recovered in a sweeping right hand turn. More spins were tried together with looping and half rolling but further attempts at aerobatics were not attempted because of the spin peculiarities. The final summary damned the Warrigal I for *Owing to the peculiar spinning characteristics...this machine is not considered suitable for any form of flying training.*[35] Further adverse comment was made by the Armament Section which reported that *this aircraft is unsuitable for any form of air gunnery or bomb training.*[36]

**Above:** The Warrigal II after its landing gear failed.

*Smith's Weekly* was an independent newspaper that was directed mainly to ex-servicemen after WWI. It mixed sensationalism, sport and satire, and published 'Where a Crash is Part of the Days Work' on 11 May 1929. This article detailed a number of RAAF accidents and included a report on the Warragul's (sic) testing. According to *Smith's* the Warragul's testing was carried out by Flt Lt C Eaton and Sgt Douglas who have been prominently before the public of late in *the search for Anderson and Hitchcock.*

*Eaton took the bus up to a height of about 5000 feet, and put it into a spin, intending to test its stability in getting out of such a predicament. But imagine his horror on discovering that it would not answer the controls! He went spinning down to almost certain death, with Douglas preparing to make a parachute descent, and got within 500 ft of the ground. Then, by an act of fate, he did the wrong thing by putting his engine full on, which did the trick, and he landed safely. How the ordeal affected him was noticed by his nervous condition when he landed.*

*Eaton has about 3000 flying hours to his credit, and is well versed in the peculiarities of aircraft. But what of a pupil pilot doing his first solo in this machine, with about 10 hours flying experience!*

*As a result of these tests, the Warragul was refused by the board as a training machine. It now lies at Pint Cook awaiting some pilot in search of a thrill to take it up for an airing.*

The article concluded that the RAAF's machines were *definitely obsolete and obviously unsafe.* Wing Cdr Paddy Heffernan repeated this story but stated that when Douglas stood up to abandon the ship, the spin stopped and they managed to bring it in for a safe landing.

The OC of 1 AD, Wing Cdr William Anderson, reported that he made four *trips totalling 3 hours 20 minutes flying in the Warrigal I and he did not consider the machine suitable for pupils in its present form on account of its unusual flying qualities.* The chief peculiarities were:

1. The sudden dropping of the right wing and nose when approaching the stall. Even though the machine righted itself if correct use was made of the controls it was thought that if this happened to a pupil low down an accident would almost inevitably result.
2. Spin recovery was slow, the spin recovery not starting until the control column was pushed well forward and even

then it took 2 to 2½ turns to stop spinning.
3. The machine would hunt fore and aft directionally.
4. Partially ineffective rudder control. Even up to cruising speed considerable amount of rudder had to be applied before it began to take effect.
5. It was impossible to perform manoeuvres such as rolling, falling leaf, etc. 'which are of little practical use; but for training pupils one would prefer to use a machine that will do all these manoeuvres well.'
6. It was found difficult to readjust the tail plane when the speed was above about 85 mph.

Williams wrote across this report a note to the Director of Training *to get a fly in this machine as soon as possible and confirm this report or otherwise.* In view of the requirement for the trainer at the FTS, the sooner it is known the better I feel.[37] As Williams was promoting Wackett in his endeavours it is easy to see why he would be concerned with an adverse report on the type.

In response to these reports Wackett replied that as *a report, intended to give qualitative values from which to make technical deductions, I regret to say that it is practically worthless. This is because no recognised, or rational, system of observation or measurement was adopted...nevertheless...the qualitative observations are in accordance with my own experience.*

*The report has served to let me know what others require in the way of improvements.*

Wackett then went on to say that he had attended to all the defects mentioned in the report. *My complete reply to the report is contained in the design of Warrigal II., and in order to permit of the details being examined, I forward herewith copies of the drawings of this type.*

*I appreciate the efforts made by the officers engaged in testing the aircraft, but I grieve to think of the utter lack of technical guidance they received from those whose duty it was to give it.* (Author's underlining.)

Wackett noted that *the only means of carrying on developmental work of this nature has been destroyed* and it was not possible to carry on the work to a successful conclusion.[38] It is presumed that he is here referring to the Australian Government's adoption of the Salmond report's recommendation that the Experimental Section be closed.

A comparison with the Moth showed that *the Warrigal fitted with a 200 H.P. engine consuming 10 gallons of petrol an hour is less efficient from a preliminary training point of view than the Moth fitted with Cirrus II, consuming 4 gallons of petrol an hour.*

*If the performance of the Moth fitted with Gypsy engine is taken the advantage of the Moth is still more outstanding as far as performance is concerned.*[39]

On 19 September P/Off Robert F.M. Dalton with P/Off S.C.C. Thompson as passenger, was flying Warrigal I at Point Cook, *when attempting a landing into wind on the aerodrome, I held off slightly high resulting in a heavy landing causing a bolt in the centre bracket of the undercarriage to collapse. The machine then slewed about 180 degrees to starboard, rendering slight damage to trailing edge of starboard lower main plane.*

Warrigal I had a total flying time of 40 hours 5 minutes at this time. The Air Board considered that Warrigal I had *now been thoroughly tried out and, although it embodies many excellent features of construction, it has been found on the whole unsuitable for the purpose for which it was designed, and it cannot be recommended in preference to "the Moth "either on the score of cost or of suitability.* As there were no spares and the Warrigal II was nearly complete it was decided to write the airframe off and return the instruments and serviceable parts to stock.[40]

Late in 1929 the Auditor-General's Office queried the construction of the two Warrigal machines for which there was no specific ministerial approval for the second aircraft. The Air Board replied that it had been made clear to the Minister *at the time ...that this would involve the construction of two machines, the parts of which would be made together. It was arranged, however, that the second machine...would not be completed until the first one had been flown and desirable modifications ascertained.*[41] The first Warrigal was to have the smaller engine (for training) while the second version was to have the larger engine and seaplane undercarriage.[42] To satisfy the Auditor-General the Minister's written approval was obtained for Warrigal II.[43]

Warrigal II was more pleasing to the eye than Warrigal I. Surviving plans show that the design was to closely follow that of the first biplane with the same fin and rudder, however the aircraft which emerged had a small fin and different rudder.[44] It was fractionally larger than its predecessor and it is thought that the wings were almost identical although interchangeability of upper and lower panels would not now be possible due to the use of slots in the upper wing panels. The 200-hp Lynx was replaced by a 385-hp Jaguar Mk. IV engine. The aircraft had acquired a decidedly angular look.

The decision to close the Randwick Experimental Section when the Warrigal II was completed coupled with the loss of the Widgeon II and its aftermath must have delayed work on the biplane. Wackett was required to submit complete stress calculations for Warrigal II. The results of these showed that the *wing strength of Warrigal...is stronger than that of Wapiti... As a result of the stressing calculations*, Sqn Ldr Harrison could see *no reason why the aircraft should not be flown.*[45]

As soon as the aircraft was completed it was taken to No. 3 Squadron at Richmond. Unfortunately, Wackett's character again brought him into conflict with his fellow officers and on 2 July the Air Board was notified that *Wackett has not yet tested Warrigal. Unable to get any decision from him, permission requested for this unit to go ahead with tests.*[46] This was granted on the 4th,[47] and the aircraft was successfully flown by F/Off Simms on the 7th, and by the 18th he had completed all tests and the biplane was flown to Point Cook.

The testing conducted by Simms must have been very superficial as he submitted a two-page report whereas that

**Above, Below, & Facing Page:** The Warrigal II tried out with floats. Note the enlarged horn balanced rudder and extra interplane struts at the junction of the centre section and the wing panels. The drawings of the floatplane version show a larger balance area but photographs of this have not been discovered. Warrigal II does not ever seem to have had a fuselage roundel applied during its service with the RAAF. (via W Bull Garing)

for the Warrigal I covered nearly 30 typed pages. Simms reported that the Warrigal II *is very easy to fly and has no peculiarities. The machine will take off in approximately the same distance as a Wapiti and once in the air is very manoeuvrable and light on the controls.*

The machine would perform all aerobatics and the problem with spinning had been rectified as *Spinning tests were satisfactorily carried out both to the left and to the right for sustained periods.* The wing slots functioned successfully. The stall was 60 mph with engine off. The gliding speed was between 70–75 mph. *The machine is very easy to land.* In conclusion he stated that the *Warrigal II was a good general purpose machine and could be used successfully for dual instruction, army co-operation etc.*[48] Cpl Eddison had *found the installation* (of the Jaguar Mk. IV) *engine satisfactory.*[49]

On 29 July F/Off T.W. Shortridge took the machine up at Mascot and when he switched the gravity tank off and over to the main tank the engine lost all revs. He switched

back and the *engine gave intermittent very short bursts but still failed to function ordinarily.*[50] He endeavoured to make a cross wind landing on the aerodrome but was obstructed by the hangars. F/Off R.H. Simms saw the crash and observed that *the machine appeared as if it was about to strike the back of one of the hangars when the engine came on with a spasmodic burst and floated him just over the obstacle.*[51] Shortbridge *did an orthodox cross wind landing on one wheel and tail skid and I consider it was entirely due to the extraordinary aerodynamic efficiency of the aircraft that I was able to land in control, although in a stalled condition.* He stalled and dropped from 20 feet, the undercarriage collapsing and the aircraft slewing around causing major damage.[52] In a statement to the Sydney *Daily Pictorial* (2 August 1930), Shortridge said that *I actually stalled, and should have been out of control on Monday when I was over the main hangar, but I was able to land the machine under control. He predicted that the machine would outclass the Wapiti.*

The repairs were carried out by Cockatoo Island Dockyard where Wackett had established an aircraft department after his resignation from the RAAF, and included a new front fuselage former, renewal of portions of the front fuselage ply and repairs to lower mainplane fabric. When No. 3 Squadron received the machine back, they were not satisfied with the repairs as a number of minor items required correction and some defects were found which could not be rectified by the squadron including:

- the front lower starboard spar which had apparently

been damaged by the undercarriage during the crash.
- lower ailerons warped about 1 inch.
- the tailplane actuating cable had a tendency to jamb on the front drum.
- the interior of the lower mainplanes was not available for inspection as the fabric had been repaired. The Squadron considered that it would have been advisable to have stripped both bottom planes.

During a test flight the engine cut out but no fault could be found. The machine was brought to flying standard and flown by F/Off Walters, with Eddison as passenger, to Point Cook on the 12 September.

The Warrigal II was inspected at 1 FTS on the 30th and it appeared that *in order to secure interchangeability of fittings in various positions on the spar it has been necessary to ignore the interference of bracing wires at the point of intersection of flying and landing wires.*[53] A number of modifications were suggested to overcome this and other perceived problem areas of the design. Tests of the spar fitting were carried out at the MSB as the *D.A.I. suspected defective design in this fitting*, but the fitting proved *satisfactory.*[54]

There is little recorded on the type until 10 September 1931, when it was issued from stores to the 'Fighter Squadron.' Sqn Ldr F.R. Scherger commenced tests on the 21st but fell ill and F/Off R.H. Simms took over the programme on 27 January 1932.

Simms noted that the *machine spins both ways smoothly and evenly with the nose moderately down. The recovery from a right spin is normal – the elevator control need not be moved beyond neutral position. In recovery from a left spin the 'stick' had to be pushed well forward.* He went on to say that the Warrigal II was an unpleasant machine to fly *due to excessive torque, an ineffectual rudder and lack of fore and aft stability. It is very hard to obtain a flying level position, the nose tending all the time to oscillate up and down the horizon giving the impression that the machine is on a 'knife edge'. If the hands and feet are taken off the controls in flight the machine does a half roll to the right.*

Pencilled notes on the report state that the unpleasantness is said to have been caused by the military load in the rear cockpit.

The machine required practically full rudder to move the nose when in a glide and the recovery from a gliding turn was very slow. When a half roll was executed to the left the machine tried to spin. *The machine 'flops' and drops its left wing on the top of a loop at all speeds entering up to 160 m.p.h.*[55]

On 6 October, Simms was carrying out a flight in the machine and had made a normal landing but *after running for a few yards I heard a crack, whereupon the machine lurched, swung to the left, and ended up face about.* The accident had been caused by structural failure of the beam to which the undercarriage attached. Repairs and modifications were to be carried out at No. 1 FTS workshops. The Warrigal II had a total flight time of 24 hours 25 minutes at this time.[56]

On 18 February 1932, the DTS considered that *this aircraft should be placed unserviceable pending the redesign and manufacture of the spar root fittings.*[57] A report nine days earlier had noted that there was movement between the front and rear portions of the fuselage.[58] The various modifications were deemed to have been carried out satisfactorily by 1 August.

The machine was then flight tested and held in the workshops before being fitted with floats for trials as a seaplane. By November the Warrigal II had only flown 6 hours as a seaplane *but with the exception of "take off" and "alighting" tests, no actual service trials have been undertaken. These "take off" and "alighting" tests prove that the float undercarriage in its present form is unsuitable, and it is suggested that it be modified...*

*With the exception of the undercarriage weakness, the Warrigal II is successful as a seaplane and it is considered will be a valuable aircraft for Bay patrol duty, and also for dual instruction when the sea is too rough for Moth Seaplanes.*[59]

It was thought that a greater fin area was required for the seaplane.

It would appear that the machine was then stored at No. 1 FTS. In February 1933 the AMS noted that in looking through the Warrigal II file, *I find that the history of this machine has been a succession of crashes and modifications due to structural failures or faults. Up to date...the machine has done a very small time in the air and the cost in time and material, of that small time, appear to be prohibitive.* He then asked for an assessment of the aircraft either as a seaplane or landplane. It was revealed that the total air time of the machine was 30 hours 20 minutes as a landplane, and 6 hours 55 minutes as a seaplane.[60]

It was considered that the faults of the Warrigal II seaplane's float undercarriage were the results of its *unconventional design*, and on account of the *unconventional design no definite assurance* could be given that the proposed modifications would eliminate its faults.[61] Williams noted on these reports that he would like the report to be criticised and analyzed and also he wanted to know how Warrigal II compared with the Wapiti.

Trials had shown that the Warrigal II biplane's performance was *down as compared with Wapiti...with little more than half the service load of the Wapiti.*[62] It was proposed to get the Warrigal II serviceable as soon as possible to fly it *in comparison with a Wapiti, so far as flying qualities are concerned.*[63]

In the meantime, the Warrigal II had been condemned as a seaplane. The aircraft had been *unserviceable for a considerable time and being a non-standard aircraft, would take some considerable time to be made serviceable, due to defective design as a Seaplane. It is considered doubtful if any modification carried out to the undercarriage of this aircraft would prove efficient.*[64]

The Air Board noted that considerable modification would be required before the type could be developed as an efficient landplane or seaplane. Since its performance was not sufficiently improved on the standard service types it was recommended *to cease to develop or operate the Warrigal type from point of view of economy*. The Melbourne Technical College requested the airframe and engine, however only the airframe went to the College and the Jaguar and Lynx engines were to go to disposal.[65] Only two tenders were received; Larkins offered £55 each while New England Airways offered £100 for the Lynx No.4215, and £250 for the Jaguar. The latter offer was accepted on 13 November 1933, thus ending the RAAF's efforts to produce its own aircraft.[66]

Norman Ellison, aviation journalist and author, was a friend of Broadsmith and devoted a chapter to Broadsmith's work in Australia in his book *Flying Matilda*, (Angus and Robertson, Sydney, 1957). Broadsmith corresponded with Ellison after he left Australia and Ellison's papers contain copies of Broadsmith's unpublished autobiography. According to Ellison there were favourable reactions in some quarters to the Avro-LASCO proposals but that strong influence by a section of the British aircraft industry led to the protracted delays which eventually saw the project rejected in favour of the De Havilland Moth. Ellison cites the announcement by the Australian Government that Sir John Salmond, RAF, had been asked to report on the state of the RAAF, as the reason that Broadsmith gave up. The Salmond Report stated that the *British industry could supply all of Australia's prospective requirements for aircraft and there was no need to establish local manufacture.*

The object of the Warrigal specifications had been to embody the characteristics which were desirable in an aircraft for use by the RAAF and to get designer's ideas as to the possibility of building some types in order that the Board might be able to judge *whether they should break away from the use of* RAF types at the present time or not, as well as the possibility of establishing an industry for the production of these types in Australia. The Board was desirous of establishing the industry *without creating what might be termed a monopoly*. Broadsmith's proposals for local manufacture were met with the assertion that if a type was in use with the RAF and it was suitable for Australian requirements it would be used by the RAAF *so long as the aircraft industry is not established in Australia*. Should the industry be established then *it would be the Air Board's policy to take that fact into consideration*. At no stage was the Board willing to commit itself to be seen to support a monopoly even though all the advice it had received noted that the only way a viable industry could be established was by one manufacture being given the small number of orders which would arise or by forming a Government aircraft factory which would oversee the work of private firms.

The contract for the Army Co-operation machine eventually went to the Westland Wapiti (See Chapter 26). It can be seen that the Australian Government would not commit itself to allowing one company to gain an ascendancy in aircraft manufacture which would be a monopoly. This was despite advice that the only way to achieve a secure manufacturing base was for some such monopoly either Government or private. A rare opportunity was lost at a time where the change to metal construction was taking place. The Wapiti, with its mixed construction, was seen as a means of introducing the RAAF to metal construction, however the acquisition of Wapiti biplanes was prolonged by delays due to demand by the UK for aircraft for India and the Middle East. In hindsight it can be appreciated that the slow acquisition of a design manufactured locally would not have changed the RAAF's overall effectiveness. The lesson that the UK could not always meet the needs of Australia was ignored.

The Warrigal was a bold attempt to produce a military training aircraft in Australia. It was saddled with too many functions and as a result could not perform any of them adequately. Its development time took too long and Wackett's personality, coupled with the loss of Widgeon II, led to conflicts and crisis of confidence which took up time which should have been devoted to developing a simple training aeroplane. Air Commodore W *Bull* Garing summed Wackett's work up when he recorded that *in many respects Wackett was perhaps ahead of his time but he never seemed to get a very happy marriage of ideas.*[67]

## Specifications

**Warrigal I**

Dimensions: Span 36 ft 6½ in; Length 25 ft 9 in; Height 9 ft 11½ in.

Wing Area 377 ft$^2$

Weights: Empty 2,148 lbs; Loaded 3,429 lbs. Military load (including crew) 506 lb.

Endurance: At 80 mph, 3 hrs.

**Warrigal II**

Dimensions: Span 37 ft 3$^1/_8$ in; Length (landplane) 26 ft 11 in, (seaplane) 31 ft 1 in.

Weights: Including Vickers gun 2,414 lb. Flight trials with full military load given as 3,647 lb.

Performance: 120 mph ground; 105 mph ASI at 4,000 ft; 96 mph ASI at 8,000 ft.

## End Notes

1. NAA ACT CRS A705 Item 69/2/278. Minute: "Training machines", Williams to DPT, 30.01.1926.
2. *Ibid.* Minute, DPT to CAS, 15.02.1926.
3 *Ibid.* Letter; "Design of New Training Aeroplane," OC, Experimental Section to Air Board, 12.02.1926.
4 *Ibid.*
5 *Ibid.* "General Training Machine. A/DTS to 1 FTS, 12.04.1926.
6 *Ibid.* Minute; "Training Machines". E Wackett, A/DTS to CAS, 3.05.1926.
7 *Ibid.* DO and I to CAS, 19.02.1926.
8 NAA ACT CRS A705/1 Item 24/7/124. Minute: "Policy - Experimental Section, R.A.A.F. Randwick". CAS to

Defence, 29.04.1926.
9 *Sydney Morning Herald,* 5.12.1928. P.15. This article stated that the fuselage was divided into four sections and could be altered from a two-seater to a single-seat scout.
10 Air Board Agendum No.776. "Purchase of Lynx Aero Engine". Meeting 28.06.1926.
11 *Ibid.* Minute: DTS to CAS, 15.12.1926.
12 *Ibid.* Wackett to Air Board, 3.01.1926.
13 *Sydney Morning Herald*, 5 December 1928, P.15.
14 Air Board Agendum No.921. Meeting 23.06.1927.
15 Letter from LASCO to Dept of Defence, 7.02.1928. Copy in RAAF Museum, Point Cook.
16 The spelling of the Warrigal, an Australian bird, was a source of constant irritation to Wackett as recorded above, however the Avro-LASCO contenders still used the incorrect spelling as recorded here.
17 NAA ACT CRS A705/1 Item 121/1/249. Manufacture of Aircraft in Australia. Letter Air Ministry to Air Board, 5.02.27.
18 *Ibid.* Letter; Broadsmith to CAS, 7.06.1927.
19 *Ibid.* Minute; DTS to CAS, 21.08.1925.
20 *Ibid.* Letter; Broadsmith to Minister of Defence (Sir William Glasgow), 16.06.1927.
21 *Ibid.* Letter; Broadsmith to Air Board, 15.06.1927.
22 *Ibid.* Letter; LASCO to Defence, 11.08.27.
23 *Ibid.* Letter; LASCO to Defence, 30.09.27.
24 *Ibid.* Minute: "Purchase of Avros 504N", 5.08.27.
25 NAA ACT CRS A705/1 Item 121/1/249. Op Cit. Extract Telegram to Williams, 15.08.27.
26 *Ibid.* Letter; Williams to Broadsmith, 7.11.27.
27 *Ibid.* Minute; Williams to Defence, 25.10.27.
28 *Ibid.* The Minister had directed in August 1927 that public tenders be invited for the construction of 504N aircraft. Contained in Minute, August 1927.
29 *Ibid.* Letter; Williams to Broadsmith, 3 02.1928.
30 NAA ACT CRS A2408/1 Item 121/2. Letterbook: Landplanes Avro. Entry dated 29.11.27.
31 Letter ; LASCo to Defence, 7.02.1928. Copy in RAAF Museum, Point Cook.
32 *Ibid.* Wackett to Air Board, 20.08.1928.
33 *Ibid.* Message, 5.12.1928.
34 Williams, R. These Are Facts, P.197.
35 NAA ACT CRS A705 Item 69/2/278. Op Cit. "Summary of Trials", 02.1929.
36 *Ibid.* Minute: "Gunnery Trials". DDI (Armament) to Dof I.
37 *Ibid.* Letter: "Warrigal I", OC 1 AD to Air Board, 4.06.1929.
38 *Ibid.* Letter; OC, Experimental Section to Air Board, 26.08.1929.
39 *Ibid.* Minute: "Warrigal I", DofS to CAS.
40 Air Board Agendum No.1344. "Disposal of Warrigal I". Meeting 18.10.1929.
41 NAA ACT CRS A705 Item 60/2/318. "Warrigal II - History of Construction Life and Disposal." Air Board to Commonwealth Audit Office, 11.10.1929.
42 *Ibid.* Minute: CAS to Financial Member, 2.12.1929.
43 *Ibid.* Memorandum: "Construction of Aircraft Warrigal II." Defence to Auditor General, 9.01.1930.
44 NAA NSW. RAAF Experimental Section Plan No.676.
45 NAA ACT CRS A705 Item 60/2/318. Op Cit. Minute; "Warrigal II Stress Calculations." DTS to AMS, 2.05.1930.
46 *Ibid.* Wireless Message; No. 3 Squadron to Air Board, 2.07.1930.
47 *Ibid.* Air Board to No.3 Squadron, 4.07.1930.
48 *Ibid.* Letter; "Tests of Warrigal II. Landplane." Simms to CO, No.3 Squadron, 21.07.1930.
49 *Ibid.* Letter: "Report on Jaguar Mk.IV. Engine - Fitted to Warrigal II." Eddison to OC, No.3 Squadron, 21.07.1930.
50 NAA Vic CRS MP116 Item Series 1. AAIC Minutes 1927–1936. Evidence of F/Off Shortbridge, 4.08.1930. With Minutes 8.09.1930.
51 *Ibid.* Evidence F/Off Simms, 4.08.1930. With Minutes 8.09.1930.
52 *Ibid.* AAIC Minutes 1927-1936. Evidence of F/Off Shortbridge, 4.08.1930. With Minutes 8.09.1930. According to the Kalgoorlie Miner of 30.07.1930, Shortridge was a pilot of Australian National Airways.
53 *Ibid.* Minute; "Warrigal II", DTS to AMS, 1.10.1930.
54 NAA Vic MP118/2 Item 69/2/544. Note to results, 27.03.1931.
55 NAA ACT CRS A705/1 Item 60/2/318. "Warrigal. II. - Tests." Date commenced: 21.09.1931.
56 *Ibid.* "Casualty Report".
57 *Ibid.* Minute: Harrison, DTS to AMS, 18.02.1932.
58 *Ibid.* "Report of failure and defect in aircraft or aircraft accessories", 9.02.1932.
59 *Ibid.* Letter: "Report of Suitability of Warrigal II as Seaplane". CO, 1 FTS to Air Board, 10.11.1932.
60 *Ibid.* Minute; "Warrigal II". AMS to DTS and DTE, 24.02.1933.
61 *Ibid.* Minute: DTS to AMS, 27.02.1933.
62 *Ibid.* Minute: DTS to AMS, 7.03.1932.
63 *Ibid.* Minute: Harrison to CAS, 8.04.1932.
64 *Ibid.* De La Rue, OC, 1FTS to Air Board. "Warrigal Seaplane", 8.03.1933.
65 Air Board Agendum No.1566. Approved 6.07.1933.
66 *Ibid.* Minute: "Disposal of Jaguar and Lynx Aero Engines and Spares", AMS to CO, 1AD, 5.09.1933.
67 Interview with Air Commodore W.H. Garing on 14.12.1987. Interview notes, RAAF Air Power Study Centre, Canberra.

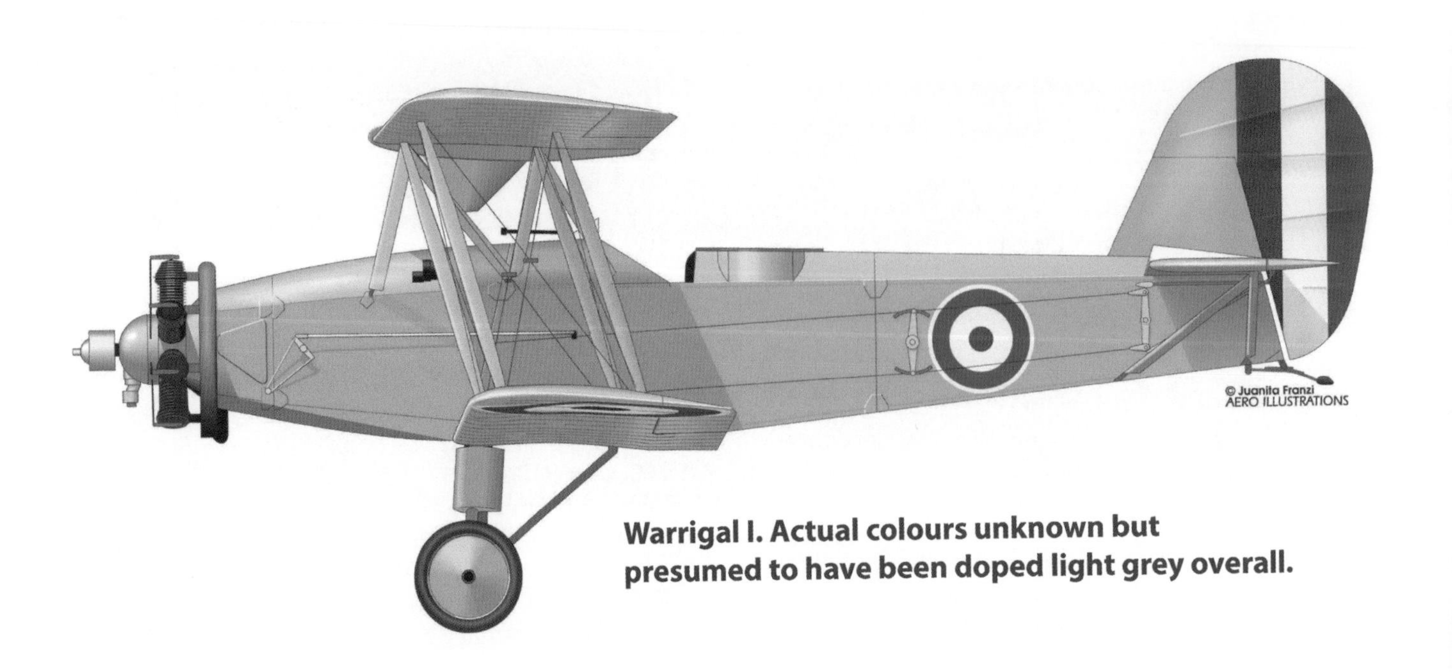


**Warrigal I. Actual colours unknown but presumed to have been doped light grey overall.**

**Warrigal II. Actual colours unknown but presumed to have been doped light grey overall.**

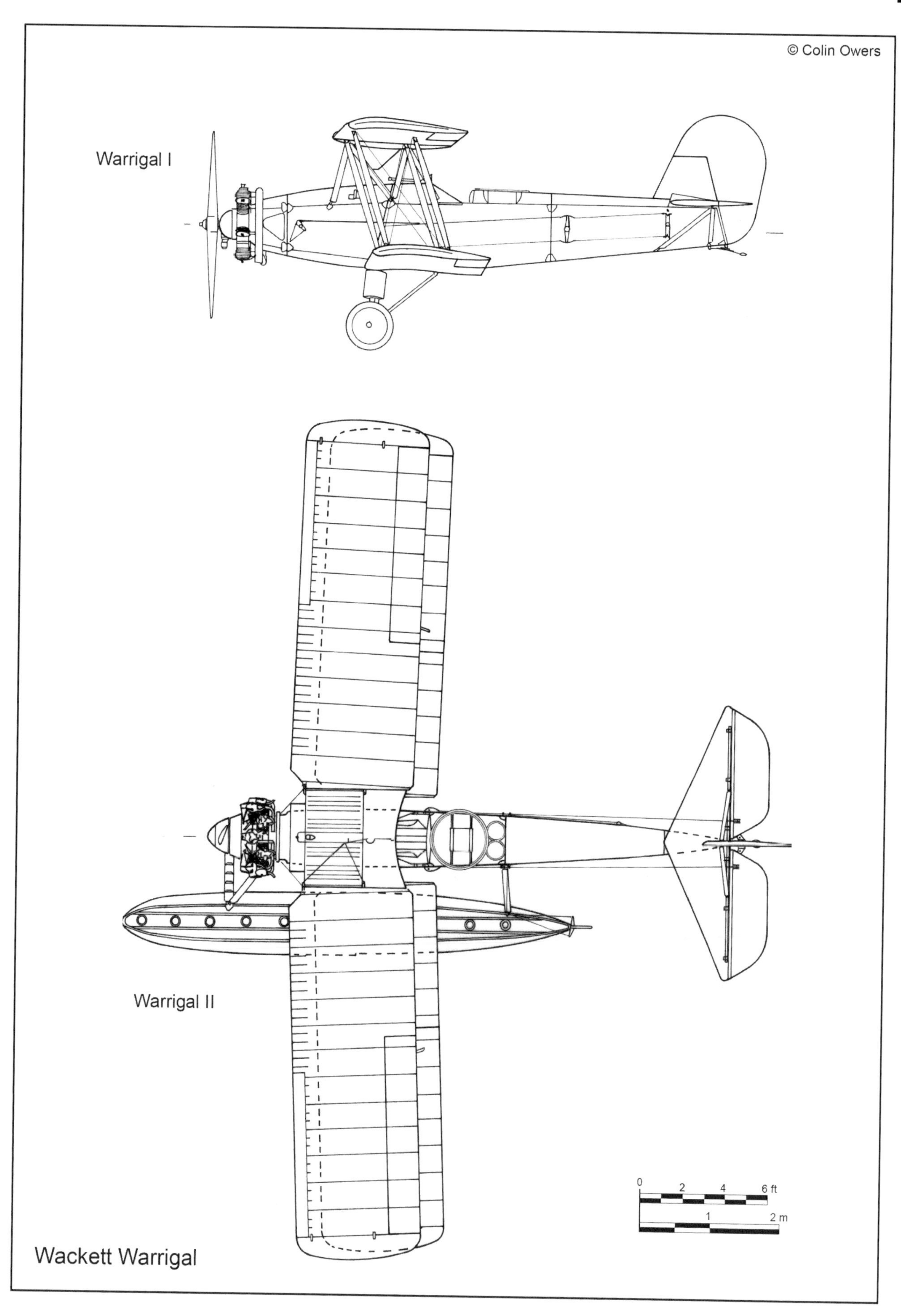
© Colin Owers
Warrigal I
Warrigal II
0
2
4
6 ft
1
2 m
Wackett Warrigal

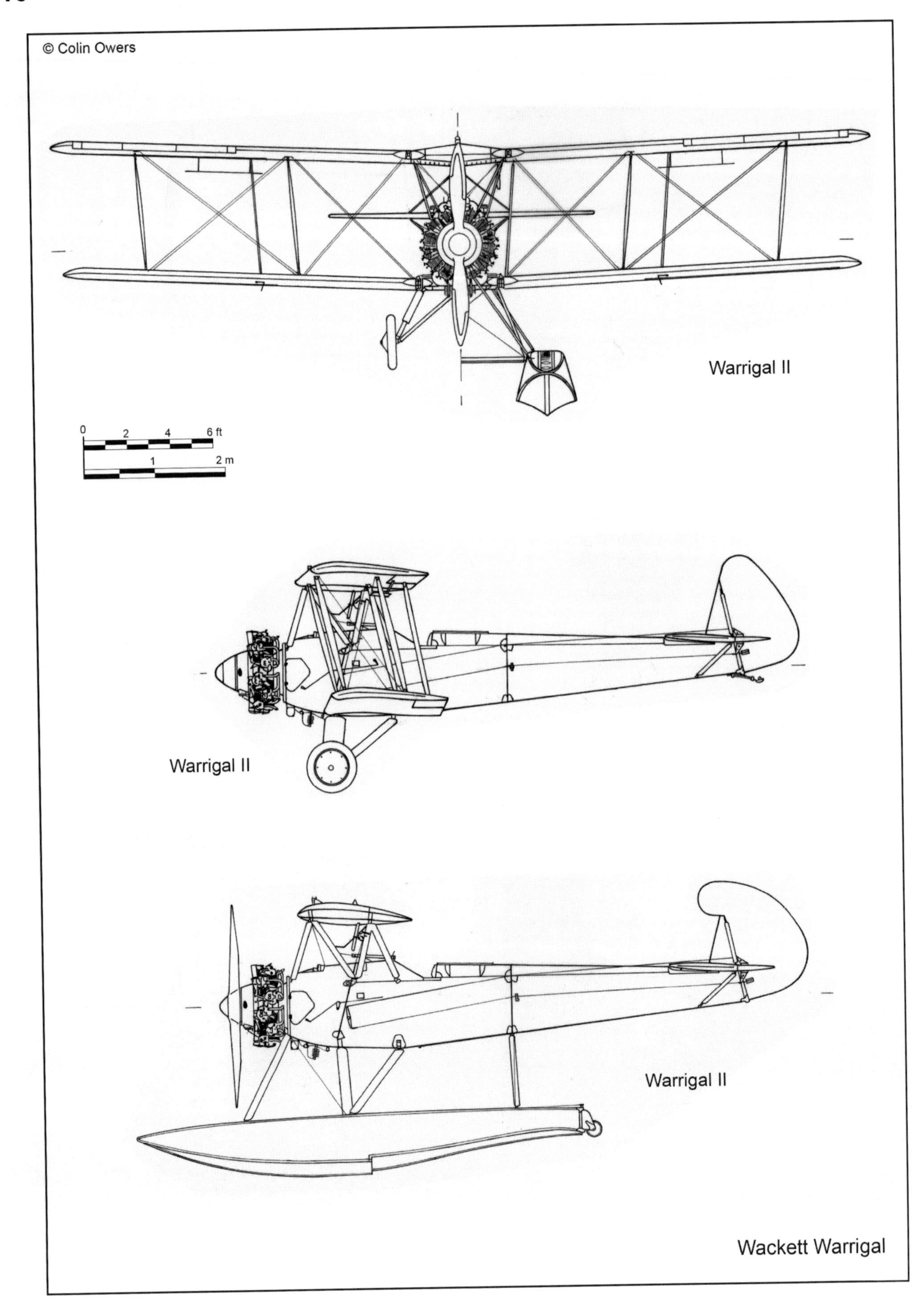
© Colin Owers
Warrigal II
0
2
4
6 ft
1
2 m
Warrigal II
Warrigal II
Wackett Warrigal

# Chapter 26. The Westland Wapiti IA & IIA

**Above & Below:** Australia's first Wapiti, A4-1, in the UK.

Air Cdre *Reg* Burrage recalls that as a young Pilot Officer in the RAAF in 1938, Francis *Dad* Bladin gave a lecture in which he said *Never be too proud to turn back if you run into bad weather conditions.* The emphasis Bladin placed on this rule was such that *Reg* felt that he *must have learnt his lesson from that disastrous flight in which one life was lost.*[1]

On 25 April 1938, eleven RAAF Wapiti biplanes left Richmond, NSW, at 0900 hours for Laverton, Victoria, after having participated in a pageant held at Richmond on the 23rd. The unit arrived at Cootamundra at 1055 hours, refuelled and left in formation for the second stage of the flight. Weather conditions had been good, however when approximately 20 miles from Cootamundra reduced visibility conditions were encountered but not such as to cause concern. When 70 miles out the following message was received by Wing Cdr Francis M Bladin's Wapiti, A5-26, the only one of the biplanes fitted with wireless: - Dust storms and bad visibility between Wagga and Benalla. Strong north wind 45 to 50 m.p.h. and slight showers over ranges.[2]

Bladin considered that *in view of...*(this)...*W/T. weather*

**Above:** A5-1 the first RAAF Wapiti IA in flight. The cowling of the Wapiti Mk. IA was a distinctive feature of these machines. (RAAF Museum)

**Above:** One of the new Wapiti biplanes is displayed for the press. Note how the fin and rudder have been marked-up for printing in the newspaper. (Argus Newspaper Collection, SLVic)

**Above:** For a short time, A5-1 bore a pennant on the rear fuselage behind the roundel and each side of the serial number. The actual colours of the pennant have still to be discovered.

*report* he would proceed, expecting the weather to improve once the ranges near Seymour were crossed.[3] The flight continued and although some bad weather was expected it was not until Seymour that the flight encountered *thick, red dust...One flight broke away and its aircraft were landed near Seymour and Yea. Shortly after this, the squadron encountered disturbed conditions, followed almost immediately by rain, hail and dense cloud. Visibility became nil.*[4] All aircraft separated and each pilot was left to act independently on his own initiative.

Flt Lt J.R. Paget reported that when the formation began to break up, he was separated from the others, *and the last I saw was F/O. Walker, W/Cdr. Bladin and the late F/O. Chalman disappearing into a thick mixture of white cloud and red dust. A few moments later F/O. Wittschieve flew over my head and I endeavoured to pick him up. Whilst watching him my aircraft went into a spin. I came out of the spin at about 5,000 ft. and glided down, saw the ground when about 200 ft from it.*[5] Paget was able to find his way back to Point Cook.

At Cootamundra F/Off Brian Reginald Walker had taken over as the lead aircraft with Bladin on his immediate right. He reported that he started to try and climb out of the dust, but *the squadron ran into conditions of such extreme poor visibility that adjacent aircraft at a distance of about one span were only visible as shadows. The squadron was still intact at a point 10 miles East of Seymour but after that I only noticed adjacent aircraft...When an aircraft on my right nearly collided with me I turned right off my course, and then turned back on to it. At this stage all other aircraft disappeared.*[6] Walker managed to fly through the clouds and dust until he calculated he should be over Point Cook, whereupon he descended through the clouds to appear in clear visibility over Box Hill. He proceeded safely to Point Cook.

Wapitis A5-32 and A5-37 forced landed with no injury and no damage. A5-33, piloted by F/Off Roland Robert Cox, suffered engine trouble and saw *a paddock and landed there as it seemed big. As I was coming down I saw* (a drain running) *diagonally across the paddock, I cleared the drain and as I was running along I saw a fence, I did not have enough engine to get over it and the machine went straight through* (the) *fence* damaging the mainplanes.[7]

F/Off Andrew Fisher Chalman in A5-19 crossed the range and like the majority of other pilots attempted a forced landing when the country became reasonably level. Chalman approached one paddock but just prior to landing he opened up his engine and climbed, lost speed, stalled and crashed.

**Above:** According to the caption this photograph shows Westland Wapiti IA biplanes A5-1 and A5-2 at Point Cook. Note the original landing gear. (via AHM of WA)

**Above:** Only the third Wapiti Mk. IA can be identified in this line up, A5-9. No message pick-up hooks are installed.

The 25 year old Chalman was killed, and his passenger, AC1 Ray Prime, was seriously injured.

Investigation of the accident revealed that a line squall had developed over the Seymour area just as the Wapitis were in that locality. This could not have been forecasted from the weather reports given to the squadron before leaving Richmond and during the flight. The line squall together with the dust conditions made flying particularly difficult and hazardous. The decision to continue the flight was deemed to have been based on a reasonable premise. Chalman's accident was thought to have been due to poor technique in carrying out the forced landing, probably due to stress caused by the adverse flying conditions. Chalman had left the Post Master General's Department to join the RAAF as a Cadet in January 1935. He was assessed as *timid* but progressed steadily to a *good average pupil* and then *average pilot*.[8] That a major tragedy had been avoided and there was only one serious crash resulting from this episode points to

**Above:** The nine original RAAF Wapiti IA biplanes lined-up for inspection. Location unknown but the presence of small children would indicate it is not at a RAAF base. The first three aircraft have message pick-up hooks installed. (AHMofWA P961671)

**Above:** Wapiti IA A5-3 with the nose cone removed shows the extension shaft the Jupiter engine. De Havilland Moth trainer A7-54 behind. (RAAF Official)

the skill of the pilots involved.

The RAAF had received Ministerial approval for the acquisition of eight Armstrong Whitworth Atlas biplanes to re-equip the Army co-operation flight of No. 3 Squadron in 1927. At the same time, it was also proposed to purchase six De Havilland Hound light bombers. The CAS (Williams) noted that it was RAAF policy to have air cooled engines and he had been in touch with De Havilland to discuss the possibility of a version of the Hound with such an engine. This was the Jupiter powered D.H.65J which was built to RAAF specifications and first flew in early June 1928.[9] In October 1927, Williams reported that *as a result of service experience the design (of the Atlas) is being modified with the view to simplifying maintenance in service.* Williams proposed to obtain the modified aircraft and by *placing our order at the same time* (as the RAF) *we will probably get an approved price.*[10] In the event the order did not proceed.

In 1928 the Air Board again considered the replacement of the RAAF's aircraft. Nos. 1 and 3 Squadrons had been *maintained in aircraft from that received with the Gift Equipment from the Imperial Government.* The Board considered that the Composite Squadrons, *Whilst offering advantage from the point of view of having a nucleus of types, these units present problems in training (particularly Citizen Forces) and are not so economical in stores, etc., as they would be if equipped with one type of machine and engine throughout.* The international situation was considered such that the adoption of a *two-seater of good performance for general purposes with its resultant economies ...would be justified.* Therefore, specific types for bomber and army co-operation were not required, the one aircraft performing both functions.

The following British machines were considered suitable

**Above:** Wapiti IA with ground crew and three parachutists. Note the man behind on the lower wing with the handle for the inertial starter for the Jupiter engine.

and were examined and flown *by our officers in England.*:

Fairey III F with Jupiter engine.
Armstrong Siddeley Atlas with Jaguar engine.
Westland Wapiti with Jupiter engine.
De Havilland Hound with Jupiter engine.

The RAF had organised a General-Purpose Competition to determine which type would be adopted by that service and the RAAF was advised to await the outcome of this competition. The Wapiti was noted as being as a general-purpose machine in service with the RAF and would probably be adopted for India. It was priced at £4,550 (wood) and £5,200 (metal) including engine.

The Hound was the cheapest of the four aircraft at £4,300. It was the latest design, of composite construction and was being produced in metal for the RAF as a light bomber. The Board recommended *that 32 De Havilland "Hounds" be purchased for the re-equipping of Nos. 1 and 3 Squadrons* for a total price including spares and freight of approximately £150,000.[11]

Two months later Williams submitted another report to the Board wherein he noted that the Hound was dropped from the *General Purposes competition...on the ground that it had a performance superior to that required for general purposes.* The type was being built by Shorts with the Napier inline engine and it was unlikely that the Jupiter engined version would enter RAF service. The Wapiti and Fairey IIIF were adopted as general-purpose types as a result of the competition and after service experience one of these two types would be adopted generally. It was considered that it would be the Wapiti and in this case *the type will be in production in England for some time to come.*[12] The Board decided to re-equip *two Service Squadrons (S.E. and D.H.9 flights) with "Wapiti's" (16 machines) plus 100% reserves.*[13] The Board recommended the adoption of the Wapiti in composite construction which it was thought would *be a convenient type to introduce metal construction into the RAAF.*[14]

Sir John Salmond was in Australia at this time to report on the state of the RAAF and the Minister for Defence asked for his views on the Board's recommendation. Salmond agreed with the choice of the Wapiti.[15] Air Board Order No.242 was raised in September 1928, for the purchase of 28 Westland Wapiti Mk.IA biplanes together with service equipment, packing, freight, engines and spares for a total price of £150,000. The order was to be kept confidential until an official announcement by the Minister.

The Wapiti was designed to Specification 26/27 and Westland utilised as many De Havilland D.H.9a parts as possible into the new design. There were eight entries to the General-Purpose Competition and it was the ability of the Wapiti to use the large numbers of D.H.9a spares in the United Kingdom and overseas which won the day for the type.

**Above:** Close-up of a Wapiti IIA showing the synchronised Vickers machine gun with feed and collector chutes. Note the ring and bead sight on the forward fuselage decking. Most photographs do not show the rear gun ring armed.

**Right:** A5-2 is fully armed with a Vickers synchronised machine gun and the rear gunner has a Lewis or Vickers K on the gun ring. The handle on the top of the Vickers is for the pilot to cock the gun. The installation of the Vickers is crude for its time as streamlining was well understood. Note the pilot's windscreen. (RAAF Museum)

**Above:** Cadet Coleman poses with a Wapiti IA undergoing maintenance in the open at Holsworthy, 1930. Note the early landing gear. (via RAAF Museum)

**Left:** View of the pilot's cockpit of a RAAF Wapiti. (via B Walker)

**Below:** RAAF Wapiti mounting a RAF light service carrier post-1918 type that replaced the wartime Cooper bomb carrier. The bombs are the 1930s replacement for the Cooper – "Bombs, Practice, Aircraft 8½ lb." (via B Walker)

**Above:** Wapitis undergoing maintenance. The oil cooler under the fuselage is well displayed.

The prototype's wings, tail surfaces, ailerons and interplane struts were stock D.H.9a components. The first production version of this large two-bay biplane had the front fuselage constructed of square section duralumin tubes with a wooden rear fuselage section. 25 of these Wapiti I biplanes were constructed. The RAAF received nine Wapiti IA biplanes, the version with the geared Jupiter VIII in place of the direct drive Jupiter VI. The Wapiti II featured a full metal fuselage and metal wings. This was followed by the major production version, the Wapiti IIA with the Jupiter VIII. The Wapiti III was used by the South African Air Force, 27 being built in that country. The Wapiti V and Wapiti VI were the last models to be built in any numbers with 35 and 16 respectively being constructed. The Wapiti VI was a dual control version of the basic type. In addition, the type was exported in small numbers to the Central Chinese Government. Like its predecessor the D.H.9a, the Wapiti saw active service in the middle-east and India using the principles of air control to keep the dissident tribes in check. The Wapiti had a long and distinguished career in the RAF. The type was to be further developed as the Westland Wallace. In all some 565 were built including some completed as Wallace biplanes.

As noted above the RAAF ordered their first batch of Wapiti airframes and Jupiter engines in September 1928. The British Air Ministry issued Instruction to Proceed No. A.M. 875845/28 on 18 October for the Australian Wapitis. The change from the Hound to the Wapiti caught the ALO in London unawares as he had taken action on the 3rd to order the Hound with split undercarriage *permitting torpedoes* to be carried.[16] In a wireless message to the Board he stated that *the first notification we received that Australia was changing their idea from the Hound to the Wapiti was a private lettergram from Sir John Salmond to the C.A.S*[17] He advised that there were no Jupiter VIII engines or Wapitis available immediately or in the next nine months except for those to meet urgent demands from Iraq and India. The British Air Ministry took eight Wapitis for Australia from the present allotment facing the risk of shortage in Iraq. *The Air Ministry are doing their utmost to meet your demand, but with the best of will in the world they cannot do any more.*[18] From surviving documents it appears that Australia was still contemplating operating the Hound together with the Wapiti, so the confusion felt by the ALO is understandable. The delay was noted and the ALO notified to *Proceed with order for Wapitis.*[19] It appears that there may have been nine aircraft diverted to Australia as the first nine RAAF aircraft were Wapiti IA biplanes. They were later converted to Wapiti IIA standard.

The uncertainty of delivery, modifications brought about by the General-Purpose Competition, changing Australian requirements, and un-availability of engines and parts led to a protracted and confused period in the execution of the contract. The Air Board asked if the Wapiti could carry a torpedo but were told that Westland would have to redesign the airframe for such an operation.[20] In September 1928, the ALO agreed *to take all metal fuselages with wood wings and tail units because going back to composite fuselage construction would further delay* the contract.[21]

**Left:** Carrying out maintenance on Wapiti IIA A5-37.

The last 12 aircraft were to be delivered without instruments as a cost savings measure, and if the Aircraft Inspection Directorate required flight trials then one set of instruments from the first 16 machines was to be used.[22] The delays in fulfilling the contract meant that the situation in Australia was such that these last 12 machines would be required *almost immediately after their arrival for F.T.S.* and it was agreed that they be fitted out upon arrival, the necessary equipment having already being purchased in view of savings effected in the cost of the contract.[23] Six Wapitis had been shipped via SS *Taranaki* without Wireless Transmission panels as supplies of necessary items were unavailable in time and the Air Ministry considered it essential *that these panels should be wired by the Service in preference to being done by contractor.*[24]

The Board was notified that *the supply of engines is the key to situation and that Air Ministry controls the delivery of these for a long time ahead.*[25] The first five engines were delivered with a plain type elbow between the carburettor and induction pipe, while subsequent engines had an exhaust heated type of elbow. The first six engines were manufactured without the modification to enable the use of mineral lubricating oil. It was concluded that these engines could be run on mineral oil but would require more frequent overhaul. The ALO noted that *we had, in order to get delivery with the aircraft, to accept*...(these engines)...*unmodified or face considerable delay in having the modifications carried out, in addition to paying the additional charges incurred thereby.*[26] The remaining 22 engines were to incorporate the necessary modifications to run on mineral oil even though the *Bristol Company objects to supply modified engines to us because their production has been batched on other lines.*[27] The engine situation was such that there were at present *79 Wapitis at Westlands and no Jupiter VIII engines available to enable them to be flight tested.*[28] Notwithstanding this the Air Ministry had promised to allow the first six engines manufactured from the end of December to go to Australia.

Westland were *considerably agitated with respect to the Jupiter VIII engine question as they are of the opinion that non-delivery of this type of engine will seriously affect demand for Wapiti aircraft.*[29] Owing to the small output of Jupiter VIII engines it was not possible for all aircraft to be flight tested. If flight testing was insisted on then this would cause *a chaotic condition at Westlands and all calculations regarding aircraft deliveries would be upset.*[30] The ALO agreed to allow Westlands to use two Air Ministry engines, which were held at the factory, in the Australian Wapiti biplanes selected for the ½ hour air test.

The urgency and resulting confusion saw the delivery of a number of engines which did not have CC machine gun synchronisation gear, this being supplied later. Of those Wapitis on Order No.242, the last six machines were to have *long distance tanks*. The last 20 machines had the split cantilevered undercarriage. The first eight were to be fitted with this undercarriage when spare examples became available at a later date. 16 machines were to have message pick up gear. Some of this confusion was the result of Australia requesting changes as the contract proceeded. Metal wings were wanted at one point but the order was too advanced for this to be done.

**Above:** This photograph is thought to show Wapitis under maintenance at Laverton. The instructional fuselage on the trestle stands to the right has plumb bobs attached to show how to brace it correctly.

Australia ordered another ten Wapitis. Order No.278 for three all metal Wapiti Mk. IIA airframes was placed on 6 June 1929. These three aircraft were also to have the extra fuel capacity of the last six machines of the first order. There were no engines included on Order No.278. The first machines on this order were received on 2 April 1930, with the last arriving a month later. The final order, No.308 of 31 December 1929, was for an additional seven Wapiti Mk. IIA biplanes. This order took 14 months to complete.[31]

When the first three metal Wapiti biplanes arrived in Australia it was discovered that the *metal wings purchased with the three all metal Wapiti Aircraft (Mark 11 A) have not been modified in accordance with Wapiti Modification No.56 but the set of spare wings supplied have been so modified.*[32] It was suggested that in *view of the present need for economy... (that) these wings should be retained in store unmodified and D.H.9.A Wood wings used.*[33] However, it was decided to fit the modified spare wings to A5-29 and to modify all the wings to standard. Documents suggest that none of these 38 biplanes were fitted for night flying at this stage.

To add to the Air Board's troubles, the *Daily Guardian* newspaper for 7 December 1928, carried an article headlined 'AIR FORCE BLUNDER. 28 OBSOLETE PLANES ORDERED.' The article went on to say that the Minister for Defence, Sir William Glasgow, had refused to state whether the Wapitis were all metal or of composite construction, but the paper had it on good authority that they were of *the wood and metal type.* In answer to the paper's allegations Williams noted that the Wapiti was first developed with the front portion of the fuselage of metal construction and the rear portion of wood. It was introduced into service in this form, but the latest type had an all-metal fuselage. In addition to the extra cost of the all metal Wapiti, the RAAF had riggers whose basic trade was carpenter and *we could not switch over from all wood to all metal in one act.*[34] However, as the manufacturer had given up making composite fuselages and it was possible to get a reduction in price due to including the Australian order with Air Ministry orders, the Wapitis supplied to the RAAF had all metal fuselages *at no greater cost than that...for the composite fuselage.*[35] Wings and tailplanes were of wooden construction.

The Wapiti was given the serial prefix 'A5' in the Australian serial number system and the first Australian Wapiti, A5-1, was christened by Lady Ryrie, the High Commissioner's wife, at Westland's Yeovil factory on 21 February 1929. The first batch of six left the UK on the SS *Taranaki* on 19 March, arriving in Melbourne on 29 April. After assembly the first test flight was conducted on 10 May by Wing Cdr W.H. Anderson.[36] No. 1 Squadron received its first Wapiti on 13 May. From this date the D.H.9 and D.H.9a biplanes were returned to store as Wapitis became available.[37] In September 1929, Williams recorded that the RAAF had *now got rid of all of our old "Avro", D.H.9 and S.E.5As. We expect to finish with D.H.9As within the next eight or nine months.* The Wapiti were *doing quite well* but the maintenance was greater than expected. *Our last batch*

**Above:** No. 3 Squadron's A5-27, with A5-13 in the background, after the cyclone at Bourke on 1 February 1932. The engines and machine guns are still wearing their canvas covers. Note that the wheel covers of A5-27 appear to be coloured. Despite the apparent amount of damage A5-27 was repaired and undertook another aerial survey in April 1933 with Dr Woolnough of the Lithgow, Newnes area of NSW. The machine was converted in November 1939 but probably had finished flying in 1938 as parts of A5-27 were used to keep A5-34 flying in March 1939. (via P.G. Heffernan)

**Left:** Dr George Woolnough (with beard) with the RAAF aerial survey team for the oil survey of late 1932. The Wapiti was A5-35 or A5-36.

**Below:** A5-14 after a hard landing, probably that of 26 November 1936. Note the serial is replaced by the large numerals '14'. (via J Hopton)

**Above:** Wapitis A5-10, A5-17 and A5-22 over St Kilda, Melbourne, 1931. (P.G. Heffernan)

*of pupils trained on "Moths" and then on D.H.9As found no difficulty in flying Wapitis and all our Citizen Force pilots are flying "Wapitis" quite well.*[38] The last of the 38 ordered arrived on 2 March 1931.

No. 3 Squadron was selected to be the first to receive the new aircraft. However, the tabulation of aircraft on issue to units as at 14 June 1929, shows that No. 1 Squadron was equipped with four Wapitis while No. 3 Squadron had three D.H.9a and four Wapitis on strength.[39] After assembly and test at No. 1 AD the aircraft were flown to Richmond, NSW. On one such flight on 28 July 1930, the Wapiti flew non-stop in poor weather using 114 gallons of fuel and 9 gallons of oil.[40] Compared with the performance of the D.H.9a biplanes the RAAF had been struggling to keep airworthy, the Wapiti must have seemed a marked improvement, however it was not in any sense a modern front line military aircraft. Following an inspection of No. 3 Squadron in late 1931, the CAS asked if the ninth Wapiti could be sent to that unit. The supply situation was such that the only way to give No. 3 Squadron a full complement was to take one from 1 FTS if that units *immediate reserve can be left two short till late February, or it can be sent now at the expense of leaving 1 Squadron one short till then.*[41] No. 1 Squadron was designated as the dive bombing squadron with No. 3 Squadron being the army co-operation squadron, however, No. 3 Squadron's pilots were given instruction in dive bombing for performing at displays and pageants. *You can put Waps into screaming dives and you can do real dives* in a Wapiti recorded Geoff Hartnell and this is confirmed by other pilots of the biplane.[42]

The Wapiti entered into all the various activities of the RAAF which had previously been performed by the De Havilland D.H.9 and D.H.9a biplanes. To the Bristol Bulldog was left the task of retaining fighting skills. The Wapiti was used for army co-operation, as a dive bomber, for photo-reconnaissance, and towing anti-aircraft drogue targets. Its range saw it undertake many mapping flights in all parts of Australia. As detailed above, several were delivered with *desert tanks* for use in Central Australia. In addition, it was used as the final trainer for aircrew. When the Hawker Demon was introduced, the Wapitis were reconditioned as trainers or used as utility aircraft. The outbreak of the 1939–45 World War saw the type maintained in service as there were no replacements available.

The first notable Wapiti flight was probably that of

**Above & Left:** Wapiti A5-12 with three others over the Sydney Harbour Bridge, with the Australian cruisers, *Australia* and *Canberra*, at the naval base at Garden Island. (via RAAF Museum & AHMofWA P0211487)

**Below:** A5-12 with the large serial and what appears to be a large 'Y' marking where the wing meets the fuselage. This machine is fitted with a blind flying hood on the front cockpit. The gun ring is missing from the rear cockpit. Just behind the fairing under the rear cockpit a cable may be discerned on the original photograph that curves around to a ring that appears to be connected by cable to the front fuselage. Whatever this attachment is meant to do, it would have to be retracted before landing. (AHMofWA P021488)

August 1929, when two Wapitis from Laverton undertook a *geological reconnaissance* of the following features of Central Australia:

1. Chain of lakes from Lake Frome to Lake Eyre.
2. Simpson Desert.
3. The country west from Alice Springs to Haasts Bluff.
4. Lake Torrens.[43]

A5-7 and A5-8 left on the 8th with F/Off J.B. Wight and F/Off A.G. Gerrand, respectively. The other members of the party were Flt Sgt Stewart (fitter), AC1 Bain (wireless operator), AC1 Thomas (photographer), and by Mr C.T. Madigan who occupied the Chair of Geology at the University of Adelaide. The aerial survey was organised by the South Australian Geological Society to examine an area of 30,000 square miles in the south-east corner of Central Australia which had never been explored. *A few prospectors may have penetrated some distance into the interior of this unknown country, but have been deterred by want of water and the uninviting character of the country. Sandhills preclude approach by motor car.*[44] The aerial survey was to try and discover promising geological features that a land party could

**Right:** Wapitis leading Kingsford-Smith's Fokker monoplane, the Southern Cross over Melbourne. (via C Eaton)

**Below:** Open formation of formation of Wapitis over Port Melbourne the day the Duke of Gloucester, Prince Henry, landed from HMS *Sussex* in 1934. Note the three Short Rangoon flying boats of No. 203 Squadron, RAF, on the water at Princes Pier, Port Melbourne Photograph taken from Flt Lt Walter's aircraft.

**Above:** A5-12 with the rear gunner's cockpit faired over to convert it into a single-seat racing machine. (via P.G. Heffernan)

then follow up. They made several flights from Alice Springs.

Observations were made by Madigan and oblique photographs were taken where required by him as well as several strips of vertical photographs of the country about 90 miles west of Alice Springs across to the McDonnell Ranges. Gerrand forced landed at Undoolya on 15 August but the Wapiti was soon repaired and the project completed in 45 flying hours for each biplane. The crews returned to Laverton on the 26th after leaving Madigan in Adelaide.

In 1931 it was proposed by the Department of Home Affairs that an aerial survey be undertaken of the Longreach district in Queensland to assess its potential as an oil producer. The Air Board was willing to carry out the work but only on the *basis of repayment of the expenses incurred* (because of) *the present financial situation.*[45]

An agreement was reached, Oil Search Ltd contributing part of the costs, but the expedition was delayed because of a drought in the area. It was essential that the aerial photography be made at a *period at which the difference in colouration of the grass is likely to be at a maximum*, hence the survey had to wait for rain.[46] The Australian climate being what it is, the Wapitis could not commence the survey until 1932. On Wednesday, 13 January, A5-27 piloted by Flt Lt A.M. Charlesworth with AC1 E.E. Skimin and Dr George Woolnough (geological adviser to the Commonwealth Government) as passengers; together with A5-13 piloted by P/Off J.C. Miles with AC1 A Fay and AC1 A.M. Stevens as passengers, left Richmond for northern Queensland. They flew to Longreach arriving on the 14th. Two photographers, Sgt F Wilson and Cpl R Moase had travelled to Longreach by train and met the aerial party there on the 16th.

The first reconnaissance flight took place on the 17th. As a result of several such flights, Dr Woolnough decided to photograph several small areas rather than one large area. Trials were carried out to determine the best altitude for the photography and a height of 9,000 feet was decided on.

The darkroom accommodation was very restrictive and so it was decided to make use of the local fire station. The dark room tent was pitched inside the station and proved satisfactory although the heat was such that the developing tank had to be cooled in a large tub of ice and water to prevent the emulsion from stripping off the film base.

Dr Woolnough was very enthusiastic about the results, and the crew completed the aerial work on the 26th. The two Wapitis arrived at Bourke, NSW, on 1 February. They were picketed down at a landing ground on the outskirts of the town as the weather report confirmed that conditions were unsuitable for photography.

At around 3.00 pm, the wind increased in velocity and Miles and Charlesworth went and checked the aircraft. Charlesworth reported that all *ropes and pickets were holding but after about 10 minutes the wind velocity suddenly increased to over 60 m.p.h. and at the height of the storm was over 80 m.p.h. Both machines broke away from their moorings and MILES and myself with the assistance of the watchman and another man endeavoured to hold them down. They were gradually blown backwards and eventually A5-27 was lifted completely into the air and landed on the tail. This caused the tail unit to become completely detached between frames 10 and 11. The undercarriage collapsed and the, machine settled down flat on the ground. In the meantime A5-13 was also lifted into the air but landed mostly on (the) port wheel. The axle was practically sheered and the radius*

**Above:** Wapiti A5-21 with three companions following the new Hawker Demon fighters.

*rod broken and the machine settled down on the starboard wheel port wing tip and the auxiliary tail skid, (the) tail skid proper having been pushed upwards.*[47]

The duration of the storm had been about 15 minutes during which heavy rain had fallen. Some indication of the fury of the storm could be gained from the damage caused to railway rolling stock. A rail truck with brakes on was driven along the line causing extensive damage to a dead end. An open truck was blown completely off the line.

An examination confirmed that A5-27 was unrepairable at Bourke and it was dismantled for railing back to Richmond. A5-13 proved to be in a better condition than Charlesworth first thought and spare parts were flown from Richmond. *The fuselage was then jacked up and improvised trestles placed under jacking points front and rear and the machine securely tied down....*(and) *the undercarriage of A5-13 was repaired.*[48]

The next day the airframe was erected and when completely satisfied with the repair work, Charlesworth permitted it to be flown back to Richmond.

The Minister of Home Affairs expressed his satisfaction at the outcome of the survey. He wrote that the *misfortune resulting in serious damage to both aeroplanes at Bourke was unavoidable. Officers and men exposed themselves to grave danger in their endeavours to prevent the damage and worked heroically to repair that damage when it had occurred.*[49] He considered that the *expedition had proved a conspicuous success, and fully justifies the expenditure involved in carrying it out.*[50]

The RAAF's Oil Survey Flight carried out another survey flight from 12 July to 13 September 1932. Charlesworth was again the OC with Miles the pilot of the second aircraft. Sgt F Wilson and LAC G.S. Brinsley were the photographers; while LAC T.L. Jackson and AC1 C.T.P. Jones were Fitter Aero to maintain the two Wapitis, A5-35 and A5-36. Dr Woolnough again accompanied the Flight to select areas for photography.

Photography was carried out on the way to the Northern Territory via NSW and Queensland. The Flight returned to Laverton via Western Australia and South Australia, thus completing a round-Australia flight with only minor problems. It was an extremely successful effort on the part of the RAAF.

Difficulties were experienced with filling the aircraft at Darwin as the only Borneo Spirit available was in eight-gallon drums, many of which contained water. The small rotary pump carried by the Flight was slow and it was found that the quickest way of refuelling the aircraft was to empty the small drums through a chamois into a 45-gallon drum and use a larger pump. *It took much time...in filling up aircraft fitted with desert tanks* as the connection between the main tank and these tanks was small. Charlesworth recommended that the connecting pipe be enlarged or that the desert tanks be given their own filler cap.[51]

Since both aircraft were fitted with desert tanks practically all the additional loading was in the rear cockpit which made the aircraft very tail heavy and with full tanks the tail incidence wheel was wound almost fully forward. It was recommended that *some sort of carrier be fitted to the bomb ribs of the main planes.* He also questioned the advisability of passengers wearing parachutes when two were carried. *On*

**Above:** Ten training Wapiti IIA biplanes in formation. A1-5 is the only one with the 'A5' prefix to the serial number. The first three Wapitis in the formation trail the undetermined cables under their fuselages. (SLVic)

*one occasion I flew Dr. Woolnough and L.A.C. Jackson neither of whom are over average girth measurement and yet they had great difficulty in getting into the rear cockpit...it is doubtful whether* (the parachutes) *could be of use under such conditions.* [52]

Following the *astonishing success* which attended the experimental survey flight round Australia, the Prime Minister, J Lyons, requested that the survey be extended to Tasmania.[53] Charlesworth and Miles, both Tasmanians, were natural selections for this flight. Other members of the expedition included Sgt F Wilson, Photographer, who had accompanied all previous expeditions, Sgt J.A. Campbell and AC Hellwig, Dr Woolnough and Mr P.B. Nye, the Tasmanian Government Geologist, who joined the party at Launceston.

The Wapiti biplanes left Laverton on 16 November, the passage of Bass Straight being without incident. So heavy and low were the clouds that only occasional glimpses of the water were obtained, and only the very tops of the rocky Hogan and Kent groups of Islands were seen.

Although clouds prevented photographic work, preliminary flights were undertaken to gain familiarisation with the country. Photographs were taken of important mineral belts but cloudy conditions and bush fires continued to hamper progress. On occasions the aircraft were *tossed and tumbled in all directions.*[54] In spite of this some successes were achieved. Dr Woolnough recorded that as *a result of the experimental operations in aerial photographic survey for geological purposes, carried out during 1932 in every State in the commonwealth and in the Northern Territory, it can be claimed with confidence that it has been proved that the new technique is capable of revealing geological structure under suitable conditions, in a way no other method is capable of doing, and in a fraction of the time and at a tithe of the cost of more conventional methods.*[55]

The following year saw the same two Wapitis carry out aerial photography of the Lithgow-Newnes-Capertee shale oil area in NSW. F/Off C.D. *Doug* Candy with Sgt Wilson as photographer flew A5-13 and A5-27 on separate occasions. It is thought that the same aircraft as were used in Queensland took part in this survey as they were set up for such aerial photography. It was on this survey was that *submarine clothing was tried for the first time, and although no very low temperatures were experienced the clothing appears to be satisfactory.*[56] However, Gp Capt J.E. Gerber, OBE, DFC, recalls that *wireless operators were not issued with Sidcot flying suits...but a long greasy wool pullover, frocks, submarine,* which was not very warm, especially in winter.[57]

In 1930 the Central Australian Gold Exploration Co lost Moth VH-UGX in inhospitable country in Central Australia and the RAAF was approached to organise a rescue mission. Sqn Ldr Wrigley advised that the Wapiti *cannot be sent owing to the absence of supplies...of the special aviation spirit required for high compression engines.*[58] Instead, four RAAF Moths were sent and a successful rescue carried out. The RAF had used the Wapiti with considerable success in the Middle

**Above:** A5-17 in floatplane configuration.

**Above:** *23/12/35. Melbourne, Victoria. Towing a Wapiti. It is said to be the first time in aviation history that a Wapiti was towed by a rowing boat. This occurred at Williamstown yesterday when the machine fitted with floats was brought alongside the Discovery II. Which sails today for the Antarctic in the search for the missing Americans, Ellsworth and Kenyon.* A5-37 on floats. (*Argus* Newspaper Collection, SLVic)

East, and it is a measure of the problems of supplying the Wapitis with correct fuel in Central Australia that the aircraft could not be used for this rescue mission, and the Moth light primary trainer was used instead.

The RAAF had developed a desert survival kit for the Wapiti. This weighed 464 lb which had *to be carried in aircraft additional to two personnel with parachutes and all tanks full...but no other items of removable equipment*, that is the

**Above:** A5-37 being lifted onto the wharf prior to being loaded onto RSS *Discovery II*.

**Left:** RSS *Discovery II* with Wapiti A5-37 on board.

Above: Skis made up for Wapiti A5-37 to be used in search for Ellsworth in Antarctica. In the event the Wapiti was not flown in Antarctica.

Above: The Wapiti float after refurbishment by the MSB. It appears that the floats were originally painted white. The exterior of the float was to be cleaned and the interiors of the compartments was to be thoroughly cleaned of the fatty coating that had been used as a protective covering. After all work had been done on the inside of the floats, they were again to be washed out to remove human sweat and other surface contaminations. Before the replacement of the top plating the entire surface of the interior of the compartments were to be given at least two coats of grey-green enamel to D.T.D. Specfn. No. 63 (R.A.A.F. Identfn. No. K.3/75). The exterior of the floats was to be given two coats of grey-green cellulose. (Source: AB Specification A.C. 54 "Reconditioning Wapiti Floats.")

machine guns, etc.[59] A5-10 had been tested with a full load representing desert equipment by F/Off M.B. Allen on 18 July 1930. He reported that the *length of runs before leaving the ground with full load were 135 and 130 paces as compared with 93 paces when normal load was carried.*[60] *In the Air the machine behaved and handled quite normally and flew "hands off" when tailplane actuating gear was wound about one and half turns beyond normal. The landing speed with full load was about 4 or 5 miles faster than with normal load but the difference in necessary landing area was almost negligible.*[61] Three desert survival kits were issued to Nos. 1 and 3 Squadrons.

In 1932 the Wapiti had the chance to show its desert capabilities. Prospector Patrick Whelan was marooned 200 miles north of Forrest on a salt lake when D.H.50, VH-UEM, of the Lasseter's Reef Gold Mining Co was damaged in a forced landing while engaged in a search for the lost gold reef. The D.H.50 was repaired and flown out by pilot Baker, but Whelan was left behind and had to be supplied by air. A Western Australian Airways (WAA) Hercules dropped several gallons of water to Whelan *but most of it was wasted by bursting on impact. Two Wapitis could safely convey water to Whelan by ammunition or other parachutes.* A5-35 and A5-32 with F/Off F.N. Wright and LAC W Thompson (W/T operator), and F/Off J.C. Miles and Sergeants J.A. Campbell (Fitter) and W.J. Cameron (Carpenter Rigger), respectively as crews, left Laverton for Parafield on 29 December 1932. They left Forrest on the 30th with a Mr Stuckey as guide, located Whelan on the salt lake and dropped supplies of

Above: *Argus* newspaper photograph showing two RAAF Wapiti seaplanes in action. (*Argus* Newspaper Collection, SLVic.)

**Left & Facing Page:** This sequence appears in a number of albums of ex-RAAF personnel. A5-19, A5-9 and A5-28 are stacked close together vertically such that the shadow of the upper machine is seen on the lower one.

food and water. A further drop was conducted on 4 January. The next day Baker landed the *derelict* D.H.50 on the lake and picked up Whelan, the Wapitis providing an escort both ways.[62] The Wapitis transmitted progress reports every half hour. The president of the Australian Wireless Institute said it should be obligatory for all aerial parties flying into the interior to carry radio equipment. The cost of such was not much compared with the cost of searches such as this one.

This exercise cost the RAAF £434.12.01 and attempts were made to recover portion of these expenses from WAA and the Lasseter's Reef Gold Mining Co. Both companies denied liability and the only concession the RAAF gained was that WAA *agreed to forgo a claim for £39 in respect of hangar accommodation provided for the Wapitis, and accommodation and meals for the Air Force personnel at Forrest.*[63]

Maps of Central Australia were extremely poor and the Army Survey Corps could not meet all the demands placed on it for accurate maps, and it was thought that aerial methods could be used with great savings in time and money. The Aerial Geological and Geophysical Survey of Northern Australia committee reached an agreement with Kingsford Smith Air Service for the Fokker trimotor *Southern Cross* to carry out a preliminary survey on 19 September 1934. A meeting of the Committee was held in February 1935, when it was decided that results were promising enough to commence the survey in detail. The RAAF was represented at the meeting by Williams who *Made it clear that while the Air Force did not specially seek the work it was, in his opinion, quite capable of carrying it out efficiently.*[64] The results of the Lithgow-Newness-Capertee flight were examined and the Committee expressed the view that the Air Force would have to improve its techniques to get the results that were required. It was decided that *in view of the high prices quoted it would be preferable to arrange for the Royal Australian Air Force to carry out this work, at least during preliminary stages, extending over the first year.*[65]

The survey team were based in Cloncurry, Queensland from April 1935. A5-32 and A5-37 were initially allocated to the flight, with the former being replaced by A5-34. The condition of A5-34 when it arrived back at Laverton after several months operating in Northern Australia was described as *fair* with the exceptions of the mainplanes which required recovering.[66] Trouble was experienced with valve seats becoming loose, wooden airscrews warping in hot moist air in coastal areas, and focal plane shutters becoming unserviceable. The RAAF noted that *aircraft crews are exposed*

**Above:** The same three aircraft in a more usual formation over the Blue Mountains, NSW, in 1938. Note the reflective properties of the aluminium dope finish. (Photograph taken by K Porteous)

*to considerable personal risks when operating in single engined aircraft over areas requiring survey*, which may be the reason that the Wapiti's role was taken over by the Tugan Gannet in 1936.[67] In all, 3,470 square miles were surveyed in 515 flying hours. As Air Commodore C.R. Taylor recalled *every time they put a Wapiti in the air in those places, they took an enormous risk.* They flew in the early morning or late afternoon as in the middle of the day the Wapiti *wasn't terribly good to maintain altitude.*[68] In May the Melbourne *Herald* reported that the air force had been denied replacement aircraft and the Wapitis had to be used *incessantly. Now, it is thought the machines are wearing out.* Wapitis were involved in two fatal crashed in the previous month and engine troubles had delayed others in Central Australia. The first machine was engaged in aerial photographic work for the North Australian Geological Survey when it was force landed at Tennant Creek, and the second was flying to the assistance of the first when it too was forced down by engine trouble at Tintinara, SA. The third machine was on its way back to Point Cook from Cloncurry where it had taken spare parts for the two Wapitis engaged in the aerial survey when it developed engine trouble and landed at Charleville, which necessitated sending a new engine from Laverton. The newspaper report ended with the statement that the Wapitis would be used for training at Point Cook after all the new Hawker Demons on order were received.

The Wapiti suffered the usual problems associated with the introduction of a new type. After two engines seized a warning light was installed on the dash board to warn of overheating. Serious trouble with leaking oil tanks was eliminated by a local modification. The CO of No. 3 Squadron thought that many *Citizen Officers unnecessarily fly the Wapiti aircraft through the gate* and Wapiti Instruction No.7/Jupiter Instruction No.10 saw the throttle gate sealed with a wire.[69] If broken the pilot had to report the circumstances on landing. Norman Mulroney recalled that *One could almost count the revs of the prop, except when one put them through the gate. They could certainly climb, for those days.*[70]

**Right:** A5-9 in flight after conversion to a Mk. IIA Wapiti. (via E Malsem)

It was found that when modifying the Wapiti to a dual control trainer the bucket parachute seat fitted in the rear cockpit caused the occupant to be elevated *to such an extent as to give insufficient power of control over the control stick* and a larger type of stick was fitted.[71] It would appear that the dual Wapiti supplied to No. 3 Squadron three years later did not have a bucket parachute seat for the instructor as the OC wrote the Air Board complaining that it was *essential that some sort of parachute seat with a substantial back rest should be provided in* dual Wapitis.[72] He went on to ask if old D.H.9a seats could be modified for use. This could not be done as those in existence were all in use at 1 FTS, however drawings were supplied for the construction and installation of such seats and it is believed that the dual Wapiti biplanes were eventually brought up to this standard.

*Experience gained by the Aircraft Depot Workshops during the rebuilding of the first three major Wapiti crashes* led to there being a necessity for holding stocks of various metal parts as there was no plant for their manufacture in Australia.[73] Quantities of duralumin sections had to be imported and fuselage members, etc, were made up by the service or by local contract. The metal construction of the Wapiti led to problems with serviceability. Minor problems occurred with broken metal parts which in most cases were due to faults in manufacture or assembly. Despite this there is no case of a Wapiti suffering major structure failure. In 1938 when A5-12 was examined after it had completed approximately *240 flying hours since last overhaul at 2,000 hours*, the fuselage *showed no evidence of fatigue cracks in the structural components that were accessible for inspection.*[74] It was concluded that while intercrystalline corrosion had occurred, it was insufficient to materially reduce the strength of the structure.[75]

In 1934 the Air Board noted that the *position regarding the Wapiti Aircraft is somewhat serious, as A.5-5, A.5-9, A.5-12 and A.5-22 require complete reconditioning or rebuilding after crashes. Being of metal construction, these airframes cannot be dealt with outside* (the) *Aircraft Depot.*[76]

Further it was stated that *Wapiti Aircraft A.5-13, A.5-27 and A.5-28 are already operating on an extension of flying times of 100 hours. It is probable that a further extension of flying time will be permitted to these Aircraft.*[77]

By 1937 the problems of training the CAF were considered to be critical and one of the major problems was the lack of modern equipment to conduct the required training of fitters and mechanics. As the Wapiti was being phased out of service it had been thought that *Wapiti air frames and Jupiter aero engines will soon be thrown up for instructional purposes. These, if not required by R.T.S., will be offered to the C.A.F.*[78]

Gp Cpt D le Rue, the CO of 1 FTS, wrote to the Air Board that engine spares were becoming more and more difficult to obtain. *There may not be sufficiently good Wapiti/Jupiter serviceability after December 1937 to keep two flights of this type in existence.*

*The position is not being helped by the fact that* (the) *Air Depot workshops are being compelled to use, in complete overhauls* (of Jupiter engines), *components which will have to be replaced at the first subsequent top overhaul.*[79]

The stage was reached where three airframes were to be kept in store after flight test so that their engines were available to 1 FTS. Two spare Jupiter VIII engines were obtained from the RAF to be used *as spares for the six part used Wapiti aircraft.*[80]

The RAAF assumed that

(i) That Wapiti aircraft will be used for training for two years.
(ii) That 100 pupils per year will pass through 1 FTS.
(iii) That each pupil will do 50 hours on 'advanced' type trainer.

Therefore, there was a requirement for *some 10,000 flying hours from our Wapitis, less a proportion taken over by Demon aircraft by their gradual introduction for training.*[81]

There were still *21 Wapitis more or less in one piece* in service.[82] While it was agreed that *we should "speed-up" the write-off of Wapiti aircraft in view of their obsolescence* (it was felt that*) until we are in a position to give F.T.S. additional advanced training aircraft I am afraid it will be unwise to write-off Wapitis*

**Above & Above Right:** A5-24, most probably following the forced landing of 13 November 1930, at Harrington, NSW. The machine hit an irrigation channel and nosed in.

**Above:** The salvage operation for A5-24 was a complicated process. The engine was removed on site and a new one installed and the machine flown out.

**Above:** In this line up of Wapiti trainers, so designated by the large serial to the fuselage, is A5-37 in landplane configuration. By at least February 1937 is was with the Cadet Squadron, 1 FTS, as a landplane. It survived until 1941. (via J Hopton)

*coming due for complete overhaul at this juncture.*[83] It was decided to write off Wapiti airframes on merit as each came up for *complete overhaul or extensive repairs.*[84] Like their predecessors, the Wapiti was used as a drill airframe at CAF halls.[85]

The engine situation was, as related above, in a worse state with only 28 Jupiters available and 11 of these unserviceable. It was considered wiser to convert some of these to components rather than undertake extensive overhauls.

Six Wapiti Mk.IIA biplanes with engines had been obtained second hand from the RAF in 1937 to ease the shortage of aircraft until the introduction of the Avro Anson and locally produced Wirraway. These were K2257, K2262, K2265, K2268, K2286 and K2287.[86] Five are recorded as shipped via SS *Somerset*, and were received on 21 February 1938, receiving serials A5-39 to A5-43. The sixth *crashed on wharf in England and* (was) *written off.*[87] The total cost of these six was £3,100, which was less than the price of one new Hawker Demon. These aircraft were described as ex-Iraq Wapitis, and were *to be given a searching 120-hour inspection at No.1 Aircraft Depot before issue to No.1 Flying Training School.*[88]

A5-40 (ex-K2265) was to be taken as a guide in preparation modification guidelines. The oxygen equipment and gas engine starters were removed from the airframes. A modified tailskid shoe giving increased bearing area was to be fitted. Bucket seats and instruments were to be fitted in the rear cockpit for instruction. It was not *proposed to fit guns to the aircraft... Bomb ribs for light series carrier are to be issued with the aircraft if available from stocks.*[89] In July 1938 the Air Board agreed to obtain four used Jupiter VIII FP engines from the RAF at £75 each in order to *maintain our Wapiti aircraft at No.1 FTS for next year or so* until Hawker Demon trainers became available.[90]

The decision as to what aircraft was available for the advanced flying course commencing in July 1939, and the

**Above:** A Wapiti playing 'skittles' at the RAAF Richmond Pageant. The suspended ball was used to knock over the 'skittles.' The structure behind the 'skittles' was probably to be blown up at the end of the display.

whole question of reconditioning Wapiti airframes *was bound up in the deliveries of Wirraway aircraft from C.A.C. and we hoped that by the middle of this year we would have had at least 12 Wirraways which we could have allotted to Service Squadrons thus releasing this number of Demons for fitting up for full control for transfer to F.T.S.*[91] It was thought that the decision to send Demons to the FTS would have to be deferred until the January 1940 course. As the Training Branch was quite satisfied with the Wapiti as an advanced trainer and having regard of future expansion requirements, it made it *necessary to keep as many Wapitis in service as possible*...(and to)... *continue our present policy of the maintenance of our Wapitis* for at least another six months.[92] This policy would enable, apart from major crashes, *a total of 15 Wapitis to be kept in service up to 1.1.40, 13 up to 1.7.40 and 10 up to 1.1.41.*[93] On 9 October 1939, there were 19 Wapiti trainers held by the RAAF. No Demon trainers were listed.[94]

In May 1939 there were 20 Wapitis available for training at 1 FTS. The Air Board was notified the following July that the ex-Iraq Wapitis A5-39, A5-40 and A5-43, all required *considerable work to make good deficiencies and rewiring.*[95] The return by 1 SFTS for May 1940 showed 10 Demons, 12 Wapitis, 1 Wackett Trainer, and 14 Ansons on strength.[96] There was a severe shortage of service aircraft for training and any problem, such as bad weather, could cause the Service Aircraft course to lag behind schedule. In these circumstances it was essential to have as many Wapitis in service as possible. An instruction was issued that *Owing to the shortage of aircraft, it is suggested that WAPITIS A5-12, 16, 39, and 42 be maintained serviceable as long as possible and be used for training.*[97] This was agreed to with A5-21 and A5-37 added to the list. The latter pair required a thorough inspection with the view to give them a 120 hour extension. A5-12 was to be left on target towing at 1 SFTS and A5-42 was allocated to 2 AD for parachute dropping. It was decided that the Wapitis *will be given another 12 months service, if major crashes are reduced to components, and*

**Above:** A gaggle, (or should that be a herd?), of Wapitis taking off before 'bombing' the 'Battleship' in the background. The destruction of such a structure in a blaze of pyrotechnics was always a highlight of RAAF Pageants. (RAAF official)

**Left:** Wapiti IA A5-14 showing Army personnel how it could pick up a message.

**Left:** Wapiti IIA A5-9 with its message pick-up hook fully extended.

*it will be noted that there are sufficient hours in the engines at present in the aircraft, and held in stores, to do this without any further overhauls.*[98]

The complement of 1 SFTS's Wapitis was drastically changed on 10 February 1941, when A5-21 and A5-39 collided east of Werribee while carrying out instrument flying. A5-21 was crewed by LAC Robert Henry Stratford under instruction from Sgt Robert John Barker. When the two aircraft collided at approximately 2,400 ft (730 m) Barker was thrown out by force collision and descended by parachute. Stratford was killed in the resultant crash. The crew of A5-39, Flt Lt Anthony Edward Robinson and LAC Robert S Osment bailed out. Osment descended by parachute, but Robinson's chute became entangled in tail and he crashed to

**Right:** A5-34 demonstrated Army co-operation with the message pick up hook. A line was suspended between two poles and the Wapiti flew through the poles, the hook grasping the rope and pulling the message bag up to where it could be retrieved by the gunner. During the Wapiti flight to Perth in October 1932, the electrical generator windmill burst during a demonstration dive damaging two ribs in the port wing and made a large hole in the petrol tanks of A5-34. The services of a welder and fabric worker were obtained from West Australia Airways to assist in repairing A5-34. (via P.G. Heffernan)

the ground with the aircraft suffering serious injuries. Both instructors were charged with neglect as they did not keep a proper lookout.

It was *desired to use Wapiti aircraft for parachute dropping, but the feasibility of this will depend on the spares available.*[99] H Williams recalls that when he was a IIA Fitter at Richmond, the Test and Ferry Flight had a Wapiti which was used to test parachutes. *The aircraft was loaded with wooden dummies to which parachutes were attached and hung on bomb racks under the wings.* These were carried to an appropriate height and dropped to test the parachutes. On one occasion *Just as the plane became airborne one parachute opened but remained fastened to the plane which brought it down rather heavily. We worked on the plane for some time repairing the damage to the wing, prop, engine bay etc.*, before it was once again airworthy.[100]

By late 1941 it was difficult to keep A5-12, A5-16, A5-37 and A5-42 in service due to lack of spares and it was considered that the withdrawal of one or all four of these Wapitis would not affect the Point Cook training programme, and that Wapiti aircraft *can be used as target towing aircraft for gunnery practices and use should be made of them as long as any can be maintained serviceable with reasonable effort.*[101]

Capt V Hodgkinson recalls that the *rear gunnery ring had been removed* from Wapiti trainer conversions. *The instructor occupied the rear cockpit which had no windscreen and was rather draughty... Our gunnery and bombing practice was carried out on a marker in Port Phillip Bay. The gun was a Vickers .303 attached to the port side of the fuselage. It invariably, jammed and it was the instructor who cleared the stoppage by climbing out over the side - minus parachute - and, hanging onto the cockpit with one hand, he cleared the stoppage with the other.*[102]

From the time of their earliest knowledge of the Wapiti, the RAAF had expressed interest in utilising the type as a floatplane *for the purpose of training flying personnel to operate the aircraft on the seaplane carrier.* In November 1928 the Air Board had recommended the purchase of a number of Wapitis with float undercarriages, however when the Chief of Naval Staff agreed that *Albatross* be equipped with Seagulls. A single Seagull was to be made from the complement of *Albatross* as required for training purposes. *As this is suitable from the Naval point of view, the Air Board is willing to concur with the arrangement rather than spend money*

**Above:** Wapiti A5-37 showing the message hook and its location when retracted. The observer/rear gunner could retrieve the message from a hatch in the floor of the fuselage. Before the days of reliable radio, messages would be dropped in weighted bags and picked up by stretching a wire between two upright poles and this was engaged by the message pick-up hook on the Wapiti.

*unnecessarily*. The proposed purchase did not go ahead and the RAAF continued to utilise their Seagulls until a suitable type *was decided on*.[103]

The Air Board was advised by the ALO in April 1929, that preliminary tests of two floatplanes sent to service units of the RAF were proceeding well. In February 1930, he noted that the Marine Aircraft Experimental Establishment at Felixstowe had issued a report on the condition of Wapiti seaplane J.9084 after approximately 18 months service as a seaplane. He arranged to inspect the aircraft *after it had been stripped of all fabric covering*. The official report had been generally unfavourable, particularly with regards to corrosion of certain parts. Westland pointed out that this was the seventh Wapiti made and was of composite construction. When asked to convert this aircraft to a floatplane the firm had made it known that neither the duralumin nor aluminium parts were anodised, nor were the steel parts cadmium plated.[104]

On inspection, the ALO reported that *the corrosion referred to is not nearly as bad as the Felixstowe Report would lead one to believe.* He concluded that the corrosion was not excessive when it was considered that the parts had undergone no anti-corrosion treatment whatsoever, and that as subsequent aircraft *all the metal parts of which are of stainless steel or receive anodic or cadmium treatment, there should be very little corrosion, provided that the aircraft receives reasonable maintenance*.[105]

Order No.257 for the expenditure of £3,000 for the conversion kit was raised in May 1929.[106] The Government announced in the 1929-30 Budget that 17 Wapiti biplanes were already on order together with sets for conversion for seaplane work.[107] It is thought that the first conversion was carried out in January 1930,[108] however it has not been determined how many were so converted. A5-17 and A5-37 are known to have been fitted with floats. Accident and status reports show that the Wapiti floatplane was in service from January 1933 to 16 September 1935, however, in early 1933 the MSB quoted to recondition the floats for £125, indicating that they may have been in service before this. It is believed that a Wapiti seaplane was still in service just prior to the Second World War.[109] A 1931 Minute, relating to the introduction of instrument flying courses in the RAAF, suggested that two Wapiti floatplanes be made available to the Seaplane Squadron at 1 FTS. This recommendation was not acted upon. In 1932 Wapiti landplanes were fitted out for instrument flying instruction.

A Wapiti was sent to Antarctic to assist in the search for the missing American explorer Lincoln Ellsworth, together with a Moth seaplane. (See Chapter 10). The Wapiti was described as a *seaplane capable of being fitted with skis so that the machine will be able to take off from and land on the sea alongside the Great Ice Barrier or to operate as a land plane from the surface of the Great Ice Barrier itself.*[110]

It was proposed that the Moth make a preliminary reconnaissance and then Wapiti A537, *a long distance Wapiti with VIIIF engine* from No. 1 Squadron, would be assembled on top of the deck house as a seaplane.[111] It would then fly to the Ross Ice Barrier at Byrd's Depot where it would be

**Above:** The remains of Brian Walker's A5-7. It is a testament to the strength of the Wapiti that he survived this accident.

**Left:** A Wapiti, possibly A5-5, over the 'Meat Wagon.'

**Below:** A5-26 in the trainer mode has the A5 serial prefix missing as do all those visible in this photograph of the line-up at Richmond in 1938.

fitted with skis, and carry out such flights as the weather permitted.[112] Gp Capt John G Townsend was then a fitter at 1 AD and recalls the *problems we had to fabricate the fittings* (for the skis) *from stainless steel; little was known of the peculiar characteristics of this metal in those early days but fortunately we had a very good welder at 1 AD and I believe the end result was very satisfactory.*[113]

In the event the seaplane Moth discovered Ellsworth and A5-37 did not fly in Antarctica.

A5-17 was apparently the first Wapiti converted to a seaplane. It was allotted to 1 AD in October 1935 for a complete overhaul and emerged as a landplane. It is not known if A5-37 had been converted to a floatplane before it was sent to Antarctica, or if it was selected in a hurry when the decision was made to send a rescue mission. A5-37 was a landplane when the subject of a report in April 1937. An immediate decision was required on the *re-allocation of A5-37 and Jupiter No. 8815 to 1 Aircraft Depot for overhaul. The airframe was in the Antarctic and...was showing signs of corrosion when taken off the "Discovery"...a certain amount of work was done by No. 1 F.T.S. workshops before the machine was placed in flying training service.*[114] It is not known if any other

**Above:** Same location, but different Wapitis formed up on A5-26. Note A5-5 the second last in this line of six Wapitis has the 'A5' prefix to its serial. All these machines have the gun ring type rear cockpit but no gun ring mounted.

RAAF Wapitis were converted to floatplanes.

On 16 April 1935, F/Off Clive Newton Edgerton took off from Laverton *for the purpose of carrying out a test flight* in Wapiti A5-31. On reaching a height of 15,000 feet he entered a steep dive but was unable to recover from same. *the structure of the aircraft failed during the test flight and the aircraft crashed at Werribee* killing Edgerton.[115] Witnesses reported that the aircraft's wings broke and folded back along the fuselage. The lower starboard wing landed in a paddock 1½ miles from the fuselage. Air Commodore P.G. Heffernan saw Edgerton's 'prang' and recalls that *Having got into a dive at T.V.* (terminal velocity), *he was unable to pull out. The crash was not caused by structural failure, he just went straight into the deck.*[116]

The AAIC reported that *the tail plane actuating gear was in full forward position...the aircraft had five ballast weights in the tail ...when there should have been six, and in addition another four in the passenger's cockpit, so that the aircraft was obviously tail light and nose heavy. Apparently the pilot had his tail actuating gear into the full forward position giving maximum lift to the tail to enable him to go into the dive.*

The speed of Edgerton's dive was so great that the blades of the airscrew were pulled from the boss by the centrifugal force.[117] The Jupiter engine was buried three feet in the ground.

Edgerton had overcome a stammering problem to be accepted as an Air Cadet in July 1932 at the age of 25. He had graduated from Melbourne University as a civil engineer and had five years experience in this field when he was accepted by the RAAF. After 12 months with No. 3 Squadron, he was transferred to 1 AD. It appears that he was being groomed for a technical career by the RAAF.

The nose heavy tendency of the Wapiti noted previously had come to official notice when Sgt R.J. Parker crashed while practising dive bombing at Point Cook in October 1934. He stated that he had *wound the wheel forward about three quarters of a turn. The machine went into a steep dive very easily and I estimated the angle of the dive was not less than 70 degrees approximately; all my weight was on the rudder bar and there was a tendency to lift out of the seat. I endeavoured to come out of the dive, but I could only move the tail plane wheel a very short distance; I immediately pulled the control column hard back still continuing to make efforts to operate the tail plane wheel, the latter would not, however, move, but at about 800 feet the aircraft appeared to answer to the elevator very slowly.*[118]

As a result of Parker's crash a set of rules for diving the Wapiti was drawn up. These were:

(a) Before going into the dive the throttle must be closed.
(b) A dive must not be continued for more than 5,000 feet (1,500 m).
(c) The angle of dive must not be steeper than 70 degrees from the horizontal.

After Edgerton's death, the AAIC recommended that the practice of power-diving Wapiti aircraft be discontinued. The Air Board did not agree for the following reasons:

1. Fast diving was not considered sufficiently dangerous or

**Above:** Two locals pose with a Wapiti Mk. IA. The RAAF carried out exercises across the Australian continent as part of its defence requirements but mainly to promote the RAAF as its independence was always under threat from the Army and Navy.

difficult when carried out under supervision.
2. No. 1 Squadron was the only unit authorised to carry out dive bombing.
3. The procedure for flight testing was not followed by Edgerton. This procedure did not include fast diving.
4. Pupils are given adequate instruction in methods of entering and recovering from a dive.

There the matter seems to have rested until 15 October 1936. On this date F/Off E.D. Scott was demonstrating dive bombing at Point Cook. He had taken his fifth pupil, Cpl Dillon, up and executed another dive.

*During the dive I heard no sound of breakage nor felt any thing peculiar in the controls of the aircraft. On recovering from the dive I did a left hand climbing turn, and was therefore looking over the left side of the machine. On levelling out to fly back to the aerodrome I noticed that the fabric had been torn from the trailing edge at the root end of the starboard lower mainplane. About 2' of the trailing edge, and also one former rib had broken away.*[119]

Fortunately, Scott was able to land without further mishap.

The AAIC report suggested that faulty maintenance was a contributory cause of the failure of the fabric, and again asked the Air Board to *review the desirability of discontinuing flying practices in Wapiti aircraft which necessitate power diving at high speed.*[120] Reference was made to Edgerton's accident and the Committee's recommendation on that occasion. There is no evidence to suggest that the Board accepted this recommendation.

The Wapiti took part in air shows and aerial derbies at venues all around the country. The 1929 West Australian celebrations saw an East-West air race across the continent from Melbourne to Perth. The RAAF were asked to participate and Williams agreed subject to the availability of aircraft. Nine Wapiti biplanes were sent under the command of Sqn Ldr J.H. Summers. Six were from No. 1 Squadron, Laverton, with the remainder from No. 3 Squadron, Richmond. Summers acted as Handicapper and Starter for the race, and two RAAF officers, Flt Lt D.E.L. Wilson and F/Off L.J. Ryan, flew in the Civil Aviation Branch D.H.50 piloted by A Murray Jones.

The RAAF aircraft did not compete in the race but provided support to the entrants. On arriving in Perth, they took part in an air pageant which included a special Wapiti race. Williams allowed two Wapitis to take part in the race as long as it was understood *that they were not to be flown full out.*[121] Others thought that two aircraft *are not sufficient to put up any kind of a show for* (the) *public.*[122] It appears that his latter view prevailed with the throttles wired to prevent the aircraft being flown full out.

The flight had problems with tyres, four blowouts being reported; three due to heavy landings and one to the tearing of the bead. A5-9 and A5-6 were delayed at Kalgoorlie with cracked oil tanks. A5-7 piloted by F/Off F.J.B. Wight crashed at Forrest on 12 October due to a damaged wheel and defective engine.

A5-15 flown by F/Off T.A. Chadwick suffered a forced landing the same day and minor damage was repaired with parts from A5-7. It was proposed to truck the latter to Port Augusta and rail it back to Point Cook. A5-2 with F/Off

**Above & Above Right:** Allan Whethers captioned this photograph *Spun in between Point Cook and Laverton in late 1939 or early 1940.* (via A Whethers)

A.L. Walters suffered a broken oil pipe and resultant forced landing on the 15th. A new engine had to be sent to enable him to return to Richmond. In all the flight was considered to have been a good training exercise in the new Wapiti biplanes.

1932 saw three Bulldog and three Wapiti biplanes provided the highlight of that year's West Australian Pageant. During the diving display by the Wapitis Sqn Ldr G Jones had the windmill generator on his machine burst, one vane going through the upper port wing, the other through the fuselage fabric puncturing the main fuel tank. Jones made a safe landing all but unconscious from the effect of petrol fumes.[123] F/Off Wright demonstrated aerial combat techniques when his Wapiti was attacked by two Bulldogs. The *comparatively slow Wapiti* putting up a creditable defence. Wright also took part in the aerial derby which completed the day's activities.[124]

The 1934 RAAF Pageant at Richmond aerodrome[125] saw demonstrations of supply dropping and message pick up by three Wapiti aircraft flown by Flt Lt A.L. Walters, and Flying Officers W.G. Compagnoni and *Doug* Candy under the direction of Sqn Ldr Bostock. An 'enemy ship' on the aerodrome was attacked by two squadrons of Wapitis and the transport was blown up in a cloud of smoke.

The display featured a game of aerial skittles played by three Wapitis. A circular weight was suspended beneath the aircraft and this was flown at large imitation bottles 15 feet high. The Wapiti had to be flown with great accuracy to skittle the bottles. A new recovery technique was demonstrated when a propeller-less Moth was hitched to a Wapiti and towed into the air. The Moth then cast off and descended in circles to safely land. The pageant was performed in wet weather with the crowd often having to shelter from the rain while interesting events were on view. The RAAF performed the whole display without incident under these trying conditions.

Amongst the multitude of tasks undertaken by the RAAF was that of spotting bushfires. From 1 February 1930, the RAAF had been enlisted by the Forests Commission in their campaign against bush fires. Fire patrols were flown by No.1 Squadron over the State Forests to the north east of the Dandenong Ranges. The Wapiti carried a wireless transmitter and reported outbreaks of fire to Laverton. Numbers were painted on roofs of prominent houses and sheds to enable the aircraft to pinpoint the position of outbreaks to within approximately 100 yards. The flights were considered part of the units training and included in regular aircrew training flights. These patrols continued well into the 1940s when civil patrols began.

Radio experimentation was carried out with the Wapiti participating in an R/T demonstration in the nature of a broadcast from the air in July 1930. Later that month a demonstration was arranged for Army personnel using an R/T tender based at Victoria Barracks, Melbourne. In October 1933 five aircraft of No. 1 Squadron flew to Yanakie to form an advanced base for operations against the RAN. A ground short wave W/T station was established and successfully maintained intercommunication with the aircraft and 1 FTS. Operations were directed from 1 FTS with flying boats reconnoitring and locating the cruisers whereupon the aircraft launched dive bomb attacks on towed targets.

In June the following year, No. 1 Squadron conducted an eight-day live-in exercise from Laverton. Exercises included:

- Squadron formation flights.
- Air drill against fighter attacks.
- Squadron bombing with 8½ lb practice and 112 lb live bombs.
- Night flying.
- Air pilotage with signal exercises during squadron cross country flights to Nyngan-Narromine and return via Junee and Hay.[126]

The exercise pointed up a number of deficiencies in the operation of the squadron in its stated role. The establishment of eight aircraft was less than the number of pilots and all pilots did not receive training in all exercises. The aircraft were fitted with Mk. IIB and Mk. VII bombsights. The establishment was requested to be changed to ten Mk. VII fitted with compasses as soon as possible. For dive bombing it was proposed to experiment with a sight

**Above:** The armourer is explaining to the crew how they load practice bombs onto the wing carriers of a Wapiti.

in the hope that 'something' might be evolved which would enable the pilot to dive at the target and the air gunner to release the bombs.

One exercise saw the squadron land and then re-arm with 112-lb bombs. The duty of loading was left to the Armament personnel and took 25 minutes. A request was made for dummy equipment to train aircraft crews in fuzing and loading 50, 112 and 250-lb bombs. It was hoped to cut the time for re-arming to five to ten minutes. There were only 15 tubular bomb racks in the unit and it was requested that the new Demon have two racks per aircraft with an extra rack per aircraft being held in the Depot as mobilisation equipment.[127]

Fire control of the 'back seat guns' was impossible and in action without R/T a squadron's defensive fire would be drawn into individual action by air gunners. (This is an indication that the doctrine that massed defensive fire would enable the day bomber to fight its way through to its target was in practice in the RAAF.) It was considered absolutely essential to have R/T (air to air) in every aircraft. The commander could not control the unit by hand signals alone. *Training without R/T involves much more flying and more subsequent landings for discussion and pointing out faults.*[128] It is not known if any of the requests of No. 1 Squadron were met.

The position the RAAF found itself in, as so clearly demonstrated by this exercise, was due to the various Governments attitude to defence spending. The deteriorating international situation was to produce a change with the Hawker Demon being introduced to No. 1 Squadron in the first week of May 1935. Unfortunately, as detailed in Chapter 14, economy was again the watch word for its selection.

The Wapiti was well thought of in the RAAF. Brian R *Blackjack* Walker recalled that *The Wapiti was an aeroplane which, in reflection, could only endear itself to you. It had a gentle stall; it certainly was not very fast in spite of having a 450 hp Bristol Jupiter. It was used for training in the Royal Australian Air Force mainly because they did not have any aeroplanes designed for (advanced) training purposes pre-war and these (Wapitis) were converted bombers.*

High level bombing wasn't really their forte as they couldn't get very high. You were lucky to get them up to 20,000 feet. I had one up to 20,000 feet once...we had to do an altitude test on the final of our training and were supposed to go to 16,000 feet and I decided to see how high it would go.

*Basically they were used for dive bombing. The only fault of the Wapiti had was what we called in those days "splurging". In other words they would sink lower as they came out of the dive and this characteristic caught two or three pilots including myself. As you*

**Left:** Close-up of parachutes slung under the lower wing of a Wapiti for testing.

**Below:** The remains of Brian Walker's A5-7. It is a testament to the strength of the Wapiti that he survived this accident.

**Right:** Students waiting for their turn watch A5-9 go past with full load of practice bombs.

**Below:** Wapitis on an outback strip being refuelled. A local Miss poses with the Wapiti. Note the canvas covers over the engine and cockpits. (AHMofWA P013472)

**Above:** Three Wapitis flying over Laverton. The remaining Bulldogs A12-2, A12-1 and A12-3 on the hard stand with Moth trainer in the background. (*Argus* Collection SLVic)

*were somewhat near the terminal velocity of a Wapiti...well over 200 mph, it generally had disastrous results.*[129]

Walker's experience with splurging occurred on 30 October 1935, at Echuca aerodrome where he was putting on a display of high spirits in A5-7 and tried to *pull my wheels through the grass and unfortunately they finished up about four feet under the grass.*

The aeroplane "splurged" into the ground, the nose dug in and it cartwheeled. I believe it bounced right over a lad who was standing on the aerodrome watching this stupid performance... (and) inevitable result. I believe he was so lucky as an interplane strut caught the handlebars of his bike and bent it up double. He brought it into the Echuca hospital later on and I remember I had to get him a new set of handlebars.

*The wreckage eventually just dug in its nose and flipped over onto its back and tossed me out. We only had a belly belt and I must have undone it because I can remember my face being dragged along the ground and it was feeling terribly hot. It was just friction and I still have a scar down my face from that accident.*[130]

Walker was taken to the Echuca District Hospital suffering from a broken jaw as well as his facial injuries and severe shock. As a result of Walker's adventure, the Secretary for Defence (Mr M.L. Shepherd) issued a Press Statement that *there was no question about the serviceability of the Wapiti machines. Although aircraft with better performance were now being acquired by the Royal Australian Air Force, Wapitis were still suitable for use in Australia and were free of structural defects.* The official verdict was that he stalled at low altitude due to pilot error on approach to landing.[131]

Allan Whetters serviced the Wapiti as an AC1, having mustered as a fitter-aero in 1934, and flew them in various squadrons after completing his pilot's training in 1936-37. At this time, they were mainly used for drogue towing. Allan recalls that the Wapiti *was a heavy aircraft. It was difficult to turn on the ground. It had a tail skid which was replaced by a plate to prevent damage to the aerodrome.* These particular aircraft skid shoes were locally developed by Mason and Cox after considerable experimentation.[132] *To turn it was necessary to use full aileron and rudder with considerable throttle. In some conditions it was also necessary to use airmen to hold the inner wing.*[133] It appears that a tail wheel was tried on A5-28. Whatever the results of the report, which has not been found, the skid remained standard.[134]

Fred Anderson agreed that *the old Wapiti...was almost impossible to turn into wind unless you* (gave) *slight stick forward and raised the tail off the ground, and (applied) fast rudder. You could turn into wind and flop the tail back on the ground.*[135] P.G. 'Paddy' Heffernan remembers that *Although the Wapiti did a good job wherever it was used, it was really not popular being very nose heavy. In fact when flown solo, 150 lbs of lead was placed in the rear.*[136] To overcome the tendency for the aircraft to nose over when taxying over rough aerodrome surfaces *additional weight is applied at the tail, it has become the practice to allow personnel to ride on the tail of the aircraft. Whilst this practise may be necessary to safeguard the aircraft, it cannot be given unqualified approval as at present carried out.*[137]

A footrest and hand grip were fitted to A5-15 and tested at 1 FTS. It was found that persons riding on the aircraft using these grips interfered with the rudder control cables. Flt Lt Walters reported that another hand grip at the rear of the fuselage was required but that the present system of sitting on the tailplane was *more comfortable, more effective as the weight is further back.*[138] Again it is not known if this was adopted as standard.

Cadet Geoff Hartnell attended No. 1 FTS from January 1936 and wrote devotedly, in diary fashion, to his mother giving his impressions of the day's events. After graduating from the Moth, he found that the *Waps are heavier than the Moth and so are not easier to shift around in formation but when they are there they will sit there.* He found it difficult for the first few minutes to get used to the responsiveness of the Moth after a period of training on the Wapiti. Air to air gunnery consisted of a Moth flying a straight course while the Wapitis went in, one at a time, *with a camera gun and shot him up. It's not as easy as it sounds* recorded Hartnell, *and to get about 19 shots at him I took about 30 dives. Once a machine is in a dive it is very difficult, almost impossible to manoeuvre the machine at all. Consequently once in a dive you stay there till you pull out.* In fact the Moth pilot became tired of the whole event and landed before Hartnell had finished his full complement of 'shots'.[139] It was RAAF policy that in order to improve forced landing techniques all landing approaches were made with the engine idling. Should it appear that the aircraft would undershoot the aerodrome the pilot would use the engine and make another approach.

Alan Whetters had read of the Wapiti being used for aerobatics but never saw any other than stall turns. Brian Walker on the other hand speaks of the *terrible things* he used to do in the Wapiti. He was an instructor on Wapitis at Point Cook at the time and would have to air test all the Wapitis before the pupils went solo.

There were three of us in this one flight at Point Cook and we used to go up with George Coleman our leader. We would turn the fuel off at a signal from our leader and would eventually run out of fuel...we would do this at 7,000 or 8,000 feet...and then we would pull them up together until the props would stop and then we would reform in formation.

*I can still remember one occasion when we glided past C Flight, who were practising formation (flying), with our props stopped, standing up in the cockpit yelling out all sorts of obscenities...Then, making sure we still had enough height, we would dive in formation and start the engines again. In fact we used to loop them in formation. So you can't say there was much wrong with the old Wapiti; it was not suppose to be aerobatic!*[140]

For its day the Wapiti was *a big aircraft for a bi-plane and the climb up the ladder to the cockpit and the unusually high seating gave me a grandiose feeling* recalled Air Cdre *Reg* Burrage. *When airborne the ponderous lumbering aircraft became a graceful bird...Stall turns on the Wapiti were sheer joy. I never experienced the nose heaviness in dives reported by other pilots... Perhaps there was so much lead in the tail that the tendency was never apparent to me, or maybe I never got around to steep enough power dives.*

*Reg* did his advanced training on the Wapiti. Two incidents remain vividly in his memory. *My altitude test which was meant to be a climb to 15,000 ft. saw me singing through a lack of oxygen at 24,000 ft. and feeling refrigerated...The other occasion I recall was when my instructor was checking me out solo on spot landings in a small circle on one of the secondary landing fields near Point Cook. The trouble was that my instructor (F/O R Cox) was standing at his observation point in the middle of the circle and as the spluttering and coughing Jupiter (throttle on idle) approached he had the indignity of having to run like a rabbit to the outside of the circle. I wasn't very popular!*[141]

The tests of the De Havilland EG-1 and EG-2 gliders in June 1942, saw the Wapiti acting as a tug, probably one of its last uses in the RAAF.[142] It had been proposed to withdraw the type from service from the second half of 1939 however it was not until the latter part of 1941 that 1 Training Group was apparently converting all its Wapitis to spares and produce. It was included on the list of obsolete types prepared in early 1944, but it is not thought that any were still flying by this time. The type achieved a remarkably long flying career in the RAAF. By August 1943, the Wapiti had disappeared from the *Returns of Flying Accidents*, and it is presumed that it was withdrawn from flying around this date, however the Squadron History for 7 CRD recorded in June 1946, that it had one Wapiti on 'Establishment' but not on 'Strength.' This is the only mention of a Wapiti at this unit and the purpose of this entry at such a late date remains a mystery.[143]

The Wapiti was not as glamorous as the Hawker Demon which replaced it, but it performed well past its prime in a variety of tasks and endeared itself to all who came in contact with it.

## Specifications:

Dimensions: Span 46 ft 5 in; Length 32 ft 6 in; height 11 ft 10 in.
Weights: Empty 3,180 lbs; Loaded 5,400 lb.
Performance: Speed: 133 mph. Range: 360 mls.
Armament: Synchronised Vickers gun; Lewis gun on observer's gun mount; Bomb load 500 lb

## End Notes

1. Letter to author, 4.07.1998.
2. NAA VIC CRS MP187/4 Item 187. Aircraft Accident Report Files, 1929–1932. 59-211 (Incomplete). "Extracts from R.A.A.F. Court of Inquiry held at No.1 Flying Training School, Point Cook, to inquire into the accident to Wapiti A5-19 which occurred at Coulthard's Farm, Whittlesea, on 25th April, 1938". Evidence of Sgt Major Oliver Studley.
3. *Ibid.* Evidence of Wing Commander F.M. Bladin.
4. *Ibid.*
5. *Ibid.* Evidence of Flight Lieutenant J.R. Paget.
6. *Ibid.* Evidence F/Off B.R. Walker.
7. NAA VIC CRS MP187/4 Item 186. Report No. 186 "Bulldog" A/12/2. Richmond, NSW. Pilot Officer L.R. Sutherland. 22.04.1938. Air Accidents Investigation Committee 28.04.1938.
8. RAAF Personnel Records.
9. The RAAF involvement in the Hound is shown by a communication from the ALO in August 1928, wherein he noted that the aircraft was undergoing trials at Martlesham and was "being sent to Australia on completion of tests whatever the result". (NAA ACT CRS A22408 Item 8/2 Aeroplanes Service General. Letterbook entry No.203, 29.08.1928). When it looked like the RAAF was not going to order the Hound, the local De Havilland agents noted that the loss of the order would mean serious financial loss to the company.
10. NAA ACT CRS A705/1 Item 121/1/249. Memo "New Aircraft for the Royal Australian Air Force." CAS to Secretary, 25.10.1927.
11. Air Board Agendum No.1085; "Re-equipment of Nos. 1 and 3 Squadrons. Williams, 1st Air Member, 21.06.1928.
12. Air Board Agendum No.1085. Op Cit. Minute: Williams, 1st Air Member, 2.08.1928.
13. NAA ACT CRS A664/1 Item 415/401/31. RAF Far Eastern Flight. Minute; "Air Force Equipment", 31.08.1928.
14. Air Board Agendum No.1085. Op Cit. Minute: 2.08.1928.
15. Williams could not have known that his choice was approved by the US as a US Naval Intelligence report on Australian aerial activities noted that the Wapiti was "such a type of plane (which) is suited to the needs of the Australian Air Force, not alone because it reduces the number of specialized units required but because of the large thinly populated or desert areas over which flying is done." (US National Archives RG38 File A-1-q, report dated 23.11.1928, Serial No.702).
16. NAA ACT CRS A22408 Item 8/2. Aeroplanes Service General. Letterbook entry No. 210, 3.10.1928.
17. NAA ACT CRS A705/1 Item 121/22/102. Purchase of "Wapiti" Jupiter. Air Board Order No. 242-248. File No.1" Wireless message, Austair, London, to Air Board, 26.09.1928. (This message is an almost verbatim copy of a message that the British CAS, H Trenchard, had suggested be sent to the Australian Government. Copy of Trenchard's memo of 25.09.1928 in file.)
18. *Ibid.*
19. *Ibid.* Undated handwritten note.
20. NAA ACT CRS A2408 Item 121/22. Wapiti. Letterbook entry No.6, 15.09.1928.
21. NAA ACT CRS A705/1 Item 121/22/102. Op Cit. Wireless message, Austair to Air Board, 19.09.1928.
22. *Ibid.* Air Ministry to Westland: "Amendments to Instruction to Proceed 875845/28", 4.01.1929.
23. *Ibid.* Minute, CAS to D of S, 25.05.1929.
24. *Ibid.* Letter, ALO to Air Board. "Air Board Order No. 242", 20.03.1929.
25. *Ibid.* ALO to Air Board, "Air Board Order No.242", 13.09.1928.
26. *Ibid.* Letter; ALO to Air Board: "Air Board Order No.242", 20.03.1929.
27. *Ibid.*
28. *Ibid.*
29. NAA ACT CRS A705/1 Item 114/6/41. Quarterly Letter from Air Liaison. Wrigley to Air Board, 18.07.1929.
30. NAA ACT CRS A705/1 Item 121/22/102. Op Cit. Air Liaison to Air Board: "Air Board Order No.242", 4.04.1929.
31. NAA ACT CRS A5954/1 Item 873/7. Manufacture of Aircraft in Australia - Formation of Commonwealth Aircraft Corporation 1935-1937. Appendix "A" - with "Deliveries of Aircraft from Orders Placed in U.K.", CAS Memo to Defence, 13.03.1936.
32. NAA ACT CRS A705/1 Item 73/1/1119. Wapiti Aircraft Miscellaneous File. Letter, DTS to 1AD: "Wapiti A.5-29", 4.09.1930.
33. *Ibid.* Minute, DTS to DTE, 2.09.1930.
34. NAA ACT A705 Item 121/22/102. Minute: Extract from "Daily Guardian" 7th December, 1928". CAS to Secretary (Defence?). 14.12.1928.
35. NAA ACT CRS A705/1 Item 73/1/1119. Op Cit.
36. *Aircraft* cutting, no date.
37. No.1 Squadron Diary. RAAF Form A50.
38. Williams to Trenchard, 12.09.1929. Williams Papers, RAAF Museum, Point Cook.
39. Minute: Estimates 1929/1930. Air Board to Defence 21.06.1929. Williams Papers, RAAF Museum, Point Cook.
40. AWM PR88/154 Item 1. AT Cole diary entry 28.07.1930.
41. NAA ACT CRS A705/1 Item 109/3/102. Visit CAS to No. 3 Squadron 11 – 18th November 1931. Air Member for Supply to CAS, Minute: "No.3 Squadron Queries", 4.12.1931.
42. Letters from Cadet (later Air Vice Marshall) G.C. Hartnell to his mother. RAAF Air Power Study Centre, Canberra.
43. 1 Squadron Unit Diary. RAAF Form A50.
44. "Central Australia Survey Flight by R.A.A.F. Wapitis." *Aircraft*, 31 August 1929, P.500.

45. NAA ACT CRS A705/1 Item 205/2/511. Survey - Longreach District - General File. Air Board to Home Affairs, 19.11.1930.
46. *Ibid.* DOI to OC, No. 3 Squadron, 16.12.1931.
47. *Ibid.* Charlesworth to CO, No. 3 Squadron. Report: "Lingreach Oil Survey", 10.02.1932.
48. *Ibid.*
49. *Ibid.* Parkhill, Minister of Home Affairs to Parkhill, Minister of Defence, 9.02.1932.
50. *Ibid.*
51. *Survey of Potential Oil Fields*, report by Flt Lt Charlesworth, undated.
52. *Ibid.*
53. NAA ACT CRS A659/1 Item 39/1/8380. "Basis For Statement In Regard To The Tasmanian Aerial Survey Flight." Notes prepared by Dr. W Woolnough, 12.12.1932.
54. *Ibid.*
55. *Ibid.*
56. NAA ACT CRS A705/1 Item 205/2/538. Air Survey of Newnes Shale Oil Area, NSW by No.3 Squadron. Bostock, CO No.3 Squadron to Air Board, 27.04.1933.
57. Letter to author, 20.06.1990.
58. NAA ACT CRS A 705/1 Item 153/1/637. Use of Aircraft during Expedition by Central Australian Gold Exploration Co. Notes on 'phone message to Acting PM (Frenton), 31.12.1930.
59. NAA ACT A705/1 Item 73/1/1109. Wapiti Aircraft. Desert Equipment. DTS to CO, 1AD, 3.05.1930.
60. *Ibid.* Wapiti Aircraft Desert Equipment. Report to CO, No.1 Sqn, Laverton, 22.07.1930.
61. *Ibid.* Report by F/Off M B Allen to CO, 1 Sqn, 22.07.1930.
62. NAA ACT CRS A705/1 Item 153/1/758. Whelan Rescue Operation.
63 *Ibid.* "Extract from Auditor General's Report 1932-33" - "Rescue of Prospector Whelan in Central Australia."
64. NAA ACT CRS A705/1 Item 205/2/690. Aerial Geological and Geophysical Survey of Northern Australia 1935. Minutes of meeting 18/19.02.1935.
65. *Ibid.* Cabinet decision of 6.03.1935. Secretary to the Survey to Defence Department, 11.03.1935.
66. 1 Squadron Unit Diary. RAAF Form A50. Entry 31.07.1935.
67. NAA ACT CRS A705/1 Item 205/2/690. Op Cit. Bladin, OC No.1 Sqn to Air Board; "North Australia Photo Survey Flight", 9.10.1935.
68. Interview with Air Commodore C R Taylor, 21.01.1988. Interview notes, Air Power Study Centre, ACT.
69. NAA ACT CRS 705/1 Item 73/1/1119. Op Cit. Letter, CO No.3 Sqn, Richmond, to Air Board, 16.07.1930.
70. ASAP News, Vol.1, No.3, P.11.
71. NAA ACT CRS A705/1 Item 73/1/1119. Op Cit. DTS to COs, 1 AD, 1 and 3 Sqns, 8.02.1930.
72. *Ibid.* Letter, Bostock, CO No.3 Sqn to Air Board, 6.01.1933.
73. Air Board Agendum No.1405. Meeting of 18.06.1930.
74. NAA Vic CRS MP1118/2 Item 69/2/875. J.T. McCormick, Superintendent, to Director of Aeronautical Inspections, Victoria Barracks, 15.05.1939.
75. *Ibid.* "Report of Examination of Wapiti Airframe A5 12." With letter of 4.11.1938.
76. Air Board Agendum No.1624: "Aircraft Reconditioning Programme for the R.A.A.F." Air Member for Supply, 22.05.1934.
77 *Ibid.*
78. NAA ACT CRS A705/1 Item 208/5/275. Training Policy Citizen Air Force 1936-37. Minute; J Mc Cauley, DT to AMP, 9.09.1936.
79. NAA ACT CRS A705/1 Item 69/13/706. Policy File Overhaul Wapiti Airframes and Engines (April 1937). Minute, CO, 1 FTS to Air Board. "Flying Training Hours - Engine Position", 5.05.1937.
80. *Ibid.* Minute: "Supply of Cylinders for Jupiter Engine", 13.10.1937.
81. *Ibid.* Minute: "Wapiti Airframes - Jupiter Engines" TS1 to D of E, 15.04.1937.
82. *Ibid.*
83. NAA CRS A705/1 Item 69/13/706. *Op Cit.* Minute from D of E, 15.04.1937.
84. *Ibid.* Minute; "Wapiti Airframes and Jupiter Engines", DE to DTS, 6.05.1937.
85. NAA ACT CRS A2408/1 Item 121/22. L14 - Letter book - Wapiti. Entry 572 of 9.12.1931. Refers to fuselages held at the North Melbourne Drill Hall.
86. Robertson, B. *British Military Aircraft Serials 1911–1979.* Patrick Stephens, UK, 1979. P.115. These aircraft were from a batch of 85 (K2236-K2320). Robertson records K2289-K2305 as Mk.IIA Wapitis (Home Service).
87. NAA ACT CRS A705/1 Item 42/301/30. "Statement of Overseas Indents for Aircraft."
88. NAA ACT CRS A705/1 Item 9/8/39. Record of Wapiti Airframes. Letter to 1 AD, "Wapiti Aircraft A5-39 to A5-43 Inclusive." No date, circa early 1938.
89. *Ibid.* Air Member for Supply to 1AD: "Wapiti Aircraft A5-39 to A5-43 Inclusive." No date, circa early 1938.
90. Air Board Agendum No.2268.
91. NAA ACT CRS A705/1 Item 9/8/39. Op Cit. Minute: "Wapiti Airframe Policy." Note by DE, 16.05.1939.
92. *Ibid.* Minute: "Wapiti Airframe Policy", note by DE, 16.05.1939.
93. *Ibid.* Memo: "Wapiti Airframes", 7.07.1939.
94. NAA ACT CRS A2670/1 Item 21/1939. War Cabinet Agenda: "RAAF Aircraft Position at 9 October 1939".
95. NAA ACT CRS A705/1 Item 9/8/39. Op Cit. 1 FTS to Air Board, 5.07.1939.
96. NAA ACT CRS A9186/18 Item 475. Operational Record Book No.1 SFTS, POINT COOK. RAAF Form A.50. Entry for May 1940.
97. NAA ACT CRS A705/1 Item 9/8/39. *Op Cit.* Minute,

15.06.1940.
98. *Ibid.* "Wapiti Aircraft". Senior Admin Staff Officer (SOA) to Air Board, 27.09.1940.
99. *Ibid.* AMDE to HQ, Southern Area, 20.06.1941.
100. Letter to author, 8.04.90.
101. NAA ACT CRS A705/1 Item 9/8/39. Op Cit. "Wapiti Aircraft". 1 SFTS to HQ, Southern Area, 31.05.1941.
102. Hodgkinson, V. "Abinto at Point Cook", *Aeroplane Monthly*, Vol 9 No.4, April, 1981.
103. Minute: "Aircraft for Seaplane Carrier, H.M.A.S. "*Albatross*". CAS to Defence, 13.02.1929. Williams Papers, RAAF Museum, Point Cook.
104. NAA ACT CRS A705/1 Item 114/6/57. "Quarterly Letter from Liaison Officer 31.1.30". Wrigley to Air Board, 6.02.1930.
105. *Ibid.*
106. NAA ACT CRS A2408 Item 121/22. WAPITI. Letterbook entry No.87, 31.05.1929.
107. NAA ACT CRS A664/1 Item 464/401/675A. Estimate of Expenditure. 1920-30. "Department of Defence, Estimate of Expenditure 1929-30, Explanatory Statement Prepared by Direction of the Minister for Defence."
108. AWM PR88/154 Item 1. A T Cole diary entry 22.01.1930.
109. NAA ACT A705/1 Item 32/10/1522. Report on RAAF Failures for period 1933 TO 30.6.1935, Reported to AAIC. Also, NAA Vic MP124/6/0 Item 415/201/764.
110. NAA ACT CRS A705/1. Ellsworth Relief Expedition to South Pole Area. "Preliminary Outline of Procedure to Adopted by "Discovery II".
111. NAA ACT CRS A705/1 Item 153/1/786. RAAF Assistance in Search for Ellsworth and Kenyon. Minute: 5.12.1935.
112. Wapiti A5-2 had been fitted with skis in the UK before delivery. A fall of snow at Westland's Yeovil aerodrome provided an opportunity to test the skis that had been ordered by the Royal Canadian Air Force. Fl Lt Douglas was reported as having improvised skis before the ship left Melbourne. AA ACT CRS A705/1 Item 153/1/786. *Op Cit.* Minute, 5.12.1935.
113. Letter to author, 29.05.1998.
114. NAA ACT CRS A705/1 Item 69/13/706. Policy File Overhaul Wapiti Airframes and Engines (April 1937). Minute; "Wapiti Airframes - Jupiter Engines". TS1 to DofE, 15.04.1937.
115. NAA ACT CRS A705/1 Item 32/10/1510. Air Accidents Investigation Committee Report No.141 of 7.06.1935.
116. Letter to author, 12.10.1990.
117. NAA VIC CRS MP187/4 Item 141. Aircraft Accident Report Files, 1929-1932. 52-211 (Incomplete). Statement by Wing Cdr E. Harrison relative to crash of Aircraft A5-31, Wapiti, which occurred at Werribee, Victoria, on 16th April, 1935. Pilot - Flying Officer C.N. Egerton (sic)"
118. *Ibid.* P.G. Heffernan notes in a letter to the author dated 12.10.1990, that Parker was lucky that his aircraft rolled onto its side as it "hit the deck".
119. NAA VIC CRS MP187/3. RAAF Preliminary Reports of Flying Accidents or Forced Landings, 1936-1939. Report: "Failure of Mainplane Fabric on A5-5", by F/Off E Scott, 15.10.1936.
120. *Ibid.* "Accident to Aircraft Wapiti A5/5".
121. NAA ACT CRS A705/1 Item 34/1/476. West Australian Centenary Celebrations. Williams in answer to Minute from DofT, 26.07.1929.
122. *Ibid.* Minute, DOI to CAS, 2.08.1929.
123. Jones, Sir G. *From Private to Air Marshal*, Greenhouse Publications, Vic, 1988. P.51
124. "Bulldogs in Action at West Australian Pageant." *Aircraft*, 1 December 1932, P.6.
125. This was a repeat of the Laverton pageant held to celebrate the 1934 Air Race and Victoria's 100th Anniversary.
126. 1 Squadron Unit Diary. RAAF Form A.50.
127. Otherwise there appears to be little recorded on Wapiti bombing activities. Proof trials of the first 250 lb (113 kg) HE Bomb took place on 24 November 1932. The CO of 1 Squadron was ordered to "load one live and fused bomb on to a Wapiti and drop it from 4,000 feet at the target... Four 8½ lb. practice bombs are to be dropped as sighters before the 250 lb. bomb is dropped." (AA ACT A705/1 Item 12/2/424. Proof Trial 250 Lb Bomb. Order 9.11.32.)
128. 1 Squadron Unit Diary. RAAF Form A.50. Appendix "A". No.1 Squadron Training Exercise 5 - 11 June 1934.
129. Interview with author, 16.07.1990.
130. Interview with author, 16.07.1990.
131. "Inquiry Into Wapiti's Crash," *The West Australian*, issue of Friday 1.11.1935, P.26. Also, AA Vic MP116 Series 3. Reports on Forced Landings and Minor Accidents. Vol.1
132. Contract Board Agendum No.13. Meeting 12.01.1937.
133. Letter to author, 16.04.1990.
134. NAA ACT CRS A2408/1 Item 121/22. L14 Letter book - Wapiti. Entry 486 of 19.10.1931.
135. Taped interview with Fred Anderson.
136. Letter to author, 23.08.1990.
137. NAA ACT CRS A 705/1 Item 73/1/1119. *Op Cit.* Letter: "Wapiti Foot Rest and Handgrip". DTS to CO, 1 FTS, 1 Sqn, 21.07.1932.
138. NAA ACT CRS A705/1 Item 73/1/1119. *Op Cit.* Report by Flt Lt Walters, OC, "B" Flight, 1 FTS.
139. Letters from Cadet (later Air Vice Marshall) G C Hartnell to his mother. RAAF Air Power Study Centre, Canberra.
140. Interview with author, 6.07.1990.
141. Letter to author, 4.07.1998.
142. For the story of these unique Australian military gliders see Isaacs, K, "The DHA Gliders - Australia's 'Wooden Warbirds'", *Air International*, UK, July 1976, Vol.11, P.22.
143. 7 CRD Unit History. RAAF Form A.50.

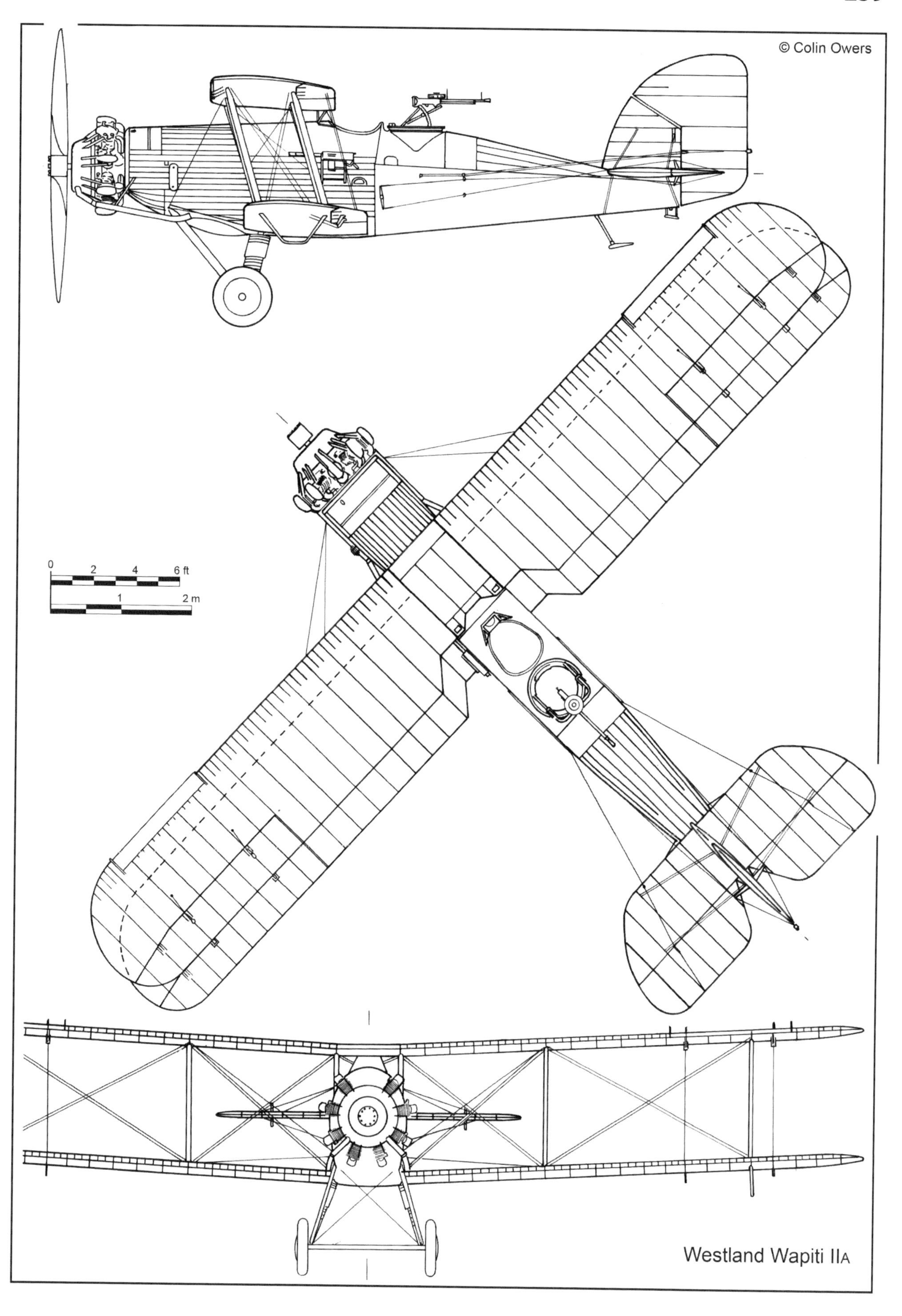
© Colin Owers
0
2
4
6 ft
1
2 m
Westland Wapiti IIA

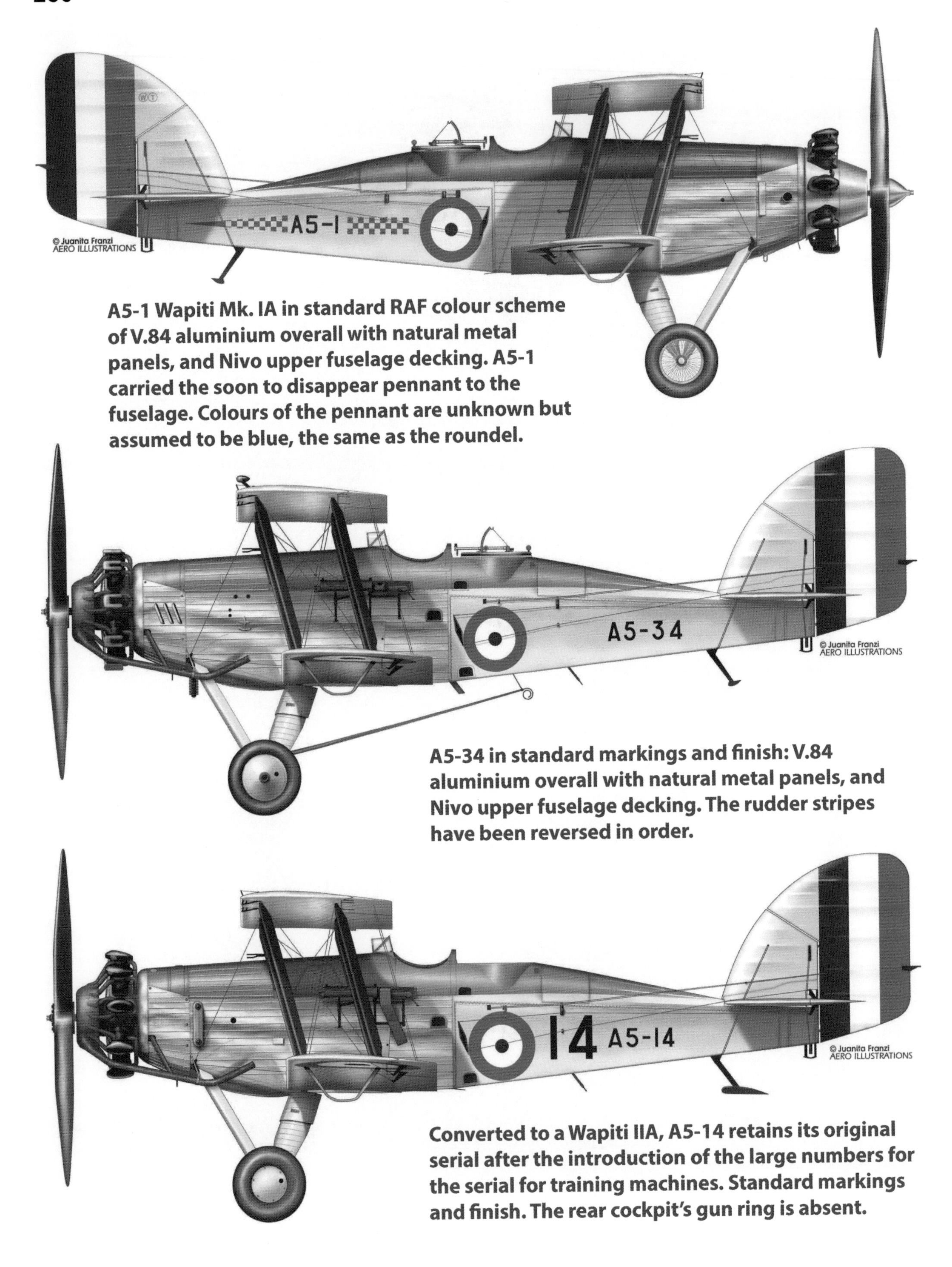


**A5-1 Wapiti Mk. IA in standard RAF colour scheme of V.84 aluminium overall with natural metal panels, and Nivo upper fuselage decking. A5-1 carried the soon to disappear pennant to the fuselage. Colours of the pennant are unknown but assumed to be blue, the same as the roundel.**

**A5-34 in standard markings and finish: V.84 aluminium overall with natural metal panels, and Nivo upper fuselage decking. The rudder stripes have been reversed in order.**

**Converted to a Wapiti IIA, A5-14 retains its original serial after the introduction of the large numbers for the serial for training machines. Standard markings and finish. The rear cockpit's gun ring is absent.**

**Right:** A5-1 in flight.

## Westland Wapiti IA & IIA – RAAF A5

### A5-1

21.02.29. Yeovil, UK. Christened by Lady Ryrie at Westland's factory.
29.04.29. Received by RAAF. 1 AD. Damaged in shipping to Australia.
25.06.29. 1 Sqn.
11.09.29. Laverton. P/Off A.C. Shaw. Forced landing due engine seizure caused by oil delivery pipe leak.
30.10.29. Sgt Jackson. Combined air and sea operation to protect Point Cook from enemy attack. Escorted A5-4 back to Laverton.
17.07.30. 1 FTS. F/Off Gerrand. Forced landing due partial seizure Jupiter 8143.
11.08.30. 1 FTS. Point Cook. Cdt D.A. Cameron. Landing accident due to soft ground. Tipped on nose breaking propeller.
20.08.30. 1 AD for repair.
21.01.31. 1 AD. A.W. Murphy, AC1 Anderson. Test flight.
22.01.31. 1 FTS.
20.05.31. Deniliquin, NSW. Cdt A.M. Bowman. When the machine touched the ground during a normal landing, a tyre blew out, the axle broke and the undercarriage collapsed. Prop was smashed. A flaw was discovered in the axle. The occupants were unhurt.
27.05.31. Returned 1 AD via rail.
26.05.31. 1 FTS. Point Cook. Cdt J.G. Glen. Accident.
17.08.31. 1 AD. A.W. Murphy, LAC Neale. Test flight. To be delivered to 1 FTS.
7.09.32. 1½ ml north-west Point Cook. Cpl L.R. Ambrose. Pupil ran into soft ground standing on nose. Prop and probable damage to front fuselage. 1 AD for repair.
(9.02.33). Repairs to be carried out at 1 FTS.
19.11.34. FTS. F/Off Douglas, AC1 Macintosh, LAC Russell. From Point Cook to Richmond for royal escort and air display. Returned 28th.
4.02.35. Point Cook. Flt Lt G.E. Douglas, Cdt D.E. Chapman. Wheel collapsed on landing.
18.02.35. Point Cook. Flt Lt G.E. Douglas, Cdt E.L. Chapman. Oleo undercarriage leg broke on take-off.
23.04.35. Laverton. Flt Lt F.N. Wright, Cdt H.H. Jackson. Tipped on nose when ran into bog.
3.05.35. Point Cook. F/Off A.G. Pither, Cdt E.L. Chapman. Tipped on nose when taxying.
26.03.36. Point Cook. Cdt G.K.K. Buscombe. Taxied into stationary A7-48, nil damage to Wapiti.
15.04.37. TFT 1,288 hours. 49 hours since last complete overhaul. Jupiter 8079.
27.03.39. 1 FTS Cadet Wing. J.8147.
26.04.39. TFT 1,963 hours.
1.08.39. 100 hours airframe life remaining.
7.09.39. 1 FTS. Cdt A.G. Wearne (solo). In attempting to cross irrigation drain surface collapsed damaging airscrew tips.
20.11.39. J8155 removed for conversion.
16.02.40. Extension of 120 hours if airframe satisfactory.
25.04.40. Issued Engineering School ex ITS.
28.10.40. Converted to Instructional Wapiti 2.
5.12.44. Converted to produce.

### A5-2

(14.08.29). TFT 64 hours 35. Jupiter 8077.
25.05.29. Flt Lt C.T. Anderson. Forced landing at Harden, NSW, due engine cut out. To Cootamundra. Delayed Cootamundra till 29th. Arrived Richmond 1210 hours.
30.09.29. 3 Sqn. Forrest. F/Off A.L. Walters. Forced landing.
15.10.29. 3 Sqn. Conoble Siding near Ivanhoe, NSW. F/Off A.L. Walters. Forced landing due engine seizure; union on oil delivery pipe coming loose.
24.10.29. 3 Sqn. Forrest. Forced landing; main and auxiliary fuel tanks empty.
(9.12.29). 3 Sqn. Forced landing at Eouoble re fractured oil pipe.

**Left:** Wapiti A5-2 after striking a fence on landing on 30 January 1931, resulting in the machine being written off. (via P.G. Heffernan)

29.07.30. 1 FTS. Point Cook. F/Off F.J. Wight. Collision with A5-11 while taxying in poor weather.
30.01.31. Point Cook. F/Off A.G. Gerrand. Struck fence when landing in darkness.
(4.05.32). 1 FTS. TFT 109 hours.
10.03.33. 1 AD. Sqn Ldr A.W. Murphy, Cpl Godwill. Test flight.
(5.10.33). 1 FTS. Defect - bonding of elevators.
8.12.33. 2 ml Essendon, Vic. F/Off W.G. Rae, Mr M.H.R. Guy, LAC K.J. Richards. Forced landing due shortage petrol, slight damage.
31.01.34. Point Cook. F/Off T.F. Percival. Heavy landing, axle bent.
1934. 1 FTS. Major crash during annual cross-country. Uneconomical to rebuild, to components. Approved 7.08.34.

### A5-3

29.04.29. 1 AD. Received from overseas.
10.05.29. 3 Sqn.
(14.08.29). TFT 84.45 hours. Jupiter 8078.
(28.02.30). 3 Sqn.
28.08.30. C Flight, 1 FTS. Point Cook. Cpl R.J. Parker. Solo practice, t/buckle unscrewed from undercarriage bracing. Machine slewed to starboard and settled on starboard plane. TFT 203 hours. Jupiter VIII J8151 TFT 204.35 hours.
21.09.31. 1 FTS. Point Cook. Cdt I.D. McLaughlin (solo). Landed in water on drome, turned over onto back, mainplanes, fuselage strained, rudder crushed, struts and airscrew broken. TFT 613.05 hours. J.VIII J.8078. To 1 AD.
23.02.32. 1 AD. A.W. Murphy, Cpl Godwill. Test Flight.
20.04.32. 1 FTS.
21.07.32. Point Cook. F/Off W.G. Rae, Cdt J.F. Hobler. Landed on soft ground and turned on nose.
23.01.33. 1 FTS. Sgt Cameron, Cdt F.B. Chapman. Instruction followed by solo practice.
1.06.33. Point Cook. F/Off R.F.M. Dalton, LAC Allen. Undercarriage failure on landing.
12.10.34. Point Cook. Cdt A.X. Richards. Bogged while taxying, prop damaged.
19.11.34. FTS. Sgt Byrnes, AC1 Hope, AC1 Torkey. Point Cook to Richmond. Royal escort and air display. Return to Point Cook 28th.
5.02.35. Point Cook. Cdt W.N. Gibson. Engine J8152 failed on first solo take-off, struck banked road, broken prop, fuselage severed forward of centre-section. Complete overhaul, bottom longerons fitted in rear bays together with patch plates.
6.02.35. 1 AD.
5.03.35. Richmond, NSW. Cdt H.F.C. Davis. Stalled too high when landing, undercarriage, bottom longerons, front fuselage damaged.
5.07.35. 1 FTS. J8145.
26.07.35. 1 AD. Sqn Ldr A.W. Murphy, LAC Hamilton. Test flight.
9.10.35. Point Cook. Cdt F.V. Sharpe. Heavy landing, undercarriage damaged, lower longeron crushed.
6.02.36. Point Cook. Cdt W.J. Keenan. Ran into drain, prop damaged.
12.11.36. R Brownell (solo). Instructor's practice.
15.04.37. TFT 1,799 hours. 487 hr since last complete overhaul. Jupiter 8080.
27.04.37. 1 FTS. Cadet W Skinner (solo). Struck fence while practicing forced landings. Main spar of tailplane bruised.
13.10.38. *Due complete Total time 2265.*
19.10.38. To be dismantled and held at FTS in present

**Right:** *Last time landed in a rubbish tip* was original caption. A5-3 had a chequered career and the date of this incident is that of 5 February 1935. (via P.G. Heffernan)

condition.
2.06.39. Completed 2663 hours recommendation for conversion.
(7.07.39). Recommended for conversion to components, together with A5-9, to allow overhaul of A5-26, A5-39 and A5-42.
25.08.39. Being converted to components.
8.09.39. Allotted Wireless School, Point Cook, for conversion for instructional purposes.
16.09.39. To components. Fuselage and mainplanes intact to Wireless School, Point Cook.
30.01.40. Allotted Engineering School, Melbourne Showgrounds.
6.05.40. Converted to components as advised by 1 FTS Memo 259/24/S of this date.

**A5-4**
29.04.29. Received by RAAF.
31.04.29 to 4.06.29. A/C Williams, Cpl Abicair. Laverton to Adelaide and return.
27.05.29. 1 Sqn.
3.02.30. 1 FTS.
18.05.30. 1 FTS. Point Cook. LAC L.M. Diprose. Forced landing due failure engine 8157.
15.07.30. Point Cook. F/Off W.G. Rae. Minor crash when undercarriage bracing wire broke.
26.03.31. 1 FTS. Point Cook. F/Off F.I. Stevens. Taking of on wet aerodrome mud and stones thrown into prop.
1.04.31. 1 AD for repair.
(27.05.31). 1 AD. To be completed to schedule following crash in May.
4.08.31. 1 AD. A.W. Murphy. Test flight. To 1FTS.
18.08.31. Training Sqn 1 FTS. Point Cook. Cdt C.D. Candy (solo). *I was practicing forced landing approaches. On my last approach seeing that I would not make the field, I opened up the engine about 50 to 100 yds back from the leeward side of the field and at a height of about 30 to 40 ft. The engine did not pick up immediately & I kept the nose down waiting for the engine to pick up. Before this occurred the aircraft received a bump which caused it to drop about 10 - 20 ft. striking a fence carrying away the port side of the undercarriage. The engine came on; I flew back & landed on the aerodrome; the aircraft landing heavily on its fuselage.* TFT 500 hours. J.8081 *torn from its mount when the two lower cylinders dug into the aerodrome*, fuselage buckled, airscrew and undercarriage broken. 1 AD for repair. The instructor, Fly Off Stevens was held responsible *in that this pupil was sent to practice approaches too early in his training.*
(18.05.32). 1 AD. Work to commence for metal rigging experience.
3.08.32. 1 AD. A.W. Murphy, AC1 Langford. Test flight.
9.08.32. 1 FTS.
28.02.33. FTS. Little River near Geelong, Vic. Cdt K.D. Salmon. Forced landing, petrol pump failure.
6.03.33. FTS. Laverton. F/Off W.G. Rae, Sgt W.A. Raymond. Forced landing due engine failure.
23.05.33. Deniliquin, NSW. Cdt A.C. Mills. Slightly damaged landing on unformed aerodrome. Cloud flying test.
7.02.34. Forced Landing Ground 3, Point Cook. P/O E.D. Scott. Hit fence, starboard king post damaged.
18.07.34. Point Cook. Sgt E.C. Sims, Cdt H.V.C. Hoskins. Forced landing, engine failure.
6.09.34. 1 Ml north-east Birregurra, near Colac, Vic. Cdt C.F. Brady. Forced landing due engine running rough, major damage undercarriage, lower mainplane, airscrew.
10.09.34. 1 AD for repair.
20.11.34. 1 AD. Sqn Ldr A.W. Murphy, LAC Woods. Test flight.
22.01.35. 1 FTS.
26.02.35. Point Cook. Cdt R.D. Welland. Taxied into drain damage to wingtip.
28.10.35. 4 ml north Whittlesea. Cdt J.R.G. Mc Donald. Forced landing due weather on cross country flight.
(9.04.36). 1 FTS. Re condemned parts being ordered into service again.
15.04.37. TFT 1,800 hours. 772 hr since last complete overhaul. Jupiter 8156.

**Left:** A5-4 as first received as a Wapiti IA. (via AHMofWA P012485)

15.10.37. 1 AD for overhaul.
9.12.37. 1 FTS. J8077.
27.03.39. 1 FTS Cadet Wing. J8144.
26.04.39. TFT 2,351 hours.
12.07.39. J8144 due for complete to 1 AD, J8143 in replacement.
1.08.39. 600 hr airframe life remain.
11.08.39. 1 FTS.
25.08.39. FTS. J8143.
12.09.39. 1 FTS. Mt Buninyong, near Ballarat, Vic. P/Off (035982) Eustance Edred Vivian Dillon, Cdt (03107) Vernon Francis Wilfred Sullivan. Struck tree during navigation exercise due poor visibility on account of low cloud and heavy rain, uneconomical to repair.
21.09.39. Issued 1 AD for conversion to component parts.
13.10.39. Approved, airframe and engine to components.

**A5-5**
29.04.29. Received from overseas.
14.05.29. Sqn Ldr R Brownell, Sqn Ldr Smart. Initial flight in Wapiti.
15.05.29. 3 Sqn.
(14.08.29). TFT 58.50 hours. Jupiter 8079.
25.03.30. 1 FTS.
22.04.30. 1 FTS. Point Cook. Flt Lt C.S. Wiggins. Undercarriage gave way during training flight.
24.04.30. 1 AD for repair.
(3.07.30). 1 AD. Being fitted with drogue target towing gear and split undercarriage.
12.07.30. 3 Sqn.
13.08.30. 1 AD. Sqn Ldr A.W. Murphy. Test flights.
21.08.30. 1 AD. Sqn Ldr A.W. Murphy, LAC Nicholas. Test drogue target.
(24.09.30). Time to fit anti-aircraft drogue for use with HMA ships is one day.
26.07.31. Forced landing - broken con rod.
(5.05.32). 3 Sqn, Richmond.
14.09.32. Sgt W.E. Brown, LAC E Keller. Forced landing, engine failure.
15.11.32. Richmond, NSW. Flt Lt U.E. Ewart, F/Off C.M. Blamey. Practice for Instructor's course, heavy landing, undercarriage damaged.
1.02.33. F/Off Candy. AA Co-op; drogue over Sydney.
14.03.33. Richmond, NSW. Sgt J.H. Buckham, Cdt B.G. Haynes. Undercarriage collapsed due seized wheel.
(1.10.33). 3 Sqn. Recommended for complete overhaul.
(22.05.34). Requires complete overhaul/rebuild after crash.
11.06.34. 1AD.
3.08.34. 1 AD. Sqn Ldr A.W. Murphy, Cpl Godwill. Test flight.
9.08.34. 3 Sqn.
24.02.35. Richmond, NSW. P/Off T.F.C. Lawrence, Sgt R.L. Horner. Accident due engine failure, undercarriage collapsed on landing.
22.05.35. Richmond for Brisbane, King's Jubilee celebrations. 3 Sqn. P/Off Hay, AC1 McNab. Returned 27th.
4.07.35. 1 FTS, J8145.
6.08.35. Point Cook. Cdt H Smith. Taxied onto soft ground tipping on nose.
15.10.36. Cadet Sqn, 1 FTS. Point Cook. F/Off E.D. Scott, Cpl Dillon. Dillon pulled out of dive too roughly during dive bombing exercise, causing excessive loading on aircraft. Fabric on starboard mainplane burst. Mainplane manufactured 11.11.28. Reconditioned 7.07.30 at 1 AD.
15.04.37. TFT 1,700 hours. 784 hr since last complete overhaul. Jupiter 8145.
2.09.37. 1 AD for overhaul.
20.10.37. Received 1 AD Workshops.
10.12.37. FTS. J8080.
(14.01.38). 1 FTS. AC1 G.M. Whitworth. Casualty.
8.06.38. 1 FTS. AC1 Whitworth (solo). Unable to stop on landing, hit fence. Damage to port and starboard lower mainplanes, airscrew.
17.08.38. 1 FTS. Point Cook. Cdt D.R. Paterson (solo). A5-17 taxied into stationary A5-5; upper port aileron damaged.
27.03.39. 1 FTS Cadet Wing. J8077.
26.04.39. TFT 2,819 hrs.

**Right:** A5-5 in Mk. IIA configuration.

1.08.39. 600 hr airframe life remain.
11.08.39. 1 FTS.
16.10.39. Awaiting issue TS, J8077.
11.03.40. 1 SFTS (ITS). Laverton. F/Sgt H.R. Baldwin (solo). Forced landing nil damage.
11.03.40. 1 SFTS (ITS). F/Sgt H.R. Baldwin, P/Off Carter. During landing practice port oleo leg lost compression due stripping of glan locking nut.
1.05.40. 1 SFTS (ITS). No. 2 Landing Field. Flt Lt E.G. Fyfe, Cdt Fletcher. Cadet stalled in gliding turn, engine failed to respond when instructor opened throttle, hit fence of forced landing field, slight damage to port wing tip skid.
28.05.40. Issued Engineering school ex ITS.
(13.06.40). Disposal.
28.10.40. Converted to Instructional Wapiti 3.

### A5-6

(25.05.29). F/Off Sherger's aircraft.
(14.08.29). TFT 62.05 hours. Jupiter 8081.
19.09.29. P/Off William Gordon Rae. To Laverton en-route to Perth.
12.03.30. 3 Sqn. Clarendon, NSW. Cdt R.E. Allman. Training accident during forced landing due mishandling petrol controls. Jupiter 8160.
(9.07.30). 1 AD. Fuselage for repair.
11.12.30. 1 AD. Sqn Ldr A.W. Murphy, TAC Matson. Test flight.
21.01.31. 1 AD. Sqn Ldr A.W. Murphy, AC1 Harford. Test flight with DH9a planes.
25.02.31. 1 AD. Sqn Ldr A.W. Murphy, Sqn Ldr Hepburn. Test of laying device for towed targets.
10.03.31. 1 AD. A.T. Cole. Delivering to Point Cook less drive to carry cable.
12.05.32. R.J. Brownell, Sqn Ldr Summers. Instructor regrading.
17.01.33. 'B' Flt, 1 FTS. Sgt Cameron, Cdt F.B. Chapman. Practice.
6.02.33. Point Cook. Cdt John Carlie Bolton McDonnell (killed) (solo). Mid-air collision with A5-8, interlocked, caught fire on impact, both totally destroyed. Jupiter 8141.
(23.03.33). Disposal recommended.

### A5-7

24.05.29. A.W. Murphy, LAC Carter. Test.
25.05.29. A.W. Murphy, Sgt Ellis. Essendon display.
8.08.29 to 26.08.29. 1 Sqn. F/0ff Wight, Sgt Stewart, AC1 Bain. With A5-8. Geographical reconnaissance of Central Australia; the area between the Qld border and the railway running south from Alice Springs and to the southern Australian Lakes.
12.10.29. Forrest, WA. F/Off F.J.B. Wight. Accident, damaged wheel due rough landing ground.
3.02.30. 1 AD. Sqn Ldr A.W. Murphy, AC1 Love.
15.07.30. Point Cook. F/Off F.J. Wight. Minor crash due flaw in axle.
20.10.30. 1 FTS. Forced landing, probably due air lock.
(28.11.30). 1 FTS. Jupiter J8147. Front outer, port landing wire fractured in flight.
24.11.31. 1 FTS. Point Cook. Cdt C.D. Candy (solo). Return from cross country flight to Deniliquin, *I held off too high and the aircraft fell suddenly on the starboard wheel. The undercarriage collapsed and I switched off immediately.* The undercarriage was wrecked, lower longeron bent, starboard lower mainplane damaged, airscrew broken. TFT 735.35 hrs. Airframe to 1 AD for complete overhaul; J.8145 to 1 AD for examination. The aircraft was fitted with parachute dropping racks at the time.
(18.05.32). 1 AD. Work to commence for metal rigging experience.
3.11.32. 1 AD. Sqn Ldr A.W. Murphy, Cpl Godwill. Test flight.
3.03.33. 'B' Flt, 1 FTS. Cdt F.B. Chapman (solo). Practice.
19.05.33. Point Cook. Cdt K.D. Salmon. Accident.
12.02.34. Point Cook. F/Off T.F. Percival. Stood on nose after landing with drift, prop and wing skid broken.
5.10.34. Point Cook. F/Off G.E. Douglas, Cdt P.O. Laverack. Accident, overshoot, fuselage damaged.
19.11.34. FTS. Sgt Reeve, AC1 Busteed, AC1 Tabner. Point Cook to Richmond. Royal escort and air display. Return

**Above:** Line-up of Wapiti Mark IA biplanes at Richmond. A5-6, A5-3 and A5-5 identified in line-up. (AHMofWA)

to Point Cook 28th.

8.05.35. Point Cook. Flt Lt G.E. Douglas. Struck tractor when landing, fractured rear spar lower port mainplane.

30.10.35. 1 FTS. Echuca, Vic. Cdt Brian Reginald Walker. Stall at low altitude, aircraft dove into ground. Extensive damage. Actually, Walker pulled out of dive too late and hit ground.

(15.11.35). Uneconomical to repair, conversion to components recommended. Jupiter 8159 badly damaged but probably repairable.

**A5-8**

8.08.29 - 26.08.29. 1 Sqn. F/Off A.G. Gerrand, AC1 Thomas, Mr Madigan. With A5-7. Geographical reconnaissance of Central Australia; the area between the Qld border and the railway running south from Alice Springs and to the southern Australian Lakes.

15.08.29. Forced landing Alice Springs, NT, due lack petrol.

28.04.30. 1 FTS. Point Cook. Diprose. Crash.

15.05.30. 1 FTS. P/Off Handover. Crash near Point Cook.

(23.11.31). 1 AD. Straight axle.

11.12.31. 1 AD. Sqn Ldr A.W. Murphy, LAC Matson. Test flight.

24.01.33. 'B' Flt 1 FTS. Sgt Cameron, Cdt F.B. Chapman. Instruction followed by solo practice.

6.02.33. Cdt Keith Aloysius Crisp (killed) (solo). Point Cook. Mid-air collision with A5-6, interlocked, caught fire on impact both totally destroyed. Jupiter 8153.

**A5-9**

7.06.29. Received at 1 AD.

2.08.29. Sqn Ldr A.W. Murphy, Bassett. Engine vibrating through gate.

7.08.29. 1 Sqn.

21.01.30. 1 AD.

(25.02.30). 1 AD. Fitting of exhaust ring. OK.

7.03.30. 1 Sqn.

26.10.30. 1 Sqn. Laverton. Accident.

25.02.31 to 14.03.31. 1 Sqn. Flt Lt F.J.B. Wight, Sgt D.A. Endean. Flight to Launceston and Hobart and return for Army Co-op exercises and survey of Huon River forestry area.

(2.03.31). 1 Sqn. Report. *Holding down lugs of oil tanks broken and channel pulled away from bottom of tanks.*

13.03.31. Forced landing at 25 ml NW Yanakie, Vic, due engine failure (air lock?).

(16.04.31). 1 FTS. 'Broken bolt at U/C V strut attachment at fuselage.'

12.02.32 to 29.02.32. 1 Sqn. Flight from Laverton to Tasmania and return. Air Pageants at Launceston (13th), Hobart (20th) and Wynyard (27th).

19.11.32. Laverton. Flt Lt F.W. Thomas, Fly Off A.R. Love. Aircraft took off across wind, controls jammed, minor accident. Airscrew broken; engine mount sheared.

21.11.32. 1 AD.

19.12.32. 1 FTS.

1.03.33. FTS. Point Cook. Sgt D.G. Cameron, Sgt T.J. Richards. Forced landing, undercarriage failure.

6.03.33. 1 AD for repair.

15.08.33. 1 AD. Sqn Ldr A.W. Murphy, AC1 Busteed. Test flight.

27.09.33. 3 Sqn.

6.03.34. Richmond, NSW. F/Off R.A. Holmwood, LAC J.E. Reynolds. Struck telephone post during approach to land, extensive damage.

9.04.34. 1 AD for repair.

12.09.34. 3 Sqn.

5.10.34. F/Off Candy. Escort for RAF flying boats.

18.10.34. F/Off Candy. Royal air escort.

28 to 29.11.34. F/Off Candy; AC1 Cherry. Richmond for Coffs Harbour and return for escort Royal party.

21.02.35. F/Off Candy, Cdt Walker. Sqn Air escort on arrival of State Governor.

2.07.35. 3 Sqn lent to 101 Fl. Lt E.G. Knox Knight, F/Off P.G. Graham. Richmond to Point Cook for annual bombing camp held on 4.07.35.

**Above:** Wapiti IA A5-7 of 1 Squadron at Maylands airfield, 12 October 1929, preparing to return to Laverton after the 1929 Transcontinental Air Race. The machine bears the pennant along the fuselage. This colourful marking may have been allowed for the Race. It appears that aircraft up to A5-10 would have carried this short-lived marking. (AHMofWA P15739 )

5.07.35. Allotted from 1 AD to 1 FTS.
22.05.36. 1 FTS. No. 2 Landing Ground, 1 ml east Werribee. Sgt R F Somerville, Sgt R J Parker. Stalled in slipstream, flew through two fences; prop, mainplanes, undercarriage damaged.
3.06.36. 1 AD, J,8081.
18.09.36. Complete overhaul. All rear longerons renewed.
15.04.37. 1 FTS. TFT 1,627 hrs. 204 hrs since last complete overhaul. Jupiter 8157.
25.04.38. 1 FTS. Yeo. F/Off F Wiltscheibe, AC1 T Otterespoor, AC1 Dolphin. Returning from Richmond Pageant, forced landing.
29.08.38. 1 FTS. Point Cook. Cdt R.G. Watt (solo). While attempting to land, stalled; bottom main beams badly damaged.
22.11.38. 1 FTS. Point Cook. Cdt T.A. Ferguson (solo). Engine failed due shortage of petrol, nil damage.
22.11.38. Forced landing Essendon, magneto trouble.
24.02.39. 1 FTS. Sgt E.E. Tuttleby, AC1 Morehouse. Forced landing due engine failure, nil damage.
(10.03.39). 1 FTS. Jupiter VIII J8151P, *engine lost power in cruising 'revs' while being flown on 'pump and gravity'.*
27.03.39. 1 FTS Cadet Wing, J.8156.
26.04.39. TFT 2,268 hours.
2.06.39. Completed 2,336 hours. Recommended for conversion.
(7.07.39). Recommended for conversion to components together with A5-3, to allow overhaul of A5-26, A5-39. Rear fuselage to be fitted to A5-40. TFT 2,372 hr 30.
15.08.39. Allotted TD for conversion for instructional purposes. Converted to Instructional Aeroplane.
20.10.39. Converted to Instructional Wapiti No.10.
24.01.40. Issued TD Showgrounds, J.8155.

**A5-10**

2.09.29. Sqn Ldr A.W. Murphy, Matson. Test flight, OK.
4.05.30. 1 Sqn. Laverton. F/Off McIntosh. Undershot landing and hit wall, major accident.
18.07.30. 1 Sqn. F/Off M.B. Allen. Test with desert equipment
25.07.30. 1 AD. Sqn Ldr A.W. Murphy, Godwill. Test Flight.
23.03.31. 1 Sqn. Laverton. F/Off A.G. Carr. Accident.
10.05.31. 1 Sqn. Laverton. Flt Lt Garrett.
12.02.32 to 29.02.32. 1 Sqn. Flight from Laverton to Tasmania and return. Air Pageants at Launceston (13th), Hobart (20th) and Wynyard (27th).
19.07.32. Laverton. P/Off A.G. Pither, AC1 H.R.B. Fitzgerald. While taxying undercarriage gave way.
9.10.32. 1 Sqn. Musk near Daylesford. Flt Lt Cecil Kenneth Shields, Sgt (205378) Lyle Richmond Charles Langley, AC2 (300122) Ernest Sutherland Yorston. Forced landing due to rain and low clouds. Crash, unfit for repair.
25.10.32. Convert to components approved.

**A5-11**

24.06.29. Received 1 AD.
20.09.29. 1 Sqn.

**Left:** P.G. Paddy Heffernan captioned this photograph was: - *Two Wapitis collided over Point Cook and Crisp and McDonald (sic) were killed.* Cdt Keith Crisp was flying A5-8 when it collided with A5-6 flown by Cdt John McDonnell. The two aircraft locked together and crashed and burst into flames killing both pilots on 6 February 1933. (via PG Heffernan)

30.10.29. P/Off Shaw. Combined air and sea operation to protect Point Cook from enemy attack. Carried out low bombing attack on ships.
29.04.30. FTS.
29.07.30. 1 FTS. Point Cook. Sgt S Austin. Collision with A5-2 while taxying in poor weather.
29.08.30. 1 FTS. Point Cook. LAC J.H. Buckham. Undershot and struck northern aerial pole on landing approach.
30.09.30. Damage to undercarriage, swung by wind.
(2.10.30). 1 FTS. Point Cook. Cpl R.J. Parker. Crash.
14.05.31. 1 FTS. Point Cook. F/Off Simms. Accident.
29.07.31. Point Cook. Cdt A McD Bowman. Major crash. Pilot landed with drift, bounced and failed to recover.
30.07.31. 1 AD for repairs.
23.02.32. 1 AD. Sqn Ldr A.W. Murphy, LAC Tout. Test flight.
20.04.32. 1 FTS.
27.05.32. P/Off H.F. Boss-Walker, F/Off G.J.I. Clarke. Major crash. One side undercarriage damaged in heavy landing, flown around again and crashed. Undercarriage, starboard mainplane, prop broken.
1.06.32. 1 AD for repair.
6.11.32. 1 AD. Sqn Ldr A.W. Murphy, AC1 Langford. Test flight.
13.12.32. 1 FTS.
8.03.33. 'B' Flt, 1 FTS. Cdt F.B. Chapman (solo). Practice and 'Pin pointing test.'
21.05.34. Deniliquin, NSW. P/Off J.R. Balmer. Struck wires while landing at unfamiliar aerodrome; rudder damaged.
19.11.34. FTS. F/Off Hely, Cpl Cottee, AC1 Briggs. Point Cook to Richmond. Royal escort and air display.
6.02.35. Point Cook. Sqn Ldr G.G. Banting, Cdt R.E. Dupont. While taxying wheel struck hole and collapsed, twisted rear fuselage, prop broken.
18.06.35. Point Cook. F/Off A.G. Pither. Forced landing following shooting off airscrew during gunnery exercise. Starboard lower mainplane damaged.
16.08.35. Cdt A.F. Chalman. Bad landing, crash, undercarriage, main beams, prop damaged.
21.10.36. 1 FTS. Linton, Vic. F/Lt R.A. Holmwood, Cdt D.G. Boehm. Forced landing, engine failure due magneto.
11.01.37. 1 AD.
15.04.37. 1 AD. TFT 1,300 hrs. Complete overhaul finished. Jupiter 8142.
20.05.37. 1 AD. Sqn Ldr A.W. Murphy, AC1 Phillips. Test flight.
17.06.37. Point Cook. 1 FTS. AC1 L.I.H. Newbound (solo). Overshot on landing, tipped on nose in drain. Airscrew and lower longeron broken.
7.06.38. 1 FTS. Sgt W.A. Whetters (solo). Aircraft test.
5.12.38. 1 FTS. Point Cook. Wing Cmdr F.M. Bladin, Cdt Guthrie. Hit mound of dirt on landing; port and starboard mainplanes, port aileron damaged, fuselage generally twisted, J.8149.
23.01.39. Arrived 1 AD with J.8149.
2.05.39. 1 AD Workshops, service.
2.05.39. 1 FTS Cadet Wing J8149.
16.10.39. 1 FTS. Awaiting 'issue Tech Sq.'
15.03.40. 1 SFTS. Cdt S.W. Clifford (solo). Inspection revealed damage caused by succession of heavy landings; bent longerons, main tank split.
18.03.40. *Star' lower longeron bent, star' front and hor strut bay 3 broken.*
15.04.40. J8148 removed.
24.05.40. Issued Engineering School ex ITS.
3.09.40. Converted to components.

### A5-12

24.06.29. 1 AD Received by RAAF.
(3.09.29). 1 AD. Loaned to Point Cook for 10 hours flying before being sent to 3 Sqn.
11.09.29. 1 Sqn.
20.09.29. 3 Sqn.

**Above:** A5-9 after conversion to Wapiti IIA configuration. Note how the lighting conditions make the wings and horizontal tail surfaces appear to be doped the same colour as the fuselage turtledeck. The machine has the "A5" prefix missing from its serial application.

2.07.30. 3 Sqn. Richmond, NSW. Flt Lt F.R. Scherger, F/Off J.R. Fleming. Test for instrument grading on service type. *I completed the test of F/O. Fleming on Wapiti A5-12, and took off myself with the intention of landing close to the Tarmac. I landed in a southerly direction towards the front of the Tarmac. The machine landed perfectly, ran about fifty yards in a straight line, and when it had almost come to a standstill, the tail went up and the machine turned over. The cause of this was the soft nature of the ground on which the machine had landed.* Soft patch of aerodrome was due to heavy rain. Engine mounting bay slightly damaged; fireproof bulkhead badly torn; rudder smashed; outer front strut broken. Damage to front longerons. Spars in upper plane definitely broken; lower planes suspect. TFT 207 hrs. Airframe to 3 Sqn, J.VIII J.8081 engine to 1 AD for repair.
3.07.30. 1 AD for repair.
29.11.30. 3 Sqn. Mascot, NSW. P/Off C.C. McMullen. Minor accident, collided with *Southern Cross Jnr* while taxing.
(5.05.32). 3 Sqn, Richmond.
29.06.32. 1 ml west Glenfield, NSW. Flt Lt A.L. Walters, Corp R Moase. Forced landing due low oil pressure and engine losing oil.
10.06.33. 3 Sqn. Richmond, NSW. Sgt J Buckland, AC1 W.C. Gates. Ran into soft ground on finishing landing run and slowly tipped on nose.
(30.11.33). 3 Sqn. Requests extension to flying time.
(22.05.34). Requires complete overhaul/rebuild after crash.
10.10.34. 1 Sqn.
18 to 27.11.34. 1 Sqn. F/Off Curnow, Sgt Fletcher, LAC Stanton. To Richmond for Royal escort and air display.
9.12.34. Laverton. P/Off P.D. Potts, Sgt E.R. Bennett. Ran into bog while taxying, prop damaged.
3.05.35. 1 FTS.
15.04.37. TFT 1,729 hours. 771 hr since last complete overhaul. No engine.
21.05.37. 1 FTS. 2 miles south Lethbridge. F/Off F.A. Wittschiebe, AC1 Groundwater, AC1 Clarke. While supervising cadets on cross country to Mortlake, successful forced landing due engine failure caused by lack petrol. No damage.
8.12.37.1 AD less engine.
(13.01.38). Airframe tested by representatives of DAI, DTS and MSB.
23.05.38. 1 FTS, J.8142.
19.08.38. Actual issue.
19.09.38. 1 FTS. Point Cook. Sgt C.R. Sladen, Cpl Ogden. Forced landing due engine trouble, no damage.
21.11.38. Forced landing Mansfield due bad weather.
18.01.39 to 3.02.39. In use training.
24.04.39. FTS Cadet Wing, J.8142.
26.04.39. TFT 2,162 hrs.
15.05.39. Completed 240 hr since last overhaul at 2,000 hours. Examination of fuselage showed no fatigue cracks. Was stored at 1 AD.
1.08.39. 600 hr airframe life remaining.
25.08.39. FTS, J.8151.
14.03.40. 1 SFTS. Point Cook. F/Off B.R. Chaseling, Cdt D.E. Sproule. Engine failure on take-off due petrol cock vibrating to 'Off"; forced landing, tailplane fabric slightly torn.
5.06.40. Issued Technical Sqn ex ITS for 120 hourly.
24.06.40. U/S at ITS for more than 2 days.
27.09.40. Will be given another 12 months service.
10.03.41 to 23.05.41. Unserviceable.
23.05.41. Serviceable at 1 SFTS.
21.10.41. Received 1 AD ex 1 SFTS.
11.41. 1 AD. Fitting universal carrier.
4.02.42. Landed Point Cook from Laverton - dropped flares near pier.
5.06.42. W Penny. Laverton to Point Cook.
17.09.43. Allotted 3 AD ex-1 AD for parachute dropping.
12.01.44. Allotment cancelled; aircraft not suitable cross-

**Above:** A5-10 in typical country operation. (AHMofWA P018448)

country flights.
25.03.44. Allotted 1 CRD ex 1 AD. To be held pending authority for commission recommended conversion of engine and airframe.
27.04.44. Approval given to convert at Technical Salvage unit.
(30.04.44). Brought in for salvage at 1 CRD.

**A5-13**
8.11.29. Sqn Ldr A.W. Murphy, Cpl Tootell.
16.11.29. Euroa, Vic, and Cootamundra, NSW. F/Off R.H. Simms. Two forced landings due broken flying wire.
9.07.30. Sqn Ldr R Brownell, Sqn Ldr Bostock. Travel flight Laverton to Point Cook and Vickers gun practice.
6.10.30. 3 Sqn. Baddaginnie, near Benalla, Vic. Sqn Ldr A.H. Cobby. Overshot on landing, port aileron, strut and undercarriage damaged during forced landing due to weather.
13.01.32. 3 Sqn. Left Richmond for aerial survey Longreach, Qld, district. P/Off Miles, AC1 Fay, AC1 Stevens, Dr Woolnough.
1.02.32. Bourke, NSW. Flt Lt A.M. Charlesworth. Damaged in storm.
8, 9 and 11.04.33. 3 Sqn. F/Off Candy, Sgt Willson. Air survey Newnes shale oil area.
27.04.33. 3 Sqn. F/Off Candy. Richmond to Brisbane for photo survey.
30.09.33. 3 ml east Blacktown, NSW. Flt Lt J.R. Fleming, Corp L.A. Milgae. Engine failure due air lock, forced landing. Fabric torn, spars bruised. Flown back 1.10.33.
29.03.34. F/Off Candy. Macquarie Marshes survey, Nyngan, NSW.
(22.05.34). Operating on an extension of 100 hours.
18.08.34. Air Firing Range Richmond, NSW. 3 Sqn. P/Off Royston Bradshaw (injured), Sgt (207425) John Evelyn Todd (CAF). Stalled while dropping message when flying down-wind, badly damaged.
16.10.34. Uneconomical to repair, approved convert to components.

**A5-14**
24.06.29. 1 AD received by RAAF.
31.10.29. A.W. Murphy, P/Off Taylor. Temperature test of engine.
7.11.29. 3 Sqn.
(8.11.29). 1 AD. Jupiter 8154. Modification test.
(9.08.30). 3 Sqn. J8154 'cracked at welding at bottom drain well.'
(13.01.32). 3 Sqn. To engine struts rendered u/s due to eyebolts coming in contact.
6.08.32. F/Off Candy. Air Pageant in Brisbane.
27.09.33. 1 AD.
9.05.34. 1 AD. Sqn Ldr A.W. Murphy, LAC Kennedy. Test flight.
23.05.34. 3 Sqn.
5.07.35. 1 FTS.
12.12.35. 1 FTS, 'B' Fl, Training Sqn. Borrowed by Seaplane Sqn for air gunnery practice.
26.11.36. 1 FTS. AC1 Jackson (solo). Casualty due inexperience, bad damage.
27.11.36. 1 AD for repair, J.8162.
15.04.37. 1 AD. TFT 1,600 hr (approx). Undergoing complete overhaul.
27.05.37. 1 AD. Sqn Ldr A.W. Murphy, AC1 Taylor. Test flight.
28.05.37. 1 AD Store S, J.8162.

**Left & Above:** A5-11 on its nose, probably the crash of 27 May 1932, judging from the damage. This Wapiti had more than its fare share of indignities performed upon it. (via P.G. Heffernan)

31.05.37. 1 FTS.
1.04.38. Cdt Wing, 1 FTS. Point Cook. F/Off R Wiley, LAC Plumb. Aircraft struck while flying in line abreast. Damage to starboard upper aileron, two ribs and trailing edge.
22.11.38. Forced landing no damage.
6.03.39. 120 hourly inspection.
27.03.39. FTS Cadet Wing, J.8157.
26.04.39. TFT 2,306 hours.
1.08.39. 200 h airframe life remaining.
25.08.39. FTS, J.8157.
16.01.40. Allotted TD for Instructional purposes with J.8152.
18.06.40. Converted to Instructional Wapiti 9, Engineering School.
(4.03.42). 1 ES, Ascot Vale. Conversion Instructional Airframes Nos. 1, 7 and 9. Converted to produce.

**A5-15**
16.09.29. Wing Cmdr A.T. Cole, Cpl Cook. Test flight, OK.
2.10.29. Deakin, WA. F/Off T.A. Chadwick. Forced landing, burst oil tank.
12.10.29. Loongana, WA. F/Off T.A. Chadwick. Forced landing, minor damage due darkness.
4.03.30. 1 Sqn. Laverton. Cdt R.J. Coto. Accident due anchor bolt port oleo cross bracing failure.
26.06.30. 1 Sqn. Laverton. Sgt Cameron. Accident.
25.02.31. 1 Sqn. P/Off H.W. Berry, LAC T.L.J. Jackson. Part proposed flight to Launceston and Hobart and return for Army Co-op exercises and survey of Huon River forestry area. At Yanaki, Vic. Minor accident, while taxying undercarriage king bolt failed, stood on nose broke prop. Repaired and flown back to Laverton.
(2.03.31). 1 Sqn. Report - *broken lugs of oil tank and channel pulled away from tank.*
(13.03.31). 1 Sqn. Laverton. P/Off H.W. Berry. Accident.
21.07.31. 1 Sqn. Test of 'adverse' dope on elevators.
7.12.32. 1 FTS. Point Cook. Sgt L.R. Ambrose, Cdt A.C. Mills. Heavy landing, undercarriage, wing tip damaged.
(17.11.32). 'B' Flight, 1 FTS. Footrest and hand grip fitted near tailplane for test.
13.03.33. Point Cook. Sgt L.M. Diprose, LAC P.S. Kennedy. Struck wire fence with tailskid.
(2.06.33). Overhaul to be carried out at FTS.
22.05.34. At FTS undergoing major repairs.
19.11.34. FTS. Flt Lt Rae, Sgt Lalor. Point Cook to Richmond. Royal escort and air display.
13.08.35. 1 FTS. ½ mile north Point Cook. Flt Lt William Gordon Rae, Cdt Thomas John Laws. Struck power lines during forced landing practice, caught fire on impact. Rae thrown out. Laws killed. Totally destroyed.
10.10.35. Approval to w/off airframe, Jupiter J.8160 to instructional engine.

**A5-16**
5.07.29. 1 AD, received by RAAF.
16.09.29. 1 AD. Test before handing to 1 Sqn.
20.09.29. 1 FTS.
5.10.29. 3 Sqn.
12.03.30. Richmond, NSW. Cadet R.E. Allman(?). Engine failure on take-off. Training accident.
(5.05.32). 3 Sqn. Richmond. During 600 hour overhaul

**Above:** *Scherger did this – landed on the only mud patch at Richmond.* A5-12 after the incident of 2 July 1930. (via PG Heffernan)

defective strut found in No.1 bay. Does not have extra fuel tank fitted.
27.01.33. 1 AD.
16.08.33. 3 Sqn.
22.05.35. 3 Sqn. F/Off Mc Lachlan, LAC Gutteridge. Richmond for Brisbane, King's Jubilee celebrations Returned 27.05.35.
09.36. 3 Sqn. Engine 8142P top overhaul.
24.01.37. 1 AD.
15.04.37. 1 AD. TFT 1,700 hr (approx). Undergoing complete overhaul.
29.07.37. 1 FTS, J.8081.
4.08.37. East Malvern, Vic. Cdt M.J. Wiber. Pupil pilot became lost, forced landing.
15.08.37. Point Cook. Cadet Sqn, 1 FTS. F/Lt J.H. Wright, Cdt A.E. Oakley. Caught in strong wind, turned onto nose. Engine plate bent, starboard lower mainplane, gravity tank, airscrew broken.
4.08.37. 1 FTS. Cdt Wiber (solo) Successful forced landing when lost bearings due low cloud.
3.09.37. 1 FTS. Cdt M.J. Wilber. Casualty.
22.11.38. Forced landing, no damage.
26.04.39. TFT 2,403 hrs.
27.05.39. FTS Cadet Wing, J.8155.
1.08.39. 200 hr airframe life remaining.
25.08.39. FTS, J.8080.
7.09.39. 1 FTS. No..1 Forced Landing Field, Point Cook. Cdt J.N. Saunders (solo). Engine failure, forced landing, struck fence damaging port and starboard lower mainplane trailing edges.
24.06.40. U/S more than 2 days awaiting change of engine.
8.07.40. Serviceable at ITS.
27.09.40. Will be given another 12 months service.
22.12.40. U/s less month at ITS awaiting parts.
29.12.40. Serviceable at a SFTS.
30.03.41. Serviceable in 3 days at 1 SFTS (oleo leg).
16.07.41. 1 SFTS. Unserviceable. Being fitted for drogue towing. Received parts of A5-42. In target tug colours.
27.10.41. 1 SFTS (ATS). Point Cook aerodrome. Sgt F.I. White (solo). On take-off reached 60 ft when engine failed completely, successfully forced landed within precincts of aerodrome but when pulling up on boundary after swerving to miss one obstacle collided with stationary grader; under-carriage, port lower mainplane damaged.
8.01.42. U/S indefinitely. (180 hourly).
20.05.42. Allotted de Havilland Co ex-1 SFTS (temp). (Would be for trials of de Havilland glider).
29.05.42. Issued de Havillands in state of disrepair, to be returned by de Havillands to be made serviceable.
21.09.42. Received 2 AD ex-de Havillands.
30.09.42. Allotted Special Duties Flight ex-2 AD.
11.11.42. Allotted 1 AD ex-2 AD for towing de Havilland glider A57-1002.
11.42. Towing de Havilland glider in trials.
24.11.42. Received 1 AD ex-2 AD.
8.02.44. Aircraft held 5 AD undergoing repairs to starboard oleo strut.
22.03.45. Approval given to convert to components.
31.01.46. 3 CRD. Converted during month, engine J.8815 converted in March.

### A5-17

18.07.29. 1 AD, received by RAAF.
(26.07.29). 1 AD. Damaged in transit to Australia.
26.05.30. 1 Sqn.
25.02.31 to 14.03.31. 1 Sqn. F/Off A.G. Carr, Sgt A.R. Murray. Flight to Launceston and Hobart and return for Army Co-op exercises and survey of Huon River forestry area.
(18.07.31). 1 Sqn. F/Off M.O. Watson. Rudder jammed one side due cables for tail light.

**Above:** A5-14 as a trainer displays the small serial with prefix and the large numerals. The biplane does not have a gun ring mounted in the rear cockpit.

12.10.33 to 1.11.33. Training flight to Perth, WA.
6.11.33. 1 FTS.
(20.11.33). Fitment of float undercarriage.
2 to 24.09.35. 1 FTS, Seaplane Sqn. Floatplane. Used for training and revision.
9.10.35. Seaplane transferred to 1 AD for complete overhaul.
27.01.36. 1 AD. At present undergoing overhaul. Mainplanes painted in experimental dope.
27.04.36. 1 FTS.
22.07.36. 1 FTS. With experimental doped wings.
15.04.37. TFT 1,218 hours. 368 hr since last complete overhaul. Jupiter 8077.
8.10.37. 1 FTS. 440 hr with experimental doped wings.
17.08.38. Ran into A5-5, slight damage.
23.02.39. 1 FTS. Point Cook. Sgt E.E. Tuttleby (solo). Hit by A5-40, airscrew broken, starboard lower mainplane damaged.
27.03.39. FTS Cadet Wing, J.8159.
26.04.39. TFT 1,709 hours.
1.08.39. 100 hr airframe life remaining.
25.08.39. FTS, J.8142.
30.10.39. Complete awaiting inspection.
16.01.40. Allotted 1 AD to Engineering school for instructional purposes.
24.01.40. Issued TD, J.8149.
15.04.40. Engineering School, J.8155.
18.06.40. Converted to Instructional Wapiti 1.

**A5-18**
16.03.31. 1 AD. A.W. Murphy, AC1 Haraford. Test flight.
(19.03.31). Transfer from 1 AD to 3 Sqn.
19.07.32. Richmond, NSW. P/Off I.D. Mc Lachlan, AC1 W.M. Orme. Major accident due engine failure on take-off. Airscrew, port mainplane and undercarriage damaged.
(12.10.32). Application to allot to 1 AD with engine OK.
18 to 27.11.34. 1 Sqn. Sqn Ldr Bladin, F/Sgt Studley, LAC Hall. To Richmond for Royal escort and air display.
28.12.34. Ballarat, Vic. P/Off J.M. Lerew, AC2 E.J. Moon, A.F. Parker. Struck post fence landing, starboard lower mainplane damaged.
30.01.35. 1 Sqn. Laverton. Sqn Ldr F.M. Bladin, (1201) LAC C.R. Meyers. Struck stationary A7-63 while taxying. Nil damage to Wapiti, severe damage to Moth.
(31.01.35). 1 Sqn.
4.03.35. Laverton. Cdt R.S. Robinson. Collision with stationary Moth.
21.04.35. Mt Egerton, Vic. Cdt Lindsay Cyril Murray (solo). During local area flying training flew too low, ducking in and out of cloud to avoid deteriorating weather, in thickly timbered country he struck a tree on a hill hidden by cloud banks. The 19-year old pilot was killed. TFT 622.15 hrs.
(4.06.35). Airframe and Jupiter 8078 conversion to produce.

**A5-19**
5.06.29. Dispatched from UK.
14.10.31. R.J. Brownell, AC Potter. Flying practice.
24.08.32. Point Cook. Sgt R.J. Parker, AC1 A.L. Grigg. Undercarriage collapsed while taxying.
22.03.33. Laverton. Sgt L.M. Diprose, Cdt J.G. Brown. Practice landings, stalled, port aileron damaged, pilot error.
10.09.33. Geelong, Belmont Common. P/Off E.D. Scott, Sgt Hazell. Accident, pilot error, airframe twisted, prop, undercarriage broken; one set mainplanes smashed.
9.04.34. 1 AD. Sqn Ldr A.W. Murphy, LAC Stanton. Test flight.
13.08.34. Richmond, NSW. F/Off C.D. Candy, LAC E.E. Skimin. Accident due weather, wind lifted tail on landing, airscrew struck ground.
28 to 29.11.34. Flt Lt Walters, LAC George. Richmond to

**Above:** A5-11, A5-7. A5-15, A5-1, and A5-3. The third aircraft in this formation is the ill-fated A5-15. This photograph was taken before A5-15's demise on 13 August 1935, as the other Wapitis survived longer, although A5-7 was written off by Brian Walker on 30 October 1935.
On 13 August 1935, Instructor Flt Lt W.G. Rae was in the back cockpit of A5-15, with pilot pupil A/Cdt T.J. Laws in front. Rae closed throttle to see if the student would carry out the correct forced landing procedure. They hit high tension wires and the machine dived into the ground and burst into flames. Rae was thrown clear but Laws was incinerated.

Coffs Harbour and return for escort Royal Party.
30.10.35. 1 FTS, Seaplane Sqn. F/Off Headlam. Cross country flight to Deniliquin, NSW. Return to Echuca overnight to investigate crash of A5-7.
28.11.35. 1 FTS, 'B' Fl, Training Sqn. Borrowed by Seaplane Sqn for crews to carry out air gunnery practice.
18.03.37. Laverton. F/Off B.R. Walker. Forced landing due damaged oil cooler.
15.04.37. TFT 1,347 hours. 959 hr since last complete overhaul. Jupiter 8077.
(6.05.37). Completed 960hr, fit 74 hr further flying.
13.04.38. 1 FTS, D Flight. F/Off A.F. Chalman. Flight test.
13 to 25.04.38. Chalman was only pilot of A5-19 for this period.
25.04.38. Coulthard's Farm, Whittlesea, Vic. 1 FTS. F/Off Andrew Fisher Chalman, AC1 (1840) Ray Prime. On flight from Richmond Pageant via Cootamundra to Point Cook with 10 Wapitis of Cadet Wing. Spun in bad weather. Chalman killed. Fitted with towing gear at time of accident.
2.05.38. A/c write off. Jupiter 8154 to components. Approved.

**A5-20**

19.02.31. 1 AD. Sqn Ldr A.W. Murphy, AC1 Dowdell. Test flight.
20.02.31. 1 AD. Sqn Ldr A.W. Murphy, AC1 Harford. Test flight. Reallotted to 1 Sqn, to be delivered on 23rd.
26.02.31. 1 Sqn. Seymour, Vic. P/Off Hiram George Scoullar, AC1 (1338) John Fredrick Yourn. Co-op in AA defence demonstration. The *Western Age* newspaper for Wednesday 4 March 1931, reported the aircraft crashed into a tree with terrific force at Seymour last Thursday. The 'plane was attached to a volunteer training camp, which was being held at Seymour, and was engaged in mock warfare manoeuvres in co-operation with troops, when it suddenly dived to the ground, struck a tree on the side of a hill and immediately caught fire. In a moment the wreckage was a mass of flames, and, although the trainees rushed to the spot, they were unable to approach the machine. The airmen's bodies were partly consumed by the flames. Totally destroyed. Both killed. TFT 6.15 hours. Jupiter 8161.
(1.03.31). 1 AD. Jupiter 8161 to be dismantled and

**Above:** A5-19 is probably newly arrived as it still bears the RAF style stencils on the fin and rudder. The pilot's seat belt from the front cockpit hangs over the fuselage side forward of the gun ring. (AHMofWA P021489)

converted.
28.04.31. Strike off approved.

**A5-21**
19.09.29. Received RAAF.
16.01.31. Exeter, NSW. Flt Lt A.M. Charlesworth; Cdt Johnson. During flight from Richmond to Point Cook machine flew low in heavy fog, struck tree, overturned, seriously damaged. Charlesworth escaped with minor injuries; Johnson was taken to Berrima hospital where he was treated for shock.
(17.03.31.) AD. Corrosion to airframe.
10.04.31. 1 AD. Sqn Ldr A.W. Murphy, AC1 Styles. Test flight.
13.04.31. 1 Sqn.
2.06.31. 3 Sqn. Sgt W E Brown. Accident.
24.07.31. Point Cook. Flt Lt S.A.C. Campbell. Pilot stalled during landing. Undercarriage, prop, lower mainplane and fuselage damaged. Three crew unhurt. Onlookers were startled by the loud crash and were alarmed to see smoke rising from the wrecked plane. There was a rush to extricate the crew as it was feared that the fuel would ignite. The smoke was caused by damage to the bomb-release apparatus that was situated on the undercarriage. Extensive repairs will be necessary to refit the machine.
29.07.31. 1 AD.
(28.10.31). Delivery from 1 AD to 1 FTS.
24.02.32. From 1 FTS to 1 Sqn, Laverton. Flying slightly left wing low, and other defects led to report of why it was released in this condition.
25 to 28.02.32. R.J. Brownell, Sgt Campbell. Laverton to Parafield, Ceduna, Forrest, Kalgoorlie, Perth.
4.03.32. R.J. Brownell, Sgt Campbell. Test Flight, Perth.
6.03.32. R.J. Brownell, Sgt Campbell. Perth to Kalgoorlie, Forrest. *Cam gear packed up. Had to take engine down and put in new cam pack.*
10.03.32. R.J. Brownell, Sgt Campbell. Test flight, Forrest.
10 to 11.03.32. R.J. Brownell, Sgt Campbell. Forrest to Ceduna, Parafield, Laverton.
21.03.32. 1 AD.
30.05.32. 1 FTS.
26.01.33. Sgt Cameron, Cdt F.B. Chapman. Instruction followed by solo practice.
28.02.33. FTS. Point Cook. Sqn Ldr F.M. Bladin, Cdt H.B. Hurley. Undercarriage failure on landing.
18.05.33. 3 Sqn.
15.11.34. FTS. Undergoing repairs.
20.11.34. F/Off Murdoch, LAC Allen. Depart Point Cook for Richmond air display.
28 to 29.11.34. Flt Lt Thompson. Flights from Richmond for Coffs Harbour to check weather along route for Royal escort.
22.05.35. Richmond for Brisbane, King's Jubilee celebrations. 3 Sqn. F/Off Compagnoni, Sgt Skillin. Returned 27.05.35.
22.01.36. Richmond, NSW. P/Off P.R. Heath. Collided with stationary Demon while taxying.
10.03.36. Richmond, NSW. P/Off B.C. Waddy, LAC Stevens. Taxied into soft ground stood on nose.
09.36. 1 FTS.

**Above:** A5-21 in flight.

17.09.36. 1 FTS. Beach 1 mile east of Point Cook. F/Off J.R. Balmer, Cdt A.E. Robinson. Wheels struck water and aircraft turned over onto its back. Airscrew, tail unit and mainplanes damaged.
8.02.37. 1 ml north of Point Cook. 1 FTS. Cdt K.H. Walsh. Forced landing due broken oil pipe.
(19.02.37). 1 FTS. Defect in oil pipe.
15.04.37. TFT 1,146 hours. 155 hr since last complete overhaul. Jupiter 8155.
20.05.37. 1 FTS. Point Cook. Cdt J.W.E. Leighton (solo). While turning across wind lifted from ground by strong wind damaging four rear longerons and undercarriage, airscrew split.
17.06.37. Point Cook. P/Off F.V. Sharpe, Cdt A.F. McGhie. Night landing, stalled at 10 ft, prop broken; undercarriage, starboard lower mainplane damaged.
26.07.37. 1 AD, overhaul and repair, J.8155.
25.11.37. FTS Cadet Wing, J.8147.
3.03.38. 1 FTS. Cdt A.K. Stielow (solo). When running engine up to max revs tail lifted, dropped heavily, four longerons bent and damage to tail end fuselage.
30.03.38. 1 AD ARS, less engine.
30.05.38. FTS, J.8151.
25.10.38. 1 FTS. Point Cook. F/Off Durant, F/Off Parker. While practicing forced landings wing tip struck ground; starboard wing tip skid broken, lower aileron slightly damaged.
24.11.38. 1 FTS. Alexandria. Cdt Lyne. During forced landing struck ground heavily on starboard wing tip; undercarriage, bottom longeron, main beam, diagonal struts broken.
8.02.39. 1 AD workshops.
24.03.39. FTS, serviceable from 1 AD, J8079.
26.04.39. TFT 1,465 hours.
1.08.39. 600 hr airframe life remaining.
17.03.40. 1 SFTS. Point Cook. P/Off A Taylor, Cdt J Hearne. On landing, collided with tractor which was hidden in dust made by a Demon taking off. Broken airscrew.
10.04.40. 1 FTS. J.8811 replaced J.8079.
27.10.40. Serviceable at ITS (1 SFTS).
10.02.41. 1 SFTS (ITS). 1 ml east Werribee, Vic. LAC (407341) Robert Henry Stratford (CAF) (killed); Sgt (2931) Robert John Barker. Collided with A5-39 at approx 2,400 ft. Instructor Barker thrown out by force collision and descended by parachute. Aircraft collided while instrument flying; both instructors charged with neglect as they did not keep a proper lookout. TFT 2,060.30 hours. Jupiter J8811 TFT 1,768.40 hours.
24.02.41. Converted to components.

### A5-22

(17.08.31). 1 AD. Awaiting exhaust. To be issued to 1 Sqn.
24.08.31. 1 AD. Sqn Ldr A.W. Murphy, F/Sgt Lockington. Test flight. Delivered to 1 Sqn.
2.07.32. Laverton. F/Off C.K. Shields, AC2 F.D. Balmer. Minor accident due slow approach, heavy landing. Undercarriage extensive damage.
(16.08.32). 1 Sqn. Magneto and petrol tank required.
16.07.33. Laverton. 1 Sqn. P/Off (251457) James Grayton

**Above:** In this line-up of three Wapiti biplanes, a civil De Havilland Moth and a Bulldog A5-34 and A5-23 are the second and third machines. Note the Handley Page slot on the upper wing of the closest Wapiti.

Brown (CAF), AC1 (205521) Percy James Swann. Jupiter 8809. Took off downwind struck high tension wires. Neither hurt, had extraordinary escape. Required complete rebuild after crash. Beyond economic repair. 8th Wapiti lost.
(31.07.33). 1 AD. Airframe and J 8809 repairs recommended.
19.06.34. Write off approved.

### A5-23

(6.09.29). Shipped via *Taranak.*
16.10.29. 1 AD, received by RAAF.
9.12.29. 1 Sqn.
18.07.30. Landed in soft mud, slight damage to airscrew.
9.09.30. Tipped on nose on landing.
(26.02.31). Allotment to 1 AD for desert equipment.
22.03.32. 1 Sqn. Flt Lt F.J.B. Wight, LAC R.T. Doran. Darwin to meet Southamptons of No. 205 Sqn RAF.
16.05.32. Laverton. Flt Lt F.J.B. Wight, AC1 Scott. Minor crash, starboard wheel collapsed on landing.
10.02.33. Point Cook. F/Off J.C. Miles, Corp Reddrop. Tail skid struck obstacle while landing, skid and longeron damaged.
(4.04.34). Extension to flying time before overhaul.
5.06.34. 1 Sqn. Landed Junee, NSW. Annual CAF training.
18 to 27.11.34. 1 Sqn. Flt Lt Simms, Sgt Murray, LAC Scott. To Richmond for Royal escort and air display. Delayed at Cootamundra, NSW on 20th with faulty magneto.
17.06.35. 1 AD.
(17.06.35). 1 Sqn. Request for a/c to replace A5-23.
3.12.35. Complete overhaul. Port and starboard rear bottom longerons renewed.
28.02.36. 1 FTS.
22.07.36. 1 FTS. With experimentally doped wings.
15.04.37. TFT 1,552 hours. 426 hr since last overhaul. Jupiter 8146.
8.10.37. 1 FTS. 339 h 35 with experimentally doped wings.
15.07.38. 1 FTS. Point Cook. F/Off Eaton, F/Off Forsyth. Instructors course, undershot during forced landing practice, tailplane struck fence, cracked spar in tailplane.
19.09.38. Due for complete overhaul, done over 2,000 hours.
19.09.38. To be disassembled and held in store at FTS.
14.04.39. FTS informed to anticipate approval (of conversion).
1.05.39. Completed 2,000 hours. In storage a long time, to components. Approved.
18.05.39. Confirmation to 1 FTS.
(1.09.39). TFT 2,086 hours.
(18.12.39). 1 FTS. Now components.

### A5-24

26.07.30. 1 AD. Starting magneto dud, changed and tested.
28.07.30. 1 AD. Wing Cmdr A.T. Cole, S,M, Oliver. Laverton to Richmond non-stop for 3 Sqn.
(25.08.30). 3 Sqn. J8141 fitted with old type manifold induction system instead of new type.
13.11.30. 3 Sqn. Harrington, NSW. Flt Lt H.E. Fraser(?) & mechanic. Visibility was bad due to dust from interior that made a thick haze. The pilot rose to 10,000 feet, but when he glimpsed the sea, he realised he was a long way off course. Fuel was running low and a landing was necessary. He circled over Harrington several times trying to find a landing ground. He went north a few miles

**Left:** A5-26 on its nose. This could be the incident of 7 March 1933.

and landed in a lagoon. The nose buried in the mud, the aircraft t remaining with its tail in the air. The crew were unhurt and walked to Harrington from where they reported their plight. A5-16 brought three officers to Harrington on the morning of the 14th. Salvage of aircraft was apparently accomplished by land and appears to have been complicated.

16.01.31. Near Exeter, NSW. 3 Sqn. Crash. Beyond economic repair.
8.04.31. Recommendation convert to spares and produce.
28.04.31. Approved.
(24.08.31). 1 AD. Conversion completed.

**A5-25**

(4.03.31). 1 Sqn.
2.08.31. 1 Sqn. Lake Gnarpurt, Vic. P/Off (253723) Raynes Waite Adrian Dickson. Major crash and submersion due low flying in bad weather.
27.08.31. Not worth cost repair, w/off approved.

**A5-26**

25.10.29. 1 AD received by RAAF.
10.03.30. 1 AD. Sqn Ldr A.W. Murphy, Cpl Hillier.
24.03.30. Flt Lt Wiggins. From 1 AD to Sydney.
25.03.30. 3 Sqn.
12.07.30. 3 Sqn. Parkes, NSW. F.S. Gardner. Heavy landing.
4.11.31. Richmond, NSW. F/Off V.E. Hancock. Forced landing due engine seizure, lack of oil.
(5.05.32.) 3 Sqn, Richmond. Extra petrol tank fitted.
12.06.32. 1 ml south-west Quakers Hill, NSW. F/off S.H. Aurousseau, Sgt F.P. Chandler. Forced landing due to engine failing shortage of petrol.
30.08.32. Richmond, NSW. P/Off J.R. Paget, LAC H Walkington. Sudden gusty wind blew machine onto prop.
7.03.33. Richmond, NSW. Cdt H Bjelke-Peterson, P/Off J.R. Paget. Undercarriage collapsed after heavy landing by pupil damaging front portion of fuselage, prop.
(9.03.33). 3 Sqn. Recommend disposal of airframe and engine.
9.05.33. 1 AD.
19.12.33. 3 Sqn.
15.12.34. Richmond for Newcastle together with three Bulldogs. P/Off Davis, Lac Stevens.
25.02.36. 3 Sqn. Richmond, NSW. P/Off E.L. Chapman. Forced landing due broken tailplane actuating gear.
28.07.36. Richmond, NSW. P/Off D Ashton-Shorter. Wheels bogged, prop, rudder damaged.
24.11.36. Sqn Ldr A.W. Murphy, LAC Miles. Practice flight.
15.04.37. TFT 1,412 hours. 154 hr since last complete overhaul. Jupiter 8143.
20/21.05.37. 1 FTS. Point Cook. Flt Lt J.R. Balmer, Cdt Mulligan. Pupil undershot during night approach, hit drain, lower longeron, main petrol tank, lower port mainplane damaged.
25.04.38. 1FTS. W/Cdr F.M. Bladin. Return journey with 10 other Wapitis from Richmond, NSW. A5-19 fatally crashed.
26.01.39. 1 FTS, 120 hourly, u/s 17 days.
15.02.39. 1 FTS. Point Cook. Cdt A.R. Hamilton (solo). Ground crew left wing tips before engine switched off, collided with A5-40; port upper wing tip and aileron damaged.
27.03.39. FTS Cadet Wing, J.8152.
26.04.39. TFT 2,056 hours.
13.05.39. Due for complete overhaul, aircraft stopped flying.
(15.06.39). Conversion, erection, or repair, along with A5-3 and A5-9, under consideration.
7.07.39. Due complete overhaul. A5-3 and A5-9 to be

**Above:** Wapiti A5-26 after a hard landing by Ashton-Shorter, Richmond, 28 July 1936. Turned over in boggy ground. (via A.D. Ferguson).

converted to components to allow this to take place.
17.07.39. Allotted to 1 AD.
18.07.39. Received 1 AD from FTS and issued workshops for overhaul.
1.08.39. 600 hours airframe life remaining.
10.10.39. J.8811 allotted to workshops for installation.
8.11.39. 1 AD. Overhaul completed, TFT 2067 hours.
9.11.39. Allotted 1 FTS ex 1 AD.
17.11.39. 1 FTS. Cdt J Hickey (solo). Soft spot on aerodrome, stood on nose, airscrew broken.
23.11.39. 1 FTS. No.2 Forced Landing Paddock. Sgt R.W. Saunders, Cdt T.G. Joyce. On final pupil allowed port wing to drop, instructor opened throttle, wing tip struck ground swinging aircraft around and over onto its back. Extensive damage to mainplanes, undercarriage, tail unit and airscrew. Stored 1 FTS.
(1.12.39). 1 FTS. Recent accident, damage to fuselage, minor external damage to wings, rudder completely damaged. Recommended return to 1 AD for examination and repair. TFT 2086 hours.
11.01.40. Allotted 1 AD for repair, J.8811.
17.01.40. J8811 repaired and fitted.
20.01.40. Allotted Engineering School, Showgrounds.
28.02.40. Still at 1 SFTS,
(28.02.40). Parts and material or repair not available, recommend conversion to components.
30.04.40. In storage 'crash' hangar No.103, 1 FTS, pending instructions.
(11.06.40). Convert to components.

### A5-27

13.11.29. 1 AD. Received by RAAF.
(10.02.30). 1 AD. Modifications after hitting fence.
13.02.30. 1 AD. Sqn Ldr A.W. Murphy, Cpl Davey.
15.02.30. 3 Sqn.
(13.04.31). 3 Sqn. Items damaged by acid.
1.02.32. Bourke, NSW. P/Off J.C. Miles. Overturned by cyclone.
(5.05.32). 3 Sqn, Richmond. Extra petrol tank fitted.
17 to 18.04.33. 3 Sqn. F/Off Candy, Sgt Willson, Dr Woolnough. Aerial survey of Lithgow, Newnes, Capertee area.
(4.02.34). 3 Sqn. Due complete overhaul.
15.03.34. Richmond, NSW. Cdt J.H. Glasscock. Starboard wheel collapsed while taxying.
(4.02.34). 3 Sqn. Due complete overhaul.
(2.03.34). Extension 100 hours recommended.
(22.05.34). Operating on an extension of 100 hours.
9.06.34. Richmond, NSW. Cdt T Primrose, AC2 Colley. Taxied into soft ground. When attempting to restart LAC S.J. Smith struck by prop - deep wound.
8.12.34. F/Off Candy. Dummy parachute dropping.
9.05.35. 1 AD.
(17.06.35). Rear cockpit instructor's seats to be fitted prior to issue to FTS for instructional purposes.
27.09.35. FTS.
17.10.35. 1 AD. Sqn Ldr A.W. Murphy, LAC McCauley. Test flight.
1.05.36. Point Cook. Cdt J.P. Godsell. Practising forced landings, ran through fence, lower mainplanes damaged.
4.05.36. 1 FTS. Cdt Godsell. Casualty due error of judgement.
15.04.37. TFT 1,526 hours. 358 hr since last complete overhaul.
(31.03.38). 1 FTS.
(1.03.39). Centre section transferred to A5-34.
1.05.39. Completed 2,000 hours. In storage a long time, to components. Approved.
(9.11.39). 1 FTS. 'Frame now converted to components.'

### A5-28

22.11.29. Sqn Ldr A.W. Murphy.
(19.10.31). 1 Sqn. Report on tailwheel.
(5.01.32). From 1 AD to 3 Sqn.
(5.05.32). 3 Sqn, Richmond. Extra petrol tank fitted.
(22.05.34). Operating on an extension of 100 hours.

**Left:** It has not been possible to determine which incident is illustrated here. The crash at Gunbower, Victoria, that ended A5-28's career was described as follows:
*Evidence of eye-witnesses show that after flying around the town three times at about 500 feet, the pilot attempted to land in a small paddock adjacent to the town. Owing to an error of judgement on the part of the pilot one wing struck the ground with the result the undercarriage and wing on one side of the machine were wrecked. The aeroplane skidded along the ground for approximately 70 yards, coming to rest just inside the paddock in which the pilot presumably had intended to land. The pilot suffered severe injuries.*
There is no mention of the machine rolling onto its back. It was noted by the Air Accidents Investigation Committee that Gunbower was approximately 40 miles off the route he was instructed to fly, and the pilot admitted he had deliberately flown to the town as he knew it was the home of one of his fellow cadets. It was held that the accident was due to Cadet A.E.L. Davies inexperience and in disobedience of orders in attempting to land in an unsuitable area.

26.11.34. F/Off W.G. Compagnoni. Richmond Air display.
28 to 29.11.34. F/Off Campagnon, AC1 Mead. Richmond for Coffs Harbour and return for escort Royal party.
4 and 5.04.35. F/Off Candy. Army co-op.
(17.06.35). Rear cockpit instructor's seats to be fitted prior to issue to FTS for instructional purposes.
27.08.35. 1 AD. Sqn Ldr A.W. Murphy, LAC Bernau. Test flight.
25.05.36. Point Cook. F/Off J R Balmer. Forced landing due engine failure.
15.04.37. TFT 1,620 hours. 512 hr since last complete overhaul. Crashed after this date. Jupiter 8150 damaged.
26.05.37. 1 FTS. Gunbower, 25 miles west of Echuca, Vic. Cdt (0353) Arthur Evan Lloyd Davies (solo). Accident while attempting forced landing. One wing struck ground and a/c skidded along ground for 70 yards, extensive damage. The pilot was severely hurt and taken to Cohuna hospital suffering from concussion and a badly smashed right ankle. Residents of Gunbower saw the plane circling over the township and when a few thousand feet up it commenced a steep descent and struck the ground at a steep angle. The fact he was in the second cockpit probably saved his life. The engine was driven into the front cockpit. Aircraft w/off. J8811.
(30.11.37). Airframe and Jupiter 8150, disposal of.

**A5-29**
15.09.30. 1 AD. Sqn Ldr A.W. Murphy, LAC Dagge. Test.
25.10.30. 1 Sqn. Altona Bay, Vic. P/Off R.J. Cato; Mechanic L.A. Richardson. Machine dived into sea about 500 yards from shore during formation practice. Major crash and immersion. The crew were saved by a fishing dinghy, fortunately the Wapiti did not sink immediately. Salvaged on the 29th using Harbour Trust barge and unloaded on the wharf at Williamstown. The remains were taken by an Air Force lorry to Laverton. First Wapiti to be written off.
30.10.30. 1 AD. Off loading and examination to stop corrosion.
19.11.30. Recommendation convert to spares and produce.
(2.04.31). Conversion carried out.

**A5-30**
20.07.32. 1 AD. Sqn Ldr A.W. Murphy, F/Sgt Lockinton. Test flight.
7.05.33. 3 Sqn. Wilberforce, NSW. P/Off Peter Herbert Martin; Sgt Myers. Forced landing, struck telephone wires. Major crash and immersion in Hawkesbury River. Landed right side up and both occupants waded ashore. Salvaged but not worth cost repair.
(4.07.33). Disposal recommended.

**A5-31**
8.09.32. 1 AD. Sqn Ldr A.W. Murphy, LAC Pieddrop. Test flight.
23.02.33. 1 AD. Laverton. Gp Capt W H Anderson. Heavy landing main fuselage members and undercarriage bent.

**Right:** Only A5-31 can be identified in this line-up of seven Wapiti biplanes at Richmond. Note that they all have their gun rings attached.

30.03.33. Wing Cmdr A.T. Cole, AC1 Siles. Practice.
12.10.33 to 1.11.33. Training flight to Perth, WA. Sqn Ldr F W F Lukis, Corp J.J. Rhyder, LAC W R Burns.
5.05.34. Laverton. Cdt J.B. Hamilton, AC2 Campbell. Accident due landing ground, tipped on nose while taxying.
5.06.34. 1 Sqn. Landed Junee, NSW. Annual CAF training.
18 to 27.11.34. 1 Sqn. F/Off Harding, LAC Bolitho, AC1 Helwig. To Richmond for Royal escort and air display.
5.12.34. Point Cook. F/Off H.R. Harding, LAC W.J. Bolitho. Bad aerodrome surface, airscrew, centre-section, lower mainplane badly damaged.
16.04.35. Werribee. 1AD. F/Off Clive Newton Edgerton (killed). Crash from dive during test flight. TFT 427.35 hours. 40 min since last overhaul. Little remained of airframe and Jupiter 8-FP 8813 was buried three feet in the ground. Egerton was testing the machine after it had been repaired following damage it received last December when it nose-dived on a sodden landing ground at Laverton. It appeared that the propeller may have broken in the air, and that the flying fragments snapped the wing struts causing the collapse of the wing. One wing was found two miles away from the crash site. It was also suggested that a fragment may have struck the pilot rendering him unconscious. This was supported by the fact that the throttle was still in the fully open position when the wreckage was examined and he had made no attempt to bail out of the machine.
21.05.35. Write off approved.

### A5-32

3.12.30. Received by RAAF. Long range Wapiti - metal type.
4.06.31. R.J. Brownell (solo). Flying practice. (Recorded as 'Wapiti A7-31').
14 to 19.03.32. Flt Sgt Stewart. Aircraft Movement Order No.93. *To test fuel arrangements on strategic air routes and to meet three Southamptons of 205 Squadron from Singapore.* Laverton - Richmond - Bourke - Charleville - Longreach - Cloncurry - Camooweal - Brunette Downs - Darwin.
16.11.32. 1 AD. Sqn Ldr A.W. Murphy, AC1 Chenery. Test flight.
18.11.32. 1 Sqn.
29.12.32 to 8.01.33. F/Off J.C. Miles, Sgt J.A. Campbell, Sgt W.J. Cameron. Left Laverton for Whelan rescue operation and return.
23 to 26.02.33. Sqn Ldr R.J. Brownell, Sgt Campbell. Laverton to Adelaide, Ceduna, Forrest, Kalgoorlie, Perth.
28.02.33. Sqn Ldr R.J. Brownell, Sgt Campbell. *Army Reconn.*
2 to 6.03.33. Sqn Ldr R.J. Brownell, Sgt Campbell. Perth to Kalgoorlie, Forest, Ceduna, Adelaide, Melbourne.
5.06.34. 1 Sqn. Return from Deniliquin, annual CAF training.
18 to 27.11.34. 1 Sqn. F/Off Carr, LAC Bainsley, LAC Webb. To Richmond for Royal escort and air display.
12.05.35. Laverton. Sqn Ldr F.M. Bladin, Cdt H L Catchlove. Forced landing, engine failure, struck fence, port lower mainplane damaged.
29.06.35. 1 Sqn. Fl Lt A.M. Charlesworth, Sgt Murray, Sgt Tonks. Left Laverton for Cloncurry carrying spares to o/haul A5-37 and to replace A5-34 in North Australian Survey Flight.
9.09.35. 1 Sqn. North Australian Survey Flight, based at Cloncurry, Qld.
10.07.35. 40 ml South-east Cunnamulla, Qld. Flt Lt A.M. Charlesworth, Sgt Tonks, Sgt A.R. Murray. Forced landing due engine failure while on long cross-country flight.
2.03.36. 1 Sqn. Port Phillip Bay. P/Off Wittscsheibe, F/Sgt Studley. Naval Co-op exercises (ranging) with HMAS *Canberra.*
1 & 6.04.36. 1 Sqn. Bush fire patrol over state forests.
21.04.36. 1 Sqn. F/Off D McLean, AC1 G.P. Hellwig. Assist in search for missing RAAF Rapide. Recalled from Bourke on 25th. To Richmond, allotted to 3 Sqn to take part in NASF from Port Hedland, WA. McLean attached to Flight as pilot.
1.05.36. 3 Sqn.
08.36. 3 Sqn. Engine 8817FR installed.
24.01.37. 1 AD.

**Above:** A5-32 with the engine and cockpit covers in place, photographed at Nyngan aerodrome, April 1935.

15.04.37. 1 AD. TFT 1150 hr (approx). Undergoing complete overhaul. Jupiter 8817.
25.05.37. 1 AD. Sqn Ldr A.W. Murphy, LAC Robinson. Test flight.
31.05.37. 1 FTS, J.8817.
21.01.38. 1 FTS. F/Off Parsons, AC1 Temple. Struck duck over small lake near Point Cook during low flying practice, interplane strut bent, one rib lower mainplane damaged.
5.04.38. 1 FTS. F/Off K Parsons, AC1 Groundwater. Over Melbourne, engine failure, forced landing in Royal Park, Melbourne. Crew walked across to Royal Park Police Station to call Point Cook. Practicing for RAAF pageant. Piston rod through the piston. Point Cook sent truck with new piston, fixed engine, flew out.
25.04.38. 1 FTS. Part formation 11 Wapitis from Richmond. Forced landing due bad weather. No damage.
2.05.38. 1 FTS. Cdt A.A. Daniel (solo). Landed, turned cross wind, wind swung aircraft into hedge. Leading edge port lower mainplane damaged.
17.08.38. 1 FTS. LAC L Mays (solo). Forced landed in field near Point Cook due engine J.8817 backfiring.
15.09.38. J.8817 to 1 AD.
18.01.39. ITS. Tullamarine, Vic. Cdt A.J.L. Williams (solo). Forced landed due shortage of petrol; fabric on port mainplane and elevator damaged.
27.03.39. FTS Cadet Wing, J.8145.
26.04.39. TFT 1,857 hours.
17.05.39. 1 FTS. Point Cook. F/Lt G.K. Buscombe, Cdt McAlister. Stalled from six feet, heavy landing, main beam bent, port oleo attachment damaged.
1.08.39. 300 hr airframe life remaining.
25.08.39. FTS, J.8145.
15.01.40. 1 SFTS (ITS). Benakka, Vic. Cdt G Mac Arthur (solo). Landed well upfield ran through fence on landing. Lower mainplanes and upper port mainplane damaged, airscrew fairing bent.
17/19.01.40. 1 SFTS (ITS). Near Essendon, Vic. Cdt A.J. Williams (solo). Hit fence on forced landing due engine losing revs, lower port mainplane spar, trailing edge and ribs damaged, fabric torn on tailplane.
10.04.40. Time expired awaiting conversion.
15.04.40. J.8817 replaced J.8145.
10.06.40. Awaiting conversion less engine.
25.07.40. Issued engineering School, Point Cook.
14.05.40. Converted to Instructional No.11.
9.08.40. Converted to components.

**A5-33**

22.12.30. 1 AD, Received by RAAF.
01.33. 1 Sqn.
2.02.33. 1 AD. Sqn Ldr A.W. Murphy, AC1 Wood. Test flight.
9.02.33. Belmont Common near Geelong, Vic. Sgt V.J. Byrnes, AC1 Cooney. Forced landing, engine failure, struck obstacle broke airscrew.
12.10.33 to 1.11.33. Training flight to Perth, WA. Flt Lt D.E.L. Wilson, Corp A.J. Abicair, LAC F.D. Hall.
9.02.34. 1 Sqn. Bush Fire Patrol over Powelltown, Taggerty, Matlock, Thompson River valley to Erica. Damaged in landing in strong winds.
16.02.34. 1 AD for repairs.
15.03.34. 1 Sqn.
5.06.34. 1 Sqn. Return from Deniliquin, annual CAF training.
18 to 27.11.34. 1 Sqn. F/Off Paget, LAC Dorana, AC1 Fitzgerald. To Richmond for Royal escort and air display.
14.05.35. Tintinara, SA. Flt Lt R.F.M. Dalton, AC1 H.R.B. Fitzgerald. Forced landing in rough country due engine failure. Moth expected on 16th with spare parts and they

would continue to Adelaide.
4 05.36 to 1.06.36. 1 Sqn. F/Off Holmwood, LAC C.T.P. Jones. To 3 Sqn, Richmond for drogue target practice.
07.36. Transferred from 1 Sqn to 1 FTS.
18.11.36. 1 FTS. F/Off E.D. Scott, Cdt Hughes. Casualty due error of judgement.
11.01.37. 1 AD.
15.04.37. 1 AD. TFT 1,000 hr (approx). Undergoing complete overhaul.
21.07.37. FTS. J.8809.
25.04.38. 1 FTS. Whittlesea, Vic. F/Off R Cox, Cpl O'Connor. Forced landing in bad weather. Part of formation 11 Wapitis returning from Richmond Pageant. Hit fence, damaged mainplanes.
11.05.38. 1 AD (J.8809) for repair.
4.08.38. J.8809 removed.
4.10.38. Issued from 1 AD to 1 FTS with J.8673.
25.01.39 to 12.06.39. In service – training.
(3.04.39). 1 FTS. Main compression rib broken.
24.04.39. 1 FTS Cadet Wing, J.8673.
26.04.39. TFT 1,281 hours.
1.08.39. 600 hr airframe life remaining.
25.08.39. FTS. J.8614.
18.01.40. 1 SFTS. Airman knocked throttle of unoccupied A5-33 causing it to roll crashing into Bellman hangar which collapsed on four Avro Cadets; airframe and engine J.8441 extensively damaged.
17.02.40. Approval for conversion.
13.03.40. Received 1 AD store for conversion. Conversion carried out in workshops
10.04.40. Converted to components.
(17.05.40). Conversion of Jupiter 8441 completed.

**A5-34**

22.12.30. 1 AD received by RAAF.
2.12.31. 1 AD. Sqn Ldr A.W. Murphy. Test flight.
3.12.31. 1 Sqn.
24.12.31. Flight to Air Pageant at Latrobe.
22.03.32. 1 Sqn. F/Off H.W. Berry, F/Sgt T.H. Stewart. Darwin to meet Southamptons of 205 Sqn RAF.
17.05.32. 2 ml west Werribee. F/Off H.W. Berry, LAC R.T. Doran. Forced landing due engine failure.
23.10.32. Maylands Aerodrome. G Jones. Windmill of small generator broke during air display.
6.03.33. Laverton. F/Off W.G. Rae. Forced landing, piston broke.
26.07.33. Laverton. Sgt R.J. Parker, AC1 N.J. Hazle. Forced landing, engine J.8816 seized.
27.08.33. West of Exford Bridge near Bacchus Marsh. P/Off E Scott, Sgt Hazell. Forced landing engine J.8817 failure, port wheel and tail skid damaged.
22.02.34. Currie, King Is, Vic. Sgt L.R. Ambrose, Sgt A.R. Murray, AC1 Langford. When landing right wing touched ground, then gust of wind struck machine. Pilot could not straighten machine and it travelled sideways some distance. Right landing wheel collapsed and the tyre was torn off the left wheel. Bad landing; damage to aileron, axle and wheel. Repaired and left for Latrobe on 1 March for Air Pageant.
5.06.34. 1 Sqn. Return from Deniliquin, annual CAF training.
18 to 27.11.34. 1 Sqn. Sgt Ambrose, LAC Campbell, AC1 Jones. To Richmond for Royal escort and air display.
04.35 to 31.07.35. North Australian Photo Survey Flight. Based at Cloncurry, Qld.
29.04.35. 1 Sqn. Flt Lt A Carr, AC1 C.T.P. Jones, AC1 A Bain. Left Laverton for Cloncurry.
13.05.35. 19 ml south Tennant Ck, NT. Flt Lt A.G. Carr. Forced landing, due loose valve seat. Repaired, proceeded in company Flt Lt Dalton to Cloncurry.
(26.07.35). 1 Sqn. Overhaul on return from Northern Australia, engine overhaul and fabric repairs - allotment to AD.
31.07.35. 1 Sqn. Returned to Laverton for O/haul. The condition was fair after several months in the north with the exception of the wing fabric which required replacing.
4.02.36 to 18.03.36. 1 Sqn. Fl Lt Carr, Cpl Abicair, LAC Bain. To Adelaide for photo survey flight, not completed, recalled.
06.36. 1 FTS.
15.04.37. 1 FTS. Point Cook. Flt Lt F Headlam, AC1 Groundwater. Landing in formation hit airman on boundary road. Airman suffered severe lacerations and concussion. Damage to fabric and front spar. TFT 1,321 hours. 119 hr since last complete overhaul. Jupiter 8812.
21.01.38. 1 FTS. F/Off Allshorn, Flt Lt Porter. While taxying airman put weight onto starboard mainplane causing aircraft to swing striking A6-5. Front interplane strut and pitot static tube damaged.
(21.01.38). 'B' Flt, 1 FTS. F/Off K.R. Parsons. Struck ducks over small lake near Point Cook.
1.03.39. Received centre section A5-27 due no Mk.2a mainplanes being available.
27.03.39. 1 FTS Cadet wing, J.8815.
26.04.39. TFT 1,861 hours.
1.08.39. 300 hr airframe life remaining.
25.08.39. FTS, J.8673.
16.01.40. Allotted TD for Instructional purposes.
18.06.40. Converted to Instructional Wapiti No.7.
(4.03.42). 1 ES, Ascot Vale. Conversion Instructional Airframes Nos. 1, 7 and 9. Converted to produce.

**A5-35**

6.01.31. 1 AD, received by RAAF.
11.12.31. 1 AD. Sqn Ldr A.W. Murphy, AC1 Brown. Test flight.
16.12.31. 1 Sqn.
12.02.32 to 29.02.32. 1 Sqn. Flight from Laverton to Tasmania and return. Air Pageants at Launceston (13th), Hobart (20th) and Wynyard (27th).

**Above:** A5-34, and another Wapiti, with Compter Swift VH-UZB during the 1939 East-West Air Race. (AHMofWA P920033)

12.07.32 to 13.09.32. 1 Sqn. F/Off J.C. Miles. Oil survey flight with A5-36. Laverton to Brisbane, Darwin, Perth, Adelaide, Laverton.
18 to 19.11.32. Sqn Ldr R.J. Brownell, LAC Fitzgerald. Laverton to Richmond, Mascot, Laverton.
29.12.32. F/Off F.N. Wright, LAC W Thompson. Left Laverton for Whelan rescue operation. Returned Laverton 8.01.33.
5.06.34. 1 Sqn. Return from Deniliquin, annual CAF training.
18 to 27.11.34. 1 Sqn. F/Lt Dalton, Cpl Turner, LAC Meyers. To Richmond for Royal escort and air display.
(17.06.35). 1 Sqn. Request for replacement a/c as A4-35 was re-allotted to AD for complete overhaul.
1.07.35. 1 AD.
17.10.35. 1 AD. Sqn Ldr A.W. Murphy, LAC Hamilton. Test flight.
27.11.35. Cootamundra, NSW. F/Off J.P. Ryland, W Fisher. Collided with A5-37 on ground in high gusty winds.
24.02.36. 1 Sqn. P/Off Wittscheibe, LAC Cooney. Target machine for HMAS *Yarra* in Port Phillip Bay.
4.03.36. 1 Sqn. Seymour, Vic. P/Off R.H. Moran, AC1 R Darlington. Army co-op, struck drain on landing smashing undercarriage, prop, mainplane. Returned by road next day.
29.07.36. 1 FTS. Cdt Armstrong, F/Off Headlam. Casualty due inexperience.
25.01.37. Laverton. P/Off F.V. Sharpe, Cdt O.J.F. Lewis. A/c stalled too high on landing. Damaged undercarriage, longerons and petrol tank.
15.04.37. TFT 1,237 hours. 218 hr since last complete overhaul. Jupiter 8159.
22.06.38. 1 FTS. Sgt W.A. Whetters, F/Off Read. Instructor's practice.
19.01.39. F/Off Hick, R Creswell. Training.
24.01.39. 1 FTS. Point Cook. F/Off A.N. Hick, AC1 A.C. McLean. Struck fence when engine failed to respond; front main cross beam, starboard oleo, lower mainplane and aileron, front port lower longeron damaged.
26.04.39. TFT 1,724 hours.
29.05.39. Cadet Wing, J.8145.
1.08.39. 300 hr airframe life remaining.
25.08.39. FTS, J.8159.
12.09.39. 1 FTS. Redesdale. F/Off A.H. Hick, Cdt G.T. Newstead. Forced landing with A5-42 due bad visibility.
27.09.39. 1 FTS. Point Cook aerodrome. F/Off A.N. Hick, Cdt K.A. Goman. Successful forced landing on aerodrome due engine failure, piston broke.
16.10.39. Awaiting inspection J.8159.
27.10.39. 1 FTS. 4 ml south west Rockbank. Sqn Ldr C.N. Douglas, AC1 R.J. Coltheart. Successful forced landing due air blockage in oil pipe.
6.12.39. 1 FTS. 1 ml west Laverton on railway line but clear rails. Point Cook. Cdt R.V. Norbury (solo), killed. Crashed when breaking formation. Write off total wreck.
12.12.39. Authority requested convert to components.
18.12.39. Approval anticipated for conversion.

### A5-36

20.11.31. 1 AD. Sqn Ldr A.W. Murphy, AC1 Wood. Test flight.
16.03.32. 1 Sqn. Oakbank via Charleville, Qld. Sqn Ldr A Hepburn, Sgt C.H. Scott. Forced landing due oil pump failure. New Jupiter 8F engine dispatched 17th.
12.07.32 to 13.09.32. 1 Sqn. Flt Lt A.M. Charlesworth. Oil survey flight with A5-35. Laverton, Brisbane, Darwin, Perth, Adelaide, Laverton.
23.10.32. 1 Sqn. Point Cook. Flt Lt Henry Thomas Johnston, Sgt (205235) Vernon Fredrick Wagstaff. Major crash during gunnery practice; when diving on ground target - commenced to recover too late, machine struck ground with considerable force. Crew escaped with minor cuts. Engine J.8818.
25.10.32. Approved unfit for repair.

**Above:** A.D. Ferguson has marked A5-35 as his aircraft in this photograph of a Wapiti formation over Point Cook, 1938. All machines have the small A5 prefix separated from the aircraft serial number. (via A.D. Ferguson)

**A5-37**

3.03.31. 1 AD received by RAAF.
22.03.32. 1 Sqn. Sqn Ldr A Hepburn, Sgt C.H. Scott. Darwin to meet Southamptons of 205 Sqn RAF.
6.07.33. Laverton. Gp Cpt W.H. Anderson, LAC Littlejohn. Bad landing, pilot error.
25.07.33. 1 AD. Sqn Ldr A.W. Murphy, LAC Neale. Test flight.
12.09.33. 1 Sqn.
5.06.34. 1 Sqn. Return from Deniliquin, annual CAF training.
18 to 27.11.34. 1 Sqn. P/Off Scott, LAC Cangford, LAC Grigg. To Richmond for Royal escort and air display.
04.35 to 09.35. 1 Sqn. Flt Lt R Simms, Cpl Kelly, LAC Langford. North Australian Photo Survey Flight, based at Cloncurry, Qld.
29.04.35. 1 Sqn. Flt Lt R Simms, Cpl Kelly, LAC Langford. Left Laverton for Cloncurry.
2.10.35. 1 Sqn. Laverton. F/Off V.G. Renowden, AC1 J.C. Stephens. Heavy landing, longeron and undercarriage damaged.
27.11.35. Cootamundra, NSW. F/Off J.M. Lerew, AC1 F.R. Schirmer. Collided with A5-35 on ground due high winds. Rudder, tail, elevators damaged.
1935. 1 FTS.
6.12.35. Ordered to return to Point Cook for fitment of floats for Ellsworth relief expedition.
23.12.35 to 16.02.36. On *Discovery II* for Ellsworth Relief expedition.
(2.03.36). FTS. Report on condition after Ellsworth Relief exhibition.
(26.01.37). 1 FTS.
15.02.37. Point Cook. Cadet Sqn 1 FTS. Cdt D.H. Hunter. Ran into drain on landing, prop, port wing tip damaged.
15.04.37. TFT 1,037 hours. 1,037 hr since last complete overhaul. Reallotted to 1 AD for complete overhaul. Jupiter 8815.
15.09.37. 1 FTS. J.8815.
25.04.38. 1 FTS. Part formation 11 Wapitis from Richmond. Forced landing bad weather. No damage.
5.02.39 to 24.05.39. In service – training.
27.03.39. 1 FTS Cadet Wing, J.8146.
26.04.39. TFT 1,595 hours.
26.07.39. 1 FTS. Point Cook. Cdt B.L. Bracegirdle (solo). During heavy landing airscrew tips hit ground, partly due to under-inflated oleos.
1.08.39. 600 hr airframe life remaining.
25.08.39. FTS. J.8152.
27.11.39. 1 FTS. Cdt C.C. Loxton (solo). Struck fence while taxying, both lower mainplanes, airscrew damaged.
19.03.40. 1 SFTS. Cdt E.B. Martin (solo). When taxying into wind strong gust caused tail to come up and drop heavily; broken back at Bay 7, airscrew split.
10.04.40. A FTS, J.8576 replaced J.8441.
7.07.40? Given thorough inspection with view to extend 120 hours.
27.09.40. Will be given another 12 months service.
2.02.41. J.8809 replaces J.8576. (Note date given as 1940).
9.05.41. Serviceable at 1 SFTS.
28.08.41. Unserviceable indefinitely (waiting spares).
22.09.41. Robbed of axle and other parts for A5-16. Recommended for conversion to components.
8.10.41. Converted to components.
7.02.42. 1 TG. Conversion.

**Above:** *CAF Pilot Johnstone dived into the sand hills doing front seat gunnery – only minor injuries* is *Paddy* Heffernan's caption to the sad remains of A5-36. The Minister of Defence had to answer questions regarding the use of the Wapiti by CAF pilots who were allowed to fly the machines on the weekend once they have reached a certain standard of training. He stated that while it could not be expected that these pilots would be as skilful as full-time service pilots, he saw no reason to change this practice. While there had been a number of accidents, the Wapiti could not be blamed. They were excellent machines and had given splendid service. (via P.G. Heffernan)

**A5-38**

18.12.33. 1 AD. Sqn Ldr A.W. Murphy, LAC Reeves. Test flight.
9.10.34. Point Cook. 1 Sq. Sgt R.J. Parker, AC1 G.P. Hellwig. Accident, overshoot. Airframe and Jupiter 8814 unfit for repair.
30.11.34. Approved.

**A5-39**

21.03.38. 1 AD store, received by RAAF. Ex-J.8503.
26.04.38. 1 AD. Ex-RAF machine, recently received.
2.05.38. Workshops 1 AD for erection.
11.07.38. Erected, inspected and flown.
27.07.38. 1 FTS, J.8503.
8.08.38. Actual issue.
9.02.39. F/Off Hick, R Creswell. Forced landings, low flying.
27.03.39. FTS Cadet Wing, J.8503.
26.04.39. TFT 823 hours.
(5.07.39). 1 FTS. Requires complete overhaul. A5-9 and A5-3 to be converted to components to allow overhaul.
1.08.39. Recommended complete overhaul after further 100 hours. 600 hours airframe life remaining.
25.08.39. FTS, J.8503.
4.09.39. For complete overhaul.
9.09.39. Allotted 1 AD for complete overhaul.
11.09.39. Complete awaiting guns 1 AD.
4.10.39. Received 1 AD ex Point Cook less engine.
21.02.40. J.8812 allotted to workshops.
10.04.40. Allotted 1 SFTS ex 1 AD.
25.04.40. 1 SFTS. Point Cook. Cdt S.M. Proud (solo). Successful forced landing following seizure of cam bearing.
30.04.40. J.8812 removed, J8080 installed.
26.08.40. Serviceable at ITS Point Cook.
15.01.41. 1 SFTS (ITS). 1/2 mile east Mordialloc, Vic, (Epsom Racecourse). P/Off H Collier, LAC D G Southwell. Instrument flying, forced landing due sever storm; under-carriage collapsed, nosed over; extensive damage to port mainplane, airscrew.
10.02.41. 1 SFTS (ITS). 1 mile east Werribee, Vic. Flt Lt Anthony Edward Robinson, LAC (400629) Robert Sydney Osment. Collided with A5-21 at approx 2,400 ft. Crew bailed out; Osment descended by parachute, but Robinson's chute became entangled in tail and crashed to ground with aircraft, seriously injured his spine and ankle. TFT 1,125.05 hours. Jupiter J8080 TFT 1,697.50 hours.
24.02.41. Converted to components.

**A5-40**

21.02.38. 1 AD, received by RAF. Ex-J.8121.
26.04.38. 1 AD. Recently received.
(28.04.38). Ex-RAF K2265. Mk IIA modified to RAAF standard.
2.05.38. Workshops 1 AD for erection.
11.07.38. Erected, inspected and flown.
9.08.38. FTS, J.8121.
6.02.39. F/Off Hick, R Creswell. Training.
6.02.39. R Creswell (solo). Steep turns, forced landings.
7.02.39. F/Off Hick, R Creswell. Training.
22.02.39. Sgt Saunders, R Creswell (passenger).

**Right:** Wapiti floatplane conversion A5-37 being loaded onto the deck of the SS *Discovery II* at Williamstown, 23 December 1935, for the journey to the Antarctic to search for the missing Ellsworth aerial expedition. (via AHMofWA Po2214900)

22.02.39. R Creswell (solo). Stall and steep turns, forced landings.
15.02.39. 1 FTS. Point Cook. Taxied into A5-26.
23.02.39. 1 FTS. Sgt R.W. Saunders (solo). Pilot attempted to turn in high wind, carried across and collided with A5-17. Starboard upper and lower mainplanes and aileron damaged, starboard front strut and cross bracing in fuselage bay broken.
5.03.39. R Creswell (solo). Cat B9. Formation.
8.03.39. R Creswell (solo). Cat B IX Formation.
21.03.39. R Creswell (solo). Cat B1 Target machine.
27.03.39. 1 FTS Cadet Wing. J.8121.(415)
26.04.39. TFT 562 hours.
1.08.39. 500 hours airframe life remaining.
22.08.39. 1 FTS. Casualty, landing during line squall, tipped on wing, slight damage..
25.08.39. 1 FTS. J.8121.
31.08.39. 1 FTS. Cdt R.W. Marks (solo). On running up tail rose and dropped 4 ft badly bending four longerons at rear fuselage.
(1.09.39). TFT 603 hours 45. No major repairs have yet been carried out. Rear fuselage A5-9 to be fitted in place downgraded rear end fuselage.
4.09.39. A120 hourly.
11.09.39. 1 FTS. Repair to fuselage 11 days.
16.01.40. Allotted TD for instructional purposes.
23.03.40. J.8121 removed. Converted to Instructional Airplane No.8.
18.06.40. Instructional Wapiti No.8.
(11.07.40). Converted to components.

### A5-41

21.02.38. 1 Ad received by RAAF. Ex-J.9001.
26.04.38. 1 AD. Ex-RAF machine, recently received.
9.05.38. Workshops for erection.
11.07.38. Erected, inspected and flown.
27.07.38. FTS. J.9001.
8.08.38. Actual issue.
27.03.39. 1 FTS Cadet Wing. J.9001.
26.04.39. TFT 530 hours.
1.08.39. 600 h airframe life remaining.
25.08.39. 1 FTS. J.8815.
16.09.39. Forced landing, damage not yet ascertained.
18.09.39. 1 FTS (ITS). 7 ml south of Edginson, near Elaine, Vic. F/Lt G K Buscombe, Cdt V.A. Hodgkinson. Forced landing, engine failure, reduction gear stripped.
16.10.39. 120 hourly 1 month.
23.10.39. 120 hourly 18 days.
10.04.40. FTS received J.8809.
22.04.40. J.8809 removed for top overhaul.
2.06.40. Issued Engineering School ex 1 FTS.
28.10.40. Converted to Instructional Wapiti 6.
(25.05.42). 1 TG. Conversion of Instructional Wapiti Airframes Nos. 4, 5 and 6.
? Converted to components. Mainplanes issued to 1 ITS.
16.04.43. W Penny. Mascot-Nowra-Mascot. *Incorrect report?*

### A5-42

21.02.38. 1 AD, received by RAAF. Ex-J.8120.
26.04.38. 1 AD. Recently received.
2.02.39(?). 1 FTS Cadet Wing. J.8120.[date given as 2.02.38].

**Above:** *Sgt Parker did this – Not a scratch*. Was Paddy Heffernan's caption to this photograph.
According to the *Western Mail* newspaper, A5-38 was wrecked when it crashed during bombing practice at Point Cook on 9 October 1934. The pilot, Sgt R.J. Parker (26), and the gunner. LAC G. Helwig (28), received only slight facial lacerations. The machine was at a height of 5,000 feet above the Point Cook target ground when it dived. It failed to straighten out and crashed with terrific force to the ground. The engine was wrenched from the fuselage and was flung more than 200 yards across the aerodrome. The undercarriage was completely wrecked. The escape of the two men from serious injury was due to the strong construction of the steel cockpits in the Wapiti machines. The only injuries sustained by either man were caused when they were dashed against the sides of the cockpits. Parker and Helwig left Laverton to carry out bombing practice after lunch at the target ground at Point Cook. The machine climbed high into the air to attain the necessary altitude for its mimic attack. It swooped down on the range and Helwig was standing by ready to release his bomb when he realised that Parker was finding it difficult to straighten out from his dive. Fighting with the controls, Parker had just succeeded in lifting the nose of the plane when the wheels struck the ground. For some distance the plane ran along the ground at a speed of more than 150 miles an hour. The wheels were torn from the fuselage by the terrific impact and the Wapiti skidded along the ground. It did not overturn but the strain flung the engine from its mountings. Members of the R.A.A.F. who were on the aerodrome saw the crash and raced to the assistance of the occupants, but before they reached the plane the crew had clambered from the cockpit. The wrecked plane was taken to Laverton aerodrome by tender.
A5-38 had a very short life with the RAAF before Parker wrote it off in this accident. (via P.G. Heffernan)

27.03.39. 1 FTS Cadet Wing J.8120.
5.04.39. R Creswell (solo). B 1. Stall & steep turns, forced landings.
26.04.39. TFT 146 hours.
8.05.39. R Creswell (solo). *Steep & stall turns - Force L & circuits.*
23.05.39. R Creswell (solo). Point Cook-Deniliquin.
23.05.39. F/Off Parker, R Creswell. Deniliquin-Benalla.
24.05.39. R Creswell (solo). Benalla-Broadford-Benalla/ Benalla-Point Cook.
15.06.39. R Creswell (solo). Steep turns, force landings.
(7.07.39). Recommended for complete overhaul. A5-3 and A5-9 to be converted to allow for overhaul.
1.08.39. 600 hr airframe life remaining.
29.08.38. J.8120 requires complete overhaul.
12.09.39. 1 FTS. Redesdale. F/Off J.C. Armstrong, Cdt L.E. Knowles. Successful forced landing with A5-35 due bad visibility.
4.10.39. 1 FTS. 2 ml north of Heathcote. Cdt R.W. Marks (solo). Forced landing due partial engine failure, rocker gear damaged.
30.10.39. 120 hourly 2 weeks.
22.03.40. J.8120 being replaced by J.8121.
10.06.40. J.8121 removed J.8817 installed.

27.09.40. Given another 12 months service.
17.11.40. Serviceable at ITS (1 SFTS).
13.04.41. Serviceable at 1 SFTS.
2.05.41. Serviceable in 3 days at 1 SFTS.
21.08.41. Allotted 2 AD ex 1 SFTS.
28.08.41. Serviceable approx 10.09.41 at 1 SFTS.
11.09.41. 2 AD, pilot will collect 16.09.
22.09.41. 2 AD. Parachute dropping.
27.09.41. C at 2 AD.
18.01.42. E Status at 2 AD.
1.02.42. C at 2 AD.
9.05.42. *Port upper and lower engine mounting damaged. Port mainplane damaged at bomb carrier attachment.*
7.12.42. C at 2 AD.
21.12.42. Allotted SHQ Richmond ex 2 AD for parachute dropping.
31.12.42. Issued SHQ Richmond ex 2 AD.
6.01.43. SHQ, Richmond Unit(?). Sgt Semple. Local flying.
13.02.43. SHQ, Richmond Unit(?). Sgt Whiting. Parachute flight.
15.02.43. SHQ, Richmond Unit(?). Grp Capt Heffernan. Local flight to Marsden Park strip.
16.02.43. SHQ, Richmond Unit(?). P/Off Blesing. Parachute flight.
17.02.43. SHQ, Richmond Unit(?). Sgt Whiting. Flare drop, Yarramundi.
10.04.43(?). Mascot. W Penny. Glider towing.
13.04.43. Aircraft to be made available on request to RTO De Havilland for towing tests.
16.04.43. W Penny. Mascot. Glider towing.
4.05. to 26.05.43. SHQ, Richmond Unit(?). Local airmanship; parachute drops; dummy drop.
1.06.43. Absent at De Hav glider towing.
4.06.43. Issued 5 AD ex 2 AD.
21 to 28.06.43. SHQ, Richmond Unit(?). Sgt Harris. From Richmond to Archerfield. Dummy drop for 3AD and then return.
14.07 to 29.08.43. SHQ, Richmond Unit(?). Dropping dummys; glider towing; Met flights and flare drops.
1.09.43. SHQ, Richmond Unit. F/Off Lewis, LAC P.E. Cutler. After landing taxied onto runway to reload flares, collided with Vultee which was parked in flight lines. TFT 944.35 hours.
14.09.43. F at SHQ Richmond.
29.12.43. Allotted 2 AD ex SHQ Richmond.
15.01.44. SHQ, Richmond Unit(?). F/Sgt Harris. Test flight.
12 & 14.02.44. Allotted to & Received SHQ Richmond ex 2AD.
11.04.44. C at SHQ Richmond.
28 & 30.06.44. Allotted to & Received 2 CRD for conversion.
8.07.44. Approval to convert to components.
15.08.44. 1 CRD. Conversion commenced. Incorrectly noted as last Wapiti in RAAF service - see A5-16.

### A5-42
?.08.39. 100 hrs airframe life remaining.
1.09.39. Due to be scrapped. TFT 2,372 hours 30.
16.09.39. To Technical Depot, Laverton. Instructional airframe.

### A5-43
21.02.38. 1 AD received by RAAF, Ex-J.8614.
26.04.38. Recently received at 1 AD.
6.07.38. 1 AD workshop for erection.
4.10.38. Issued from 1 AD to 1 FTS.
5.10.38. 1 FTS. J,8614.
5.10.38. Slight damage taking off for Point Cook.
4.10.38. 1 FTS. Laverton. F/Off Buscombe. Accident while taxying downwind.
9.03.39. R Creswell (solo). Cat B IX Formation.
13.03.39. 120 hourly inspection.
27.03.39. 1 FTS Cadet Wing. J.8164.
26.04.39. TFT 351 hours.
29.04.39. F/Off Hick, R Creswell. *Circuits, Force Landings Steep T.*
1.08.39. Recommended for complete overhaul after further 300 hours. 600 hours airframe life remaining.
25.08.39. 1 FTS. J.8576.
6.11.39. 120 hourly 11 days.
13.11.39. 120 hourly 5 days.
22.11.39. 1 FTS. Sqn Ldr E.E. Douglas, Sgt Huskinson. On test flight noticed starboard side undercarriage damaged, pilot informed, landed cross wind on port wheel, undercarriage collapsed.
4 and 11.12.39. Awaiting supplies starboard lower mainplane.
20.12.39. Approval granted assemble wooden mainplane and centre section.
19.03.40. 1 SFTS. Point Cook. P/Off A Taylor, Cdt Davidson. Landed slightly out of wind, tipped onto starboard aileron and wing tip.
(28.03.40). Accident caused by socket fitting coming loose. No other details.
10.04.40. FTS J.8576 replaced with J.8145.
30.04.40. J.8145 removed.
5.06.40. Issued engineering School ex FTS.
28.10.40. Converted to Instructional Wapiti 5.
(25.05.42). 1 TG. Conversion of Instructional Wapiti Airframes Nos. 4, 5 and 6.

### Instructional Wapiti No.4
(25.05.42). 1 TG. Conversion of Instructional Wapiti Airframes Nos. 4, 5 and 6.
A5-3 and A5-42 are possible candidates for this airframe.

### Unidentified incidents:
04.07.1934. Engine trouble necessitated the forced landing of a RAAF Wapiti a few miles north of Macedon, Vic, and yesterday (the 5th) a tender was despatched from Point Cook to bring the damaged plane to Point Cook for

**Above:** What Raynes did to A5-25, Lake Gnarpuit, 2.08.31. Lake Gnarpuit is one of the nine saline lakes making up the Western District Lakes and a recognised wetland.

The Melbourne *Age* newspaper reported on Tuesday, 4 August 1931, that an Air Force plane, flown by P/Offs R. Rickson (sic) and Cunningham, of the CAF, made a forced landing on the shores of Lake Corangamite, near Colac, on Sunday. Neither pilot was injured, but the machine was damaged, and was to be brought back to Point Cook for repairs. Information received by the Air Board shows that the pilots were forced low by cloud, and that the accident occurred in attempting to land. Citizen Air Force pilots were entitled to the use of a Wapiti machine on alternate Sundays for training purposes.

repairs. It was ascertained that the damage to the Wapiti was estimated at £1000. Neither the pilot (Sgt-Pilot J.H. Buchan) nor the observer (Flt-Sgt A.E. Reddaway) was

Injured. The usual inquiry will be held by the Air Board.

14.05.1935. Flt Lt Dalton and companion suffered forced landing owing to engine trouble, about 1 mile from Tintinarra in fairly rough country. A Moth from Laverton was sent with spare parts. Newspaper report said they were on their way from Melbourne to Adelaide.

# Appendix 1. RAAF Doping Practices 1921–1939

**Above:** These three RAAF D.H.9a bombers all have the gun ring on the rear cockpit. They appear to be in three different colour schemes. The closest, A1-2X appears to be a dull colour (grey) overall. The middle machine is V.84 aluminium overall, while the far machine has the same colour as the first, but the fabric of the fuselage appears to be V.84. If this was an experiment of scheme is unknown. Unfortunately, the serials cannot be read. The photograph was dated as 6 July 1927.

That the dope and practices adopted by the Australia followed British practice is shown by a 1934 Minute entitled 'Doping Schemes.' This Minute by Sqn Ldr Harrison, the Director of Technical Services (DTS), records that *Originally in 1920, the R.A.A.F. used clear Acetate dope in conformity with R.A.F. practice.*[1]

The first AAC aircraft were delivered in standard RAF camouflage. This consisted of P.C.10 dope on upper surfaces with clear doped under surfaces with minor variations depending on type; e.g. the D.H.9 and D.H.9a had grey ply panels; some of the Avro 504K trainers were in a clear doped scheme. P.C. stood for Protective Colouring and the brown dope was designed to protect the fabric from the sun's rays and not as camouflage. Under RAAF Technical Order A3-8 issued in September 1921, the Avro 504K was no to have identification rings painted on the main planes. *With the exception of the identification rings and identification numbers on both sides of the body, and the tricolour markings on the rudder, the whole of the fabric surfaces including the undersides of the planes and tail are to be pigmented with Nitro P.C. 10 covering.*

Technical Order No. 51 in 1921, stated that service grey was to replace black japan for painting engine cowlings and metal fittings.

Included in the Imperial Gift were large quantities of dope. Air Agendum No.209 relates how the P.C.10 dope supplied with the Gift machines became useless after being stored too long and the successful efforts made to reconstitute it.

In 1923 the Air Board recorded that *the majority of machines on issue to units have been marked unserviceable pending a thorough examination and overhaul. As this will necessitate a renewal of all fabric covering a quantity of dope is urgently required.*[2] It is thought that this may have been the spur which led to the Munitions Supply Board (MSB) manufacturing aircraft dope in Australia.

RAAF Equipment Standing Orders Pt.3 noted, under the title 'Identification Colours and Respective Coverings for Aeroplane Dopes', that clear and pigmented oil varnish would no longer be used on the fabric surfaces of aircraft. They were to be replaced by nitro-varnished as follows:

Khaki (P.C.10) 'Nivo'; Brown (P.C.12); Aluminium (V.84); Red (V.R.3); White (V.W.3); Blue (V.B.2); Black (V.Bl.4) and Clear (V.114). Until a supply of these dopes was available, the planes and other surfaces were to be left unvarnished and without identification colours and stored until the receipt of Nitro varnishes.

These dopes were specified for the finish of the AA&ECo constructed Avro 504K trainers.[3]

There was only one change made to dope covering; this was the change from P.C.10 to V.84 after *researches in Britain which shewed that V.84 was a much superior dope covering. Its advantages are so outstanding that no change back to the use of P.C.10 will, at any time be contemplated.*[4] For William's epic flight around Australia in 1927 one D.H.9 and the D.H.50 were coated with V.84 whilst the other D.H.9 was finished in P.C.10. *The superiority of V 84 doping scheme...was apparent by comparison of the wing fabrics of the machines* under the severe conditions of the flight.[5] It appears that this 'new' doping scheme was introduced in late 1926 or early 1927.[6] V.84 Protective Covering (Aluminium) was the standard RAAF finish for fabric covered components. It could be used over

**Left:** Wapiti IA A5-1 with the checked pennant to its fuselage. The origin and colours of this marking have not been ascertained. (via RAAF Museum)

**Left:** A poor but interesting photograph of Wapiti IA A5-2 with the numeral '3' in a circle on the fin, the purpose of which is not known.

A.W.D. (All Weather Dope), clear dope, or cellulose enamel.

The above comments on V.84 are noteworthy as in 1921 the Fairey IIID Floatplanes were to be supplied in a doping scheme to be approved by the representatives of the Air Ministry.

*This should include four coats of A.M.A. dope followed by two coats of P.C.12 and two coats of V.84 on the upper surfaces.*[7] This was described as a doping scheme suitable for a tropical climate.

L.J. Wackett, the Technical Staff Officer, complained most vigorously that *it appears that the Fairey 3D. Seaplanes have been doped with aluminium covering. My experience is that this is not so satisfactory as Khaki pigment.*

*The P.C.12 is a khaki pigment and it is difficult to understand how both doping schemes have been incorporated.*

*As it is understood that the Cordite factory will be able to supply our requirements in nitro pigments, it is not considered necessary to import same.*[8]

(Note: P.C.12 was a chocolate brown dope which was used mainly in the Middle East and by the RNAS, whilst P.C.10 was the dope which was mainly used in Europe by the RFC during World War I. P.C.10 has unfortunately been described as khaki green when it was actually a brown shade.)

Air Board Agenda No. 268 of 28 July 1922, noted that pigmented oil varnish as used *for some considerable time past* for doping machines, has always been unsatisfactory *owing to the fact that after application the varnish has a tendency to chip off.* The MSB was now in a position to supply all Nitro Pigmented Dopes. Technical Order No. 11 Issue No. 1 read as follows:

*Clear and pigmented oil varnish will no longer be used on fabric surfaces of aircraft. They will be replaced by Nitro varnishes as follows:*

Khaki (P.C.10)

Nivo, brown (P.C.12)
Aluminum (V.-84)
Red (V.R.-3)
White (V.W.-3)
Blue (V.B.-2)
Black (V.B.L.4)
Clear (V.114)

*Until a supply of these are* (sic) *available, planes and other surfaces will be left unvarnished and without identification marks, and will be stored pending receipt of nitro varnishes.*

The large stock of pigmented oil varnishes was to be used up providing the efficiency of the machines was not impaired.

The reconditioning of De Havilland D.H.9a biplanes by Matthews and Hassall, under Contract No.658 in 1925, was to RAAF Specification 2.A.C.10. This specified that all fuselage plywood was to be cleaned and covered with cotton fabric, which was to be protected by two coats of approved grey paint and one coat of clear varnish. The undercarriage was given two coats of grey paint and one coat of varnish. All metal fittings were to be given two coats of black japan. Fabric covered surfaces received four coats of pigmented nitro cellulose dope P.D.N.12, two coats of aluminium covering V.84 and one coat of Transparent Oil Varnish T.O.V. dope.[9] From photographic evidence RAAF D.H.9a biplanes were doped V.84 overall. Later in their careers those which survived to receive slots were given a different scheme which appears to have seen the ply and metal fuselage panels doped grey with fabric surfaces left in V.84. No documentation for this scheme has been found. The last D.H.9a machines appear to have been V.84 aluminium overall.

Reconditioned aircraft were to be marked with the letter 'R' on the fin or rudder on the starboard side in a suitable position.[10]

In late 1925, A1-9 was reconditioned by Matthew and Hassall under Contract 658. From the weekly reports it appears that there were:

Four coats P.D.N.12, followed by
Two coats V.84 aluminium, then
Identification markings,
One coat T.O.V., varnish finish.

In 1926 the RAAF changed from acetate dope to partial use of pigmented nitro dope (P.D.N. A.2), retaining acetate dope for the sticking down of tapes, on account of its slightly greater adhesive qualities. The change was influenced by the slightly reduced costs of nitro dope.

1928 saw a return to the use of acetate dope *when the (Air Member Supply) was a R.A.F. officer on loan.*[11] It would appear that this was done to conform with standard RAF practice. Doping schemes then laid down included night flying and tropical schemes which were never used and were subsequently eliminated.

In late 1930 inquiries were made into Cellon doping schemes which *did not require the usual ventilation and heating arrangements in the dope shop.*[12] It was felt that this type of dope would be of great value to the RAAF and the MSB was asked to develop a similar dope which would be able to *cope with conditions such as are met at No.3 Squadron where facilities for control of doping conditions are not available.*[13] The MSB made up samples of this 'adverse' dope for service trials. Satisfactory trials were carried out on the elevators of Wapiti A5-15 of No. 1 Squadron over 58 flying hours. It is thought that this dope was then introduced into service as K.N.I.V. Dope, Adverse.[14]

The first Wapiti biplanes operated by the RAAF appeared in an exercise over Port Phillip Bay with a long checkerboard pennant marked on their rear fuselages. The pennant started just behind the roundel and carried to the stern with a break for the serial. A5-1 and A5-10 appear so marked in newspaper photographs. Whether this was a 'one off' application for this demonstration or an experimental squadron marking has not been determined. In any case it was short lived.

The CAS visited No. 3 Squadron on 11 November 1931, and wrote that some of the Wapiti biplanes of that unit had doped aluminium side panels. The CO, Sqn Ldr Bostock, wrote back addressing the concerns that the CAS had raised and he pointed out that the two Wapitis that had aluminium painted panels had been delivered to the Squadron so painted. He wrote that the *method of covering the metal sides of aircraft of this unit is as laid down in Order Part 3, Serial No. 256, 16/3/31 and Workshop Instruction No. 8, Sheet No. 2, which stipulated two coats of Enamel Cellulose, Grey Green, and one coat of Dope Nitro Aluminium for all metal work.* Bostock then described how a Wapiti of No. 1 Squadron had arrived with bare and polished cowls. This was in accordance with Wapiti Instruction No. 14 of 14 January 1932. He then asked for portable buffs as used by No 1 Squadron, if this was to be the necessary finish. His letter had Anderson, the Air Member for Supply advising the CAS that the workshop instructions quotes were in the process of being brought up to date. *The correct finish is laid down in Wapiti Instruction No. 14 recently issued.* Portable buffs should not be necessary to keep the cowlings clean. 'Bright' as used by No. 3 squadron *seems to infer a mirror surface, which, of course, is not intended.*

The standard Wapiti scheme was detailed on 'Wapiti Instruction No. 14 Colour Scheme' and listed on RAAF HQ Routine Orders on 4 January 1932. This described the scheme as:

*The exhaust collector ring and engine cowl were not painted. All wooden and metal cowling from the nose to aft of the gunner's cockpit was doped grey-green. All other metal panels were left "bright" (polished unpainted metal). All other fabric areas were doped with V.84. Axle and strut fairings were painted with grey-green enamel and finished with V.84 dope. This colour scheme was to be strictly adhered to, Unit Commanders could use squadron or flight colours on the wheel fairings.*[15]

**RAAF**
**Aircraft General Instruction No. 35**
**Paints & Varnishes for Use in Aircraft**

| Ident No. | Nomenclature and Specification | Uses | Application by |
|---|---|---|---|
| ENAMEL | | | |
| K4/84 | Air drying black | General protection of wood & metal | Brush or spray |
| K4/71 | Air drying white | | |
| K4/ 4 | Air drying grey | | |
| K/75 | Cellulose grey-green D.T.D. 63 | Interior of cockpits, metal fuselage members, tanks, cowlings, etc. | Brush or spray |
| K3/79 | White; special for seaplane hulls | Seaplane hulls & floats | Brush only |
| K4/108 | Stowing black | General use for metal parts | Brush or spray |
| LACQUER | | | |
| K3/76 | Cellulose undercoat, khaki | For lacquered airscrews & glued-on fabric of fuselages. | Brush or spray |
| K3/77 | Cellulose finishing, dark green | | |
| K3/82 | Oil, lion | External preservation of aero engines. For seaplane metal fittings both as a protective coat & sealing on to woodwork. | Brush or spray |
| PAINT | | | |
| K4/86 | Antisulphuric black BESA X 19 | Accumulator boxes | Brush only |
| K3/69 | Battleship Grey flat BESA 4X 2 | Cowlings | |
| K4/237 | Compass, spirit resisting black | Compasses | Brush or spray |
| K4/238 | Compass, spirit resisting white | | |
| K3/70 | Dope resisting white BESA 3X 4 | On wood & metal parts liable to come in contact with dope fabric | Brush only |
| K3/66 | Undercoating, grey BESA X 16 | First coat pointed woodwork | |
| VARNISH | | | |
| K4/141 | Copal pale exterior BESA 3X 6 | External woodwork | Brush or spray |
| K4/142 | Copal pale interior BASA 3X 7 | Internal woodwork | |
| K3/74 | Seaplane BESA X 17 | For external woodwork | Brush or spray |
| Source: NAA ACT A705 Item 62/1/164. Date of issue 4 January 1932. | | | |

The grey green referred to was K3-75 Cellulose. This enamel could be sprayed while a lead-based paint was prohibited. It was used in addition to the above on fuselage members, tanks, and the inside of cowlings.[16]

This photograph shows A7-38 and A7-48 were given a colourful scheme with the upper wing stripe. The third Moth appears to be a solid colour overall.

It is thought that RAAF Bulldog fighters were finished the same as their British counterparts. Research by Ian K Baker suggests that the top fuselage deck was painted in Nivo. Contemporary colour art work by Gerald Muir shows a green top deck. All remaining fabric covered parts were doped in V.84 and metal panels were highly polished.[17]

A submission made by the MSB in January 1934, pointed out that the continued use of acetate dope would require a

**Right:** This photograph of a crashed D.H.60 Moth was in an album of a former member of the RAAF. As colourful markings were frowned on, it was at first thought it may have been taken in the UK, however other photographs of RAAF Moths so marked have come to light. (via P.G. Heffernan)

**Above:** This photograph shows A7-38 and A7-48 were given a colourful scheme with the upper wing stripe. The third Moth appears to be a solid colour overall.

major investment in overhauling and upgrading the plant which produced the dope. The doping scheme then in force was:

(1) Pigmented Cellulose Acetate Dope (A.D.P) 4 coats.
(2) Aluminium Protective Covering (V.84) 2 coats.

The decision was made to return to the use of nitro cellulose dope for the following reasons:

(a) The present use of acetate dope in the R.A.F. was influenced by conditions which did not occur in Australia. The materials for the manufacture here of nitro cellulose dope are obtainable from supplies normally carried for the manufacture of explosives, whereas those for the

**Above:** The mystery colourful Moth leads A7-53 and A7-38 from a grass strip. These photographs were taken before 16 March 1936, the date A7-38 was written off. The serial of the colourful Moth has not been determined to date. (via B Walker)

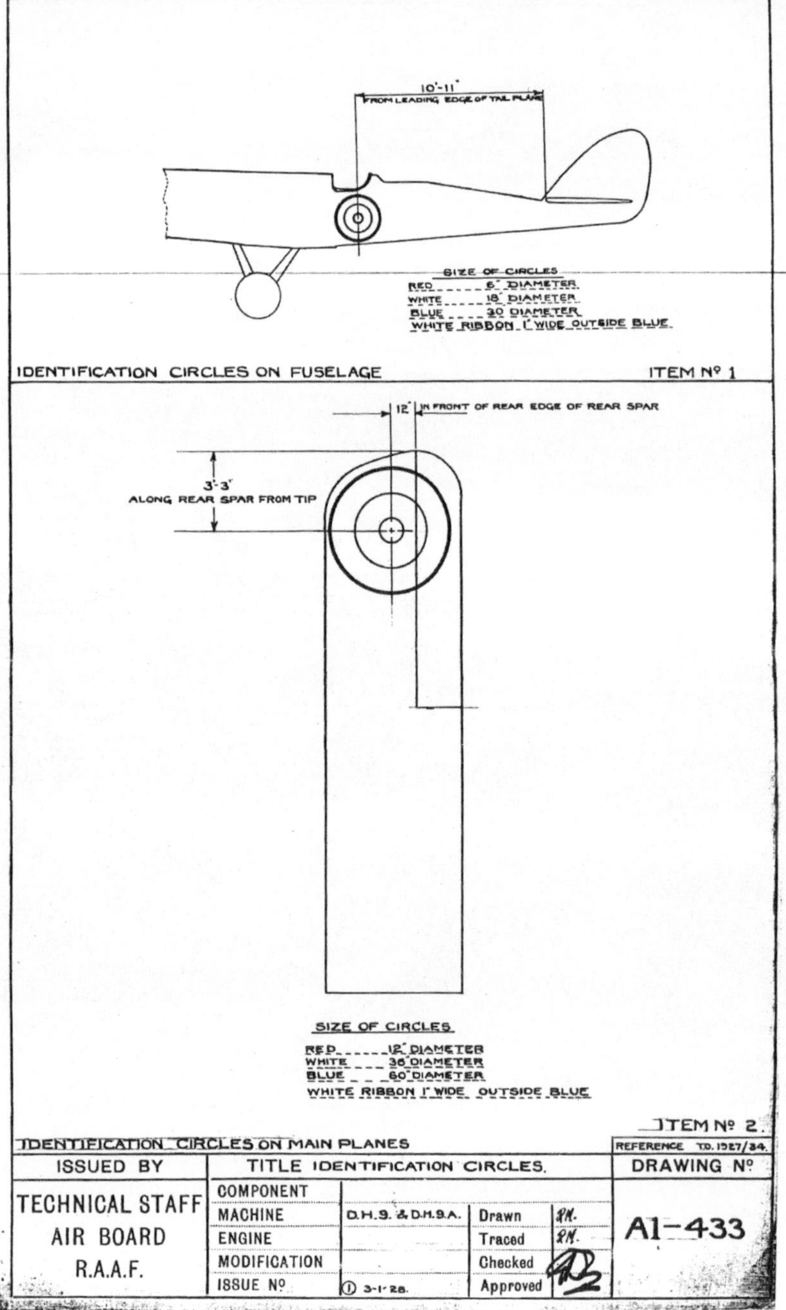


**Left:** Typical RAAF drawing showing the application of national markings to the De Havilland Metal Moth. (Note that the terminology of Roundels has not come into effect and they are referred to as Circles.)

**Right:** This drawing shows the proposed Squadron markings for RAAF Demons. Their style and colours followed those used by the RAF but were rejected by the RAAF.

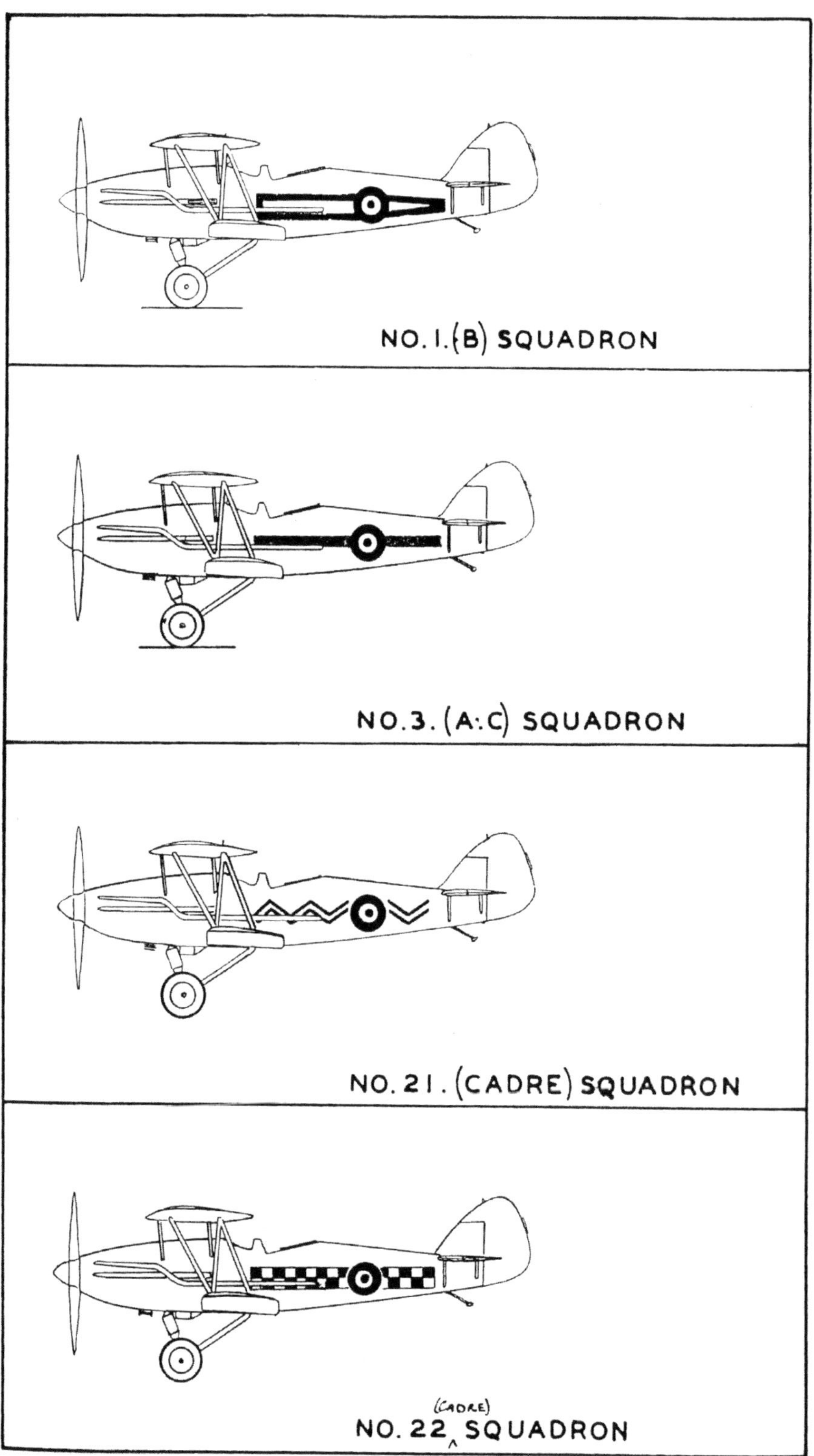


manufacture of cellulose acetate dope have to be provided as a special activity. This was not the situation in Britain. The demand for dope in a war situation would be so small compared with the demand for explosives that the two purposes (ie the manufacture of dope and explosives) could readily be served by the same manufacturing processes.

(b) Nitro dopes are slightly superior in tightening and weathering qualities, and are less affected by changes in atmospheric conditions.

(c) Nitro dope is slightly more inflammable, but this was considered to be negligible since the danger of fire arose chiefly from the fuel and the danger from the dope was insignificant in comparison.

Jets

Introduction
Home and dry

(d) The adhesive quality of nitro dope was thought to be capable of being rectified by suitable adjustments in the proportions of the ingredients. The cost was only slightly more than half that of cellulose acetate dope, and finally, conformity with RAF practice was considered of no moment.

The MSB was supplying nitro cellulose dope to QANTAS and Western Australian Airways and had previously supplied it to the RAAF. The consumption of dope in the RAAF over the preceding 12 months was given at 646 gallons (2,936 litres) at a cost of £963. The Defence Committee agreed to abandon cellulose acetate dope for the RAAF on 31.05.1934, the change over to the new dope, nitro cellulose dope P.D. No.12, being by a gradual process.

Experimentation continued with tests of P.D.N. 12 - Modified No.421 Mixing 3, being tried on Wapiti A5-17 and A5-23 mainplanes in 1936. After 12 months service the results were very satisfactory. It is not known if this mix was adopted as standard.

In 1938 it was decided to cease cotton nitration for aircraft dope materials at the MSB as aircraft dopes of Australian manufacture were now available. The Air Board wanted the MSB to provide back up, but it is thought that this was not done and private enterprise took over the supply of all RAAF dopes. British Australian Lead Manufacturers Pty Ltd (BALM) won the first such contract.

It was noted in 1935 that the *present practice, and the practice in force for years, has been to cover the identifying colours with a coat of transparent covering, except where the aircraft has been doped to a night flying scheme (and)... It is to avoid the transparent covering with its attendant difficulties that the new colours are being tried out.* The new colours referred to were of a semi-gloss finish.[18]

Two years later the new identification colours were noted as not complying with B.S. Spec.D.103, but that the existing nomenclature would be retained (viz. V.R.3, V.W.3, V.B.2, and V.BL.4 for red, white, blue and black respectively), but that the specification numbers would be included instead of the British specification, the necessary amendments being issued and effective from around 21 July 1937.

## Unit Markings

For a display by the RAAF in 1926, the units were allocated a 'Unit Marking' that consisted of the wheel covers painted a particular colour:

| | |
|---|---|
| 1 FTS | Blue |
| 1 Squadron | Red |
| 3 Squadron | White |
| 101 Flight | Yellow |
| RAAF HQ | Green |
| Experimental Section | Normal |

In 1936 the COs of RAAF Richmond and Laverton wrote to the Air Board noting that a *certain amount of difficulty is being experienced at this station in identifying at a distance* Demons of Nos. 3 and 22, and 1 and 21 Squadrons respectively, and asking if *information be given...as to whether any scheme of markings exists for similar types of aircraft in different units in the Service?*[19] These officers knew of the colourful markings carried by their RAF counterparts in the UK, and the drawings of suggested markings would have made the RAAF aircraft every bit as colourful with checks and geometrical markings on the fuselages. Unfortunately, conservatism expressed itself with permission being granted for No. 21 Squadron to *carry a special marking. This marking is to consist of a blue band, five inches wide, painted above and below the national marking on each side and top of the fuselage.*[20] The same day No. 22 Squadron was advised that its markings would consist of two five inch wide bands. On 2 November the Unit diary recorded that all No. 21 Squadron's Demons had been so marked. These markings proved satisfactory and four months later permission was granted for them to be carried onto the bottom of the fuselage as well *as this would assist in the identification of the aircraft from below.*[21] Permission was duly granted in Weekly Order No.415 of 19 April 1937. The markings were eventually to be carried by other aircraft of these squadrons.

This seems to have been the scheme in force until the declaration of war. Green and brown camouflage only appearing gradually on Australian aircraft until the start of the Pacific War. In March 1940, the ADD General Staff of the 3rd Military district complained that aircraft presently being used for army co-operation with anti-aircraft companies were silver in colour and were required to fly with their navigation lights on and this *greatly detract from the value of training because of the ease with which initial pick up of aircraft can be obtained and target held.*[22] The Army suggested that a camouflaged aircraft be used and that it fly without lights, however it was not until 23 January 1942, that a camouflaged Demon was allocated to Southern Command for AA Co-op.

## Seaplanes

RAAF Standing Orders noted that when seaplanes were moored out they were to be *taken up at least once every month and the tow strap and the hull thoroughly inspected. The fouling of the hull will be removed and the hull repainted.*[23]

What this anti-fouling colour was is not known with certainty. In 1927 the Liaison Officer reported that Paint Anti Rust Blue was no longer available had been replaced by Seaplane Varnish. Paint Anti Rust Blue appears to have been an anti-fouling paint. Seven Gallons of Seaplane Varnish and three gallons of Sozol Rust Preventative were ordered in lieu of the former. In June 1928 it was noted that Southampton wooden hulls and floats were coated with Seaplane Varnish

**Facing Page:** The only surviving Southampton hull is displayed at the RAF Museum, Hendon, UK. The restored hull is finished in the same scheme that would have been applied to the RAAF Southamptons.

Research has shown that the color of the upper surface of the Seagull III hull was most probably green.

**Left & Right:** The sole surviving remains of a Seagull III in the Solent Sky Museum, Southampton, UK. (via B Rybbans)

**Above:** F-Off A.M. Murdock at the seaplane flight, Point Cook, 1932, with one of the refurbished Seagull III amphibians in the late (grey) colour scheme. Note the Moth floatplane in the background.

BCSA Specification No. 217. In late 1929 experiments were carried out on Southampton A11-2 at the Seaplane Squadron. This appears to have been tests of a Taubmans AMS Ltd varnish, sample RS. In 1931 Sherwin Williams Ltd prepared an Enamel White Marine for floats and hulls.[24] A 1933 entry states that Enamel White Special was not as suitable as other enamels. In August the same year the MSB was asked about manufacturing and supplying *enamel white* for seaplane hulls.[25] From this fragmentary evidence and contemporary British practices it seems evident that the Southampton flying boats were finished in varnished natural wood hulls, giving a red-brown colour, with white anti-fouling finish applied to the hull bottom. All fabric covered surfaces were V-84 Aluminium.[26]

It was though that the Seagull hulls were initially the same colour as the Southamptons, however research by R Lambert, P Malone and F Harris, has shown that the Seagull III hulls were initially Brunswick Green and later, after refurbishing, in a grey enamel, called Battleship Grey in the article ('Brown Seagulls Dismythed,' *ModelArt Australia* No.52,), the hull bottom remaining white, and all fabric covered areas being V.84 aluminium. It is thought that the Grey scheme was only applied to the last few surviving Seagull III amphibians. The hulls were varnished as the Report on the Papuan Survey Flight of 1927-28 records that before leaving the steps of both Seagulls (A9-5 and A9-6) were *given one coat of white Ripolin enamel, and the hulls were given one coat of Taubman's Marine Varnish. The vanish soon came off where it was in contact with the sea water, and by the time THURSDAY ISLAND was reached there was little enamel left on the steps. These were re-enamelled at SAMARI and the hulls were varnished. Both enamel and varnish peeled.*[27]

The operational environment of the Seagull V led to it having a unique finish. The metal hull was first treated with boiled Linseed Oil but this coating did not resist marine growth and *when applied over painted finish practically useless as anticorrosive.*[28] It was decided to apply one coat K4/10012 Creparokato Grey followed by the appropriate camouflage colour then to apply a coating of DTD122P Lanoline diluted with white spirit. This coat resisted marine growth, had good adhesion and was easily removed. Colin Harvey can still remember the lanolin that coated his hands whenever he flew in or serviced the type. Wings and tail surfaces were V.84 aluminium. After the outbreak of war many of the remaining Seagull V amphibians were camouflaged.

## Floatplanes

Moth floatplanes were finished the same as their land-based counterparts with the floats given two coats of zinc-chromate primer (Aviation BALM No.63-1048) followed by two coats of aluminium pigmented cellulose enamel (Spec D.T.D.63 BALM No.958.)[29] According to RAAF Specification AC54 'Reconditioning of Wapiti Floats,' the exterior of the floats was to be given two coats of grey-green cellulose. The special finish applied to the Antarctic floatplanes is given in the chapter on the Moth.

## National Insignia and Serial Application

The RAAF followed RAF practice in markings with only little variation, this was most evident in the case of application of underwing serials. The RAF had applied underwing serials to trainers since the 1914-1918 War and during 1927 this became general; however, the RAAF did not follow suit until the purchase of the Avro Anson. The roundel and rudder stripes were the same proportions and positioned the same as on their RAF counterparts. Roundel colours were lighter than present day colours and close to those adopted in the 1914-1918 War. It must be remembered that the Australian climate was harsh and this would have had a marked effect on roundel colours.

Until August 1930 RAF rudder stripes were red at the trailing edge as they had been in the 1914-1918 War. After this date the colours were reversed to avoid confusion with French Air Force machines. The RAAF followed suit, RAAF HQ Routine Orders of 24 October 1930, referred to the colour marking on aircraft rudders as follows:

It has been decided that the sequence of colour markings on the rudders of aircraft are to be in accordance with the following:

That part of the rudder which lies behind the rudder post is to be divided into three vertical strips of equal width which are to be coloured red, white and blue respectively; the red strip being next to the rudder post, the blue at the trailing edge and the white between.

This is a reversal of the present sequence of colours.

Units are to carry out the conversion as opportunity offers, but all aircraft must bear reversed colour marks by 1st. January, 1931.

*Aircraft issued from No.1 AD are to have the revised colours marks incorporated prior to issue.*[30]

This is very evident in photographs of Bulldogs. When the RAF abandoned rudder stripes completely in 1934, again the RAAF followed British practice but only on newly delivered aircraft, such as Hawker Demons, Supermarine Seagull V amphibians, Avro Cadet trainers and Ansons. National insignia proportions also followed RAF standards for that particular type, no attempt being made to bring the whole of the RAAF into line with the current standard.

## RAAF Serial Numbers

Air Board Agendum No.123 of 12 August 1921, set out the 'Numbering of Aeroplanes, Seaplanes, etc' as proposed by Sqn Ldr P.A. McBain, the Director of Equipment. The prefix consisted of the group letter and the section number that had already been allocated for the purposes of Stores Accounting:

A - Aircraft
B - Engines

**Left:** Painting the roundel on Wapiti IIA A5-35 after an overhaul.

**Below:** Wapiti IIA A5-16. Note the placement of the serial, its size and the lack of the A5 prefix. (via B Walker)

C - Motor transport
D - hand tools
E - Armament
F - Photographic equipment

Thus, each type of aircraft had an 'A' number serial prefix. RAAF Technical Order No.32 of October 1921, listed the identification numbers for RAAF aircraft which would replace the RAF serial. The latter were used for some time after this order was promulgated.

The initial allocation was:

D.H.9a type.............................. A.1-1 to 29
S.E.5a type.............................. A.2-1 to 35
Avro 504K type......................... A.3-1 to 47
D.H.9 type................................ A.6-1 to 28
Fairey 3 D type......................... A.10-1 to 9
Flying Boats............................. A.11-1 to 18

*No identification numbers are to be painted on the rudder or rudders. The identification number is to be painted on both sides of the body, midway between the identification rings and the leading edge of the tailplane.*[31]

Serials were carried at the rear of the fuselage in 8-inch letters. White on P.C.10/P.C.12 and black on clear doped or V.84 finishes. At some time in the late 1930 the serial was adopted as the aircraft number and displayed in large numerals. It is thought that this was only carried out on training machines as Wapitis, Moths and Seagull V

**Above:** Wapiti A5-16 of 1 Development Unit, Laverton, January 1944, in the all-yellow World War II trainer scheme with blue and white roundels. (RAAF official)

amphibians have been noted as so marked.

In 1939 it was decided to adopt RAF colours and marking practices. From late September low visibility red and blue roundels were specified together with camouflage for the RAAF's front-line aircraft, Ansons, Wirraways, Seagull V amphibians and Demons. Photographs show these aircraft with modified roundels, sometimes this was done very crudely. Squadron codes were introduced at the same time. They comprised a single code letter for each squadron marked in front of the roundel on both sides of the fuselage. The letter was to be 48 inches high and six inches thick. Where there was insufficient space to take the nominated length, this could be reduced. The code was grey on camouflage surfaces and black on aluminium finishes. There was no individual aircraft letter. The red/blue roundels proved not to be visible enough and white was reintroduced in early 1940. Red was deleted on Japan's entry into the war to ensure that there would be no confusion with the solid red Japanese *Hinomaru*, the roundel being blue and white.[32]

In April 1943 an instruction was issued that required all training aircraft at Elementary Flying Training Schools were to be painted camouflage Yellow (K3/185) on all surfaces. All single and twin engined aircraft at Service Flying Training Schools were to have their engine cowlings painted yellow. Aircraft withdrawn from training for other duties were to carry operational camouflage.[33]

The markings on ambulance aircraft were the Geneva Crosses – a red cross usually on a white background. These were usually carried on the sides of the aircraft.

The red cross on the upper surfaces of the aircraft was to be painted on the fuselage opposite the junction of the wings and the fuselage and in size approximating to the width of the fuselage at this point. The RAAF Gannets were so marked.[34]

## End Notes

1. NAA ACT CRS A705/1 Item 62/1/201. Dope Covering V-84 - Experimental.
2. NAA ACT CRS A705/1 Item NN. Air Board Agendum No.448, Decision. 21.09.1923.
3. Air Board Agendum No.114.
4. NAA ACT CRS A705/1 Item 62/1/201.
5. RAAF Museum - Williams papers. "Report on Reconnaissance Flight Round and Through Central Australia, 21st July to 10th September, 1927".
6. MSB Agendum No.907. 17.03.27. This refers to the new

doping scheme in the RAAF and the 12 months supply of dopes lists V.84 but no P.C.10.

7. NAA ACT CRS A705/1 Item 199/2/12. Schedule for the supply and delivery of Fairey General Purpose Seaplane Type 3.D.
8. NAA ACT CRS A705/1 Item 199/2/12. TSO to Director of Equipment, 24.08.1921.
9. NAA ACT CRS A705/1 Item 69/4/126 Part 4. Appendices H-J. Appendix I.
10. Section IV. Extracts from Technical Orders. Contained in NAA ACT CRS A705/1 Item 69/4/126 Pt. 5.
11. NAA ACT CRS A705/1 Item 62/1/201
12. Ibid.
13. A705/2 Item 62/1/201. DTS to CO, No.1 Squadron, Laverton. 17.07.1931
14. NAA ACT CRS A705/1 Item 62/1/201. Dope Covering V-84 - Experimental. CO, No.1 Squadron to Air Board. 14.12.1931.
15. NAA ACT CRS A705/1 Item 73/1/1119. Wapiti Aircraft Miscellaneous File. "Draft Wapiti Colour Scheme."
16. NAA ACT CRS A705/1 Item 62/1/164. Paints And Varnishes. 1 AD to Air Board. Proposed Technical Order. 26.11.1931.
17. Ian K Baker's "Aviation History Colouring Book", Part 2, Revised 1994.
18. NAA ACT CRS A705/1 Item 62/1/201. Air Board to MSB. 15.08.1935.
19. NAA ACT CRS A705 Item 62/1/234. Markings Of Demon Aircraft. Minute; "Markings - Demon Aircraft." CO, RAAF, Richmond to Air Board, 17.07.1936.
20. Ibid. Letter; DSD to CAS. 30.10.1936.
21. Ibid. Letter; CO, Richmond to Air Board. 21.01.1937. Exactly the same letter came from Laverton on the 27th.
22. NAA ACT CRS A705/1 Item 208/3/488. Army Co-Operation Southern Command. ADD General Staff, 3 MD to Director Operations and Intelligence, RAAF. 30.03.1940.
23. RAAF Equipment Standing Orders Pt.3, Chapter III, "Aircraft Rigging and Hull Inspection." Contained in NAA ACT CRS A705/1 Item 69/4/126 Pt.5.
24. Sherwin Williams Co of Cleveland, Ohio, was established by Henry A Sherwin in 1866. By 1871 Sherwin, Williams and Co began to manufacture their own coatings. The interwar years saw a proliferation of specialist coatings with marine and aircraft finishes included. In 1928 the company introduced its Aero Enamels. It would appear the RAAF was interested in their marine finishes.
25. AWM PR88/154 Item 1. AT Cole diary entry 10.08.1933.
26. NAA ACT CRS A2408/1 Item 62/2 , "Dopes and Paint Tests", and Item 62/3 "Dopes and Paint Supplies". Various entries in Letterbooks.
27. NAA ACT A9376 Item 36. RAAF – Report on Papuan Survey Flight by F/Lt Packer, 27 September 1927 to 19 January 1928.
28. NAA ACT CRS A705/1 Item 9/5/273. Seagull V and Walrus Aircraft General Technical File. Radio message; F/Off Stochen to Air Board. 23.07.1942.
29. RAAF Specification AC57.
30. NAA ACT CRS A705 Item 9/1/109. Colour markings of Rudders of Aircraft.
31. RAAF Technical Order No.1.
32. Aircraft General Instruction C.11, 22.09.1939.
33. NAA ACT CRS A705/1 Item 9/7/585. Anson Aircraft Maintenance. Instruction: "Aircraft Camouflage", by Air Member for Engineering and Maintenance, 19.04.1943.
34. This marking came about from 1 Air Ambulance Unit, RAAF, of the AIF, asking for a definite policy in regard to the marking of Geneva Crosses on the aircraft. DDMS, 1 Aust Corps, to G.III (AIR). 14.09.1941. AWM 54 File 14/2/9.

# Appendix 2. HMAS *Albatross*

**Above:** A rare photograph of *Albatross* showing the forward E III H catapult that was installed in 1936.

In June 1924, S.M. Bruce, the Prime Minister, announced the first major rearmament program that Australia had embarked on since the end of World War I. The purchase of new warships dominated the program. Two long-range cruisers, two submarines, and an aircraft carrier were ordered. The cruisers were HMAS *Australia* and HMAS *Canberra,* the submarines, HMAS *Otway* and *Oxley,* while the aircraft carrier was not an aircraft carrier in having a flight deck, but was HMAS *Albatross,* a ship that would carry seaplanes in the fashion of the early carriers of the past war. The Navy Board noted that the correct designation of the ship was 'Seaplane Carrier.'[1] This apparently came about due to the British announcing to the Dominion Governments in February 1924, that they were not upgrading the Singapore Naval Base. This decision made the Australian Government initiate a naval expansion program.

The two cruisers were to be built in Britain rather than locally, thereby saving £1,000,000. This saving would then be used to build the Seaplane Carrier at the Cockatoo Island Dockyards, keeping the Dockyard employed, and public opinion, as well as the Labour Party opposition, on side. It would be a counter to the aircraft carriers being introduced into the Pacific by Japan.

The RAN had operated aircraft from its ships in World War I. HMAS *Brisbane* embarked a Sopwith Baby seaplane in mid-1917, while HMAS *Sydney* and HMAS *Australia* launched Sopwith Pup fighters in December that year. The following year *Australia* was equipped with a Sopwith 1½ Strutter two-seat reconnaissance machine and a Sopwith 2F.1 Camel fighter. The end of the war saw the aircraft returned to the RAF and plans for an Australian naval air arm were in abeyance.

In order to get experience with operating aircraft, one of the RAAF Avro 504K conversions to the floatplane version was carried by *Australia* for two months in July 1920. On 29 September a second Avro embarked on *Melbourne* for a Pacific cruise. (See Chapter 1). These cruises showed that the aircraft would have to be designed to operate from a ship.

In 1921 the RAAF came into being and was to provide air support for the Army and Navy. Six Fairey IIID floatplanes were purchased in 1921 and appeared with Australian Naval Aircraft serial numbers but were soon renumbered with RAAF numbers after it came into existence. (See Chapter 13).

The seaplane carriers of World War I were laid down on hulls being built or already existing. They were converted to carry aircraft with all the problems that modifications for a use that the ships were not designed for, brings to the surface. *Albatross* was the first seaplane carrier to be designed before steel was cut.[2] The problems with Albatross started even before she was built as the RAN had not prepared any specifications. The Admiralty's Director of Naval Construction was asked for assistance and was told that the ship was to have a speed of 21 knots and a cost of £1 million. The Naval Constructor in charge of the Admiralty's Aircraft Section is on record as retorting – *a more unsatisfactory way of producing an aircraft carrier I do not know, and I cannot imagine.*[3]

Naval Constructor Stephen Payne was to say later that the *hull was designed around three holds, three cranes and 21 knots.*[4] Payne had the assistance of naval architect Mr Woolnough who attended the weekly Admiralty meetings that saw the design progress. The *Albatross* was designed around the Fairey IIID.

*The Bulletin* magazine was very conscious of Australia's defence and published the following article after the launch of *Albatross*:

*H.M.A.S. Albatross, was launched at Cockatoo Dockyard,*

**Above & Above Right:** HMAS *Albatross* on the slipway at Cockatoo Island, Sydney Harbour.

**Above:** HMAS *Albatross* after its launch on 23 February 1928. The *Albatross* was obsolete by the time it reached the Australian fleet.

**Above:** A flag bedecked *Albatross* in Sydney harbour with three Supermarine Seagull III biplanes on the forward deck during the celebrations accompanying the opening of the Sydney Harbour Bridge on 19 March 1932.

**Above:** This view shows the three cranes and mixed RAAF and Navy crew on the *Albatross*.

**Above:** An aerial view of HMAS *Albatross*.

*Sydney last week. but if RAAF equipment is not added to, there will be no seaplanes for the. vessel to carry when it is ready for service at the end of the year (says a Melbourne paper). It Is stated that the three Fairey 3D. Seagulls at Point Cooke, bought in 1921, are not suitable for carrier work. The only other aircraft are the two new Supermarine Southampton flying boats. They are too big to be carried by the Albatross, unless partly dismantled. The Albatross can carry nine seaplanes, six -erected and. three partly dismantled. When a 'plane has to take the air the vessel is stopped and the seaplane is lowered to the surface of the water*

**Right:** RAAF and RAN crew on the deck of *Albatross*.

**Right:** Operating the Seagull III amphibians required the ship to stop. This photograph was taken in New Guinea.

*by means of a crane. Similar methods will be used when a 'plane wishes to return home. Later the vessel may be fitted with a catapult for launching aircraft Defence authorities are watching developments in seacraft construction overseas, and may purchase new equipment.*[5]

What is interesting is that *The Bulletin,* usually up to date on defence matters, makes no mention of the Seagull III amphibians that had been purchased for the *Albatross* and had been delivered in 1926. Six of the Supermarine Seagull III amphibians were financed from the 1925 Navy vote as they were to form a fleet co-operation flight. As described in Chapter 19, they were utilised for surveying the Great Barrier Reef before they were required for *Albatross.* In fact, the Minister for Defence, Sir Neville Howse made

**Left:** Note that the amphibians have their undercarriage down.

**Right:** The Supermarine Seagull III will always be associated with HMAS *Albatross*.

**Left:** Two Seagull III amphibians on *Albatross*. One on the deck being attached to the second crane, and one already on the crane. It is easy to understand that trying to launch or recover the aircraft in anything but calm seas was a hazardous affair.

a statement on 1 July 1926, wherein he admitted that the Seagull III amphibians would probably be used up in training *it being anticipated that improved types would be available for the seaplane carrier.* As described in Chapter 19, the British lost interest in the boat amphibian the expected improved Seagull did not eventuate until Williams pressed for the design of the Seagull V.

*Albatross* was designed with a high freeboard containing the three holds. Each hold could accompany three Fairey IIID biplanes or an aeroplane of similar dimensions. Three cranes were positioned such that they could lift the aircraft out of the holds and over the side of the ship, reversing the process on landing. Provision was made for a catapult to be installed later. On receiving plans from the UK, the keel of *Albatross* was laid on 16 April 1926.

On 1 July 101 Fleet Co-operation Flight was formed with the Seagull III and moved to Richmond soon after. The Fairey IIID floatplanes stayed at Point Cook as trainers.

On Thursday, 23 February 1928, the Governor General's wife, Lady Stonehaven, launched *Albatross* at the Cockatoo Island Dockyards. The Sydney Morning Herald recorded the event as follows:

H.M.A.S. *Albatross*, the first seaplane carrier forming a unit of the Royal Australian Navy, was successfully launched at Cockatoo Island Dockyard yesterday morning. A short religious service was conducted from the launching platform by the Rev. A. G. Rix, rector of St. John's parish, Balmain, after which her Excellency Lady Stonehaven christened the vessel with a bottle of Australian wine, using a pair of silver scissors to cut the red, white and blue ribbons. "I name this ship Albatross." said Lady Stonehaven. "I am proud that she is the result of Australian workmanship, and I congratulate those who have so faithfully and skilfully constructed her. May she prove a valuable addition to the Royal Australian Navy, and may God's protecting care be over all who voyage in her."

*Lady Stonehaven then pulled the lever releasing the huge vessel— it is about 420ft long, with a beam of 57ft — and the Albatross glided down the ways in stately fashion to the accompaniment of cheers by the large crowd of spectators, and the strains of "Advance Australia Fair," played by the naval band. It was a wonderful sight, and thrilled those who witnessed it. The warship was then taken in tow for transfer to the cruiser wharf, where the machinery will be installed.*[6]

Such was the interest in the launching that the Lady Stonehaven's speech was broadcast to the nation.

The Government had reversed the decision of 1915 to continue with the RAN Fleet Air Arm before *Albatross* was launched. It had been decided that the RAAF would provide the aircraft, pilots and maintenance personnel for the ship, the Navy to supply the observers and wireless telegraphists. RAAF pilots could train as pilots, such a one being J.E. *Joe* Hewitt whose career and changing ranks between the Navy and Air Force before he transferred permanently to the RAAF, is detailed in his autobiography *The Black One.*[7]

*Albatross* was fitted out with 12,910-hp Parsons geared turbines with two shafts, and four Yarrow boilers. Dimensions were a length of 443¾ feet; a beam of 60 feet and a displacement of 4,800 toms with a draft of 16¼ ft. No. 101 Flight embarked on 25 February and the Seagull III amphibians, with their wings folded, were lowered into the ship's hangars through the 41 feet x 20 feet hatch. By chance the Seagull III's dimensions with wings folded were very close to that of the Fairey IIID in similar condition. According to Wg Cdr J.H. McCorrisston *Albatross* could only carry six Seagull III amphibians. Three were three bays on each side. One aircraft was carried in each of two bays with two in the centre. The two rear bays were utilised as workshops.[8]

The new RAN cruisers *Australia* and *Canberra* had been built with a catapult base, but no catapult, and did not carry aircraft at this time. *Albatross* worked up by exercising with these ships, her aircraft operating as a reconnaissance element for the cruisers. In July and August, Lord and Lady Stonehaven made a vice-regal tour of New Guinea. Albatross carried the Wackett Widgeon II amphibian in addition to her Seagull IIIs.

In November 1929, there was a combined exercise with the RAN and RAAF in Port Phillip Bay. The Seagull IIIs carried out an attack on RAAF facilities but the attacking fleet was located by a Southampton and the RAAF 'fighters,' De Havilland Moth biplanes, carried out mock attacks and it was concluded that the Seagulls were sitting targets when being hoisted in or out or on the deck of the ship.

On 23 April 1933, the effects of the Great Depression saw *Albatross* paid off into the Reserve Fleet in Sydney Harbour. She had worked winter cruises to New Guinea, spring cruises to southern states, training exercises and combined operations, but for the next five years she would not leave Sydney Harbour.

A Type E III H catapult was finally fitted to *Albatross* at Garden Island in early 1936. Catapult trials were held with a metal hull Seagull V, but the anticipated return to sea did not occur. She remained in reserve until 19 April 1938, when she was accepted by the British Admiralty as part payment for the new cruiser, HMAS *Hobart.* After receiving a 'full dress' farewell by the crews of other ships of the Royal Australian Navy in port, the seaplane carrier, left Sydney Harbour shortly after 2 o'clock in the afternoon on Monday, 11 July 1938, bound for Great Britain. As the ship pulled out of her berth at Garden Island, the crews of the fleet ships in harbour cheered her while RAAF Seagull V amphibians flew in formation overhead.[9]

## Endnotes

1 NAA 200/3. Navy Board. 19.05.1925.

2 The British monitors of WWI were designed to carry seaplanes as an adjunct to their gun armament.

3 Isaacs, K. "First of the Line," *Naval Historical Review,* October 1977.

**Above:** The cranes of *Albatross* folded down when not required.

**Above:** A Seagull V with *Albatross*. The type did not operate from the ship.

4 *Ibid.*
5 *The Bulletin*, 1 March 1928.
6 *Sydney Morning Herald* (Sydney), 24 February 1928. P.10.
7 Hewitt, J.E. *The Black One*, Langate Publishing, Australia. 1984.
8 Interview with Wg Cdr J.H. McCorriston of Bulleen, Vic, 15 March 1989. RAAF Air Power Study Centre, Canberra.
9 "Farwell to the Albatross", *Sydney Morning Herald*, (Sydney), 12.07.1938.

# Bibliography


*Aircraft of the Royal Australian Air Force*, Big Sky Publishing P/L, Australia. 2021

Affleck, A.H. *The Wandering Years*. Longmans, Green & Co, Australia. 1964.

Alcorn, J. *AMC DH9A, Vol.1 & Vol. 2*. Windsock Datafile, Albatros Productions, UK, 2010.

Barnes, CH. *Bristol Aircraft since 1910*, Putnam, UK, 1964

Bennett, J. *Highest Traditions – The History of No. 2 Squadron, RAAF.* AGPS, 1995.

Bennett, J. *The Imperial Gift – British Aeroplanes which formed the RAAF in 1921.*

Booth, G. *33 Days*, Greenhouse Publications, Australia, 1988.

Brearley, N. *Australian Aviator*, Rigby, Australia, 1974.

Brook, W.H., *Demon to Vampire; The Story of No.21 (City of Melbourne) Squadron*, Glen Waverley, Vic, 1986.

Brownell, Air Commodore R.J., *From Khaki to Blue*, Military Historical Society of Australia, Canberra, Australia, 1978.

Bruce, JM. *British Aeroplanes 1914-1918*, Putnam, UK. 1957.

Bruce, J.M. *De Havilland Aircraft of World War I*, Arms and Armour Press, UK, 1991.

Bruce, JM. *Vickers Vimy*, Albatros Productions, UK, 1994.

Bruce, JM. *Airco DH9*, Windsock Datafile No.72, Albatros Productions, UK, 1998.

Bruce, JM. *The Aeroplanes of the Royal Flying Corps (Military Wing)*, Putnam, UK, 1992.

Bruce, J.M. *Bristol Scouts*, Windsock Datafile No. 44, Albatros Productions, UK. 1994.

Bruce, JM, Page, G & Sturtivant, R. *The Sopwith Pup*, Air Britain, UK, 2002.

Campbell-Wight, S. *An Interesting Point. A History of Military Aviation at Point Cook 1914–2014.Air Power Development Centre, Canberra. 2014.*

Chinn, G. *The Machine Gun*, Vol. 1. Bureau of Ordnance, USN, 1951

Coulthard-Clark, C. *The Third Brother – The Royal Australian Air Force 1921–39*. Allen & Unwin, Australia, 1991.

Coulthard-Clark, C. *Edge of Centre – The eventful life of Group Captain Gerald Packer*, RAAF Museum, 1992.

Davis, M. *Airco, The Aircraft Manufacturing Company*, Crowood Press, UK, 2001.

*Gipsy I Aero Engine*, AP1420, Air Ministry, UK, 1931.

Green, W & Swanborough, N. *The Complete Book of Fighters*, Greenwich Editions, UK, Revised Edition, 2004.

Grenfell Prince, A. *The Skies Remember – The Story of Ross & Keith Smith*, Angus & Robertson, Australia, 1966.

Hare, P. *RAF BE2/BE2a/BE2b*, Windsock Datafile No.163, Albatros Productions, UK, 2014.

Hartnett, L. *Big Wheels and Little Wheels*, Gold Star Publications, Australia, 1964.

Hewitt, J.E. *The Black One*. Langate Publishing, Australia. 1984.

Jackson, A.J. *De Havilland Aircraft*, Putnam, UK, 1962.

Jackson, A.J. *Avro Aircraft since 1908*, Putnam, UK, 1965.

Jones, G. *From Private to Air Marshal.* Greenhouse Publications, Australia, 1988.

Isaacs, K. *Military Aircraft of Australia 1900–1918*. AWM, Australia. 1971.

Lamberton, W.M. *Fighter Aircraft of the 1914–1918 War*, Harlborough Publications, UK, 1960.

Lamberton, W.M. *Reconnaissance & Bomber Aircraft of the 1914–1918 War*, Harleyford Publications, UK, 1962.

Lewis, P. *The British Fighter Since 1912*, Putnam, UK, 1965.

Miller, H.C. *Early Birds*. Rigby Ltd, Australia. 1968.

Moss, H. *10,000 Hours*. Hesperian Press, WA, 1988.

Neal, R.J. *A Technical & Operational History of the Liberty Engine: Tanks, Ships and Aircraft 1917–1960*. Speciality Press, USA, 2009.

Parnell, N & Boughton, T. *Flypast – A Record of Aviation in Australia*. AGPS, 1988.

*R.A.F. Flying Training Manual, Part 1 Flying Instructions.* AP129, Air Ministry, UK, 1929.

*R.A.F. Flying Training Manual, Part II Applied Flying.* AP928, Air Ministry, UK, 1927.

*RAF Flying Training Manual, Part III. Seaplane Flying.* AP 1098, Air Ministry, 1928.

Rayner, H. *Scherger*, Australian War Memorial, 1984.

Robertson, B. *British Military Aircraft Serials 1911–1979*, Patrick Stevens Ltd, UK, 1979.

Schaedel, C. *Australian Air Ace*. Rigby Ltd, Australia. 1979.

Simons, G.M. *The History of the DH84 'Dragon.'* The International Friends of the DH89, UK.

Sinclair, J. *Wings of Gold*, Robert Brown & Assoc, Australia, 1978.

Smith, P.C. *Combat Biplanes of World War II*. Pen & Sword, UK, 2015.

Sturtivant, R & Page, G. *The S.E.5 File*, Air-Britain Publication, UK, 1996

Sturtivant, R & Page, G. *The D.H.4/D.H.9 File*, Air-Britain Publication, UK, 1999.

Taylor, H.A. *Fairey Aircraft since 1915*, Putnam, UK, 1974.

Wackett, L.J. *Aircraft Pioneer*. Angus & Robertson, Australia. 1972.

Walker, B. *Black Jack - 50 Years as a Pilot; 1935–1985*, Banner Books, Australia, 1984.

Williams, Sir R. *These are Facts*, AWM & AGPS, Canberra. 1977.

Wilson, D. *Alfresco Flight*. RAAF Museum, 1991.


## Articles


'A New De Havilland Commercial Aeroplane – The D.H. 50 with 240 H.P. Siddeley "Puma" Engine.' *Flight*, 9 August 1923. P.46.

Boughton, T. 'The Strange Case of the DH-50.' *Man and Aerial Machines*, Nos. 24 & 25. 1991.

'De Havilland "Moth", 60 H.P. 'Cirrus' Engine.' *Flight*, 5 March, 1925, P.72.

Denny, O. 'An Airman Remembers – My Nine Years in the RAAF,' *ASAP News*, No.2.

Isaacs. K. 'Historic Flight,' *Defence Force Journal,* date unknown.

Kightly, J. 'The Supermarine Southampton – The RAAF's Southamptons.' *Flightpath*, Vol.29 No. 4, 2018.

'Report on Accidents to Aircraft,' *Aircraft*, Oct–Dec 1927, P.302.

'Seaplane for G.G. of Australia – The Ubiquitous D.H.50 Fitted with Floats.' *Flight*, 1 April 1926, P.53.

Sturtivant, R. 'Avro Anson, The Chronicles of 'Faithful Annie.' *Air Enthusiast*, UK, No.42. P.41.

'The De Havilland Dragon.' *Flight*, 22 December 1932. P.135.

In addition, various issues of the UK journal *Flight*, the Australian *Aircraft* magazine, the Journal of the Aviation Society of Australia, the ADF Serials Military Aircraft Group website, and newspapers on the National Library of Australia website, TROVE, have been consulted.

Printed in Great Britain
by Amazon